Oxford Studies in Social History
General Editor: Keith Thomas

The English Urban Renaissance

The English Urban Renaissance

Culture and Society in
The Provincial Town 1660–1770

PETER BORSAY

CLARENDON PRESS · OXFORD

Oxford University Press, Great Clarendon Street, Oxford OX2 6DP
Oxford New York
Athens Auckland Bangkok Bogota Bombay Buenos Aires
Calcutta Cape Town Dar es Salaam Delhi Florence Hong Kong Istanbul
Karachi Kuala Lumpur Madras Madrid Melbourne Mexico City
Nairobi Paris Singapore Taipei Tokyo Toronto Warsaw
and associated companies in
Berlin Ibadan

Oxford is a registered trade mark of Oxford University Press

Published in the United States
by Oxford University Press Inc., New York

© Peter Borsay 1989

Reprinted 1998

ISBN 0 19 820255 5

Printed in Great Britain
by
Ipswich Book Company, Suffolk

To Anne

PREFACE

About two of the clock in the afternoon, on the fifth of . . .
September, a fire broke forth in the western part of the town of
Warwick, which by a violent and tempestuous wind, was so
swiftly carried through the principal and chief trading parts of the
town, that within the space of half an hour, several places, and
far distant from each other, were all in flames at once . . . And,
within the space of 4 or 5 hours, it had wholly consumed (except
two or three houses) all the High Street, Sheep Street, and
Church Street entirely; part of the Jury Street, New Street, and
many buildings about the Market Place; together with (the most
to be lamented loss) the great and ancient church of St Mary's,
and several . . . buildings in other parts of the town.

Memorials, 9 Sept. 1694

THUS a letter to the Bishop of Worcester, written four days after the
catastrophe, describes the fire of Warwick of 1694. Urban conflagrations were not necessarily notable events. Damaging fires were a
common occurrence in early modern towns, and Warwick itself had
suffered a number during the seventeenth century.[1] What made the
fire of 1694 exceptional was the sheer extent of the destruction (it was
one of the most devastating of the period), and the response to it.
Customarily, the rebuilding that followed a disaster took place along
lines similar to that of the pre-fire landscape. Yet during the
reconstruction at Warwick traditional vernacular architecture was
dramatically abandoned for fashionable classical town planning. This
book began life as an attempt to answer the question, why should this
have happened? It soon became clear that the search for a solution was
going to take me beyond the narrow confines of a specific academic
discipline or geographical location. Within Warwick itself it was
evident that the post-fire reconstruction of the town was part of a
wider economic, social, and cultural revival, originating in the years
after the Restoration. Moreover, a glance at the fortunes of other towns
during this period suggested that what was happening in Warwick was
not unique. Throughout the middle and upper reaches of the urban

---

[1] *VCH Warwickshire*, viii (London, 1969), 513; Corporation Accounts, 1692/3,
Warwickshire CRO, CR.1618 (Warwick Borough Records), W. 13/5.

system can be discerned a new wave of prosperity, the most striking sign of which was the cultural refinement and prestige it brought to those towns which were affected. Therefore, the rebuilding of Warwick was part of a much broader urban renaissance, and it is this that forms the subject of my book. The use of the term 'renaissance' should not be seen to herald the discovery of yet another major historical movement. The English Urban Renaissance was small fry when compared with the great Italian Renaissance. Yet there are parallels between the two movements that justify a respectful allusion to the latter. Both represented cultural revivals, in the case of English towns after a period of decline and even crisis; both were an urban phenomenon; both were associated with high culture, and with the absorption and propagation of classical art and thought; and finally, both were extraordinarily diverse but integrated processes, embracing a broad range of cultural forms (from the visual and physical to the abstract and cerebral), whose nature and development were inextricably tied to wider economic and social forces.

This book concentrates on the provincial town, though frequent reference will be made to London, since it fully participated in the Urban Renaissance and in many respects led it. But the metropolis was a unique case, for the pace and scale of change was markedly different from that in the provinces, and it deserves a study of its own. Moreover, forcing the capital to take a back seat for once permits the vitality of the mass of lesser centres to emerge. The Introduction outlines the nature of the urban system in the early eighteenth century before discussing the history of the early modern town, suggesting that a decisive change in fortunes occurred in the century after the Restoration. The Urban Renaissance emerged both as part and product of this new context. The following two sections explore different forms taken by the cultural revival. Part Two examines landscape and architecture, beginning with the basic unit of the domestic dwelling, before widening the focus to take in the middle ground of street and square, and the broader panorama embodied in urban prospects, planning, and public buildings. Part Three turns to fashionable leisure. After a general review of the performing and intellectual arts, it progresses to more detailed studies of recreational arenas of display, and of sport. If Parts Two and Three are primarily concerned with establishing the material forms of the Urban Renaissance, Part Four concentrates on its social analysis. Initially, the socio-economic foundations of the movement are investigated. Two chapters then examine its underlying

motives, the pursuit of status, civility, and sociability, and the way
these assisted in the development of a broader élite. The limits of this
élite are revealed in a further chapter, which looks beyond the world of
the polite, to show how the growth of fashionable urban life had a
culturally divisive impact on society. The implications of the thesis
presented in this study, both for towns and the nation as a whole, are
summarized in Part Five. By this stage it should be clear that
Warwick's innovative response to that fateful afternoon in late 1694
was only a part of a much broader renaissance that was permanently to
alter the face of English towns.

P. B.

ACKNOWLEDGEMENTS

My first debt is to all those historians, and scholars from other disciplines, whose publications are referred to in the footnotes and bibliography. Without their research it would have been impossible to write much of this book. The original doctoral thesis on which this study is based was supported by the then Social Science Research Council, and I have subsequently received several grants towards the costs of research and typing from the trustees of the Pantyfedwen Fund at Lampeter. I am grateful for this assistance. Some of the material in Chapters Six and Seven, and Appendix 6 has already appeared in two published essays of mine, and I would like to thank the editor of the *British Journal for Eighteenth-Century Studies* and the secretary of the Georgian Group for allowing the material to be reprinted here. During the course of my work I have incurred many debts to individuals. I should like to thank the staff of the Beinecke Library, the British Library, the Institute of Historical Research, the town council offices at Preston, the Shakespeare Birthplace Trust, and the Yale Center for British Art; the public libraries at Bath, Hereford, Lancaster, Preston, Taunton, and Warwick; the university libraries at Lampeter and Lancaster; the city record offices at Bath, Bristol, and York; and the county record offices of Herefordshire, Lancashire, Somerset, Warwickshire, and Wiltshire. Earlier drafts of parts of this study have been read at various conferences and meetings, and I have benefited from the comments of those who attended these sessions, as I have also from the insights and enthusiasm of my Special Subject groups at Lampeter. Maureen Hunwicks typed the manuscript with daunting speed and accuracy. Jonathan Barry responded promptly to an anxious phone call and provided me with a copy of his excellent thesis on Bristol. Richard Chamberlain-Brothers, Michael Farr, and Michael Turner greatly assisted me with their specialist knowledge of Warwick, and Sonia Spurdle with hers of French. Bruce Clarke, David Hey, Rosamond McGuinness, Angus McInnes, Joyce Miles, John Quinn, and Sarah Pearson have provided me with references or information, and the RCHM have kindly allowed me to consult their forthcoming volume on Whitehaven. I am particularly indebted to Pat Murrell who has brought to my attention, or directly provided me with material from the Hervey *Letter-Books*, the *Suffolk Mercury*, and the Cullum collection of manuscripts in the Suffolk Record Office. I must also thank Mrs E. Byers for permitting me to consult extracts from her catalogue of the Cullum Correspondence and Hanson Letters. Keith Thomas kindly read the whole of the type-script, and Christine Ferdinand copy-edited it. I am obliged to them both for their valuable suggestions, as I am also to the staff at OUP, particularly Ivon Asquith, for their help in producing this book. I should like to express my gratitude to all those who have guided my education, especially David Watson, Roger Hughes, the late Robert Heaton, the staff of the history department at the University of Lancaster, and Alan Everitt and Eric Evans, who examined my doctoral thesis. Geoffrey Holmes, who supervised my thesis, stimulated my interest in the subject and directed my early work with skill and consideration. I owe him a great deal. Finally, I wish to thank my family: my parents who have unstintingly encouraged and assisted my education, and Anne, whose intellectual and emotional support has contributed incalculably to the completion of this book.

CONTENTS

LIST OF ILLUSTRATIONS

Fig. 1 is reproduced by courtesy of Leeds City Council, Department of Leisure Services; Figs. 2, 3, 7, 8, 10, 11, 12, 13, 15, 22, 23, and 26 by courtesy of the Royal Commission on the Historical Monuments of England; Fig. 4 by courtesy of the Birmingham Public Libraries, Local Studies Department; Figs. 5, 14, 18, and 24 by courtesy of the Avon Community Leisure Department (Bath Reference Library); Fig. 6 by courtesy of The British Library; Figs. 9, 21, and 25 by courtesy of B. T. Batsford Ltd.; Fig. 16 by courtesy of York City Art Gallery; Figs. 19 and 20 by courtesy of the Museum and Art Gallery, Tunbridge Wells Borough Council; and Fig. 27 by courtesy of the Trustees of The British Museum.

LIST OF MAPS

Map 1 is based upon J. Fish and C. Bridgeman's plan of Warwick (*c*.1711) by courtesy of the Warwickshire County Record Office.

Map 2 is based upon *A Map of Bath showing the Principal Buildings of Architectural Interest*, compiled by Ernest F. Tew (1966).

LIST OF TABLES

ABBREVIATIONS

AO	Archives Office
BCA	Bath City Archives
BE	*Buildings of England*
CRO	County Record Office
EcHR	*Economic History Review*
Estimate	Warwickshire CRO, CR.1618, WA.4, 'An Estimate of the Loss Sustained in and by the Late Fire . . . 1694'
Fire Act	6 Gul. III, c. 1, 'An Act for the Rebuilding the Town of Warwick . . .'
HMC	Historical Manuscripts Commission
Memorials	Warwickshire CRO, CR.1618, WA.4, 'Memorials of . . . the Late Dreadful Fire'
Newdigate Diaries	Warwickshire CRO, CR.136/582–637, Diaries of Sir Roger Newdigate (1751–1806)
Pigott Diary	Beinecke Library (Yale), Osborne Shelves, f.c. 80, Diary of E. Pigott (1770–83), 2 vols.
PCMSS	Preston Corporation Manuscripts
Racing Calendar	*An Historical List of . . . Horse Matches*, compiled at various times by J. Cheny, R. Heber, and B. Walker, annual vols. (London 1730–71)
RCHM	Royal Commission on Historical Monuments
RO	Record Office
Students Diary	Bath Reference Library, 38/43, 'Diary of a Tour Undertaken by Three Students' (1725)
TBAS	*Transactions of the Birmingham Archaeological Society*
TRHS	*Transactions of the Royal Historical Society*
VCH	*Victoria County History*
YCA	York City Archives

Spelling and punctuation have been modernized. Prices are given in seventeenth- and eighteenth-century units of currency. All counties referred to are those before local government reorganization in 1974. All dates before 1752 (the reform of the calendar) are given in the Old Style, though in the text the year is taken to have begun on 1 January. In the notes dates between 1 January and 25 March are listed with both years.

I
INTRODUCTION

1

The Urban Scene

1. THE URBAN SYSTEM

Today the United Kingdom is one of the most urbanized countries in the world, with about two-thirds of its fifty million inhabitants living in communities of over 20,000 people.[1] It takes a leap of the imagination to visualize the pre-urbanized world of later Stuart and early Georgian England. In 1700 only one in four of the population of five million[2] lived in the 600 to 700 towns[3] that were scattered across the nation like small islands amidst a sea of villages, hamlets, and fields. Moreover, the contrast between then and now is even sharper. By our standards the vast majority of early eighteenth-century towns would seem little more than villages. Many possessed a population of only 1,000 people, some barely over 500. At the turn of the century there were scarcely seventy settlements of over 2,500 inhabitants, and a mere three cities of over 20,000. One of these was the 'monstrous city' of London with half a million souls. The provinces could boast only two cities, or one per cent of the population, that fell within the modern demographic measure of urbanism.[4]

But twentieth-century standards can be misleading. With late Stuart England possessing only a tenth of today's population, the true statistical yardstick of a town was bound to be lower. Moreover, head-counts are only one way, and a rather crude one at that, of defining a town. Economic organization, social and political structure, culture, and spheres of influence are equally important factors.[5] Henley-in-Arden in the woodland zone of north Warwickshire had a population

[1] E. E. Lampard, 'The Nature of Urbanization', in D. Fraser and A. Sutcliffe (eds.), *The Pursuit of Urban History* (London, 1983), 26, 46.

[2] C. W. Chalkin, *The Provincial Towns of Georgian England* (London, 1974), 3, 17.

[3] P. Clark and P. Slack, *English Towns in Transition 1500-1700* (London, 1976), 7-8; Chalklin, *Provincial Towns*, 4-5.

[4] P. J. Corfield, *The Impact of English Towns 1700-1800* (Oxford, 1982), 8-9.

[5] Clark and Slack, *Towns in Transition*, 2-7; Corfield, *English Towns*, 4-6; J. Patten, *English Towns 1500-1700* (Folkestone, 1978), 21-8.

of between 500 and 700 in the late seventeenth and early eighteenth
centuries. Yet this tiny settlement was a regularly accredited market
town, accommodated a range of distinctly urban trades and services
(including five inns in 1663), possessed its own 'proletariat', quite
different from that of the surrounding countryside, and even enjoyed
a form of 'rudimentary civic organization'.[6] The Henleys of England
demonstrate the importance of defining towns qualitatively rather
than quantitatively, and by the standards of their own time. However,
such places occupied the very margins of the urban system. Above
them climbed a hierarchy of towns that grew increasingly complex and
sophisticated the further it ascended.

An individual community's position in this hierarchy depended
primarily upon the degree of influence it exercised over its surrounding countryside, for this relationship was the *raison d'être* of the
mass of towns at this time. Bearing this criterion in mind, four broad
categories of settlements can be distinguished: commercial towns,
regional centres, provincial capitals, and the metropolis.[7] The vast
majority of towns, between 500 and 600 or over four-fifths of the
total, were accommodated in the bottom tier of the system. Individually they had a population of between about 500 and 2,500 in 1700,
and their livelihood depended largely upon the commercial services
they offered. Most were small-scale marketing centres, though the
category also includes a substantial number of minor and medium-
sized ports, and an expanding body of thoroughfare towns. Within
this lower division there was an important distinction between the
larger and smaller centres, a distinction that grew sharper during our
period as their economic fortunes diverged.

The smaller towns were the bedrock of the urban system. In the
later seventeenth century a third of the towns in Hampshire, two-fifths
of those in Kent, and half of those in East Anglia and Warwickshire
had populations of around 1,000 or under.[8] Despite the size of this

[6] P. Styles, *Studies in Seventeenth-Century West Midlands History* (Kineton,
1978), 205-12.
[7] Clark and Slack, *Towns in Transition*, 8-10; Patten, *English Towns*, 51-5;
Chalklin, *Provincial Towns*, 4-17; W.G. Hoskins, *Provincial England* (London, 1963),
86-8; P. J. Corfield, 'Urban Development in England and Wales in the Sixteenth
and Seventeenth Centuries', in D. C. Coleman and A. H. John (eds.), *Trade, Government, and Economy in Pre-Industrial England* (London, 1976), 221-3; A. Dyer,
'Warwickshire Towns under the Tudors and Stuarts', *Warwickshire History*, iii, No. 4
(1976/7), 125-8.
[8] A. Rosen, 'Winchester in Transition 1580-1700', in P. Clark (ed.), *Country
Towns in Pre-Industrial England* (Leicester, 1981), 175; C. W. Chalklin, *Seventeenth-*

category relatively little is known about its members. However, Tonbridge (600–800 people) in Kent and Kenilworth (about 1,000 people) in Warwickshire were probably representative of this type of settlement.[9] Both consisted of no more than a handful of main streets, two or three at Tonbridge, three or four at Kenilworth. Houses were relatively loosely dispersed, except in the vicinity of the market cross, with considerable gaps between individual dwellings or blocks of them. Long stretches of the main thoroughfares at Kenilworth were lined with trees and fields. Both communities enjoyed a wide range of simple trades and services, such as those provided by innkeepers, butchers, bakers, shoemakers, tailors, blacksmiths, and carpenters, and Tonbridge hosted a regular weekly market. Industry played only a minor role in their employment base. Above all, both places were deeply influenced by the close physical and economic proximity of the countryside.

Whereas the smaller commercial towns served only their immediate localities, the larger ones presided over a wider area and were frequently referred to in more expansive terms. Defoe described Petworth as a 'large handsome country market town', Tamworth as 'a fine pleasing trading town', Farnham and Basingstoke each as a 'large populous market town'; and in 1750 it was claimed of the thorough-fare settlement of Stony Stratford, that it 'has so extended its limits, that it ought to be reckoned among the large market towns'.[10] The larger commercial towns generally possessed populations of between 1,500 and 2,500 in the early eighteenth century, were often situated on navigable rivers or important roads, frequently hosted major inter-

Century Kent (Rochester, 1978), 28; Patten, *English Towns*, 251; Dyer, 'Warwickshire Towns', 125; E. A. Wrigley and R. S. Schofield, *The Population History of England 1541-1871* (London, 1981), 217-18.

9 C. W. Chalklin, 'A Seventeenth-Century Market Town: Tonbridge', *Archaeologia Cantiana*, lxxvi (1961), 152-62; J. Powell, *A Parson and his Flock: Kenilworth 1690-1740* (Kenilworth, 1981); J. Fish, 'The Survey of the Manor of Rusden with the Honour and Part of the Manor of Kenilworth', Warwickshire CRO, CR.143/A; J. D. Marshall, 'The Rise and Transformation of the Cumbrian Market Town 1660-1900', *Northern History*, xix (1983), 128-209; M. Noble, 'Growth and Development in a Regional Urban System: The Country Towns of Eastern Yorkshire 1700-1850', *Urban History Yearbook* (1987), 1-21; R. W. Unwin, 'Tradition and Transition: Market Towns of the Vale of York 1660-1830', *Northern History*, xvii (1981), 72-116. We will know much more about this type of community when the results of the project on English small towns 1600-1850, based at Leicester University, are published.

10 D. Defoe, *A Tour through the Whole Island of Great Britain*, ed. G. D. H. Cole and D. C. Browning (London, 1962), i. 132, 142, 180; ii. 82; *British Courant or the Preston Jnl.*, No. 278, 1-8 June 1750.

regional markets, and could usually boast at least a few sophisticated trades and services. Typical of this type of community was Stratford-upon-Avon, with around 2,000 inhabitants in 1700. After a period of crisis during the late sixteenth and early seventeenth centuries, Stratford subsequently began to enjoy a phase of prosperity based especially on malt processing and a long-distance trade in cheese and corn. Underpinning this revival was the completion of a river improvement scheme in 1671, which enhanced the town's position as the furthest navigable point along the Avon, improving its access to Bristol, and extending its capacity to trade in a wide range of consumables and bulky goods. In the 1750s it was home to James Keating, printer, bookseller, and proprietor of the town's first newspaper, the title of which, *The Stratford, Shipston, and Alcester Journal*, hinted at a group of smaller satellite market centres that fell under Stratford's influence.[11]

Like a number of the larger commercial towns Stratford was the hub of a miniature region. However, its influence was too limited to constitute a true regional centre. This accolade fell to a group of important towns that were able to exert a major impact on an extensive hinterland. They constituted the second tier of the urban system, and in 1700 numbered sixty to seventy members among their ranks, and enjoyed populations of between about 2,500 and 11,000. A major component of this second category of the hierarchy were those places that contemporaries called 'the capital city of a county', a 'shire town', 'assize town', or just plain 'county town'.[12] In practice many counties contained more than one of these types of centre, especially if the shire covered a large area or its terrain was topographically divided. In addition to their formal county towns, Lancashire had Preston, Derbyshire had Chesterfield, Lincolnshire had Stamford, Shropshire had Ludlow, Buckinghamshire had Aylesbury, and Kent had Maidstone, while the huge expanse of Yorkshire boasted additional centres at Wakefield, Beverley, and Doncaster. County centres rarely serviced the whole area of their home territory equally, and many would have drawn their clientele from neighbouring regions. Lichfield

[11] J. M. Martin, 'A Warwickshire Market Town in Adversity: Stratford-upon-Avon in the Sixteenth and Seventeenth Centuries', *Midland History*, vii (1982), 26–41; L. Fox, *The Borough Town of Stratford-upon-Avon* (Stratford-upon-Avon, 1953), 48, 61–5; Chalklin, *Provincial Towns*, 18.

[12] D. Defoe, *The Complete English Tradesman*, 1745, repr. (New York, 1970), 58; G. Miège, *The New State of England*, 3rd edn. (London, 1699), *passim*; E. Chamberlayne, *Angliae Notitia*, 18th edn. (London, 1694), *passim*.

catered to the gentry of Warwickshire and Derbyshire, as well as Staffordshire, Bury St Edmunds to those of Cambridgeshire, Norfolk, and Suffolk.[13] But the support of a particular county, or a substantial portion of it, was critical to the livelihood of these towns.[14] One factor that strengthened the close connection between a county town and its shire was its position as a regional administrative capital. The nature and value of this role can be seen in Morant's description of Chelmsford, as 'much frequented on account of its conveniency for public business. Here the assizes, the general quarter sessions, petty sessions, and county courts are held; here the commissioners for the land and window tax sit as often as is required; here elections of knights of the shire are made; and here is a county gaol. It has a very convenient shire house'. Such was the work generated by the duchy and county palatine courts at Preston that one visitor described 'the staple trade of this place' as 'the business of law'.[15] During the early modern period the level of provincial legal and political activity expanded considerably, and the county towns were major beneficiaries of this. Their administrative function was further enhanced by the fact that as cathedral cities many were also diocesan centres.

Shire towns today may appear rather sleepy places, cut off from the main stream of economic life. Nothing could have been further from the truth in the years after 1660.[16] Most were thriving trading communities, sometimes possessing markets of national significance, such as that for horses at Northampton, fruit at Maidstone, and wool at Cirencester.[17] Many were centres of a multi-faceted craft economy, and a number fostered important industrial enterprises, such as the

[13] A. Hughes, 'Warwickshire on the Eve of the Civil War: A "County Community"?', *Midland History*, vii (1982), 45–6; Defoe, *Tour*, i. 51; ii. 80; J. Money, *Experience and Identity: Birmingham and the West Midlands 1760–1800* (Manchester, 1977), 82; Newdigate Diaries, *passim*.

[14] A. Everitt, 'Country, County, and Town: Patterns of Regional Evolution in England', *TRHS*, 5th ser., xxix (1979), 88–105.

[15] P. Morant, *The History and Antiquities of the County of Essex* (London, 1768), ii. 1; J. Crofts, 'A Lakeland Journey 1759', ed. B. G. Hutton, *Trans. of the Cumberland and Westmorland Antiquarian and Archaeological Soc.*, new ser., lxi (1961), 289; Defoe, *Tour*, ii. 268.

[16] P. Clark (ed.), *The Transformation of English Provincial Towns 1600–1800* (London, 1984), 26–7.

[17] Defoe, *Tour*, i. 113–14, 282; ii. 86–7; S. and N. Buck, *Buck's Antiquities* (London, 1774), iii, Maidstone; and also H. B. Rodgers, 'The Marketing Area of Preston in the Sixteenth and Seventeenth Centuries', *Geographical Studies*, iii (1956), 46–55; Rosen, 'Winchester', 170–6; Buck, *Antiquities*, iii, Guildford, Leicester; Defoe, *Tour*, i. 144–5, 291; ii. 14, 113, 145–6, 238.

hosiery trade in Leicester and Nottingham, and brewing and silk weaving in Derby.[18] Most also enjoyed a burgeoning trade in consumer goods and professional services. One characteristic which they all shared was the high status of their residents and visitors, a feature they carefully cultivated, even to the extent of accommodating and protecting groups of Roman Catholic gentry, as at Durham, Winchester, and York.[19] Given their image, it is not surprising that shire towns also became focal points for the provision of fashionable culture and leisure after the Restoration.

Two further types of towns occupied the regional tier of the urban hierarchy. The first of these comprised the larger ports and dockyards, the most notable of which in 1700 were Yarmouth (with roughly 11,000 people), Plymouth (8,500), Ipswich (8,000), Portsmouth (7,500), Hull (6,000), Chatham, King's Lynn, and Liverpool (all about 5,000).[20] Of the second type were those towns that acted as centres of rural-industrial regions. These included Colchester (with roughly 9,000 inhabitants in 1700), Manchester (8,000), Leeds (7,000), and Tiverton (5,000) in the textile trades, and Birmingham (8,000) and Sheffield (3,500) in the manufacture of metalwares.[21] They were concerned predominantly with providing a range of marketing and general services for industries whose basic production was dispersed throughout the surrounding countryside. Ports, dockyards, and industrial centres were among the most dynamic towns during the period, and by 1750 several had ascended a further rung of the urban ladder.

A handful of provincial capitals constituted the élite cadre of the system. It is impossible to be precise about which cities occupied this third category, but in 1700 there were probably seven candidates: Norwich (with a population of around 30,000), Bristol (20,000), Newcastle-upon-Tyne (16,000), Exeter (14,000), York (12,000),

---

[18] Everitt, 'County and Town', 98–105; Defoe, *Tour*, ii. 88, 145, 157; Buck, *Antiquities*, iii, Derby, Leicester, Nottingham; Students Diary, fos. 79, 82; HMC, *Verulam MSS*, 231.

[19] Defoe, *Tour*, i. 186; ii. 249; Rosen, 'Winchester', 179–80; F. Drake, *Eboracum: Or, the History and Antiquities of the City of York*, 1736, repr. (East Ardsley, 1978), 241.

[20] These population figures are generally working estimates. P. J. Corfield, 'Economic Growth and Change in Seventeenth-Century English Towns', in C. Phythian-Adams *et al.*, *The Traditional Community under Stress*, Open University English Urban History Course (Milton Keynes, 1977), 42.

[21] Corfield, 'Economic Growth', 42; K. Grady, 'The Provision of Public Buildings in the West Riding of Yorkshire *c*.1600–1840', Ph.D. thesis (Leeds, 1980), 13.

Chester (8,000), and Shrewsbury (7,500). By the mid-eighteenth
century they had been joined by Birmingham, Liverpool, Manchester,
and perhaps by one or two other thrusting regional centres.[22] The
members of this tier earned their special status because of the
enormous range and depth of their influence, which was substantially
greater than that of a county town. In the 1720s Newcastle was called
'the great emporium of all the northern parts of England, and of a
good share of Scotland', and it was said of the two great western
ports that 'Bristol has the trade of south Wales; Liverpool great part
of the trade of north Wales; Bristol has the south west counties of
England, and some north of it, as high as Bridgnorth, and perhaps to
Shrewsbury; Liverpool has all the northern counties, and a large
consumption of goods in Cheshire and Staffordshire are supplied'.[23]
The influence of Norwich, Exeter, Birmingham, and Manchester may
have been geographically more limited, but the depth of their impact
on East Anglia, the far South-West, the West Midlands, and the
North-West was considerable.[24] York held sway throughout the North
as an administrative and social centre (since 1542 it has been the seat
of the northern province of the anglican church, which included all
the six northern counties as well as Nottinghamshire and Cheshire),
and Chester and Shrewsbury derived much of their significance from
servicing the urban desert of Wales.[25] The provincial capitals were
universal towns whose prosperity rested upon a wide range of
functions. All were major trading centres with markets and shops that
spilled out over a wide area of their streetscape. Several were great
ports, some at the head of navigable river systems that penetrated
deep inland, allowing them to command the trade of a huge hinterland. All, York and Chester excepted, were closely associated with
industry, either as the centre of a manufacturing region or, in the case

[22] Corfield, 'Economic Growth', 42; Clark and Slack, *Towns in Transition*, 46–61;
Chalklin, *Provincial Towns*, 13–16.
[23] T. Cox, *Magna Britannia et Hibernia, Antiqua et Nova* (London, 1720–31), iii.
608; Defoe, *Tour*, ii. 257.
[24] P. J. Corfield, 'A Provincial Capital in the Late Seventeenth Century: The Case of
Norwich', in P. Clark and P. Slack (eds.), *Crisis and Order in English Towns 1500–1700*
(London, 1972), 263–310; W. G. Hoskins, *Industry, Trade, and People in Exeter 1688–
1800*, 2nd edn. (Exeter, 1968), *passim*; M. Wise, 'Birmingham and its Trade Relations
in the Early Eighteenth Century', *University of Birmingham Historical Jnl.*, xi (1949),
72–9; Money, *Experience and Identity, passim*.
[25] J. Hutchinson and D. M. Palliser, *York*, Bartholomew City Guides (Edinburgh,
1980), 55–74; Defoe, *Tour*, ii. 75–7; I. Mitchell, 'The Development of Urban Retailing
1700–1815', in Clark, *Provincial Towns*, 261–2.

of the ports, as the base for a number of specialized industrial processes. Most, as county or cathedral towns, were administrative capitals, and all supported a rich diet of fashionable culture.

Crowning the whole urban edifice, and in a division all of its own, was London. In 1700 it was home to one in every ten Englishmen and was sixteen times the size of its nearest rival. Throughout the early modern period its growth had been spectacular, from about 120,000 inhabitants in 1550, to 200,000 by 1600, and 490,000 at the beginning of the eighteenth century. By the last period it was incomparably the greatest centre of marketing, trade, business, craft manufacture, consumption, administration, and recreation in Britain.[26]

The concept of an urban hierarchy is valuable in helping us to grasp the general pattern of English towns in the years 1660 to 1770. But it also suggests a uniformity and rigidity about the urban scene that is belied by the local context and the swift pace of change. Some regions were far more urbanized than others. Market centres were much thicker on the ground in the South-West, the South Midlands, and East Anglia, than in Cumbria, the North-East, and the Welsh Border counties. In the 1670s Essex, Suffolk, and Norfolk were among the most urbanized areas in the country, with about a third of their inhabitants living in towns. On the other hand, the East Midlands had a distinctly rural profile in the later Stuart period, with only about twenty per cent of Leicestershire's population, and scarcely fifteen per cent of Lincolnshire's inhabitants (if towns with probably less than 400 people are excluded) living in urban settlements.[27] Even within county boundaries there could be considerable variations. In the Forest of Arden zone of Warwickshire towns were few and far between, whereas the periphery of the area was circled with a number of prosperous trading centres, mediating between the county's woodland and Feldon economies. Defoe thought it 'remarkable of Bedfordshire, that though a great part of the county lies on the north side of the Ouse

---

[26] Clark and Slack, *Towns in Transition*, 62–81; Corfield, *English Towns*, 66–81; A. L. Beier and R. Finlay (eds.), *London 1500–1700: The Making of the Metropolis* (London, 1986), especially p. 48, which contains the most recent estimate of the capital's population.

[27] A. Everitt, 'The Market Towns', in P. Clark (ed.), *The Early Modern Town* (London, 1976), 191–2; K. H. Burley, 'The Economic Development of Essex in the Later Seventeenth and Early Eighteenth Centuries', Ph.D. thesis (London, 1957), 7–11; J. Patten, 'Population Distribution in Norfolk and Suffolk during the Sixteenth and Seventeenth Centuries', *Trans. of the Institute of British Geographers*, lxv (1975), 48–9; A. Dyer, 'Growth and Decay in English Towns 1500–1700', *Urban History Yearbook* (1979), 65; Chalklin, *Provincial Towns*, 320.

. . . yet there is not one market town in all that side . . . but Bedford only'.[28]

One factor which makes it difficult to paint a single comprehensive picture of the later Stuart and early Georgian urban system is the fact that its form was altering under the impact of demographic and economic change. The years 1660 to 1770 were ones of substantial but selective urban expansion, affecting some areas, such as the West Midlands, South Lancashire, and the West Riding of Yorkshire, far more than others. Moreover, the nature of the growth that was underway began to disturb the very basis of the urban hierarchy. There had been traditionally a close association between the size of a town and its regional influence. Certain types of centres were now emerging which failed to fit this pattern. The dockyards tended to be 'inward-looking and secretive' communities,[29] and the new industrial towns were increasingly able to generate their livelihoods from within their own boundaries. At the opposite end of the spectrum, resorts and thoroughfare towns enjoyed a geographical impact considerably greater than their size would suggest. In the long term, such new settlements pointed towards an urban system defined more by the economic and social function of its members than by their external influence. But this trend should not be exaggerated. The continued rural location of industry and the comparatively small scale of resort development ensured that for our period the relationship between an urban centre and its immediate hinterland continued to be the major characteristic that determined a town's status.

2. THE TUDOR AND EARLY STUART TOWN

If, in the century after the Restoration, the English town remained recognizably the same creature, these were nevertheless years of considerable and positive change, even of transformation. The scale of this may appear unremarkable when judged against the urban upheaval of the Industrial Revolution, but when compared with the years *before* 1660, as properly should be the case, the pace of progress was impressive. Therefore, to understand the context of post-Restoration urban development we must briefly explore the Tudor and early Stuart town. The picture that confronts us is a confused one,

---

[28] Dyer, 'Warwickshire Towns', 124-5; Defoe, *Tour*, ii. 112-13.
[29] Corfield, *English Towns*, 45.

since historians are divided about the fate of urban communities during this period. Some paint a picture of crisis and decline, while others take a less pessimistic line.[30] But few analysts would portray the period as one of general urban development, and most would probably argue that the debit side outweighed the credit one.

Three main periods of acute problems have been detected: the early Tudor years, the late sixteenth to early seventeenth centuries (with the 1590s and 1620s particularly bad decades), and the Civil War. On these occasions the communities most seriously affected were those occupying the middling and upper ranks of the urban hierarchy. There is no unanimity among historians as to the precise timing or gravity of this trio of crises. In practice, few would want to argue that the period was one of unremitting gloom. At the very least the years between the mid- and late sixteenth century, and about 1605 and 1620, provided a respite. Moreover, several centres which initially suffered serious setbacks began to show signs of recovery before the mid-seventeenth century: Norwich and York as early as the reign of Elizabeth, Stratford-upon-Avon and Winchester rather later, though the progress of the Hampshire capital was rudely halted by the events of the 1640s.[31] Most significant, there was a substantial body of towns which undoubtedly enjoyed stability and even prosperity for much of the period. These included largish ports such as Hull and Yarmouth, and industrial/marketing centres like Colchester, Worcester (at least until the mid-1620s), and Exeter.[32] Perhaps the most successful towns were some of the smaller ones. Free from the burdens of their larger neighbours, they were able to benefit, particularly after the 1570s, from a surge in inland trade. Also in this group should be included the

[30] The debate has generated a considerable literature. Among the 'crisis school' are Clark and Slack, *Crisis and Order*, 1-56; C. Phythian-Adams, 'Urban Decay in Late Medieval England', in P. Abrams and E. A. Wrigley (eds.), *Towns in Societies* (Cambridge, 1978), 159-85; D. Palliser, *Tudor York* (Oxford, 1979), 201-25. For a more optimistic approach see Dyer, 'Growth and Decay', 60-72; S. Reynolds, 'Decline and Decay in Late Medieval Towns', *Urban History Yearbook* (1980), 76-8; A. R. Bridbury, 'English Provincial Towns in the Later Middle Ages', *EcHR*, 2nd ser., xxxiv, No. 1 (1981), 1-24; N. R. Goose, 'In Search of the Urban Variable: Towns and the English Economy 1500-1650', *EcHR*, 2nd ser., xxxix, No. 2 (1986), 165-85.
[31] J. F. Pound, 'The Social and Trade Structure of Norwich 1525-1575', *Past and Present*, xxxiv (1966), 61-2; Palliser, *Tudor York*, 260-87; Martin, 'Stratford-upon-Avon', 36-8; Rosen, 'Winchester', 150-5.
[32] Clark, *Country Towns*, 12; Corfield, 'Urban Development', 227-8; W. T. MacCaffrey, *Exeter 1540-1640*, 2nd edn. (Cambridge, Mass., and London, 1975), 160-73; A. Dyer, *The City of Worcester in the Sixteenth Century* (Leicester, 1973), chaps. 7-11.

nascent industrial communities, such as Birmingham, Leeds, and Halifax, along with their less dynamic companions, like tiny Ledbury in Herefordshire, enjoying after 1570 'possibly its period of greatest prosperity'.[33]

The years between the late fifteenth and mid-seventeenth centuries were clearly not ones of unabated crisis. On the other hand, the pressures faced by towns during this period were daunting enough, and few centres would have entirely escaped their damaging influence. These difficulties were of two types, the first of a natural genesis, the second human in origin.[34] Towns were frequently buffeted, and occasionally racked to their foundations by the awesome forces of nature. Ports could suffer enormous damage through the encroachment or withdrawal of the sea. But the most widespread natural impediments to urban prosperity were disease and fire. On top of a persistently high level of mortality, towns were subject to waves of epidemic illness, especially in the mid-sixteenth and early seventeenth centuries. Among the chief killers were a mysterious virus disease, probably a form of influenza, and bubonic plague. When an epidemic struck it could devastate a town. In the 1550s York lost a third or more of its population, and a similar proportion in the plague of 1604. One in six of the inhabitants of Salisbury in 1604, and one in five of those of Loughborough in 1558 and Leicester in 1610–11 died during the epidemics of these years. In 1558–9 10 per cent of Stratford-upon-Avon's citizens were scythed down by flu or typhus, and at least 16 per cent by plague only five years later. Nor were these visitations exceptional events. Loughborough suffered four major epidemics and five minor ones between 1545 and 1631, Leicester about eleven plague attacks between 1558 and 1639.[35]

[33] Everitt, 'Market Towns', 168–204; Clark, *Country Towns*, 13; V. Skipp, *The History of Greater Birmingham: Down to 1830* (Birmingham, 1980), 38–46; W. G. Rimmer, 'The Evolution of Leeds', in Clark, *Early Modern Town*, 281–6; M. E. François, 'The Social and Economic Development of Halifax 1558–1640', *Proceedings of the Leeds Philosophical and Literary Soc.*, Literary Historical Section, xi, Part 8 (1966), 217–80; J. Hillaby, *The Book of Ledbury* (Buckingham, 1982), 95–6.
[34] Patten, *English Towns*, 56–76.
[35] Palliser, *Tudor York*, 124–5; P. Slack, 'Poverty and Politics in Salisbury 1597–1666', in Clark and Slack, *Crisis and Order*, 169; N. Griffin, 'Epidemics in Loughborough 1539–1640', *Trans. of the Leicestershire Archaeological and Historical Soc.*, xciii (1967–8), 27, 32; J. E. O. Wilshere, 'Plague in Leicester 1558–1665', *Trans. of the Leicestershire Archaeological and Historical Soc.*, xciv (1968–9), 46–7; Martin, 'Stratford-upon-Avon', 30; P. Slack, *The Impact of Plague in Tudor and Stuart England* (London, 1985), especially chap. 5.

Fire was less profligate with human life, but its effects may have been equally debilitating. The widespread use of inflammable building materials, the closely packed nature of properties, and the presence of trades in which fire was a major tool of production made towns highly vulnerable to regular and large-scale conflagrations. Some of these could be devastating. Norwich is reported to have lost 718 dwellings in 1507, Tiverton 400 in 1598, and Oxford about 300 in 1644. Moreover, recent research suggests that serious fires occurred more frequently than we might imagine, even in the same town; Dorchester had three between 1613 and 1625, Stratford-upon-Avon five between 1594 and 1641.[36] Quite apart from the loss of life and property, pestilence and fire could lead to severe short-term dislocations in the life of the community. Trading and production might grind to a halt, creating unemployment and poverty. Partly as a consequence of this, partly as a direct result of the crisis, the demand for public assistance escalated dramatically. During epidemics these problems were sometimes exacerbated by an unseemly flight of the leading citizens, leaving civic government impoverished and seriously weakened.

If disease and fire are attributable to the blind forces of nature, the human hand was evident in three further ailments that afflicted English towns: economic depression, poverty, and warfare. A number of centres experienced serious difficulties as a consequence of long- and short-term changes in the structure and operation of the economy.[37] Two aspects of this were critical. First, there was a decided shift in the location of some major industries away from the larger towns towards the countryside and smaller urban settlements, where labour was cheap, plentiful, unregulated, and carried few social overheads. A second feature was the inherent volatility in the demand for manufactured goods, particularly for textiles. Changes in fashion, international warfare, and harvest failures (which raised food prices and depressed the demand for industrial products), created an ongoing series of trade crises.

[36] E. L. Jones, S. Porter, and M. Turner, *A Gazetteer of English Urban Fire Disasters 1500-1900*, Historical Geography Research Ser., No. 13 (Norwich, 1984), 16, 32, 39; S. Porter, 'The Oxford Fire of 1644', *Oxoniensia*, xlix (1984), 295-6; S. Porter, 'Fires in Stratford-upon-Avon in the Sixteenth and Seventeenth Centuries', *Warwickshire History*, iii, No. 3 (1976), 97-105.

[37] Clark and Slack, *Towns in Transition*, 97-110; N. R. Goose, 'Decay and Regeneration in Seventeenth-Century Reading: A Study in a Changing Economy', *Southern History*, vi (1984), 57-61.

Economic depression, with its attendant unemployment and under-employment, also contributed to the soaring problem of urban poverty,[38] as did epidemics, crop failures, and the loss of institutional relief in the wake of the Reformation. But the most important under-lying cause of pauperism was the rapid growth in the national popu-lation from the mid-Tudor years. This increased the number of mouths to feed, forced up the prices of foodstuffs faster than wages, and stimulated a wave of subsistence migration from country to town in pursuit of illusory relief and employment opportunities. The effect on urban centres was to create a growing reservoir of poor and semi-poor, whose numbers could escalate alarmingly during a period of crisis. At Warwick, one in every four families may have needed relief during the harvest failure of 1586-7, and at Stratford-upon-Avon in 1601 about a third of the inhabitants were receiving aid after a period of fire and dearth. During the Salisbury epidemic of 1604-5 probably 20 per cent of the population obtained some type of public assist-ance, while in that of 1627 the proportion rose to almost one in every two.[39]

Poverty placed a heavy burden on the economic and administrative resources of a town. A similar case could be argued for warfare. Even where the theatre of military action was overseas, towns could suffer from the dislocation of international trade, the cost of billeting troops, and heavy taxation to pay for the conflict.[40] When a town was directly caught up in the fighting, as during the Civil War, the effects could be traumatic. Preparations for defence, and the impact of an attack or a calculated fire-raid, might lead to the wholesale destruction of a community's building stock. During the siege of Gloucester in 1643, 241 houses, barns, stables, and outbuildings were lost; during that of Taunton in 1645, two-thirds of the town was destroyed; and the firing of Axminster in 1644 by the Parliamentarians almost totally devastated the town.[41] Raiding, looting, and extortion were also a

---

[38] C. Phythian-Adams, *Desolation of a City: Coventry and the Urban Crisis of the Later Middle Ages* (Cambridge, 1979), 55, 61-2, 219-20.

[39] A. L. Beier, 'The Social Problems of an Elizabethan Country Town: Warwick 1580-90', in Clark, *Country Towns*, 58; Martin, 'Stratford-upon-Avon', 34; Slack, 'Poverty and Politics', 170, 172.

[40] Phythian-Adams, *Coventry*, 62-3; Rosen, 'Winchester', 157-8.

[41] S. Porter, 'Property Destruction in the English Civil Wars,' *History Today*, xxxvi (Aug. 1986), 36-41; S. Porter, 'The Fire-Raid in the English Civil War', *War and Society*, ii, No. 2 (1984), 27-40; S. Rudder, *A New History of Gloucestershire* (Cirencester, 1779), 205; I. Roy, 'The English Civil War and English Society', in

serious and continuous problem for a number of centres. The presence
of an unhealthy garrison of troops could savagely increase the civilian
mortality rate (at Banbury during 1642–5 it probably trebled), while
the general impact of military action severely disrupted trade and
temporarily damaged many towns' economies. All in all, the conflicts
of the 1640s must have sent a shock wave through the urban system.[42]

3. THE POST-RESTORATION TOWN

At best, the Tudor and early Stuart years were mixed ones for the
nation's towns, and the period ended on a pronounced down-beat.
Undoubtedly there were signs of progress, but there were also
formidable problems. However, in the century after the Restoration
the whole tenor of urban life subtly but indubitably altered. The
extent of this change should not be exaggerated. There was no urban
revolution. But, if before 1660 the fortunes of English towns had been
regularly checked by bouts of crisis and uncertainty, then afterwards
they were carried along on a gathering tide of prosperity.[43]

Underpinning this transformation was a fresh and significant phase
of development in the national economy, which injected a new
buoyancy into its urban components. Three general features of this
revival stand out. First, though towns were still subject to bouts of
economic depression, these no longer seemed quite as prevalent or
severe as before, suggesting that urban economies had acquired a new
inner strength that enabled them to weather short-term crises. Second,
whereas in the sixteenth century a degree of rivalry had characterized
the economic interaction between town and country, and at the
former's expense, interdependence now became the keynote of their
relationship. This was achieved by the two sectors concentrating on
different but related functions: the rural one on basic agricultural and

B. Bond and I. Roy (eds.), *War and Society: A Yearbook of Military History* (London,
1975), 30; S. Porter, 'The Destruction of Axminster in 1644', *Devon and Cornwall
Notes and Queries*, xxv (1985), 243–5.

[42] Roy, 'Civil War', 31, 37; I. Roy, 'England Turned Germany? The Aftermath of
the Civil War in its European Context', *TRHS*, 5th ser., xxviii (1978), 136–42; Clark,
Country Towns, 15.

[43] Chalklin, *Provincial Towns*, 17–25; P. Borsay, 'The English Urban Renaissance:
The Development of Provincial Urban Culture *c*.1680–*c*.1760', *Social History*, No. 5
(1977), 581–603; A. McInnes, *The English Town 1660–1760*, Historical Association
(London, 1980), 35–6, Clark, *Country Towns*, 15–31; Clark, *Provincial Towns*, Introduction.

industrial production, the urban one on marketing, finishing processes, crafts, and services. Third, towns now began to enjoy the benefits of successfully adapting to the special difficulties and opportunities they faced during the early modern period. If the older draperies would not sell then it was important to build a new textile industry based on more fashionable materials. If cloth manufacture itself was uneconomic then perhaps it was better to abandon it altogether for other trades, or to develop a more broadly based service and consumer economy. By the late seventeenth century the lessons of the years of crisis had been learnt, and with some profit.

Economic prosperity meant that many of the problems that had so depressed towns before 1660 no longer appeared so acute. Poverty remained an endemic and serious feature of urban society. But improved employment opportunities, a widespread rise in living standards, and developing administrative arrangements for public relief were probably helping to take the edge off the problem.[44] A similar case can be made for disease and fire. Epidemics of flu, smallpox, and typhus continued to reap their grim harvests, particularly between the 1720s and the early 1740s (one in thirteen of Nottingham's population died during an epidemic in 1741-2), but their impact no longer appears quite as awesome. A major reason for this was the sudden disappearance of plague, after three centuries of carnage. Loughborough and Leicester suffered their last significant visitations in 1631 and 1639, and the final great wave of the disease struck English towns in 1665-6.[45]

There is no reason to believe that the incidence of urban fires diminished after 1660. Under the impact of urbanization it may even have increased, though the nature of the sources makes it difficult to

[44] Clark, *Provincial Towns*, 30-2; C. B. Phillips, 'Town and Country: Economic Change in Kendal *c*.1550-1700', in Clark, *Provincial Towns*, 110; P. Ripley, 'Poverty in Gloucester and its Alleviation 1690-1740', *Trans. of the Bristol and Gloucestershire Archaeological Soc.*, ciii (1985), 185-99.

[45] Corfield, *English Towns*, 109-20; J. D. Chambers, 'Population Change in a Provincial Town: Nottingham 1700-1800', in D. V. Glass and D. E. C. Eversley (eds.), *Population History* (London, 1965), 343; A. B. Appleby, 'The Disappearance of Plague: A Continuing Puzzle', *EcHR*, 2nd ser., xxxiii, No. 2 (1980), 161-73; P. Slack, 'The Disappearance of Plague: An Alternative View', *EcHR*, 2nd ser., xxxiv, No. 3 (1981), 469-76; Griffin, 'Epidemics in Loughborough', 30-2; Wilshere, 'Plague in Leicester', 62-4; J. Taylor, 'Plague in the Towns of Hampshire: The Epidemic of 1665-6', *Southern History*, vi (1984), 107; I. G. Doolittle, 'The Effects of the Plague on a Provincial Town in the Sixteenth and Seventeenth Centuries', *Medical History*, xix (1975), 334.

18 *Introduction*

establish any secure chronology. Only after the 1760s is it clear that a sharp and permanent decline set in. Yet fire was no longer quite the spectre that had haunted towns in earlier years. Despite the considerable physical growth of many communities there is little evidence that the scale of individual conflagrations was growing. Moreover, many of the most prosperous and expanding centres seem to have escaped serious damage altogether. This was probably due to the increasing adoption of non-inflammable building materials, especially brick and slate instead of timber and thatch, which not only decreased the chances of a fire starting, but also introduced natural firebreaks into the landscape, which reduced the risk of minor incidents flaring up into major disasters.[46] Improvements in fire-fighting equipment, particularly the growing use and sophistication of fire-engines, the development of urban piped water supplies, and the tightening up of regulations to prevent the occurrence and spread of conflagrations also ameliorated the problem.[47] In early eighteenth-century York the corporation employed four teams of uniformed fire-men and maintained a battery of eight engines, the equipment being regularly checked and used.[48] Catastrophes, of course, continued to occur. What is remarkable is the way towns rapidly recovered and even profited from disaster. In the late seventeenth century the two most serious provincial fires were those at Northampton (1675) and, as we have seen, Warwick (1694). Yet both communities displayed extraordinary resilience in quickly and fashionably rebuilding their shattered landscapes. By 1736 the *Northampton Mercury* could boast 'there has

---

[46] Jones *et al.*, *Gazetteer*, 42, 60-2; E. L. Jones, 'The Reduction of Fire Damage in Southern England 1650-1850', *Post-Medieval Archaeology*, ii (1968), 141-2.

[47] Council Minutes, 18 Dec. 1724, 11 Dec. 1727, PCMSS; Guild Roll 1702, PCMSS; Hereford Common Council Proceedings, July 1700 and Apr. 1705, Hereford City Library; Council Minutes, 29 June 1747, BCA; Chamberlain's Accounts, 1712/13, BCA; H. Cunnington (ed.), *Some Annals of the Borough of Devizes* (Devizes, 1925), 208; K. A. Macmahon (ed.), *Beverley Corporation Minute Books 1707-1835*, Yorkshire Archaeological Soc., Record Ser., cxxii (1956), 11; J. Nichols, *The History and Antiquities of the County of Leicester* (London, 1795-1815), i, part 2, 435, 445; A. L. Clegg, *A History of Dorchester, Dorset* (London, 1972), 125; R. Jenkins, 'Fire-Extinguishing Engines in England 1625-1725', *Trans. of the Newcomen Soc.*, xi (1930-1), 15-25; S. Porter, 'Fire Precautions in Early Modern Abingdon', *Berkshire Archaeological Jnl.*, lxxi (1981-2), 71-7; S. Porter, 'The Oxford Fire Regulations of 1671', *Bulletin of the Institute of Historical Research*, lviii, No. 138 (1985), 251-5.

[48] House Book, 6 Dec. 1711, 19 July 1712, 24 Oct. and 8 Dec. 1720, 12 Dec. 1722, 29 Jan. 1723/4, 10 Apr. 1724, 2 June 1728, 3 Feb. 1728/9, 16 Dec. 1734, 29 Jan. 1750/1, 23 May 1755, 5 Feb. 1759, YCA.

been a friendly emulation and contest betwixt the two agreeable inland towns of Warwick and Northampton, ever since the dreadful calamity which laid them both in ashes, whither of the two exceeds the other in the beauty of its structure and the regularity of its plan. It is sufficient to say that neither of them is to yield to any other town in England'.[49]

After the 1650s English towns were largely spared the trauma of civil war, though the Jacobite campaigns created a small amount of damage.[50] But international conflict escalated to quite new levels, especially during the wars against France. A number of ports and manufacturing towns, such as Colchester, Exeter, and Weymouth, suffered particularly from privateering and the general dislocation of trade.[51] On the other hand, many more were either unaffected or benefited. The latter group included the expanding naval dockyards, 'safe' ports beyond the operating zone of enemy raiders, like Liverpool, and those towns at the centre of industrial regions that supplied military hardware and munitions, such as Birmingham, Leeds, and Halifax.[52]

Economic prosperity, allied to the easing of pressures which had long beleaguered the town, provided a favourable background for *positive* urbanization. In the century before the Civil War, the proportion of the nation living in towns had probably risen significantly.[53] But much of this growth was of a *negative* nature, since it caused or exacerbated many of the problems faced by these communities. The urban sector may have carried more people, but it was ill-equipped to bear such a burden. In the years after 1660 urbanization continued. Whereas in 1600 about 8 per cent of the total population lived in settlements of over 5,000, by 1700 this had doubled to 16.5 per cent; and those inhabiting places of over 2,500

[49] Jones *et al.*, *Gazetteer*, 18-19; extract from the *Northampton Mercury*, letter headed Warwick, 30 Apr. 1734, Warwickshire CRO, CR.15/96.

[50] R. Patten, *The History of the Late Rebellion*, 2nd edn. (London, 1717), 112, 128, 132-3.

[51] Morant, *Essex*, i. 79; Hoskins, *Exeter*, 30; S. McIntyre, 'Towns as Health and Pleasure Resorts: Bath, Scarborough, and Weymouth 1700-1815', D.Phil. thesis (Oxford, 1973), 297.

[52] *VCH Warwickshire*, vii (London, 1964), 85-6; Defoe, *Tour*, i. 43, 105-8, 136-9, 230-1; ii. 198; R. Davis, *The Rise of the English Shipping Industry* (Newton Abbot, 1972), 38; G. S. Holmes (ed.), *Britain after the Glorious Revolution* (London, 1969), 26-32.

[53] Corfield, 'Urban Development', 222-3; Patten, *English Towns*, 120-4.

increased from just under 19 per cent in 1700, to 22.5 per cent by
1750.[54] However, more critical than these growth rates was the positive
context in which they occurred. Towns now possessed the economic
capacity to absorb larger numbers without debilitating themselves.
Demographic expansion therefore became a genuine sign of health
and a true stimulus to urban development. Moreover, from about
1700 the most dynamic area of urbanization was no longer the metropolis, as had been the case for much of the early modern period, but
the provinces. Whereas during the first half of the eighteenth century
London's share of the national population stayed fixed at 11.1 per
cent, provincial towns of over 2,500 people increased their proportion
from 7.5 per cent to 11 per cent. As one commentator has suggested,
'England's urban world was becoming notably multi-centred rather
than focused upon a single city'.[55]

If, in the years after the Restoration, the general urban climate
improved, there were still problems to be faced by individual
communities. The most serious threat, itself a by-product of urban
prosperity, was that posed by competition. Between about 1680 and
1730 Barnstaple lost ground to its close rival Bideford, and in the
North-West 'the trade' of Chester was 'much eclipsed by the neighbouring greatness of Liverpool'. However, in both cases natural forces
contributed to decline, with the silting up of the Taw and the Dee.
Stafford suffered as a manufacturing centre from its proximity to the
rapidly industrializing regions of the West Midlands and the Potteries,
and as a marketing and social centre from the superior attractions of
nearby Lichfield.[56] Undoubtedly the communities most vulnerable to
competition were the smaller commercial towns. One estimate
suggests that by 1770 perhaps as many as a third of the market towns
of Tudor and early Stuart England had become extinct; another, that
in the century after 1690 the number of marketing centres fell by
about a fifth among a group of sixteen 'metropolitan Western
England' counties. The central problem was that the smaller towns
were unable to compete with the superior commercial facilities offered
to both buyers and sellers by their larger neighbours, a trend exacerbated by improvements in road and water transport. But the extent of

[54] Corfield, 'Economic Growth', 40; Corfield, *English Towns*, 8-9.
[55] Corfield, *English Towns*, 10.
[56] Defoe, *Tour*, i. 259-62; W. G. Hoskins, *Devon* (London, 1954), 115, 328, 336;
British Courant, No. 289, 17-24 Aug. 1750; K. R. Adey, 'Seventeenth-Century
Stafford: A County Town in Decline', *Midland History*, ii, No. 3 (1974), 164-7.

the decline of the smaller centres was much less marked in some regions than others, and was often a slow process. Moreover, the loss of these minnows of the urban system should not disturb our overall view, since many may only have been nominally towns in the first place.[57]

After competition, the most serious threat to a town's livelihood was that posed by fluctuations in the demand for specific products and services. The danger was keenest in those places heavily dependent on a single trade, particularly one where demand was potentially volatile. In this respect textile centres were greatest at risk, and there were a number of casualties among their ranks. Though prosperous in the late seventeenth century, the Essex cloth industry went into long-term decline from about 1700, as the Spanish and Portuguese markets for its products were frequently disrupted and began to shrink. Towns such as Coggeshall, Braintree, Bocking, and Colchester were seriously affected, though their demise was a protracted and uneven affair. From the 1720s a similar fate hit the towns of the even more successful Devonshire serge industry, because of a falling-off in the Dutch entrepôt trade and a decisive swing of fashion in favour of Norwich stuffs.[58] The impact of economic fluctuations, along with that of competition, therefore ensured that the course of urban progress in post-Restoration England was not always a smooth one. But it should be noted, for example, that the Essex and Devonshire textile towns enjoyed many years of prosperity before deterioration set in, and the larger centres that suffered set-backs, such as Chester, Exeter, Colchester, and Worcester, were often able to cultivate a broader service and consumer role that cushioned them against long-term decline.[59]

---

[57] A. Everitt, 'Urban Growth 1570-1770', *Local Historian*, viii, No. 4 (1968), 120; J. Chartres, 'Markets and Marketing in Metropolitan Western England in the Late Seventeenth and Eighteenth Centuries', in M. A. Havinden (ed.), *Husbandry and Marketing in the South West 1500-1800* (Exeter, 1973), 64; and also Clark, *Country Towns*, 30-1; Corfield, *English Towns*, 20-1; J. Chartres, 'The Marketing of Agricultural Produce,' in J. Thirsk (ed.), *The Agrarian History of England and Wales*, Vol. v, *1640-1750, Part 2, Agrarian Change* (Cambridge, 1985), 409-14; Noble, 'Regional Urban System,' 3, 16-17; Unwin, 'Tradition and Transition', 79, 114-15. For views that question the thesis of small town decline see Marshall, 'Cumbrian Market Town', 128-209; Dyer, 'Growth and Decay', 65-6; A. Dyer, 'The Market Towns of Southern England', *Southern History*, i (1979), 123-34.

[58] A. F. J. Brown, *Essex at Work 1700-1815* (Chelmsford, 1969), 1-26; Hoskins, *Devon*, 128-9; C. Wilson, *England's Apprenticeship 1603-1763* (London, 1967), 290-3.

[59] *British Courant*, No. 289, 17 Aug. 1750; Mitchell, 'Urban Retailing', 261-2, 275-7; Defoe, *Tour*, i. 222; R. Newton, *Eighteenth-Century Exeter* (Exeter, 1984),

Moreover, the general buoyancy of the economy meant that the opportunities for success far outweighed the risks of failure. It is this favourable climate and the way it stimulated individual communities that will now be explored.

The three springboards of urban development were commerce, industry, and services. Market centres, thoroughfare towns, and ports all directly benefited from commercial expansion. English overseas trade at least trebled in value between 1650 and 1750, with an initial surge during the so-called Commercial Revolution of 1660-88.[60] Though much of the early growth was concentrated on London, from about 1700 the provincial ports became the dynamic sector, progressively eroding the metropolis's dominance.[61] Inland trade, quantitatively more important than that overseas, but difficult to measure statistically, also expanded impressively. It is estimated that between 1637 and 1715 the output of scheduled road carrying services from London more than doubled with the greater part of the rise occurring in the years after 1681.[62] Three main factors were responsible for the escalating level of commercial activity: the increasing penetration and exploitation of overseas markets, particularly in southern Europe, the Orient, the West Indies, and North America; the extraordinary development of London, which (allied to advancing local economic specialization) generated huge inter-regional movements of goods;[63] and improvements in the communications infrastructure, which did much to enhance the flow of trade. The extent of navigable inland waterways almost doubled from around 685 miles between 1600 and 1660 to about 1,160 miles by the early eighteenth century; and from the latter period, turnpiking made considerable progress so that by the 1750s the majority of the nation's trunk-roads had been treated.[64]

23-7, 65-71; Brown, *Essex*, 111-12; G. Talbut, 'Worcester as an Industrial and Commercial Centre 1660-1750', *Trans. of the Worcestershire Archaeological Soc.*, x (1986), 91-102.

[60] D. C. Coleman, *The Economy of England 1450-1750* (London, 1977), 133-45; W. Minchinton (ed.), *The Growth of English Overseas Trade in the Seventeenth and Eighteenth Centuries* (London, 1969), 1-63, 78-118.

[61] Corfield, *English Towns*, 34-5; Wilson, *England's Apprenticeship*, 273-5.

[62] J. Chartres, 'Road Carrying in England in the Seventeenth Century: Myth and Reality', *EcHR*, 2nd ser., xxx, No. 1 (1977), 77-8; J. Chartres, *Internal Trade in England 1500-1700* (London, 1977), 9-38.

[63] E. A. Wrigley, 'A Simple Model of London's Importance in Changing English Society and Economy 1650-1750', *Past and Present*, xxxvii (1967), 55-63.

[64] T. S. Willan, *River Navigation in England 1600-1760* (London, 1964), 133; W. Albert, *The Turnpike Road System in England 1663-1840* (Cambridge, 1972), 14-56.

In their role as market centres, towns were the engines of the commercial system, pumping goods to and fro along the arteries of trade.[65] Three types of communities benefited particularly. First, there were those dedicated to feeding the gargantuan appetite of the metropolis. From Farnham, Guildford, and Croydon came corn; from Abingdon, Faringdon, and Chertsey malt; from Reading, Henley-on-Thames, and Maidenhead malt, meal, and timber; from High Wycombe and Marlow malt and meal; from Dorking, St Ives (Cambridgeshire), and Peterborough poultry; and from Maidstone corn, timber, and 'very great quantities of fruit, such as Kentish pippins, runnets, etc., which come up as the cherries do, whole hoy-loads at a time to the wharf called the Three Cranes in London'.[66] Second, there were the market towns located in regions of rapid economic growth and specialization. The industrialization of the West Riding of Yorkshire and the West Midlands brought immense business to their urban markets, through which were exported local manufactured products and imported raw materials and·food for a working population less and less able to provision itself as it concentrated on industrial production. The expansion of the metallurgical and extractive industries in South Yorkshire and north Derbyshire not only profited established towns in the area, but even led to the establishment of small new markets, such as those at Thorne (which obtained a market charter in 1659), Dronfield (1662), Winster (1690), and Penistone (1699).[67] Third, there were the towns with excellent external communications, notably those situated on turnpiked roads and navigable rivers. Lincoln's economy, which had stagnated during the Tudor and early Stuart period, only began to recover with the local navigation schemes of the late seventeenth century, which linked it to the Wash and the Trent, and later the Aire and Calder scheme of 1699–1701, which enabled Lincolnshire's vast resources of wool and corn to be easily channelled through the city and into the industrial West Riding of Yorkshire.[68]

In 1700 at least twelve of the leading thirty provincial towns were

[65] A. Everitt, 'The Food Market of the English Town 1660–1760', in *Third International Conference of Economic History* (Munich, 1965), 59–71.

[66] Defoe, *Tour*, i. 79, 113–14, 142, 144–5, 153, 157, 284, 291, 298, 300; Goose, 'Seventeenth-Century Reading', 61–4.

[67] Defoe, *Tour*, ii. 199–200, 204–8; D. Hey, *Packmen, Carriers, and Pack-Horse Roads: Trade and Communications in North Derbyshire and South Yorkshire* (Leicester, 1980), 163–70.

[68] J. W. F. Hill, *Tudor and Stuart Lincoln* (Cambridge, 1956), 206–10, J. W. F. Hill, *Georgian Lincoln* (Cambridge, 1966), 100–1, 139–40; Defoe, *Tour*, ii. 92, 199.

ports, reflecting the critical role played by water-borne transport in the economy. The coastal centres that benefited most from the commercial expansion of the period did so because of certain specific advantages. The most important of these was the possession of a prosperous hinterland that required a sea-based outlet through which to trade. Liverpool grew fat on the textiles, salt, and coal of the North-West, and earthenware from the Potteries; Whitehaven on Cumbrian coal; Newcastle and Sunderland on Tyne and Wear coal; Hull on West Riding cloth, South Yorkshire ironmongery, Derbyshire lead, and East Midlands hosiery; Bristol on Black Country metalwares, West Country cloth, Welsh coal and wool, and Cornish tin; and Exeter (until the 1720s) on Devonshire serges. A number of these ports experienced prodigious growth. Bristol increased from about 20,000 inhabitants in 1700 to become the leading provincial town in 1750 with a population of 50,000; Newcastle from about 16,000 in the 1660s to around 29,000 by 1750; Hull from 7,000 in 1700 to 13,000 by the late 1760s; Whitehaven from probably no more than 200 at the Restoration to over 9,000 by 1762; and Liverpool from about 1,500 in the 1670s to perhaps 22,000 by 1750.[69] Less dynamic, but in a way no less buoyant, were those centres servicing a rich agricultural region. In the early eighteenth century the ports of East Anglia and the south coast, particularly King's Lynn, Wells, Yarmouth, Chichester, and Portsmouth, were dispatching huge cargoes of grain to Europe during the unprecedented export boom in corn.[70]

The full exploitation of a port's hinterland depended upon good communications. Therefore, among the most successful seaboard towns were those which headed extensive internal navigation systems. By the late 1720s, Bristol could be reached by river from as far inland as Hereford and Leominster along the Wye and the Lugg, Welshpool along the Severn, and Stratford-upon-Avon and Bath along the

[69] Chalklin, *Provincial Towns*, 13–20; F. Hyde, *Liverpool and the Mersey: The Development of a Port 1700–1970* (Newton Abbot, 1971), 12; Davis, *Shipping Industry*, 39; J. Ellis, 'A Dynamic Society: Social Relations in Newcastle-upon-Tyne 1660–1760', in Clark, *Provincial Towns*, 193–4; G. Jackson, *Hull in the Eighteenth Century* (Oxford, 1972), 337; E. Gillett and K. A. Macmahon, *A History of Hull* (Oxford, 1980), 186–7, 198; J. Lowther, *The Correspondence of Sir John Lowther 1693–1698*, ed. D. Hainsworth, Records of Social and Economic History, new ser., vii (Oxford, 1983), p. xxii; C. M. Law, 'Some Notes on the Urban Population of England and Wales in the Eighteenth Century', *Local Historian*, x, No. 1 (1972), 22–6.

[70] Chartres, 'Marketing of Agricultural Produce', 448–53; Defoe, *Tour*, i. 72; Davis, *Shipping Industry*, 203–4; J. H. Andrews, 'The Port of Chichester and the Grain Trade 1650–1750', *Sussex Archaeological Collections*, xcii (1954), 102–3.

Warwickshire and Somerset Avons; using the Humber and the tributaries that emptied into it, Hull's watery tendrils penetrated as deep as York, Leeds, Wakefield, Bawtry, Derby, Burton-upon-Trent, and Lincoln; and from King's Lynn, employing the Ouse and the rivers of the Wash, could be reached Stamford, Peterborough, Bedford, Cambridge, Bury St Edmunds, and Thetford, prompting Defoe to comment that 'by these navigable rivers the merchants of Lynn supply about six counties wholly, and three counties in part, with their goods'.[71] A port's influence stretched seawards as well as inland, and some of the leading trading centres were those able to capture or share a particularly rich export/import market. During the first half of the eighteenth century between fifty and sixty per cent of the ships entering Hull from overseas had travelled from Scandinavia and the Baltic, and on the west coast, ports such as Whitehaven, Lancaster, Liverpool, Bristol, and Bideford, profited from the considerable short-haul trade with Ireland, and their contact with the dynamic economic regions of North America and the West Indies.[72]

At the same time the mounting volume of traffic that crowded the nation's network of roads was bringing prosperity to those stopping-off places or halts which were devoted to servicing the needs of travellers for horse power, refreshment, and accommodation.[73] Andover was 'a great thoroughfare on the direct western road', Canterbury 'the thoroughfare for London to France by Dover', and there was 'a great deal of travelling through' Cirencester 'from the northern to the western parts of England'. It was said of East Grinstead that 'as it is the great thoroughfare to Lewes, it has good trade', of Guildford that 'the chief trade of this town now depends on travellers and the corn market', while it was argued that 'Brentwood and Ingatestone, and even Chelmsford', were 'thoroughfare towns . . . chiefly maintained by the excessive multitude of carriers and passengers, which are constantly passing this way to London, with droves of cattle, provisions, and manufactures for London'.[74] On the Great

[71] Willan, *River Navigation*, 68, 150–2; W. E. Minchinton, 'Bristol: Metropolis of the West in the Eighteenth Century', *TRHS*, 5th ser., iv (1954), 71; Defoe, *Tour*, i. 73.

[72] Jackson, *Hull*, 335; J. E. Williams, 'Whitehaven in the Eighteenth Century', *EcHR*, 2nd ser., vii (1956), 393–404; W. Stout, *The Autobiography of William Stout of Lancaster 1665–1752*, ed. J. D. Marshall (Manchester, 1967), 36–52; Davis, *Shipping Industry*, 36–9; P. G. E. Clemens, 'The Rise of Liverpool 1665–1750', *EcHR*, 2nd ser., xxix, No. 2 (1976), 211–25; W. G. Hoskins, *Old Devon* (London, 1971), 55–6.

[73] Everitt, 'Food Market', 67–8.

[74] P. L. Powys, *Passages from the Diaries of Mrs Philip Lybbe Powys*, ed. E. J. Climenson (London, 1899), 61; Buck, *Antiquities*, iii, Canterbury, Guildford; Rudder,

Introduction

North Road, Stamford, Grantham, Newark-on-Trent, Doncaster, Wetherby, and Chester-le-Street were all established staging posts reaping the benefits of the contemporary growth in mobility.[75]

If post-Restoration urban prosperity owed a great debt to commercial expansion, scarcely less important was the contribution of industrial growth. Rising real incomes, the exploitation of new overseas markets, and the requirements of large-scale warfare, led to a marked expansion in the demand for manufactured goods.[76] The impact of this on urban communities has to be assessed with care, since a good deal of production was located in the countryside. But towns were heavily involved in servicing rural industry, and they often accommodated whole or substantial portions of particular manufacturing processes. Textile production was the most important large-scale industry of the period, and was principally located in east Devon, Essex, Norfolk, the West Country, and the rapidly developing regions of the West Riding and south Lancashire. All these areas supported major cloth towns. By 1700 Exeter and Colchester were both reaching their peak as textile centres, but more sustained expansion was experienced by Norwich (whose population rose from about 20,000 in 1650, to 30,000 by 1700, and 36,000 by 1752), and the rising stars of Manchester (with about 5,000 people in 1660, 10,000 to 12,000 by 1717, and almost 20,000 by 1758) and Leeds (3,750 inhabitants in 1600, 6,000 by 1700, and 12,000 by 1750).[77] Among the lesser luminaries were the cloth towns of the West Country, such as Frome, Devizes, Bradford-on-Avon, Warminster, and Trowbridge, whose early eighteenth-century well-being is still evident in their landscape.[78] By this period the most dynamic sector of the hosiery industry was situated in the East Midlands, where the introduction of the knitting-frame brought growth particularly to Nottingham (whose

Gloucestershire, 344; T. B. Burr, *A History of Tunbridge Wells* (London, 1766), 269; Defoe, *Tour*, i. 37; Morant, *Essex*, ii. 1.

[75] Defoe, *Tour*, ii. 103, 181, 209, 249; A. Everitt, 'The English Urban Inn 1560–1760', in A. Everitt (ed.), *Perspectives in English Urban History* (London, 1973), 95; J. Thirsk, 'Stamford in the Sixteenth and Seventeenth Centuries', in A. Rogers (ed.), *The Making of Stamford* (Leicester, 1965), 72.

[76] Coleman, *Economy of England*, 158–68; Wilson, *England's Apprenticeship*, 185–205, 288–312.

[77] Law, 'Urban Population', 22–6; Corfield, 'Provincial Capital', 266–7; Chalklin, *Provincial Towns*, 22, 33; Grady, 'Public Buildings in the West Riding', 13.

[78] Defoe, *Tour*, i. 280–1; K. H. Rogers, 'Trowbridge Clothiers and their Houses 1660–1800', in N. B. Harte and K. G. Ponting (eds.), *Textile History and Economic History* (Manchester, 1973), 138–62; *VCH Wiltshire*, viii (London, 1965), 93, 110–11.

population rose from about 7,000 in 1700 to 12,000 by 1750) and Leicester. However, like the cloth trade, pockets of production were scattered throughout the country, as for example the bustling industry in Tewkesbury.[79] The expansion of the metalwares trade had its most dramatic impact on Birmingham and Sheffield: the former mush-roomed from perhaps 4,400 people in 1676 to over 23,000 by 1750, the latter from about 3,500 in 1700 to 12,000 by the mid-eighteenth century. Other centres also prospered from the manufacture of ironwares, such as Walsall, Wolverhampton, Barnsley, Ross-on-Wye, Tewkesbury (nails), Chichester (needles), and Gloucester (pin-making and bell-founding).[80]

Among the most important industrial centres were the ports. This was a consequence of a number of advantages they enjoyed. First, they were naturally the home of shipbuilding. The eastern seaboard towns were particularly strong in this field because of the huge carrying capacity required by the Tyne and Wear coal trade. Originally centred on East Anglia, by the early eighteenth century the focus of the industry had shifted decisively to the North-East, especially Whitby, Newcastle, South Shields, Scarborough, Stockton-on-Tees, and Sunderland.[81] Second, ports were increasingly landing a range of valuable imports, such as sugar and tobacco, that required processing before they could be sold. Since many of these were destined for re-export, it was logical to locate the relevant plant at the point of entry and exit. Third, ports were ideally equipped, because of their command of water, to handle bulky fuels and raw materials. For these reasons cities such as Newcastle (including North and South Shields), Liverpool, and Bristol emerged as major industrial complexes. In the early 1700s the Shields salt industry, at the mouth of the Tyne, was one of the key centres of production in the country, and in Newcastle

---

[79] J. Thirsk, 'The Fantastical Folly of Fashion: The English Stocking Knitting Industry 1500-1700', in Harte and Ponting, *Textile History and Economic History*, 60-73; Chambers, 'Nottingham', 343-4, 351; Defoe, *Tour*, i. 208, 217. 277; ii. 42, 88-9, 145, 181, 270; HMC, *Verulam MSS*, 241; Rudder, *Gloucestershire*, 738; *VCH Gloucestershire*, viii (London, 1968), 144; T. Rath, 'The Tewkesbury Hosiery Industry', *Textile History*, vii (1976), 140-53.

[80] Chalklin, *Provincial Towns*, 22-3; M. Rowlands, *Masters and Men in the West Midlands Metalware Trades before the Industrial Revolution* (Manchester, 1975); Defoe, *Tour*, ii. 51, 183, 185; HMC, *Verulam MSS*, 239; J. Spershott, *The Memoirs of James Spershott*, ed. F. W. Steer, Chichester Papers, No. 30 (1962), 17; P. Clark, 'The Civic Leaders of Gloucester 1580-1800', in Clark, *Provincial Towns*, 313; M. Lobel (ed.), *Historic Towns Atlas*, i (London, 1969), Gloucester, 13.

[81] Davis, *Shipping Industry*, 61-6; Defoe, *Tour*, i. 40-3, 347; ii. 252.

itself a whole district was devoted to the manufacture of glass, where in the 1730s there were at least seven glasshouses, a number that by 1772 had risen to sixteen. From the 1690s works began to appear along the Mersey at Liverpool to process rock salt from the expanding mines in Cheshire, and during the following century sugar boiling (a visitor noted eight refineries in 1760), glass manufacture, pipemaking, pottery (by 1761 there were at least 117 potters), ropemaking, and the production of watches and clocks were all important industries in the town. During the eighteenth century Bristol supported a similarly wide range of manufacturing processes, such as glass making (there were fourteen or fifteen glasshouses in the 1720s), sugar refining, soap boiling, brass and copper smelting, earthenware production, brewing, and distilling.[82]

4. SOCIAL AND CONSUMER CENTRES

In addition to commercial and industrial growth, the resurgence in urban fortunes owed much to a third factor, the rising demand for high-status social and consumer services. This led to the development of many towns as centres of fashionable society, places where the more affluent could engage in conspicuous consumption, and recuperate, recreate, and reside in some elegance. These communities and the cultural world which they embraced are the major focus of this book.

A number of provincial centres must have remained relatively unaffected by the market for leisure and luxury services. Defoe found Harwich 'a town of hurry and business, not much of gaiety and pleasure', and discovered of Yarmouth 'that there is little encouragement to assemblies, plays, and gaming-meetings . . . as in some other places'.[83] Towns were often too poor and small, or too wrapped up in their own basic economic activities, to cultivate or attract fashionable society. On the other hand, it is surprising how many centres

---

[82] J. Ellis, 'The Decline and Fall of the Tyneside Salt Industry 1660–1790: A Re-examination', *EcHR*, 2nd ser., xxxiii, No. 1 (1980), 45–52; H. Bourne, *The History of Newcastle-upon-Tyne* (Newcastle-upon-Tyne, 1736), 155, 178; J. Brand, *History and Antiquities of the Town and County of Newcastle-upon-Tyne* (London, 1789), ii. 42–7; Defoe, *Tour*, ii. 115, 251; T. Barker, 'Lancashire Coal, Cheshire Salt, and the Rise of Liverpool', *Trans. of the Historic Soc. of Lancashire and Cheshire*, cii (1951), 83–101; G. Chandler, *Liverpool* (London, 1957), 330–51, 432; Buck, *Antiquities*, iii, Liverpool, Bristol; Minchinton, 'Bristol', 77–8; Students Diary, fos. 127–8.

[83] Defoe, *Tour*, i. 36, 69.

benefited at least a little from this trade. Tiny Eye and Harleston on
the Suffolk/Norfolk border, both with populations of about 850 in
1670, still possess inns with specially constructed assembly rooms of
the early to mid-Georgian period. Petworth, with around 1,000 souls
in 1700, supported a cluster of prosperous 'luxury' tradesmen and a
number of resident gentlemen, and was described in the mid-1720s as
'full of gentlemen's families, and good well built houses, both in the
town and neighbourhood'.[84] However, it is clear that the places which
developed most successfully as social centres were of three types:
county towns, provincial capitals, and resorts.

The old shire towns had in many respects borne the brunt of the
crises of the Tudor and early Stuart years. But even before the
Restoration signs of recovery were evident, as heavy dependence upon
a single industry gave way to a more diversified economy of luxury
trades and services. Though the transition was often a protracted and
painful one, the rich harvest reaped in the century after 1660 more
than compensated. Communities like Warwick, Winchester, Salisbury,
and Gloucester, which had suffered severely from the strain of
poverty, industrial decline, and warfare, blossomed as social centres
during what was to be the golden age of the county town.[85] In
such places commerce and industry might take second place to
the more refined needs of society. Miège reported that Durham was
'so far from being well traded . . . that it is one of the best retiring
places of the North, free from the noise and hurry of trade, where
one may live plentifully, and breathe good air at an easy rate'; Defoe
discovered Derby to be a 'town of gentry rather than trade', and
Winchester 'a place of no trade', other than that generated locally,
and 'no manufacture', and yet enjoying 'a great deal of good
company'. Lybbe Powys echoed these sentiments, when she wrote of
Winchester in 1760 that 'no place this summer is more gay than this,
prodigious deal of company resorting to the camp . . . here is no
manufacture, no navigation, and of course no trade'. This is not
to suggest that county centres eschewed all contact with commerce
and manufacture. Most were places of considerable business activity,
to which their social roles added a valuable extra dimension: such

[84] R. Keverne, *Tales of Old Inns*, 2nd edn. (London, 1947), 50-2; HMC, *Portland MSS*, vi. 151-2; G. H. Kenyon, 'Petworth Town and Trades 1610-1760, Part One', *Sussex Archaeological Collections*, xcvi (1958), 57-79; Defoe, *Tour*, i. 132.
[85] *VCH Warwickshire*, viii. 507, 513; Rosen, 'Winchester', 170-84; *VCH Wiltshire*, vi (London, 1962), 78, 129-31, 140-3; Clark, 'Civic Leaders', 313.

was the case at Maidstone, where Defoe found 'a town of very great business and trade, and yet full of gentry, of mirth, and of good company'.[86]

The multiplicity of functions displayed by county centres like Maidstone was a feature of the provincial capitals. All were able to exploit rich seams of both business and pleasure, such as Exeter, 'full of gentry and good company, and yet full of trade and manufacture also', and Shrewsbury, 'full of gentry and yet full of trade too'. Similar claims could be made for Norwich, Bristol, Newcastle-upon-Tyne, and Chester.[87] Even towns which had only recently ascended to the rank of provincial capital, and done so as commercial or manufacturing communities, such as Liverpool, Birmingham, and Manchester, soon developed into important centres of culture and consumption. All three hosted regular assemblies from an early date and were among the first provincial towns to develop classical squares; Birmingham and Manchester possessed thriving musical and theatrical facilities; and Birmingham and Liverpool appear to have been widely used by the local gentry for recreation and shopping.[88] Among the provincial capitals, the most prestigious social rendezvous was York. Ever since the dramatic decline of its woollen textile industry under the early Tudors, it had swung decisively away from basic manufacture towards an administrative and service-based economy. By the early eighteenth century pleasure, and those who sought it, were critical to York's livelihood. As one writer declared, 'what has been, and is, the chief support of the city at present, is the resort to and residence of several country gentlemen with their families', and another wrote that 'here is no trade indeed, except such as depends upon the confluence of the gentry'. The city's position as the fashionable metropolis of the North was strengthened in the 1730s by a burst of civic and commercial investment in a theatre, racecourse, assembly room, and walk. In 1736 Drake, the distinguished historian of York, could confidently claim, 'that though other cities and towns in the kingdom run far beyond us

[86] Miège, *New State of England*, 39; Defoe, *Tour*, i. 115, 186; ii. 157; Powys, *Diaries*, 80.

[87] Corfield, 'Provincial Capital', 263–310; B. Little, *The City and County of Bristol* (London, 1954), 150–80, 203–37; Ellis, 'Social Relations in Newcastle', 192–6; Mitchell, 'Urban Retailing', 261–2.

[88] See Appendices 1, 3, 4, 5; Money, *Experience and Identity*, 80–94; Newdigate Diaries, *passim*; N. Blundell, *The Great Diurnall of Nicholas Blundell*, ed. J. J. Bagley, Record Soc. of Lancashire and Cheshire, cx, cxii, cxiv (1968–72), *passim*.

in trade and hurry of business, yet there is no place, out of London, so polite and elegant to live in'.[89]

Of the regional centres and provincial capitals, York was probably the town most devoted to leisure. But for undiluted pursuit of pleasure most contemporaries would have turned to one of the growing body of specialist resorts. These developed around the innumerable medicinal wells and springs scattered throughout the country, and were initially visited primarily for reasons of health. Though there are signs of a more sophisticated regime emerging at the spas under the early Stuarts, it was only after the Restoration, and especially from the 1690s, that a number of them began seriously to cater for the leisured visitor and evolve into genuine holiday resorts.[90] Several offered their patrons the opportunity to bathe in as well as drink the waters. In such circumstances it was natural that as demand expanded and diversified, the resources of the coastline should also be exploited. Sea-bathing was practised in Kent and Lancashire in the 1720s, and at Scarborough, Brighton, and on Tyneside in the following decade, but it was not until the middle of the century that the seaside resort began to develop on a substantial scale.[91]

The queen of the spas was Bath. A victim of the Reformation, the Civil War, and industrial decline, it underwent a spectacular recovery from the late seventeenth century to become the most fashionable of all provincial towns. Between the 1660s and 1750 its resident population quadrupled from about 1,500 to 6,000, and this takes no cognizance of the thousands who flocked to the resort during the season. Development occurred in a series of lurches forward rather than through steady expansion: there were spurts of growth between the 1690s and early 1700s, the mid-1720s to mid-1730s, and the late 1740s to early 1770s.

[89] Hutchinson and Palliser, *York*, 39–74; *VCH York* (London, 1961), 166–70, 198–200, 245–50; Drake, *Eboracum*, 240–1; Defoe, *Tour*, ii. 234.

[90] R. Lennard, 'The Watering-Places', in R. Lennard (ed.), *Englishmen at Rest and Play: Some Phases of English Leisure 1558-1714* (Oxford, 1931), 1–79; J. A. R. Pimlott, *The Englishman's Holiday* (Hassocks, 1976), 21–48; McIntyre, 'Health and Pleasure Resorts', *passim*; J. Barrett, 'Spas and Seaside Resorts 1660–1780', in J. Stevenson *et al.*, *The Rise of the New Urban Society*, Open University Urban History Course (Milton Keynes, 1977), 37–70.

[91] J. Whyman, 'A Hanoverian Watering-Place: Margate before the Railway', in Everitt, *Urban History*, 139; Blundell, *Diurnal*, iii. 52, 81; *A Journey from London to Scarborough* (London, 1734), 36; Pimlott, *Englishman's Holiday*, 49–64; Bourne, *Newcastle*, 181; J. K. Walton, *The English Seaside Resort: A Social History 1750-1914* (Leicester, 1983), 10–18; E. W. Gilbert, 'The Growth of Inland and Seaside Health Resorts in England', *Scottish Geographical Magazine*, lv (1939), 16–35; E. W. Gilbert, *Brighton: Old Ocean's Bauble* (London, 1954), 1–110.

By the end of the last period the city had burst its traditional physical limits, filling the surrounding orchards, fields, and hills with some of the most urbane classical architecture to be found in Europe.[92] The only real pretender to Bath's crown was Tunbridge Wells, which was established on a virgin site in the early seventeenth century, with the area around the wells seriously developed from the 1670s or 1680s. Though, like Bath, able to attract a nationwide and prestigious clientele, it never expanded at the rate of the Somerset spa, and remained a loose agglomeration of separate settlements, which in 1766 Burr optimistically suggested 'all united together, form a considerable town'.[93]

The remaining spas depended upon a more regionally oriented trade. Scarborough drew its patrons principally from Scotland and the North. Although in 1700 a visitor could complain, 'I can yet see nothing but close-stools and drying fish . . . the company there was but few, most Scotch and no diversion at all', from the 1720s there was a growth in fashionable tourists and an improvement in facilities, which secured the town's position as the leading resort after Bath and Tunbridge.[94] The next two most prominent northern spas were Harrogate and Buxton. The former was already firmly established by 1700, with about twenty 'bathing' or lodging houses in the Low Harrogate area and 'a great confluence of gentry' during the season, but like Buxton it was only during the late eighteenth century that it began to emerge as a major resort. In the Midlands and the West the most important secondary spas were Hotwells on the outskirts of Bristol, under serious commercial development from the 1690s, Cheltenham from the late 1730s (though there had been earlier attempts), and Malvern by about the 1750s. In the South, London was the magnet around which a host of miniature watering-places clustered, such as Islington, Sadler's Wells, and Hampstead, but only Epsom really evolved, from the last decades of the seventeenth century, as a substantial, independent, and fashionable resort.[95]

[92] R. Neale, *Bath 1680-1850: A Social History* (London, 1981); S. McIntyre, 'Bath: The Rise of a Resort Town 1660-1800', in Clark, *Country Towns*, 198-249; B. Cunliffe, *The City of Bath* (Gloucester, 1986).

[93] A. Savidge, *Royal Tunbridge Wells* (Tunbridge Wells, 1975); C. W. Chalklin, 'The Making of Some New Towns c.1600-1720', in C. W. Chalklin and M. A. Havinden (eds.), *Rural Change and Urban Growth 1500-1800* (London, 1974), 233-5, 243-4, 248-9; Burr, *Tunbridge Wells*, 98-9, and *passim*.

[94] McIntyre, 'Health and Pleasure Resorts', 190-4, 197-204, 264-80; Defoe, *Tour*, ii. 247; Warwickshire CRO, CR.1368 (Mordaunt MSS), i, fos. 66-7.

[95] B. Jennings (ed.), *A History of Harrogate and Knaresborough* (Huddersfield, 1970), 219-38; R. G. Heape, *Buxton under the Dukes of Devonshire* (London, 1948),

One of the major attractions of the spas was undoubtedly the medical services which they offered. But the line between recuperation and recreation was a thin one, and contemporary accounts stress the opportunities for unadulterated leisure to be found at the larger resorts. Misson noted of Bath in the 1690s, that 'thousands go hither to pass away a few weeks, without heeding the baths or the waters, but only to divert themselves with good company', and by 1727 it could be claimed that there was 'no place in Europe that affords more' opportunity for 'diversion and pleasure'. Defoe called the Somerset spa 'the resort of the sound rather than the sick'; a writer advised in 1745 that 'this is the place in all England to enjoy good health and to turn it to account'; and in 1767 John Penrose regretted that 'one would imagine, the gentry who resort hither, were lovers of pleasure more than lovers of God.'[96] Other spas attracted similar comments. At Tunbridge Wells the 'company and diversion' were 'the main business of the place'; at Scarborough it was suggested that the 'amusements and the pleasure of seeing company induces many to come who are not really in want of water'; and in 1734 Dr Thomas Short complained that the inns found at watering-places were 'no longer the hospitals of invalids, but too often the rendezvous of wantonness, and not seldom, of mad frolics'.[97] By the early eighteenth century the leading spas had discovered that pleasure was big business, as they rapidly developed into full-blown holiday resorts.

To a large extent, success for a spa depended upon the range and quality of facilities that it offered. Good external communications, such as turnpike roads, frequent coach services, and comfortable staging inns *en route*, were of the first importance. Extensive,

19-41; B. Little, 'The Gloucestershire Spas: An Eighteenth-Century Parallel', in P. McGrath and J. Cannon (eds.), *Essays in Bristol and Gloucestershire History*, Bristol and Gloucester Archaeological Soc. (1976), 170-99; G. Hart, *A History of Cheltenham* (Leicester, 1965), 124-37; B. S. Smith, *A History of Malvern* (Leicester, 1964), 172-5; W. Wroth, *The London Pleasure Gardens of the Eighteenth Century*, (Michigan and London, 1979), *passim*; F. L. Clark, 'A History of Epsom Spa', *Surrey Archaeological Collections*, lvii (1960), 1-41.

[96] H. Misson, *M. Misson's Memoirs and Observations in his Travels over England*, trans. Mr Ozell (London, 1719), 14; Cox, *Magna Britannia*, iv. 733; Defoe, *Tour*, ii. 34; L'abbé Le Blanc, *Lettres d'un François*, quoted in A. Barbeau, *Life and Letters at Bath in the Eighteenth Century* (London, 1904), 81; J. Penrose, *Letters from Bath 1766-1767*, ed. B. Mitchell and H. Penrose (Gloucester, 1983), 174.

[97] Defoe, *Tour*, i. 126; HMC, *Verulam MSS*, 237; T. Short, *History of the Mineral Waters of Derbyshire, Lincolnshire, and Yorkshire*, quoted in Jennings, *Harrogate and Knaresborough*, 233.

commodious, and preferably modern accommodation, a ready supply of servants and fresh produce, and the availability of a wide variety of medical and recreational services also weighed heavily on visitors' minds. Not least in importance was the provision of an efficient postal service, since the need to keep in touch with the world of business and politics, as well as with separated loved ones, was a pressing concern. It was in the provision of such facilities that the larger urban spas scored heavily. The roads to Bath were lined with good coaching inns, and one of the city's most illustrious heroes, Ralph Allen, initially rose to prominence as a pioneer of the postal system.[98] In the long run the host of smaller rural spas was unable to compete with such services, and many, like tiny Astrop in Northamptonshire, vanished into obscurity, to leave the field to a more urbanized body of resorts.[99]

All social centres provided a growing range of luxury trades and retail outlets. Georgian England experienced what has been called a 'consumer revolution', during which the purchase of products that were more than basic necessities became an integral part of many people's lives.[100] As producer, displayer, and distributor, towns played a central role in servicing this new demand. For much of the seventeenth century London dominated the trade in luxury goods, and subsequently it remained the nation's undisputed leader and trend-setter in this field. But, as demand broadened under the later Stuarts, provincial towns also began to cater for the needs of the sophisticated shopper. It was no longer necessary to turn to the distant metropolis to purchase fashionable goods. Sir John Mordaunt hinted at these changes when, writing in 1698 from his Norfolk country seat to his wife in the capital, he directed that 'if you have not sent the paper I wrote for to hang my rooms with, do not buy it until you hear from me again, being told I may have it at [King's] Lynn'.[101]

The swing towards a more diversified and consumer-oriented

---

[98] *A Step to the Bath* (London, 1700), 117-54; M. Baker, *Discovering the Bath Road* (Tring, 1968), *passim*; Keverne, *Old Inns*, 89-92; B. Boyce, *The Benevolent Man: A Life of Ralph Allen of Bath* (Cambridge, Mass., 1967), 10-23, 40-55.

[99] C. Fiennes, *The Journeys of Celia Fiennes*, ed. C. Morris (London, 1947), 31-2; *BE Northamptonshire*, 2nd edn. (Harmondsworth, 1973), 96.

[100] N. McKendrick, 'The Consumer Revolution of Eighteenth-Century England', in N. McKendrick, J. Brewer, and J. H. Plumb, *The Birth of A Consumer Society* (London, 1983), 9-33.

[101] L. Stone, 'The Residential Development of the West End of London in the Seventeenth Century', in B. C. Malament (ed.), *After the Reformation* (Manchester, 1980), 182-3; P. Jenkins, *The Making of a Ruling Class: The Glamorgan Gentry 1640-1790* (Cambridge, 1983), 243; Warwickshire CRO, CR.1368, i, fo. 2.

economy is a common feature of social centres: for example, it can be detected at Norwich, York, Chester, Colchester, King's Lynn, Ipswich, Winchester, Preston, and Newmarket.[102] At Northampton the number of distinct crafts and trades recorded in the apprenticeship registers rose from forty-five in the years 1562 to 1601, to eighty-three 1654 to 1705, and 114 between 1716 and 1776, and at Warwick the range of different occupations in the town may have doubled between the late sixteenth and late seventeenth centuries.[103] Bath was naturally a consumer's paradise, with an expanding volume and variety of fine craftsmen and retailers. Among the fastest growing trades in the city, to judge from the apprenticeship registers, were those of cabinet-makers, where the number of enrolments rose from one in the years 1724 to 1737 to fourteen between 1741 and 1760, jewellers from one to seven, and milliners and lacemakers (taken together) from none to eleven. The opportunities for individual consumption are vividly displayed in the surviving bills of the Warwickshire country gentleman George Lucy, who during a series of visits to the spa in the mid-eighteenth century purchased china, port, shalloon, ribbons, and silk; a 'fine beaver hat', a 'brown lace wig', 'brown dress bag wig', and 'black silk bag'; various 'shaving', 'dressing', 'powdering', and medical services; and a 'three-quarter frame burnished gold and . . . case' for a portrait of himself painted by the resident Gainsborough. When the Cornish clergyman John Penrose stayed in 1766, he filled the vacant hours by visiting

'several shops . . . that we might see fine things. I suppose there is nothing in the kingdom curious or valuable, but you might serve yourself of it here . . . Among other places we went to Mrs Smith's, a shop where artificial flowers are made and sold. There we saw a made auricula, which gained the florist's prize . . . the maker . . . was afterwards threatened with a prosecution of the imposture'.[104]

[102] U. Priestley and A. Fenner, *Shops and Shopkeepers in Norwich 1660-1730* (Norwich, 1985); *VCH York*, 167, 218-19; Mitchell, 'Urban Retailing', 261-2, 272-3, 275-7; A. F. J. Brown, 'Colchester in the Eighteenth Century', in L. Munby (ed.), *East Anglian Studies* (Cambridge, 1968), 155-61; V. Parker, *The Making of King's Lynn* (Chichester, 1971), 14-16; M. Reed, 'Economic Structure and Change in Seventeenth-Century Ipswich', in Clark, *Country Towns*, 114, 130-1; Rosen, 'Winchester', 177-9; Borsay, 'Provincial Urban Culture', 585, 587; P. May, *The Changing Face of Newmarket: A History from 1600 to 1760* (Newmarket, 1984), 40-1.

[103] A. Everitt, *Ways and Means in Local History* (London, 1971), 37; P. Borsay, 'A County Town Renaissance: Warwick 1660-1760', 26. See also Everitt, 'County and Town', 98-105.

[104] McIntyre, 'Rise of a Resort Town', 215-21; Neale, *Bath: A Social History*, 54-5; Warwickshire CRO, L6 (Lucy MSS)/1305, 1308, 1310-20; Penrose, *Letters*, 123.

It is not the intention of this study to examine in detail the development of the new urban consumer economy, but it may be instructive to focus briefly on one particular luxury trade, that in time-pieces, to suggest the level of provision that existed. Voters Lists of 1715 record the presence of three watchmakers and clockmakers in Norwich, and five in York. At the latter it was a custom to waive a number of clockmakers' admission fees to the city's freedom, if they undertook work for the corporation. In 1706 John Terry offered a clock worth £25 for the Thursday Market, in 1732 Henry Hindley was required to make 'a very good and handsome eight-day clock and case for the Lord Mayor's house and another for the Common Hall', and eighteen years later John Smith's fee was an eight-day chronometer for Ousebridge Hall. Over forty clockmakers have been identified as working in Chester between the Restoration and 1770, even though the craft 'was not a particular speciality' of the city. In Bristol the number of clock and watchmakers noted in the freedom and apprentice records rose from five per decade 1640–1700, to eleven per decade 1700–50, and thirty-one per decade 1750–75.[105] As provincial capitals, Norwich, York, Chester, and Bristol might be expected to support a pool of specialist craftsmen. However, middle-ranking regional centres with populations between 4,500 and 6,000 in the 1750s also enjoyed the services of a surprisingly large number of watchmakers and clockmakers. Preston had five registered as in-burgesses in the Guild Roll of 1702, three in 1722, eight in 1742, five in 1762, and five in the Poll Book of 1741. Among the collection of timepieces housed at Angel Corner in Bury St Edmunds are instruments made by eleven different Bury craftsmen operating in the eighteenth century (five in the years before 1770), and at Warwick about eighteen different watchmakers and clockmakers have been identified as working during the century (fourteen before 1770).[106] But such statistics conceal as much as they reveal. Many men may have

---

[105] W. A. Speck, *Tory and Whig* (London, 1970), 119; List of Voters in the York City election Feb. 1714/15, information from Ella and Geoffrey Holmes; House Book, 23 May 1706, 9 Mar. 1731/2, 11 Dec. 1750, YCA; N. Moore, *Chester Clocks and Clockmakers* (Chester, n.d.), 17–19; J. Barry, 'The Cultural Life of Bristol 1640–1775', D.Phil. thesis (Oxford, 1985), 133.

[106] R. Meyrick, *The John Gershom Parkington Memorial Collection of Time Measurement Instruments*, Catalogue Mark III (1979); W. A. Seaby, *Clockmakers of Warwick and Leamington to 1850* (Warwick, 1981). My figures are calculated from these pamphlets. In the latter I have tended to exclude those simply engaged in clock maintenance.

been engaged in the manufacture and maintenance of timepieces who are described simply as smiths or braziers. Others, labelled as clockmakers, were much more than this. Nicholas Paris senior, based in Jury Street, Warwick in the late Stuart and early Georgian period, was also a gilder, gunsmith, fire-engine and water-pump maker, wrought-iron smith, and general blacksmith.[107] Nor can mere statistics ever describe the extraordinary intricacy, ingenuity, and versatility such men displayed in the practice of their craft.

The Tudor and early Stuart years had been ones of difficulties and problems for English towns. However, from the late seventeenth century the gloom began to lift, and many urban communities started to enjoy a resurgence in their fortunes, due to the expansion in commerce, industry, and the demand for social and consumer services. This provided the essential economic foundations for a change in the *quality* of urban life. It was a transformation that was symbolized by the clockmakers and luxury craftsmen who came to ornament the shopping streets of eighteenth-century towns. Their sophisticated workmanship not only enhanced the economic well-being of the urban system, but also contributed to a revival in its cultural prestige. One of the most striking manifestations of this cultural renaissance was the reshaping and refining of the architectural fabric of the town, and it is this which will be explored in the following three chapters.

[107] W. Seaby, *The Paris Family of Warwick 1670-1750* (Warwick, n.d.); Borsay, 'Provincial Urban Culture', 586.

II

LANDSCAPE

2

The House

A central feature of the Urban Renaissance was the renewal and transformation of the landscape. Not only was a town's physical form the most overt sign of its prosperity and status, dominating the first impressions of any visitor, but it also expressed the social and cultural aspirations of those who resided there. In the mid-seventeenth century the visual appearance of provincial towns must have seemed generally undistinguished and in some cases even shabby. The majority of urban centres were neither big enough to possess any serious architectural pretensions, nor wealthy enough to engage in any other than modest improvements. Since the reign of Elizabeth there had been a significant upgrading in the domestic accommodation of the more substantial citizens, but this tended to concentrate on interior comfort rather than external elegance. Whatever grandeur the larger towns displayed was primarily a legacy of the distant rather than the recent past. By far their most impressive structures were the cathedrals, abbeys, churches, castles, and fortifications erected during the medieval period. But these were fading glories. After a century and a half of neglect and depredation, many were in a serious state of disrepair or already ruinated. In the 1690s Miège reported that the walls at Canterbury were in a 'decayed condition', called those at Gloucester 'standing remains', described Hereford as possessing 'a strong castle, now ruined' and Shrewsbury 'a stately abbey whose remains are still extant', and declared the sixteen churches that Colchester had once supported, many of which were critically damaged in the siege of 1648, to be a 'sad monument to this day of the civil wars'. Even in the early eighteenth century, after the tide of prosperity had turned, Defoe could still write of Canterbury that 'the many ruins of churches, chapels, oratories, and smaller cells of religious people, makes the place look like a general ruin a little recovered'. In a similar vein, he discovered at Launceston 'little else but marks of antiquity, for great part of it is so old, as it may, in a manner, pass for an old, ragged, decayed place', and he described Lincoln as 'an ancient, ragged, decayed . . . city, it is so full of the ruins of monasteries and religious houses, that in short, the very barns, stables, outhouses, and, as they showed me, some of the very hog-sties, were built church-fashion'. The Bucks' prospects of the 1730s and 1740s confirm that this medieval heritage lingered long.[1]

At the Restoration the provincial townscape was characterized by its rather old-fashioned nature and modest architectural pretensions (medieval buildings excepted). Within a century this image had substantially altered. The larger towns could boast some of the finest public and private buildings of the period, and many of the smaller centres had acquired at least a veneer of modernity. During this revival three broad trends were visible. First and foremost was the declining impact of the vernacular tradition of building and its replacement by classical architecture. This led to the formation of a major new stratum in the urban landscape, one that thrust the town into the forefront of fashion, and whose influence extended well into the nineteenth century. A second feature was the emergence of a more convenient and comfortable physical environment, at least for wealthier inhabitants and visitors. Third, parts of the townscape acquired a more ordered, integrated, and therefore 'urban' appearance. This was a natural result of the stress which classical architecture placed on uniformity, allied to a novel contemporary concern to exploit the town's potential for the development of large-scale building forms. To explore these cohesive tendencies, this part of the book is arranged on a deliberately progressive basis, beginning with the basic unit of construction, the house, then widening the focus to take in the street and square, before finally viewing the town as a whole, particularly the influence of planning on it.

Before venturing into a detailed examination of the changes taking place a number of qualifications need to be made. The architectural renaissance was a selective process. The towns most affected were generally the larger and more prosperous ones, and within individual communities the areas that benefited most were those occupied by the more affluent. Positive developments have also to be weighed against negative ones. The very economic prosperity that made urban renewal

---

[1] Miège, *New State of England*, 42, 45, 54, 58, 95; Defoe, *Tour*, i. 118, 257; ii. 91; Buck, *Antiquities, passim*.

a possibility also threatened its success. Greater commercial and manufacturing activity brought with it an increasing volume of traffic, trading, dirt, industrial plant, and pollution. On market-days the busier towns would have been almost awash with animal muck (and stank accordingly), as hundreds of horses, cattle, sheep, geese, and so on were driven through and sold in the open streets. The elegant iron palisades which the more respectable citizens erected in front of their fine houses were as much a device to protect their properties from the effects of this invasion as a piece of decoration. Urban authorities were increasingly concerned about the adequacy of their thoroughfares and trading facilities to cope with this traffic, and, as we shall see, they made considerable efforts to improve the situation.

Industry exerted a growing impact on the urban environment. The finishing processes in textile production were frequently located in the town. Fiennes graphically describes how at Exeter woven serges were soaked in urine, soaped, and passed through the fulling mills, then dried and stretched on open-air tenter frames (which occupied 'huge large fields . . . almost all round the town'), before being dipped into coal-fired vats of boiling dyes. All this was none too pleasant for those employed in the tasks, or for their neighbours. Other textile towns must have been similarly affected. In 1730 Tiverton had no less than fifty-six fulling mills operating, and maps and views of Leeds show the town surrounded by several fields of tenter frames (see Fig. 1).[2] In the larger ports the wide range of refining, smelting, and manufacturing plant must have left its mark on the environment. The Bucks' prospects of Liverpool and Bristol show clusters of conical chimneys belching out smoke, and among the first sights that confronted Pope on entering Bristol in 1739 was that of 'twenty odd pyramids smoking over the town (which are glasshouses)'.[3] The metalware towns were among those most vulnerable to industrial pollution. One visitor to Sheffield described how the 'houses [were] dark and black, occasioned by the continued smoke of the forges', another complained how 'disagreeable' was 'the excessive smoke from the great multitude of forges which this town is crowded with'. Of 'Black Barnsley', it was said, 'the very town looks as black and smoky as they were all smiths that lived in it', and at Birmingham the added aggravation of aural

[2] Fiennes, *Journeys*, 246–7; Hoskins, *Devon*, 128; J. Cossins, *A New and Exact Plan of the Town of Leeds* (1725); Buck, *Antiquities*, iii, Leeds.

[3] Buck, *Antiquities*, iii; A. Pope, *The Correspondence of Alexander Pope*, ed. G. Sherburn (Oxford, 1956), iv. 201.

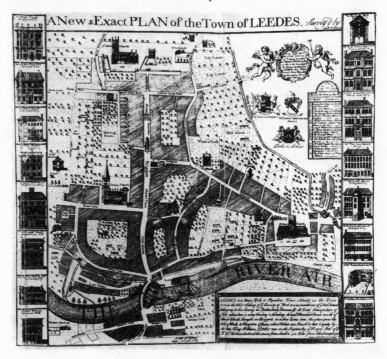

Fig. 1   A New and Exact Plan of the Town of Leeds, surveyed by J. Cossins, pub. 1725

pollution prompted one writer to claim that 'we hear nothing here but the noise of hammers and anvils'.[4] Though industrialization posed a gathering threat to the quality of life and visual appearance of towns, the extent of this should not be exaggerated. Much, perhaps the majority of basic production, continued to take place in the countryside. Where manufacture did intrude into the town, its most disagreeable plant and processes were usually located on the periphery, relatively out of harm's way. It was probably only in the later eighteenth century that the large-scale degradation of the urban environment associated with the Industrial Revolution began to set in. In the 1720s Manchester could still be described as 'a spacious, rich, and populous inland town . . . with handsome broad streets', and

[4] Defoe, *Tour*, ii. 183, 185; HMC, *Verulam MSS*, 240; Cox, *Magna Britannia*, v. 657.

Salford as 'a populous, beautiful town', and even in 1768 a visitor to the former discovered it to be 'handsome, full of good houses', and 'well paved'.[5]

The architectural renaissance needs to be qualified in one final respect, that of chronology. The date of its arrival and the speed with which it altered the urban fabric varied considerably from place to place. For most, though not all centres, innovation came slowly. Such were the obstacles to reshaping a townscape which had often evolved over many centuries that dramatic change was rarely possible. In general, the new fashions arrived piecemeal—a new house here, a revamped façade there.

Classical ornament had been used in the more important provincial urban buildings since at least the late Tudor period: for example, in the timber-framed front of Stanley Place, Chester (1591), the Old Gaol at Banbury (c.1610), the porch of Trinity Guildhall, King's Lynn (1624), the old Guildhall at Bath (1625), and Peacock's School, Rye (1636).[6] But these were only tantalizing hints of things to come. Well into the mid-seventeenth century, grand timber-framed and jettied houses were still appearing on the streets of major cities like Bristol and Exeter, and smaller but similarly styled properties continued to be erected at Norwich and Totnes until, and even after the end of the century.[7] However, the tide of fashion began to turn decisively against vernacular and in favour of classical architecture shortly after the Restoration. The underlying stimulus for change came from the general revival in the urban economy, but the immediate trigger was provided by the rebuilding of London after the Great Fire of 1666. The muted but undeniably classical style in which the metropolis was reconstructed created a model that profoundly influenced provincial attitudes.

The first large-scale evidence of change can be seen in the rebuilding of Northampton, after much of it was destroyed in a

[5] Buck, *Antiquities*, iii, Manchester; HMC, *Verulam MSS*, 232.

[6] J. Summerson, *Architecture in Britain 1530 to 1830* (Harmondsworth, 1970), 98-9; *VCH Oxfordshire*, x (London, 1972), 30; Parker, *King's Lynn*, 145; J. Wood, *A Description of Bath*, 2nd edn., repr. (Bath, 1969), 316-17; *BE Sussex* (Harmondsworth, 1965), 598.

[7] Summerson, *Architecture in Britain*, 101-2; D. Portman, *Exeter Houses 1400-1700* (Exeter, 1966), 81-2, and frontispiece; A. Gomme, M. Jenner, and B. Little, *Bristol: An Architectural History* (London, 1979), 84-7; M. Laithwaite, 'Totnes Houses 1500-1800', in Clark, *Provincial Towns*, 68, 70; *The Norwich Survey 1971-1980*, 2nd edn. (Norwich, 1980), 12.

disastrous blaze in 1675. The simple but elegant post-fire house established in London probably provided the prototype for reconstructing the town's properties, and well into the eighteenth century Northampton was viewed as a model of urban architecture. Fire also initiated a substantial remodelling of the landscapes at Warwick (1694), Buckingham (1725), Blandford Forum (1731), Stony Stratford (1742), and Wareham (1762).[8] Lacking the opportunity created by such wholesale destruction, most towns took a gentler run into the classical phase. However, for a number of communities natural change must have appeared dramatic enough. The booming ports and industrial centres of the later Stuart period experienced considerable physical growth. By the 1720s Bristol, Liverpool, Bideford, Whitehaven, Manchester, Birmingham, Nottingham, Leeds, and Frome all had sizeable pockets of the new architecture.[9] Other places advanced more slowly, though no less impressively. In the mid-1720s Stamford was noted for 'the ruins of many ancient buildings', and could still be described as a town where 'the buildings are not very handsome'. Only fifty years later those comments would have seemed incomprehensible after Stamford had undergone its own local revival and developed into one of the finest classical towns of the Georgian period.[10] During the early decades of the eighteenth century dwellings displaying vernacular features were still being erected on the main thoroughfares at Bath,[11] yet by the 1770s the spa had emerged as the jewel in the crown of an urban architectural renaissance whose influence spread the length and breadth of the country.[12] The basic building block of this movement was the house, and it is to the development of this that we now turn.

    [8] Jones *et al.*, *Gazetteer*, 52-7; *BE Buckinghamshire* (Harmondsworth, 1973), 76; RCHM, *Dorset*, iii, Part i (London, 1970), 16-40; *British Courant*, No. 278, 1-8 June 1750; *BE Dorset* (Harmondsworth, 1972), 439.
    [9] See various references below.
    [10] F. Howgrave, *An Essay of the Ancient and Present State of Stamford* (Stamford, 1726), 11; Students Diary, fo. 21; J. Harris, 'The Architecture of Stamford', in Rogers, *Making of Stamford*, 83-6; RCHM, *Stamford* (London, 1977), *passim*.
    [11] W. Ison, *The Georgian Buildings of Bath* (Bath, 1969), 116-23.
    [12] J. H. Plumb, *The Growth of Political Stability in England 1675-1725* (Harmondsworth, 1969), 20; E. L. Jones and M. E. Falkus, 'Urban Improvement and the English Economy in the Seventeenth and Eighteenth Centuries', in P. J. Uselding (ed.), *Research in Economic History*, Vol. 4 (Greenwich, Conn., 1979), 197; A. Henstock, 'Town Houses and Society in Georgian Country Towns. Part 1: Architecture', *Local Historian*, xiv, No. 2 (1980), 68-75; McInnes, *English Town*, 28-31.

2. THE DEVELOPMENT OF THE HOUSE

The late seventeenth-century town's stock of housing, old-fashioned as it may have seemed, was no medieval fossil. The early modern period had seen considerable alterations and improvements in the dwellings of the more affluent. Much of this change was the product of a major expansion in urban and rural building activity between about 1570 and 1640, which historians have called the Great Rebuilding.[13] A wide variety of towns appear to have participated in this movement, such as Ludlow, Worcester, Tewkesbury, Ledbury, Warwick, King's Lynn, Totnes, Oxford, Yarmouth, Dartmouth, and Plymouth,[14] but its impact was not universal. Burford experienced a period of substantial reconstruction between the late fifteenth and early sixteenth centuries, which effectively pre-empted the Great Rebuilding, while at Banbury its arrival was delayed until the mid-seventeenth century. Further north, there is little evidence of its presence in Stamford, and it seems to have bypassed York altogether, as it probably did the four most northerly English counties as a whole.[15] More significant, it now appears that the Great Rebuilding was only the first phase in a longer process of reconstruction, the second phase of which ran from about 1660 to 1739 and was of far greater quantitative importance than its predecessor. The presence of a twin-phased rebuilding movement can be seen in Broad Street, Ludlow, where detailed investigation has revealed two 'great rebuilds', the earlier one spanning the century from about 1540 to 1640, the later one that from about 1680 to 1780. These have created a rich and complex building fabric, in which the classical facades of the second rebuilding are often no more than an elegant mask, hiding a warren of medieval or first rebuilding timber-framing (see Fig. 2).[16]

[13] W. G. Hoskins, 'The Rebuilding of Rural England 1570-1640', *Past and Present*, iv (1953), 44-59.

[14] D. Lloyd, *Broad Street*, Ludlow Research Paper No. 3 (Birmingham, 1979), 45-8; Dyer, *Worcester in the Sixteenth Century*, 161-5; *VCH Gloucestershire*, viii. 126-31; Hillaby, *Ledbury*, 103-12; *VCH Warwickshire*, viii. 427-9, 434-5; Parker, *King's Lynn*, 12-13; Laithwaite, 'Totnes Houses', 68-72; W. G. Hoskins, 'The Great Rebuilding', *History Today*, v (1955), 104-6.

[15] M. Laithwaite, 'The Buildings of Burford: A Cotswold Town in the Fourteenth to Nineteenth Centuries', in Everitt, *Urban History*, 69-71; *VCH Oxfordshire*, x. 29; RCHM, *Stamford*, pp. xlii-xliii; Harris, 'Architecture of Stamford', 82; *VCH York*, 161; Hoskins, 'Rebuilding of Rural England', 48.

[16] R. Machin, 'The Great Rebuilding: A Reassessment', *Past and Present*, lxxvii (1977), 33-56; Lloyd, *Broad Street*, 45-62; A. Dyer, 'Urban Housing: A Documentary Study of Four Midland Towns 1530-1700', *Post-Medieval Archaeology*, xv (1981), 217.

Fig. 2. Broad Street, Ludlow, west side. In the centre No. 39 (Venetian
Window House, refronted *c*.1760), and south of it No. 38 (1768)

The earlier part of the reconstruction process, the traditional period
of the Great Rebuilding, concentrated particularly on the inside of the
house. Standards of personal comfort and convenience had been
relatively low in medieval dwellings. In fourteenth- and fifteenth-
century Burford and Colchester, two- and even one-roomed properties
were occupied by men of some substance.[17] In such circumstances, the
first call on any new input of building capital would be to improve
basic domestic facilities and fittings. Principally this involved creating
a greater quantity and variety of living space, either by adding new
rooms or subdividing existing ones through the insertion of ceilings
and partitions. The construction of permanent stairs facilitated access
to the newly created space, and the level of general comfort and
privacy was enhanced by the erection of chimneys and the growing use
of curtains and window glass.[18] These changes brought welcome
practical improvements to the internal arrangements of the house, but

[17] Laithwaite, 'Buildings of Burford', 69–77; M. W. Barley, *The English Farmhouse
and Cottage* (London, 1972), 19.

[18] See the works cited in notes 13–14 above; and Barley, *English Farmhouse, passim*;
E. Mercer, *English Vernacular Houses* (London, 1975), 28–32; Dyer, 'Urban Housing',
207–17.

its façade and general structure, though showing signs of the transition ahead, continued to be built in the vernacular tradition. The second phase took the process much further. With essential interior comforts catered for, new capital was directed especially towards the public face of the house and the pursuit of fashion. This resulted in the transformation of the domestic façade through the adoption of classical architecture.

The transition to a new style of construction posed an enormous challenge. How were property owners to understand what classicism required, and how were builders, nurtured in a different tradition, to deliver this? A major programme of re-education was necessary. To some extent this could be realized at an informal level, simply by seeing and doing. Craftsmen working in London or on country houses, where the new architecture had advanced more rapidly, and provincial townsmen visiting such places, were able to absorb valuable design ideas and practical skills. But this was necessarily a slow method of learning, and encouraged an incomplete and superficial appreciation of the new style. More rapid and thorough results could be achieved by exploiting the technology of the printing-press. Ever since the Renaissance, classicism had been a highly literate architecture, and printed manuals and treatises were widely available on the continent. English publications, which drew heavily on these European texts, first began to appear in the mid-seventeenth century, though at this stage the output of the genre was still very limited. The turning-point came with the emergence of Palladianism, an austere and academic interpretation of classicism that encouraged a bookish approach to design. The movement's earliest literary monuments appeared in 1715, with the first volume of Campbell's *Vitruvius Britannicus*, and Dubois' and Leoni's translation and redraughting of Palladio's *I Quattro Libri dell'Architettura*. These were rather exclusive publications, and it was not until the late 1720s that the idea that the medium is the message eventually filtered through to a wider public, as the trickle of architectural texts of earlier years turned into a flood.[19]

Behind this outflow from the presses lay an increasingly publicity-

[19] For architectural publications and their impact see J. Summerson, *Georgian London* (Harmondsworth, 1962), 72-5; Summerson, *Architecture in Britain*, 363-6; D. Cruickshank and P. Wyld, *London: The Art of Georgian Building* (London, 1975), 83-4; Harris, 'Architecture of Stamford', 83-6; K. A. Esdaile, 'The Small House and its Amenities in the Architectural Handbooks of 1749-1827', *Trans. of the Bibliographical Soc.*, xv (1917-19), 115-32.

oriented building profession, creating a new breed of author-architects, men such as James Gibbs (1682-1754), William Halfpenny (?-1755), Edward Hoppus (?-1739), Batty Langley (1696-1751), Robert Morris (1701-54), and Isaac Ware (*c*.1707-66).[20] They used print to advertise their own designs and boost their personal practices. But writing in itself also became an important aspect of their careers, and a number of them produced a sizeable output of books and pamphlets, some of which ran into several editions: Langley and Halfpenny can be accredited with almost twenty identified items each. These volumes were generally of four types. First, there was the reprint of a classic text, such as Dubois' and Leoni's (1715-16), and Ware's (1738) English versions of Palladio's *Four Books*, or Leoni's translation of Alberti's *Architecture* (1726). A second category encompassed books of drawings and designs, sometimes lavishly produced, as in Campbell's *Vitruvius Britannicus* (1715-25). Third, there were the more theoretical works, concentrating on discussion and speculation, such as Robert Morris's *Lectures on Architecture* (1734-6), or John Wood's *Origin of Building* (1741). Finally came the genuine building manual or pattern-book, packed with practical information, from how to establish detailed measurements and costings, to descriptions of the different types of bricks and glass that were available. Richard Neve's *City and Country Purchaser* (1703), and Batty Langley's *Builder's Chest-Book* (1727) fall into this group. In reality the four categories overlapped a great deal. The manuals, though concentrating on practical matters, usually contained a good dash of theory and some reference to Renaissance authorities. Isaac Ware's encyclopaedic *Complete Body of Architecture* (1756), as its name suggests, was all categories rolled into one. However, the four types of books did represent a certain social reality, with the clients probably focusing their attention on the more expensive classic texts, illustrative and theoretical works, and the craftsmen on the generally cheaper manuals. It could therefore be argued that the former publications generated demand while the latter satisfied it. Between them such volumes provided consumer and producer with a crash-course in the new architecture, which greatly facilitated a proper understanding of classicism, and encouraged its swift dissemination. The end result can be seen in the radical fashion by which the façade of the traditional town dwelling was transformed. The frontage was affected in four

[20] H. M. Colvin, *A Biographical Dictionary of British Architects 1600-1840* (London, 1978).

critical areas: the plane in which it was built, the relationship of its component parts, the application of ornament, and the use of building materials.

3. THE CLASSICAL FAÇADE

The façade of the vernacular urban house was frequently uneven in appearance. This was partly due to the presence of projecting window-cases, and of timber-framed walls which had buckled. It also resulted from the widespread practice of jettying one floor out over another, so that in taller properties several storeys tumbled forward precariously into the road. Such a building was to be anathema to the new architecture, which required a frontage that was constructed in a single plane set at right angles to the street. In practice, door-cases and ornamental features were permitted to project a little, but the degree of this was to be kept to a minimum. The earliest classical town houses were built with the steeply hipped roof and dormer windows favoured by the Dutch, but later this was perceived as an inappropriate visual deviation from the single-plane ideal, and replaced by a lower pitched roof, preferably concealed behind a parapet.

One development that considerably enhanced the flush appearance of the façade was the adoption of the sash-window. When this was opened the glass pane remained within the surface of the wall rather than projecting from it, as it did in the traditional casement-window. Sliding windows and shutters had probably been used on a limited scale for some time. But the true sash system, employing a counter-balancing device, appears to have been an English invention of the late 1660s or early 1670s. Some years passed before it became established in the provincial town. Important houses were still being built or refronted with mullioned and transomed windows at Chichester in 1696 and Tewkesbury in 1701.[21] However, it was about this time that sashes began to appear in the more prestigious urban dwellings. An early example in Bristol can be traced back to 1690, though traditional fenestration continued to be employed for new 'classical' houses after this date. Wood pinpoints the arrival of sash-windows in Bath to 1695

[21] H. J. Louw, 'The Origin of the Sash-Window,' *Architectural History*, xxvi (1983), 49–72; D. Cruickshank, *A Guide to the Georgian Buildings of Britain and Ireland* (London, 1985), 27; Cruickshank and Wyld, *Art of Georgian Building*, 161–5; J. Woodforde, *Georgian Houses for All* (London, 1978), 112–20; Spershott, *Memoirs*, 10; *VCH Gloucestershire*, viii. 131.

or 1696, and in the early eighteenth century they were being used in York (Middlethorpe Hall, *c*.1700), King's Lynn (Clifton House, *c*.1708), and Manchester (St Ann's Church, 1709–12). Before long the new fashion swept all before it, like the double-glazing vogue of today. In the 1730s the York authorities ripped out the old windows from several of the city's medieval public buildings and replaced them with sashes, and at Preston the corporation was requiring their use in town building leases. Such windows became a hallmark of the new architecture. In the early eighteenth century John Macky could write of the 'handsome houses, sash-windowed on each side' of the street by which one entered Ludlow, and note that some of 'the finest houses' at Winchester are 'as handsome as one can see anywhere, all sashed and adorned after the newest manner'.[22]

Towards the end of the vernacular phase, the façades of new urban dwellings began to reflect a growing concern for order and balance. This was to be a harbinger of the central role played by proportion and symmetry in the design of the classical town house. No deviation was permitted from these principles. Langley proclaimed 'true proportions . . . the fundamentals and very life of architecture', and Ware wrote that 'proportion is established upon rule: there is no apology for an unneedful violation of the truth of the science in this article'.[23] When it came to the mysteries of mensuration the pattern-books were in their element. It was recognized that there existed two types of proportion. The first, as Neve argued, was 'between the parts and the whole, whereby a great fabric should have great apartments, great lights or windows, great entrances . . . in fine, all the members and parts great, proportionable to the building'. In a similar vein Ware warned that 'it would be absurd to see a great house divided into a multitude of closets, or a little house consisting only of a hall and dining-room'.[24] The second form of proportion was that 'between the parts themselves . . . considering their breadths . . . lengths', and

[22] Gomme *et al.*, *Bristol*, 88, 90–1; Wood, *Bath*, 220; RCHM, *York*, iii (London, 1972), p. lxxxii; Parker, *King's Lynn*, 89–90; Students Diary, fo. 51; House Book, 23 Dec. 1734, 10 Aug. 1737, YCA; Drake, *Eboracum*, 301; Council Minutes, 6 Apr. 1736, PCMSS; J. Macky, *A Journey through England and Scotland* (London, 1722–3), ii. 13, 138.
[23] B. Langley, *The Builder's Chest-Book*, 1727, repr. (Farnborough, 1971), p. iii; I. Ware, *A Complete Body of Architecture*, 1768, repr. (Farnborough, 1971), 294; J. Wood, *The Origin of Building*, 1741, repr. (Farnborough, 1968), 72; B. Denvir, *The Eighteenth Century: Art, Design, and Society 1689–1789* (London, 1983), 36.
[24] R. Neve, *The City and Country Purchaser and Builder's Dictionary*, 1726, repr. (Newton Abbot, 1969), 64; Ware, *Body of Architecture*, 294.

'height'.[25] The detailed dimensions of the five classical orders were controlled by a unit called the module, either the diameter, or in the case of the doric order, half the diameter of the column at its base.[26] Doors were to be constructed on the double-square principle, with their height twice their width, though this could be varied a little, as long as a proportionate relationship was retained between the parts.[27] A similar latitude was allowed in the case of windows, but for a general model Ware and others recommended that the height of those on the first or principal floor be twice their breadth, that on the chamber floor 'the best measure . . . is the diagonal, which is once and a half the breadth', and that 'the attic storey should have the windows square'.[28] Finally, to arrange the various elements of the frontage into a uniform composition, it was essential to follow the laws of symmetry. As Langley insisted, 'place your windows in such order that those on the right of the door be equal to those on the left, and those in the storeys above . . . directly above those below'.[29] In theory the dictates of the architectural manuals enmeshed the façade in a web of proportion and symmetry from which the component parts could not escape. In practice, however, this was a good deal less rigid than it seems, since nothing could prevent clients and craftsmen adapting, bending, or ignoring the rules. But the visual appearance of surviving buildings suggests that contemporaries generally placed a high premium on designing a well balanced and pleasingly proportioned frontage to their houses.

The façade has always been the show-case of a house and this was especially so for an urban dwelling. Commercial pressures to maximize the availability of street space favoured a compact frontage,[30] and tended to create an unbroken line of buildings that excluded any view of their side or rear walls. In these circumstances it was natural that the façade should become the special focus for any decorative show, and that this should be relatively elaborate to compensate for the restricted

---

[25] Neve, *Dictionary*, 64.

[26] Ware, *Body of Architecture*, 24; Neve, *Dictionary*, 110-13, 197; Langley, *Chest-Book*, 42-53.

[27] Ware, *Body of Architecture*, 439-41; Neve, *Dictionary*, 124; Cruickshank and Wyld, *Art of Georgian Building*, 83-4.

[28] Ware, *Body of Architecture*, 60-1; and also Neve, *Dictionary*, 282; Langley, *Chest-Book*, 132; Cruickshank and Wyld, *Art of Georgian Building*, 157-60.

[29] Langley, *Chest-Book*, 132; Neve, *Dictionary*, 282; Ware, *Body of Architecture*, 319-21.

[30] W. and J. Halfpenny, R. Morris, and T. Lightoler, *The Modern Builder's Assistant* (London, 1757), 36.

space available. Medieval and early modern town architecture had developed a corpus of external ornamentation that was particularly varied in the case of timber-framed properties, where rich patterning and carving could be executed comparatively cheaply.[31] The Urban Renaissance wholly abandoned this tradition of vernacular decoration and replaced it with one founded on classicism. The new package contained a wide range of elements. The most important were the five orders: tuscan, doric, ionic, corinthian, and composite. These could be applied, in whole or in part, to windows, doorways, and the surface of the wall. For example, the cornice which crowned the top of many a town house façade was normally left to stand on its own, without any trace of the column or remaining entablature that should have accompanied it. Other decorative devices included arches, keystones, pediments, aprons, quoins, string-courses, balustrades, parapets, scrolls, vases, urns, carved masks, statuary, and various fabric treatments, such as rusticated stone or patterned brickwork.[32] The use of classical ornaments was governed by rules that controlled not only their dimensions, but also their relationship towards each other. It was thought quite inappropriate to place doric columns over ionic ones, or rusticated stones over smooth ones.[33] However, the critical factors determining the choice of decorative features were fashion and status. These forces will be examined in Chapter Nine.

Underpinning the strictly architectural aspects of the Urban Renaissance was a revolution in building fabrics. This involved the replacement of traditional materials (such as rubble stones, cobbles, pebbles, flints, turfs, clay blocks, thatch, and timber-framing infilled with wattle and daub), with brick, ashlar stone, tile and slate. Brick had been employed continuously in England since at least the late twelfth century. During the Great Rebuilding there was a marked growth in its use, particularly in the erection of chimneys, and in the construction of the more substantial houses in East Anglia and the South-East. However, it was the late seventeenth century that witnessed the dramatic upturn in the exploitation of brick that was eventually to consign many vernacular materials to obsolescence.[34] In

---

[31] *VCH Oxfordshire*, x. 29–30; Laithwaite, 'Buildings of Burford', 67.

[32] Cruickshank and Wyld, *Art of Georgian Building, passim*.

[33] Ware, *Body of Architecture*, 33, 133.

[34] R. W. Brunskill and A. Clifton-Taylor, *English Brickwork* (London, 1977), especially 29–43; A. Clifton-Taylor, *The Pattern of English Building* (London, 1962), chap. 10; Barley, *English Farmhouse*, 67–9, 188–91, 205–10, 246–8; Mercer, *Vernacular Houses*, 129–33; Jones and Falkus, 'Urban Improvement', 200–3.

1795 Aikin wrote of Manchester, 'towards the latter end of the last century and the beginning of the present, the traders had certainly got money beforehand, and began to build modern brick houses, in place of those of wood and plaster'. This was a trend that would have been visible in a host of other towns of this time, such as York, Beverley, Lincoln, King's Lynn, Warwick, Tewkesbury, Salisbury, and Chichester.[35]

To contemporary observers brick became a powerful symbol of a community's architectural status and economic prosperity. Writing of Preston, probably in the 1680s, Kuerden described the 'handsome buildings . . . here and there interwoven with stately fabrics of brick building, after the modish manner, extraordinarily adorning the streets which they belong unto'. Fiennes, touring England during the transitional years at the end of the seventeenth century, was particularly sensitive to the advance of the new material. At Canterbury she found 'the buildings are handsome . . . most are of brickwork; its a flourishing town. . . .' She thought Deal 'looks a good thriving place, the building new and neat brickwork', and Newcastle-upon-Tyne she considered 'a noble town . . . its buildings . . . of brick mostly or stone'. Other places she recorded as still predominantly timber-framed, such as Coventry, where 'the buildings are most of timber work and old', and Sandwich, 'a sad old town, all timber building'. Almost a century later, when Rudder compiled his history of Gloucestershire, brick was still an architectural and economic marker. He described the developing spa of Cheltenham as consisting 'of one handsome street . . . the buildings are chiefly of brick', affirmed that in the county town 'the buildings are chiefly of brick, whereas formerly they were of wood', but noted that in Thornbury, stranded by the arrival of the turnpike, 'Some of the houses are built of brick, a few of stone, but the greater part seem to be wood buildings: and from the present condition of them, the town appears to be declining.'[36]

[35] J. Aikin, *A Description of the Country from Thirty to Forty Miles round Manchester* (London, 1795), 182; RCHM, *York*, iii, pp. lxxx–lxxxi; I. and E. Hall, *Historic Beverley* (York, 1973), 3; Hill, *Stuart Lincoln*, 211; Parker, *King's Lynn*, 102–7; P. Borsay, 'The English Urban Renaissance: Landscape and Leisure in the Provincial Town *c.*1660–1770', Ph.D. thesis (Lancaster, 1981), 156–62; *VCH Gloucestershire*, viii. 126, 130–1; Rudder, *Gloucestershire*, 738; A. Clifton-Taylor, *Six English Towns* (London, 1978), 24–36, 82–3; *VCH Wiltshire*, vi. 70.

[36] [R. Kuerden], *A Brief Description of the Borough and Town of Preston*, with occasional notes by J. Taylor (Preston, 1818), 8; Fiennes, *Journeys*, 113, 123, 128–9, 209; Rudder, *Gloucestershire*, 81, 334, 750.

Modern machine-made bricks tend to have a dull, utilitarian finish and to look much the same as each other. Yet in the eighteenth century the material was a remarkably rich and flexible one, capable of introducing a good deal of variety into a façade, without upsetting its visual coherence. A wide range of bricks was available. Neve listed eighteen different kinds, though four basic types were generally recognized. The cheaper and lower quality products were place bricks, made to inexacting standards with poorish earth, and samel bricks, stacked on the edge of the kiln and therefore crumbly in texture; the better and more expensive ones were stocks, carefully moulded with higher quality ingredients, and rubbers or cutting bricks, normally used for decorative work. Colours could differ considerably depending upon the type of earth used. Earlier on, it was fashionable to create dramatic effects by employing fiery red hues, or by mixing purple and red bricks together. Later, colours were more muted, and in London at least, austere grey stocks became very popular. Once the basic raw material had been decided upon, it could be laid or bonded in a variety of ways, which either enhanced the overall smoothness of the finish, or created subtle patterns in the wall. Great skill was required in the cutting or rubbing of bricks, known as gauged work, so as to smooth them or alter their shape. Such bricks were used especially for ornamental features like pilasters, quoins, string-courses, cornices, and most widely of all, window arches, where they were often arranged to form a decorative fan. Occasionally gauged bricks were laid across the whole facade, set in a thin layer of white putty, to create the smoothest of finishes. But this was very expensive, and a cheaper imitation, known as tuck-pointing, could be produced by building up the edge of ordinary bricks with red mortar to give the appearance of having been rubbed smooth, and then inserting a pencil line of putty between the layers of mortar. Such ingenuity was an indication of the degree to which the common brick could be manipulated in the interests of fashion.[37]

In some towns brick arrived very late, or scarcely at all, in the eighteenth century. Stamford, Banbury, Burford, Bath, and Warminster fall into this category. Yet among them only Banbury was backward in responding to classical influences. What they all shared in common was that they lay on the limestone belt that snakes from north Yorkshire down to Dorset, and therefore enjoyed a ready supply of

[37] Neve, *Dictionary*, 37-56; Langley, *Chest-Book*, 62-4; Ware, *Body of Architecture*, 57-61; Cruickshank and Wyld, *Art of Georgian Building*, 178-91.

excellent building stone.[38] So long as this was cut to even faces with square edges to form ashlar, then it was a perfectly acceptable material. Indeed, in many brick towns stone acquired a superior status, and was employed in the construction of the more important buildings. The greatest part of the rebuilding after the fire at Blandford Forum in 1731 was executed in brick, though Portland stone was imported for the church and town hall. Often stone would also be used as a dressing in a predominantly brick façade to highlight ornamental features, such as quoins, string-courses, windows, and door-cases. Occasionally a brick front would be stuccoed to give the impression of ashlar. However, the relationship of one material to another varied from place to place. Where stone was common, brick could acquire a social kudos of its own. The leases granted for the houses built in Bristol's Queen Square and Orchard Street stipulated the use of brick for the façade, but permitted all other walls to be constructed of stone. The Bull Inn at Burford was ambitiously refronted, largely with brick, in about 1715, apparently so that it stood out from its neighbouring stone buildings and its competitors in the victualling trade (see Fig. 3).[39] The other newly favoured building materials were tile and slate, which increasingly replaced thatch for roofing. Tiling was also exploited, especially in the South-East, as a cover for timber-framed walls. Towards the middle of the eighteenth century special mathematical or brick tiles appeared, which were designed to imitate fashionable Georgian brickwork: Lewes, Guildford, Canterbury, and Salisbury still contain fine examples that can easily mislead the casual observer.[40]

The emphasis placed on obtaining a flush façade, the rigorous pursuit of proportion and symmetry, the employment of classical ornament, and the use of the new building materials helped to radically alter the appearance of the English town house. But this transformation in design was achieved not through a wholesale reconstruction of the landscape, but by a judicious combination of

[38] RCHM, *Stamford*, pp. lxiv–lxvii; *VCH Oxfordshire*, x. 33–4; M. S. Gretton, *Burford Past and Present* (London, 1945), 29–30; Ison, *Bath*, *passim*; *VCH Wiltshire*, viii. 93–4; R. W. Brunskill, *Illustrated Handbook of Vernacular Architecture*, 2nd edn. (London, 1978), 187, 189.

[39] RCHM, *Dorset*, iii, Part 1, 18; Cruickshank and Wyld, *Art of Georgian Building*, 192–7; Gomme *et al.*, *Bristol*, 95–6, 101; *BE Oxfordshire* (Harmondsworth, 1974), 516.

[40] Clifton-Taylor, *English Building*, 265–71; Brunskill and Clifton-Taylor, *English Brickwork*, 40–3, 75; Brunskill, *Handbook of Vernacular Architecture*, 60–3, 86–93; *VCH Wiltshire*, vi. 70.

Fig. 3. The Bull Hotel (refronted *c*.1715), High Street, Burford

pragmatism and compromise. One imagines that most townsmen were
either financially unable or personally unwilling to totally rebuild
their comfortable vernacular dwellings, a good number of which had
been only recently erected or improved during the late Tudor and
early Stuart Great Rebuilding. On the other hand, it is clear that many
citizens did wish to give their homes some type of less expensive
but fashionable face-lift, and possessed the means to do this.
Consequently, it was often the case that the new architecture was
introduced into the townscape not so much by erecting new buildings,
as by wholly or partially refronting existing ones. Today, even the most
practised eye can be taken in by this elegant deception, since many a
vernacular house hides behind a perfect classical façade. In Broad

Street Ludlow, only seven properties have exposed timber fronts, whereas another twenty-two are almost entirely timber-framed behind a skin of brick or plaster (see Fig. 2).[41]

The full cosmetic treatment would require completely rebuilding a façade in brick or ashlar, perhaps with a parapet to conceal a traditional gabled or steeply hipped roof. Where the old house contained jettied storeys, refronting necessitated either cutting back the line of the property to the ground floor, or extending it forward to that of the topmost projection, so as to achieve the desired single plane. A superficial but cheap improvement could be executed simply by plastering, tiling, or weather-boarding over the unfashionable front to conceal the old building materials and imitate the new ones. In Norwich Fiennes found 'their building timber . . . they plaster on laths, which they strike into squares, like broad free-stone on the outside', and Neve knew of a 'house that is plastered in imitation of brickwork. . . . This house has been done this 20 years, and yet looks very well, and passes for a brick house with common passengers, though it be only timber plastered over.' The actual building work involved in refronting must have temporarily left many a home in a state of semi-exposure, and provoked not a little local comment. As a visitor to Dartford recorded in 1723, 'we went to see the church, accompanied by our landlord, who, I doubt not, is with great justice esteemed as one of the chief wits of this place; and he gave us a specimen of it, as we went along, by asking one of his neighbours, who had pulled down the front of his house, with a very facetious air, how long it had been since he kept open house?'[42]

---

[41] Lloyd, *Broad Street*, 46; RCHM, *York*, iii, p. lxxix; House Book, 3 Feb. 1702/3, 21 Mar. 1744/5, YCA; Hall, *Beverley*, 38; R. Thoresby, *Ducatus Leodiensis: Or, the Topography of the Ancient and Populous Town and Parish of Leeds*, 2nd edn., ed. T. D. Whitaker (Leeds, 1816), 39; Henstock, 'Town Houses', 69; RCHM, *Stamford*, pp. xliii, lix; *VCH Warwickshire*, viii. 430-1; Fox, *Stratford-upon-Avon*, 49; Hillaby, *Ledbury*, 103-4, and plates 107-10; Laithwaite, 'Buildings of Burford', 85; *BE Oxfordshire*, 513-21; *VCH Gloucestershire*, viii. 130-1; Clifton-Taylor, *Six English Towns*, 24, 83; Clegg, *Dorchester*, 147-8; *VCH Wiltshire*, vi. 78-84; Laithwaite, 'Totnes Houses', 88; Parker, *King's Lynn*, 89-90.

[42] Fiennes, *Journeys*, 148; Neve, *Dictionary*, 224-5; HMC, *Portland MSS*, vi. 75. I am grateful to Geoffrey Holmes for bringing the last reference to my notice.

Coherence

3

Street and Square

Classicism transformed the public face of the house. But the impact of the architectural renaissance struck much deeper than this. Changes in the design of individual dwellings were accompanied by a new consciousness of the relationship between buildings. It seems that traditionally the majority of town houses had been designed as discrete structures. Classicism modified this approach. Individual properties were now to be perceived and treated (where possible) as part of a wider fabric, with their specific identities subsumed beneath a larger architectural form, such as a street or square. The development of these units was to give a coherence to the urban landscape that altered not only its appearance, but also its very nature.[1]

1. THE STREET: BUILDINGS

The foundation of this more unified townscape was the street, which was remodelled under the influence of two complementary pressures. The first of these sought to integrate the separate buildings that flanked the highway, the second to improve the quantity and quality of space within it. Together they gave the street an integrity and elegance that it had never displayed before. Critical to its visual unity was the design of its various parts. Vernacular town houses had been built in a very flexible and pragmatic way. Structural concerns predominated over aesthetic ones, and the local and personal requirements of each building were more important than slavishly reproducing an architectural model.[2] As a result, houses displayed a good deal of individuality. One property might contain jettying, another not. The position and size of doors and windows varied considerably, as did the use of decorative timber work, and many façades sported some piece of

[1] Cruickshank, *Guide*, 20; T. Sharp, *English Panorama* (London, 1950), 37-8.
[2] Brunskill, *Handbook of Vernacular Architecture*, 25-6; Mercer, *Vernacular Houses*, 1-2.

idiosyncratic carving, such as a grotesque figure, head, or mask. However, a number of houses were consciously erected as part of a larger scheme. The Abbey Cottages in Church Street Tewkesbury, probably of the fifteenth or early sixteenth century, originally formed a continuous block of over twenty separate dwellings. The extent of this project was exceptional, and examples from York, King's Lynn, Winchester, and Coventry suggest that six to nine homes was more typical. It is unlikely that such units constituted more than a small minority of a town's total housing stock. Most were probably either small speculative ventures in the provision of cheap accommodation, or almshouses for the poor and infirm, as in Church Street Stratford-upon-Avon. Moreover, there is little to suggest that they were conceived by their builders as pieces of *street* architecture.[3]

The generally loose relationship between vernacular buildings must have seriously undermined the visual integrity of the pre-industrial street. The arrival of classicism was to substantially modify this picture. Here was a highly theoretical architecture based on archetypal building forms and universal rules, which were intended to override local tradition and personal fancy. Moreover, as classicism practically developed within the constraints of the English townscape, it tended to eschew the wilder fantasies of its baroque substyle in favour of a general moderation and simplicity.[4] The outcome was an approach to building design that contained individual expression within relatively narrow parameters, increased the similarity between neighbouring properties, and over time enhanced the coherence and identity of the street.

Contemporaries were fully conscious of the virtues of a uniform street architecture, applauding its presence, encouraging its construction, and criticizing any deviations. John Wood argued that the High Street in Bath 'wants only regularity to make it a picture to such as enter the city at the north gate', and suggested of the existing houses, 'I could wish to see some of them rebuilt, to add to the beauty of the rest'. Sir Edward Moore, on whose estate much of the expanding port of Liverpool was being erected in the late seventeenth century, tried hard to establish a common house design for each road. When one builder thwarted his plans, he complained that 'This man should have

---

[3] *VCH Gloucestershire*, viii. 29–30; C. Platt, *The English Medieval Town* (London, 1976), 66–9; M. Airs, *The Buildings of Britain: Tudor and Jacobean* (London, 1982), 97–8; *BE Warwickshire* (Harmondsworth, 1966), 419.

[4] K. Downes, *English Baroque Architecture* (London, 1966), 97.

built two dormer windows as others did: but when he had got me fast
and he was loose, he would build none, but made the house like a
barn, much to the disparagement of the street.' At the developing
port of Whitehaven, Sir John Lowther, writing probably in the later
1690s, saw his 'chief care being to have the streets laid out regularly,
and that the houses in each street should be made uniform so far as it
could be, and carried on in the same range, and built contiguous to
each other'. Some sixty years later a Scottish visitor testified to
Lowther's success, when he noted how 'you will be struck with the
good appearance of Whitehaven at your approach, and more so, when
you enter it, with the regularity of the streets and goodness of the
buildings'. Other favoured towns attracted similar approval. Fiennes
discovered the buildings at Pontefract to be 'so even and uniform as
well as lofty, that it appears very magnificent', and Miège described
how after the fire of 1675 at Northampton, the town 'was soon raised
up again, more uniform and beautiful than ever it was before'.[5] Today
we are largely inured to the attractions of the terraced street. During
the Industrial Revolution it dominated town planning to such an
extent that it now appears utilitarian and monotonous. But in the
post-Restoration years uniform streets were a novel and appealing
feature, islands of ordered elegance amidst a sea of vernacular idio-
syncracy.

2. THE STREET: SHAPE AND SPACE

In the development of the new street just as important as the design of
the flanking properties was the treatment of the space between them.
Traditional town thoroughfares were often constricted in size and
irregularly shaped, features which came to attract much criticism. The
highways in the old city at Bath were notoriously narrow and uneven,
and visitors and residents from the time of Pepys onwards were not
slow to air their views on the matter. In the 1740s Wood complained
that among the 'narrow ways within the walls of Bath . . . there is not
a street, lane, alley, or throng whose sides are straight, or whose
surface is upon a true depending line, to give them the least beauty',

    [5] Wood, *Bath*, 332; E. Moore, *Liverpool in King Charles the Second's Time*, ed.
W. F. Irvine (Liverpool, 1899), 127; Lowther quoted in Chalklin, 'New Towns', 240;
Crofts, 'Lakeland Journey', 289; Fiennes, *Journeys*, 94; Miège, *New State of England*,
80.

and two decades later Samuel Derrick could still bemoan the fact that 'the streets of the city are so narrow, that two carriages can scarcely pass one another'.[6] York suffered from similar problems. In the 1690s Fiennes thought that 'for one of the metropolis and the see of the Archbishop it makes but a mean appearance, the streets are narrow and not of any length', a view repeated sixty years later, when, in spite of improvements, Lybbe Powys still found 'the streets (hardly deserving such an appellation) . . . extremely narrow'.[7]

The new fashions in urban design represented a strong reaction against the 'picturesque' characteristics of vernacular streets. A broad, straight, and open thoroughfare became the model.[8] The classical house itself helped to develop this ideal. Traditional town dwellings frequently possessed an overhanging facade that cut into the free space occupied by the highway. Where a narrow road was flanked by tall houses with several layers of jettying, the space above ground floor level became progressively eroded, and the street was almost enclosed. Defoe described how 'the timber-built houses' in Coventry projected 'forwards and towards one another, till in the narrow streets they were ready to touch one another at the top', and in the 1730s Drake explained that in his native York, 'our streets being but narrow, and these buildings projecting very much at the top . . . in some streets they now almost meet on each side. This renders the place closer'.[9] The overall effect was to reduce both the volume of the street, and, by restricting the passage of light and flow of air, the quality of its environment. The flush façade required in the construction of the classical house avoided these problems, and in the long run helped considerably to open up urban thoroughfares.

When planning new streets developers now paid considerable attention to line and width. At York, where in the mid-1740s an elegant new thoroughfare was being constructed between Davygate

[6] S. Pepys, *The Diary of Samuel Pepys*, ed. R. Latham and W. Matthews (London, 1970-83), ix. 233; Students Diary, fo. 114; Cox, *Magna Britannia*, iv. 733; Wood, *Bath*, 352; S. Derrick, *Letters Written from Liverpool. Chester. Cork. the Lake of Killarney, Dublin, Tunbridge Wells, Bath* (London, 1767), ii. 105.

[7] Fiennes, *Journeys*, 76; Powys, *Diaries*, 17; and also *A Diary of a Journey through the North of England Made by William and John Blathwayt of Dyrham Park in 1703*, ed. N. Hardwick (n.p., 1977). 20; Revd Sir J. Cullum's Journal of a Tour of the Yorkshire Area (1771), fo. 141. Suffolk RO, E2/44/1. For the narrow streets in Bristol see HMC, *Verulam MSS*, 250; Pigott Diary, i, article 495.

[8] *Diary of a Journey . . . Made by William and John Blathwayt*, 26; J. Black, *The British and the Grand Tour* (London, 1985), 225-6.

[9] Defoe, *Tour*, ii. 83; Drake, *Eboracum*, 279.

and Coney Street, the corporation agreed to amend their original proposals so as 'to make the . . . street more uniform and take off the curves, angles, and corners that spoil the regularity thereof'. While describing how his plans for making a straight road in Liverpool were frustrated by a small plot of land, Sir Edward Moore revealed the premium that he placed on street design:

> If it had not been for this piece of land, I had made Fenwick Street as straight as any street in town. But this being none of my land, I was forced to wind the street in that place: for before I did it, I sent to Mr Crosse's agents, and would have given fifty pounds for bare six yards of ground, which was a hundred times the purchase, and they said they would sell none.

Despite this set-back, Moore seems to have been generally successful in planning his estate, at least judging from Defoe's description of the streets of 'New Liverpool' as 'straight, clean, and spacious'. When Defoe visited Bideford in Devon he saw 'a new spacious street . . . a great length, broad as the High Street at Exeter'. This was the fine Bridgeland Street, developed by the town's Bridge Feoffees in the 1690s, with careful controls to produce a wide thoroughfare flanked by uniform houses.[10] Redevelopment after a large-scale fire was sometimes seen as an advantageous occasion to execute road improvements. The rebuilding acts at Northampton, Warwick, and Blandford Forum made provisions for street widening, and at Warwick these were extensively used. Though the formal powers provided at Northampton were limited in scope, builders appear to have followed closely the new trends in road construction. Fiennes described how the rebuilt town 'opens a noble prospect to your sight a mile distant . . . the streets [are] as large as most in London except Holborn and the Strand', and later visitors commended the thoroughfares for being 'spacious and wide' and of 'uncommon breadth'.[11]

Although urban expansion and post-fire reconstruction provided an excellent opportunity to introduce the new fashions in street design, these two processes affected only a minority of town thoroughfares.

---

[10] House Book, 14 June 1745, YCA; Moore, *Liverpool*, 150; Defoe, *Tour*, i. 260; ii. 69; M. Goaman, *Old Bideford and District* (Bideford, 1970), 26–7; Hoskins, *Devon*, 336–7.

[11] 27 Car. II; 6 Gul. III, c. 1; 5 Geo. II, c. 16; Borsay, 'Landscape and Leisure', 144–51; Jones *et al.*, *Gazetteer*, 53–4; H. M. Colvin, 'The Bastards of Blandford: Architects and Master-Builders', *Archaeological Jnl.*, civ (1948), 181–2; *VCH Northamptonshire*, iii (London, 1930), 32–3; Fiennes, *Journeys*, 118; Defoe, *Tour*, ii. 86; Students Diary, fo. 5.

Most were long-established features of the landscape, accommodating a diversity of vested interests among their inhabitants, and displaying a complex pattern of landholding, all of which made change very difficult. However, by a combination of judicious expenditure, the manipulation of town leases, and a little legal compulsion, advances were possible.[12] Fishergate Lane in Preston was widened in 1713 with the aid of an act of Parliament, by which owners whose property was to be used in the project received compensation from an assessment raised on the town.[13] The majority of improvements progressed on a more piecemeal basis. In York, as we have seen, the problems of the physical environment were particularly acute. From the late 1720s the corporation pursued a policy of using strategically placed properties, either belonging to the city or specially purchased by it, to enlarge the highways. In some cases this involved the acquisition of relatively unencumbered land, such as a garden, in others, the demolition of a building and its reconstruction on a smaller portion of the same plot, the space released being added to the street.[14] From the mid-eighteenth century the authorities at Bath began to tackle the tortuous roads of the old town. During the 1750s and 1760s Cheap Street, Southgate Street, Walcot Street, Broad Street, and Horse Street were widened. Sometimes this was effected by making the grant of new corporate leases or the renewal of old ones conditional on the lessee rebuilding the dwelling to a different ground plan.[15] Though such an approach was inevitably patchy and protracted in its impact, it suggests that civic leaders had long-term plans for remodelling the urban landscape, and that they were able to sustain these over several decades.

A major factor influencing the trend towards wider and straighter streets was the mounting strain placed on urban communications by the growth in inland trade and private travel. The problems that could face a town, and the need for improvements, were very evident in York. Pressure from the commercial traffic that plied its way between

[12] M. Lobel, 'Some Reflections on the Topographical Development of the Pre-Industrial Town in England', in F. Emmison and R. Stephens (eds.), *Tribute to an Antiquary* (London, 1976), 160.

[13] Council Minutes, 20 Apr. 1713, 11 Aug. 1720, PCMSS.

[14] See references below to street improvement in York; and House Book, 26 Apr. 1731, 7 Dec. 1741, 1 Feb. 1741/2, 28 Apr. and 14 July 1742, 27 Jan. 1745/6, YCA; *VCH York*, 208–9.

[15] Council Minutes, 26 Apr., 18 June, and 4 July 1753, 4 Oct. 1756, BCA; McIntyre, 'Rise of a Resort Town', 230–1.

the quayside and the city centre led to an agreement in 1744 to widen Far Water Lane, so as 'to make it more convenient for carriages, being the only carriageway to and from the Staith'.[16] No less severe were the demands of personal mobility, with York's leisure and consumer services attracting more and more prestigious visitors, residents, and their cumbersome vehicles.[17] In 1729 the city negotiated with the churchwardens of St Helen's Stonegate for permission 'to cut off part of their churchyard, so far as to answer the opening of Blake Street, and to lay it to the street so as a coach may drive with greater ease and conveniency'. In all likelihood this was a response to a contemporaneous scheme to build new assembly rooms in Blake Street, which would considerably increase the strain on communications in the area. Though the erection of the rooms went ahead, the proposed road alterations proved abortive. However, the scheme was not forgotten. Eighteen years later, during the construction of the new street linking Davygate and Coney Street, the site of Davy Hall became vacant and was used to relocate the offending churchyard.[18] Many of the properties acquired in order to widen the highways at York, like the churchyard of St Helen's Stonegate, were situated on street corners, since these were the natural bottle-necks in the urban road network. Such considerations were clearly in the corporation's mind, when in 1731 it agreed to bargain for so much of a house on the corner of Spurriergate, 'as shall be necessary for widening and making the said corner more commodious for turning of coaches and carriages'.[19]

If practical needs provided much of the impetus behind street improvements, aesthetic considerations also played a part. In 1673 the Lord of the Manor at tiny Henley-in-Arden in Warwickshire granted a centrally located house and garden to the high bailiff, with the intention that the site should be cleared and 'laid wast and open to the street, for the better ornament of the said town', and the Warwick rebuilding act referred to 'ornament' as one of the two motives for widening the town's highways.[20] A factor that must have particularly enhanced the attractiveness of broad and straight thoroughfares was that they permitted the uniform qualities of classical house design to be properly appreciated, and the street viewed as an architectural whole.

16 House Book, 10 Dec. 1744, 29 Jan. 1744/5, YCA.
17 Drake, *Eboracum*, 241.
18 House Book, 29 Oct. 1729, 14 June 1745, YCA.
19 Ibid. 1 Dec. 1731; Drake, *Eboracum*, 292.
20 Styles, *West Midlands History*, 210; Fire Act, 6.

Some of the most serious problems facing established streets were not a consequence of any inherent fault in their construction. Many had originally been wide thoroughfares that had become progressively colonized as existing premises crept forward into the highway, temporary market stalls fossilized into permanent shops and shambles, and town halls and market crosses were erected on prestigious island sites. So extensive were these additions that they frequently created new alleys and passages, as in the High Street at Ludlow, which was split up into three narrow lanes and an attenuated street. The impact of these changes was to seriously undermine the appearance and effectiveness of many urban thoroughfares.[21] From the late seventeenth century civic authorities began a sustained campaign to sweep away these objectionable accretions. After the fire at Blandford Forum, the Guildhall, the permanent shambles, and a set of almshouses were removed from their location in the middle of the Market-Place, and following the blaze at Wareham, the centrally placed shambles, together with a block of tenements called the Throng were pulled down.[22] During the reconstruction work at Warwick in the 1690s, the Market Cross that straddled four of the town's main streets was dismantled, as in the 1760s were the crosses that occupied the marketplaces at Hull and Kendal. The central roads at Gloucester were packed with a veritable procession of buildings. A local act of 1750 provided the powers to uproot many of these, including the High Cross, the King's Board (or Butter Market), and the tower of the previously demolished Holy Trinity, all of which filled the middle of Westgate Street.[23]

The clearance of the High Street at Bath offers a revealing case-study in how major changes could be executed over a period of time. In the early eighteenth century the city's Guildhall occupied an island site at

[21] Platt, *Medieval Town*, 50-1; M. Aston and J. Bond, *The Landscape of Towns* (London, 1976), 97; M. Beresford, *New Towns in the Middle Ages* (London, 1967), 142; M. Beresford, *History on the Ground*, rev. edn. (London, 1971), 158-67; D. Lloyd and M. Moran, *The Corner Shop*, Ludlow Research Paper No. 2 (Birmingham, n.d.), 23-8; R. Millward, 'The Cumbrian Town between 1600 and 1800', in Chalklin and Havinden, *Urban Growth*, 222-3; W. Potts, *A History of Banbury* (Banbury, 1958), 34; Hillaby, *Ledbury*, 46-7; G. H. Tupling, 'Lancashire Markets in the Sixteenth and Seventeenth Centuries', *Trans. of the Lancashire and Cheshire Antiquarian Soc.*, lviii (1945), 1-20.

[22] Jones *et al.*, *Gazetteer*, 53; Colvin, 'Bastards of Blandford', 186-7, and plate xxvi(b); RCHM, *Dorset*, iii, Part 1, 22-3, and plate 104.

[23] Memorials, 20 Oct. 1695; Gillett and Macmahon, *Hull*, 205-6; Millward, 'Cumbrian Town', 226; Rudder, *Gloucestershire*, 90; Lobel, *Atlas*, i. Gloucester, 14.

the south end of the street, close to the Abbey, and on market-days
the rest of the highway was cluttered up with temporary stalls (see Map
2). The corporation began to tackle the problem in 1744 by extending
a court on the east side of the road that already accommodated the
town shambles. However, Wood claimed in 1749 that this area needed
to be further enlarged 'so as to contain all the stalls which on market-
days encumber the street', and he also argued that the Guildhall
should be removed. These opinions clearly had some support in the
city. In 1760 it was agreed to build a new town hall, and a committee
was appointed to supervise the arrangements. This was the beginning
of a saga of false starts that continued until the late 1770s, when the
old hall was finally demolished and a new one erected opposite the site
of its predecessor, but outside the body of the highway. The removal
of the market stalls progressed more expeditiously. By the end of the
sixties the authorities had considerably expanded the area of the old
shambles, and were directing almost all the open-street traders to
move there. The result of these and later changes can still be seen
today, both on the east side of High Street, with its fine Guildhall and
thriving indoor market to the rear, and in the broad thoroughfare that
leads up to the now fully exposed north flank of the Abbey.[24]

3. THE STREET: QUALITY OF SPACE

The trend to remodel the basic structure of the street (its shape and
volume) was paralleled by one to enhance the quality of space within
it. This focused on three principal aspects of the highway: its surface,
cleansing, and lighting. Some caution is necessary in assessing the
impact of new developments in these areas. First, the problem of how
to obtain an adequate standard of road surfacing and street sanitation
had exercised urban authorities for several centuries and inspired a
variety of solutions. But the long-term effectiveness of these remains
doubtful, particularly since the situation was still so poor in many late
Stuart towns.[25] Second, the value of any improvements has to be

[24] Council Minutes, 10 Jan. and 8 Mar. 1744/5, 19 May 1760, BCA; Wood, *Bath*,
339; J. Wood, *A Plan of the City of Bath* (1736); Derrick, *Letters*, ii. 105; McIntyre,
'Rise of a Resort Town', 231; Ison, *Bath*, 35-7.

[25] Platt, *Medieval Town*, 48-50, 70-2; C. Platt, *Medieval Southampton: The Port
and Trading Community AD 1000-1600* (London, 1973), 171; S. Reynolds, *An
Introduction to the History of English Medieval Towns* (Oxford, 1977), 128; Gillett and

weighed against the mounting strain that was being placed on urban roads, so that a measure of progress was necessary simply to maintain the status quo. Even allowing for these qualifications, substantial advances were made due to a new sense of inventiveness and purposefulness in tackling the problems that existed.[26]

From the late seventeenth century a variety of towns were involved in projects to maintain or enhance the surface of their public highways and spaces. Between about 1680 and 1750 paving schemes were introduced into Wisbech, Penzance, Nottingham, Bristol, and Scarborough. In early eighteenth-century Preston, St John's Weend, Church Gate Barrs, and the Market-Place were the subject of long-term improvement plans which included paving, and in the late 1720s the Market-Place, Corn Rails, and Shambles at Devizes were paved or pitched.[27] A valuable general innovation was the replacement of the open gutters that had scored the surface of many streets, posing a serious hazard to mobility and sanitation alike, with less obtrusive drainage systems.[28]

Any progress achieved in remodelling the street surface would be wasted if it were not supported by adequate cleansing arrangements. Especially important was the need to dispose of domestic and commercial waste, which might easily accumulate to a level where it seriously impeded the flow of traffic and offended visitors. Provisions for the public removal of rubbish had existed for centuries, though they were usually of only a limited nature. By at least 1656 Preston boasted an official scavenger, but considerable doubt must exist as to the adequacy of his services, since he was also town beadle, swineherd, and sexton, and his name comes to our attention in the records because he was 'very negligent' in his duties. Moreover, at Preston, as in the majority of towns, it is clear that the tasks of street cleansing and waste disposal fell predominantly on private householders. The Guild Orders of 1662 required 'all and every the inhabitants . . . every Saturday night, and every night in each fair, [to] sweep and cleanse

Macmahon, *Hull*, 30-3, 110; J. H. Thomas, *Town Government in the Sixteenth Century* (London, 1933), chaps. 5-6; Clark and Slack, *Towns in Transition*, 96; Dyer, *Worcester in the Sixteenth Century*, 205-7; Borsay, 'Landscape and Leisure', 98-100.

[26] Jones and Falkus, 'Urban Improvement', 193-233.

[27] Ibid. 212; McIntyre, 'Health and Pleasure Resorts', 243; Council Minutes, 23 May 1704, 17 July 1710, 8 Feb. 1710/11, 4 Apr. and 11 Aug. 1720, 20 Nov. 1738, 15 Feb. 1738/9, 6 June 1739, 13 Mar. 1740/1, PCMSS; Cunnington, *Devizes*, 237-8.

[28] Gillett and Macmahon, *Hull*, 202; Council Minutes, 30 Mar. 1752, BCA; *VCH Wiltshire*, vi. 89.

their street causeways before their houses and shops unto the channel
. . . and also [to] carry away their dung or dirt into their backsides, or
any other convenient place out of the streets'.[29] There are signs that
from about the 1670s urban authorities began to devote greater
attention and resources to the problem of highway sanitation. Public
scavengers were appointed at Leicester in 1686, Hereford in 1694, and
Lincoln in 1707, the one at Lincoln specifically to tackle the notorious
warren of lanes and alleys in the lower part of the city. The salaries of
the scavengers at Hereford and Lincoln were to be raised by a special
rate levied on the inhabitants, thereby transferring practical responsibility from private citizens to permanent contractors or officials, who
could guarantee the work was regularly executed. At Hereford the
scheme was soon upgraded, when in 1697 the expenditure on it was
increased from £8 to £15 a year (raised to £16 in 1700), a sum large
enough, given contemporary wage rates, to provide a substantial
measure of service.[30]

Some towns were remarkably inventive in their approach to the problems of waste disposal and street cleansing. In 1673 the authorities at
Bideford ordered thirty empty 'tobacco hogsheads strongly looped, or
some other fit vessels' to be placed at strategic points in the port,
which were to be used for personal refuse and to be regularly emptied
by the town scavenger. Liverpool introduced a similar public dustbin
service. In 1719 the corporation negotiated an eleven-year agreement
with two contractors, 'to take away all the muck and dirt in the streets
and passages of this town twice every week', and to facilitate rubbish
collection the men were permitted 'to make a convenient hole with an
iron grate over it at every street end'. Bath exploited the advances made
in the spa's piped water supplies, when in 1742 it was agreed that 'a
pump shall be erected in Westgate Street where the old cock and
cistern formerly stood, in order to keep the said street clean, and two
other in proper places in the Market-Place'.[31]

An important sign of the new commitment to street improvement
was the growing use of local acts of Parliament, which were often

[29] A. Hewitson (ed.), *Preston Court Leet Records* (Preston, 1905), 64–5; Guild Roll
1662, fo. 140, PCMSS; A. Hewitson, *History of Preston* (East Ardsley, 1969), 57–8.

[30] Jones and Falkus, 'Urban Improvement', 212; Nichols, *Leicester*, i, Part 2, 437;
Hereford Common Council Minutes, 8 Nov. 1694, Nov. 1697, Dec. 1700, Hereford
City Library; Hill, *Stuart Lincoln*, 211.

[31] A. G. Duncan, 'Bideford under the Restored Monarchy', *Trans. of the Devon
Association*, xlvii (1915), 312–15; J. A. Picton (ed.), *City of Liverpool: Municipal
Archives and Records* (Liverpool, 1886), 64; Council Minutes, 11 Oct. 1742, BCA.

expensive and time-consuming to obtain. Such legislation was not an entirely new phenomenon. Northampton had acquired a paving act as early as 1431 and Cambridge in 1543. But during the eighteenth century towns procured local acts on an unprecedented scale, especially from the middle years of the century onwards.[32] Many of these dealt wholly or partially with streets, such as the ones passed for Bristol (1700 and 1748), Norwich (1700), Liverpool (1748 and 1762), and Gloucester (1750). Some towns were particularly active in this field. Bath, where there was constant pressure from the tourist trade to enhance the amenities, obtained a whole battery of street-related acts in 1708, 1720, 1739, 1757, and 1766, while Hull, where proposals for legislation had failed in 1734-5, rapidly caught up in the middle of the century with acts in 1755, 1762, and 1764.[33]

This type of locally oriented legislation appears to have had three underlying motives. First, it was a means of establishing or confirming a town's authority to execute improvements, particularly where these involved some threat to the sensitive domain of private property. A parliamentary imprimatur gave the civic leaders the confidence to go ahead with substantial changes without being constrained by the fear of costly and lengthy litigation. Second, many of the new acts were concerned with introducing rating schemes. These were essential for effective street maintenance, since they provided the means by which responsibility could be transferred from the whims of individual householders to the security of a full-scale service which could be publicly monitored. Third, and most innovative of all, several acts sought to modify the traditional structure of local government by vesting improvement powers in specially constituted bodies of officials. These became known as improvement commissions, and were to play a critical role in urban administration during the early Industrial Revolution. Salisbury was the first provincial town to acquire such a body in 1737. Although only a few urban communities had followed suit before 1748, their popularity grew with the Liverpool act of that

---

[32] Thomas, *Town Government*, 40-1; Clark, *Country Towns*, 20-1; Jones and Falkus, *Urban Improvement*, 209-20.

[33] Bristol Common Council Proceedings, 9 Mar. 1698/9, 21 Oct. 1700, Bristol AO; S. and B. Webb, *The Manor and the Borough: English Local Government from the Revolution to the Municipal Corporations Act* (London, 1908), i. 455-6; W. Enfield, *An Essay towards the History of Liverpool* (Warrington, 1773), 17; Rudder, *Gloucestershire*, 90; Council Minutes, 11 Nov. and 1 Dec. 1707, 22 Mar. 1707/8, 28 June 1708, 6 Feb. 1720/1, 18 July 1739, 12 and 24 Jan., and 28 Mar. 1757, BCA; Wood, *Bath*, 373-7; McIntyre, 'Rise of a Resort Town', 239-41; Gillett and Macmahon, *Hull*, 199.

year, and by 1769 a total of fifty-two had been established (including those for London). Their emergence was a recognition of the mounting demands being placed on urban government, and of the determination of town leaders to meet these expectations by creating a more sophist-icated administrative structure.[34]

Street legislation was not confined to paving and cleansing, but was also directed towards a third factor that substantially influenced the quality of public space, the degree of light available. During the daytime this was governed by the width of the highway and the line of the flanking buildings. The development of broader thoroughfares and the decline of jettying would have helped a good deal in these respects. However, after nightfall the only factor that could affect the supply of light, the moon apart, was the use of artificial illumination. Before the 1680s this was almost entirely based on the candle-lit lantern hung outside individual premises. During the seventeenth century advances were achieved in the extension of lighting hours and the introduction of a measure of public financing, but street lighting remained generally confined to a limited time span (for example, dusk to nine p.m. on moonless nights between November and January), and was left largely to householders under direction from the urban authorities.[35] This combination of candle power, short hours, and private responsibility could have done little to relieve the blanket of darkness that enveloped the town every night. However, from the end of the seventeenth century the gloom began to lift a little. The key technical innovation was the introduction of oil-burning lamps, harnessed to a glass or reflector to enhance their luminosity. In the half century between the late 1680s and the mid-1730s, at least sixteen provincial towns experimented with these more powerful lamps: Canterbury (1687), York (1687), Exeter (1689), Norwich (1692), Hereford (1695), Preston (1699), Bristol (c.1700), Warwick (1701/2), Bath (1701/2), Hull (1713), Wisbech (1715), Liverpool (1718), Coventry (1725), Salisbury (1727), and Birmingham and Sheffield (both by 1735).[36] Many other towns probably followed suit.

[34] *VCH Wiltshire*, vi. 89, 110; Jones and Falkus, 'Urban Improvement', 213–17.

[35] M. Falkus, 'Lighting in the Dark Ages of English Economic History: Town Streets before the Industrial Revolution', in Coleman and John, *Pre-Industrial England*, 248–73, is a key study of the subject; Thomas, *Town Government*, 56–7; Dyer, *Worcester in the Sixteenth Century*, 205; Picton, *Liverpool Municipal Archives*, 64–5; *VCH York*, 162.

[36] The dates are the earliest I can find for these towns. In some cases they refer to no more than the experimental use of the odd lamp, though this often led to more

Though the spread of oil street lighting was superficially impressive, few communities were suddenly transformed into evening oases of light. The introduction of the new technology was often tentative and could require several decades to become fully established. Preston is a case in point. In late December 1699 the corporation agreed to erect four 'convex lights' at strategic points in the town, 'for the better going in the streets . . . in the winter evenings in the decrease of the moon, or when clouds interpose'. These four lamps could have done only a little to dispel the evening darkness and were probably perceived as an experiment. Though initially the servicing costs were to be born by the town (three of the lights were gifts of local gentlemen), it was intended that in the long run the expenses should be transferred to private householders. If this failed, then the lamps were to be dismantled. The subsequent fate of the scheme is a little unclear. In 1707 and 1710 the corporation agreed to continue meeting the maintenance costs, though at the latter date only three lights were in operation, and there is the distinct impression that the service had been allowed to deteriorate. This seems to be confirmed by an order of 1711 that required the repair of the remaining lamps and permitted a further one to be purchased. Nothing is heard on the subject for the next two decades, until in 1731 the town bailiffs were ordered to 'buy eight new lamps for the better lighting of the streets'.

The case of Preston exemplifies the cautious way in which the new lighting was sometimes adopted. Other towns were less conservative: Liverpool erected forty-five lamps in 1718, York at least fifty in 1723-4, and Salisbury twenty-two in 1727, while presumably the larger centres that obtained improvement acts containing lighting clauses, such as Norwich, Bristol, and Bath, also set up a substantial number of lights. A critical factor influencing the level of provision and its long-term

ambitious schemes. The notes refer both to the first example and subsequent usage, and should be used as the sources for later references in this section. Falkus, 'Lighting in the Dark Ages', 257-60; T. Allen, *A New and Complete History of the County of York* (London, 1828-31), i. 180; House Book, 25 Nov. 1723, 29 Jan. 1723/4, 23 Apr. and 20 Aug. 1724, YCA; F. Blomefield, *An Essay towards a Topographical History of the County of Norfolk*, 2nd edn. (London, 1805-10), iii. 427; Webb, *Manor and Borough*, ii. 555-6; Hereford Common Council Minutes, 7 Nov. 1695, Hereford City Library; Small Order Book, 22 Dec. 1699, PCMSS; Council Minutes, 8 Dec. 1707, 16 Jan. 1709/10, 5 Nov. 1711, 17 Dec. 1731, 21 Nov. 1739, PCMSS; Bristol Common Council Proceedings, 23 Oct. 1699, 21 Oct. 1700, Bristol AO; Warwickshire CRO, CR.1618, W.13/5, 1701/2; Chamberlains Accounts, 1701/2, 1702/3, 1704/5, 1706/7, 1707/8, 1712/13, BCA; Wood, *Bath*, 375-6; McIntyre, 'Rise of a Resort Town', 240; Picton, *Liverpool Municipal Archives*, 65; *VCH Wiltshire*, vi. 110.

quality was that of finance. Few authorities were willing or able to meet the costs of installation and maintenance, especially where a substantial project was involved, and therefore the successful development of street lighting depended upon the evolution of urban rating schemes. These permitted or required householders to transfer their responsibilities to a public or private contractor by the payment of a regular sum. The more important cities, like Bristol, Norwich, Coventry, Salisbury, and Bath, were quick to exploit this method of financing. By the 1760s oil street lighting supported by rating schemes was firmly established throughout the country. In 1766 a visitor to Bath, where the value of the new facilities was appreciated from an early date, noted that 'the streets here are so well illuminated in the night with lamps, that you may walk about as well as by day'. In the following year even a modest provincial town like Kendal acquired the means to roll back the tide of darkness, when, following an act of Parliament, '4 dozen of globe lamps' were ordered for the town, and an annual rate levied to service them.[37]

4. THE SQUARE

At the heart of the new classical townscape was the redeveloped street. On the one hand, its enhanced identity was derived from the adoption of a uniform domestic architecture, which allowed the street to emerge as a whole unit rather than a jumble of discrete buildings; on the other hand, its new character resulted from improvements in the shape of the thoroughfare, and the quantity and quality of space within it. Straighter and broader roads, the clearance of physical obstructions, sturdier surfaces, and more efficient cleansing and artificial lighting all contributed to this process. Taken together, these advances in street design went a good way towards ordering and 'civilizing' the vernacular landscape. However, such was the force of the trend towards regularity that it spread beyond the traditional thoroughfare and led to the introduction of novel architectural features. By 1700 one of the most important elements in Renaissance urban planning, the square, was beginning to make its appearance in provincial towns. It was to demonstrate, even more emphatically than the street, how the identity

[37] Penrose, *Letters*, 54; G. H. Martin, 'Street Lamps for Kendal: A Note on Inland Transport in the 1770s', *Jnl. of Transport History* (1965), 37-43.

of the private house could be subsumed under a much larger architectural unit.

The square arrived in England in the 1630s with the piazza designed by Inigo Jones in London's Covent Garden. But it was only after the Restoration, during the explosion of the metropolis's fashionable West End, that this new form of residential accommodation effectively caught on. The building of Bloomsbury and St James's Squares began in the 1660s, and by the turn of the century Soho, Golden, and Red Lion Squares had been added to their number.[38] Where London led, the provinces soon began to follow. The earliest examples (see Appendix 1) are probably the square laid out in the centre of Whitehaven from about the 1680s, and that at Warwick as part of the town's reconstruction after the fire of 1694. By the mid-1720s at least a further seven had been started and largely completed. Four of these were located in Bristol (Queen, St James's, Orchard, and Dowry Squares), and the others in Birmingham (the Square), Manchester (St Ann's Square), and Liverpool (Derby Square). Fifty years later another six had joined their ranks, three in Bath (Kingsmead, Beaufort, and Queen Squares), two in Bristol (King and Brunswick Squares), and one in Manchester (St James's Square). No doubt there are others to be discovered. Only occasionally did these provincial piazzas match the scale and sophistication of their continental or metropolitan prototypes. A number covered only a tiny area, such as the Square at Warwick, Orchard Square Bristol, Beaufort Square Bath, and St James's Square Manchester. The development of the larger ones was frequently spread over a lengthy period, with construction grinding to a halt during the recurring troughs in the building cycle. Many of the Bristol squares took over two decades to complete. So it would be wrong to overdramatize the impact of the Renaissance square on the provincial town, though where they existed they were undoubtedly a notable feature.

The aesthetic success of the square depended upon its architectural homogeneity. One way to achieve this was simply to impose uniform façades on each of the houses involved in a scheme. Such was the approach adopted in the earliest projects, as at Queen Square Bristol and the Square Birmingham (see Fig. 4). A more novel solution was to treat the whole side of a square as one building, even though in reality

---

[38] Summerson, *Georgian London*, 27–51; N. G. Brett-James, *The Growth of Stuart London* (London, 1935), 366–404; K. Downes, *The Georgian Cities of Britain* (Oxford, 1979), 39–43.

Fig. 4. The North Prospect of St Philip's Church, Birmingham (1709–15, tower completed 1725), drawn by W. Westley 1732

it consisted of a number of quite separate dwellings, and front it with the type of grand façade that might adorn a palace or a gentleman's country house. The first hint of this approach can be seen in St James's Square Bristol (*c*. 1707–16), where the two central bays on its east side were projected forward a little, decorated with long and short quoins, and capped with a giant triangular pediment.[39] However, in this case the overall result was very tame and bore little resemblance to the true palatial treatment. This, despite a number of other precursors, had to await the talents of John Wood in Bath, with his influential design (imposing enough to grace any Palladian country villa) for the north side of Queen Square (see Fig. 5). The palace-façade concept provided a radical solution to the problem of merging individual houses into a larger structure, since from the exterior the identity of each dwelling was reduced to no more than an entrance door. Inside, a variety of domestic plans might be found, but these differences were not permitted to upset the external mask of uniformity.[40]

Just as care was taken in the street to safeguard and enhance the quality of space between the buildings, so also with the square. Wood described how 'all kinds of private nuisances are prohibited in the building leases of the houses fronting Queen Square [Bath]; the streets are to be cleaned and lighted by virtue of the same leases; and the inside of the square is kept in repair by the same power'. In 1755 his son sought to protect the area from commercial graffiti, when he threatened to prosecute 'all persons . . . sticking up playbills, advertisements, etc., on the gate-piers and obelisks of' the square.[41] In the centre of several of the larger squares, such as Queen Squares Bristol and Bath, and the Square Birmingham, an ornamental garden was planted, surrounded by a stone balustrade or iron railings.[42] The horticultural arrangements in Queen Square Bath were particularly elaborate: 'the four quarters of the square' were 'inclosed with espaliers of elm and lime trees', and 'planted with flowering shrubs', and the intersecting footpaths were arranged to form a striking geometric pattern. These original features, along with later additions,

[39] W. Ison, *The Georgian Buildings of Bristol* (Bath, 1968), 149–52; Gomme *et al.*, *Bristol*, 98–100.

[40] Cruickshank, *Guide*, 32–4; J. Summerson, 'John Wood and the English Town-Planning Tradition', in J. Summerson, *Heavenly Mansions* (London, 1949), 90–2; Ison, *Bath*, 105–4; Wood, *Bath*, 345–7.

[41] Wood, *Bath*, 347; *Bath Advertiser*, No. 5, 15 Nov. 1755.

[42] Wood, *Bath*, 345; J. Hill and R. K. Dent, *Memorials of the Old Square* (Birmingham, 1897), 17, 124; Students Diary, fo. 121.

Fig. 5.   Queen Square (1729–36), Bath. Drawing of the north side (right) and west side (centre) by T. Malton the younger, for an aquatint, pub. 1784

were noted by a visitor in the 1760s, who discovered 'in the inside of the square . . . a garden with fine gravel walks, confined by a handsome balustrade of stone, with four noble iron gates opening into it, and in the midst of all is a large circular piece of water, in whose centre is an obelisk . . . seventy foot high, which looks beautiful'.[43]

Several squares provided the setting for a new church. The square at Whitehaven accommodated St Nicholas's; Old Square, Warwick, the rebuilt St Mary's; St Ann's Square, Manchester, the church of the same name; and Derby Square, Liverpool, St George's. Small chapels were also erected close to Queen Square, Bath, and Dowry Square, Bristol.[44] This echoed what was a long-established relationship between churches and public spaces. During the medieval period abbeys and parish churches had frequently provided a focal point for the development of a market-place.[45] There had also emerged adjacent to many of

[43] Wood, *Bath*, 345, and plan opposite 312; Penrose, *Letters*, 67.

[44] Lowther, *Correspondence*, 49–50; Borsay, 'Landscape and Leisure', 176–8; Aikin, *Manchester*, 186; B. F. L. Clarke, *The Building of the Eighteenth-Century Church* (London, 1963), 43–4; Wood, *Bath*, 312–15; Ison, *Bristol*, 158.

[45] W. G. Hoskins, *The Making of the English Landscape* (Harmondsworth, 1970), 292–5; Aston and Bond, *Landscape of Towns*, 96; Tupling, 'Lancashire Markets', 1–3.

the great cathedrals a close to accommodate the resident clergy. In their original form these precincts were generally only loosely organized, but as they were exposed to the new 'uniform' architecture a number began to acquire the feeling of a square. During the Civil War and Interregnum the closes at Winchester and Salisbury had been seriously neglected and maltreated. The buildings of the former were ransacked, and the latter became a meat market, rubbish dump, and playground. However, after the Restoration both were extensively and handsomely redeveloped in the voguish classical style.[46] Similar fashionable rebuilding occurred in the closes at Lichfield, Worcester, Bristol, and Exeter.[47] The new church of St Philip's Birmingham was originally erected (1709-15) on a green-field site, but as fine new buildings such as Temple Row (begun in 1719) sprang up on the edge of the churchyard, an area emerged that possessed many of the characteristics of a square (see Fig. 4). By 1781 William Hutton could claim of it,

If we assemble the beauties of the edifice [St Philip's], which covers a rood of ground; the spacious area of the churchyard, occupying four acres; ornamented with walks in great perfection; shaded with trees in double and treble ranks; and surrounded with buildings in elegant taste; perhaps its equal cannot be found in the British dominions.[48]

[46] Rosen, 'Winchester', 182; *VCH Wiltshire*, vi. 78; Defoe, *Tour*, i. 184, 189; Fiennes, *Journeys*, 5-6, 47; Macky, *Journey*, ii. 14, 38.

[47] Defoe, *Tour*, ii. 80; *BE Staffordshire* (Harmondsworth, 1975), 187-9; *BE Worcestershire* (Harmondsworth, 1968), 314-16; Students Diary, fo. 120; *BE South Devon* (Harmondsworth, 1952), 160-2.

[48] B. Little, *Birmingham Buildings: The Architectural Story of a Midland City* (Newton Abbot, 1971), 10-12; W. Hutton, *An History of Birmingham to the End of the Year 1780* (Birmingham, 1781), 249.

4

Prospects, Planning, and Public Buildings

The development of the street and square contributed much to the emerging elegance and amenity of the town's built environment. It also, by emphasizing the collective rather than individual treatment of structures and spaces, suggests a new contemporary concern with the form of the town *as a whole*. From the Restoration onwards there are signs that the urban landscape was increasingly perceived and treated as an integral body rather than a collection of independent parts. Moreover, there was a rising tide of investment in buildings which projected a sense of corporate identity. The following chapter will explore these trends from three standpoints: maps and prospects, planning, and public buildings.

1. MAPS AND PROSPECTS

One of the most effective ways of grasping the entirety of a town's form is by creating a visual image of it. Through the medium of maps and prospects a complete urban landscape can be held in the mind's eye, contemplated, and if desired, reorganized. Before the mid-sixteenth century, Englishmen seem to have been curiously reluctant to produce such pictorial representations. The only reasonably complete medieval plan of an English town is Ricart's bird's-eye view of Bristol made in about 1480 (and included in his manuscript chronicle of the city), while the earliest known complete map of London dates from as late as the 1550s.[1] Only in the reign of Elizabeth

---

[1] R. A. Skelton and P. D. A. Harvey (eds.), *Local Maps and Plans from Medieval England* (Oxford, 1986), especially 3–39, 309–16; J. E. Pritchard, 'Old Plans and Views of Bristol', *Trans. of the Bristol and Gloucestershire Archaeological Soc.*, xlviii (1926), 326–7; P. Glanville, *London in Maps* (London, 1972), 18–20, 72; P. D. A. Harvey, *The History of Topographical Maps* (London, 1980), 66, 81, 91, 137.

does a concerted interest in urban cartography emerge, culminating in John Speed's *Theatre of the Empire of Great Britain* (1612). Inset into the county maps of this collection were plans of seventy-three towns, three-quarters of which probably constituted new surveys.[2] Speed's atlas was an important landmark, but the following half century witnessed little progress in the science of town mapping, in all likelihood because the domestic market for the product remained limited. The *Theatre* had been preceded by three abortive attempts to publish national compilations (inserted into other material), and by 1600 fewer than a dozen individual surveys of English towns had been printed.[3] This early phase of development owed as much to overseas entrepreneurs as to those at home. The first substantial collection of English town plans was that published in Cologne as part of Braun and Hogenberg's multi-volumed *Civitates Orbis Terrarum* (1572–1618). Of the seven known maps of London that appeared before 1600, four were produced abroad, and all but one was probably engraved by a foreigner; of the seven identified plans of Bristol printed before 1671, only Speed's was published in Britain. Moreover, these early maps were often highly inaccurate and of little practical use. Scientific surveying techniques were still in their infancy, and the tradition of the attractive but imprecise picture-map predominated.[4]

From the 1660s in the case of London, and rather later in the provinces, the town map entered a fresh phase of growth and development.[5] Many urban centres acquired new two-dimensional surveys, which were often regularly updated through the issue of later editions. At Bristol there were fine new surveys in 1671 by James Millerd (new edition 1673, further revised in 1684, 1696, and 1728–30) and in 1742 by John Rocque (published 1743, reissued in a smaller version in 1750, of which three further editions had been printed by 1759). York, in addition to a military survey of about 1673, obtained new maps in 1697 (B. Horsley, surveyed 1694), c.1727 (J. Cossins, revised 1748), 1736 (F. Drake), and 1750 (P. Chassereau). At Bath original surveys appeared in 1694 (J. Gilmore, which by 1731

[2] R. A. Skelton, 'Tudor Town Plans in John Speed's *Theatre*', *Archaeological Jnl.*, cviii (1952), 109–20.

[3] The latter figure excludes those in Braun and Hogenberg's *Civitates*. Skelton, 'John Speed's *Theatre*', 110–13; Beresford, *History on the Ground*, 154–8.

[4] Skelton, 'John Speed's *Theatre*', 110–11; Glanville, *London in Maps*, 18; Pritchard, 'Plans and Views of Bristol', 326–34; Harvey, *Topographical Maps*, chap. 10.

[5] J. B. Harley, *Maps for the Local Historian* (London, 1972), 12–13; Glanville, *London in Maps*, 22, 25.

had passed through five editions), 1736 (J. Wood, surveyed 1735), *c*.1740 (T. Thorpe), and 1750 (*A New and Correct Plan*, revised *c*.1760).[6] Such plans were so highly valued that the civic fathers would frequently support or reward the surveyor responsible and proudly decorate their public buildings with his product.[7] Urban maps were also to be found in general compilations. Many county surveys included town insets, like that of Chichester in Emanuel Bowen's *Sussex* (1749), and those of Exeter and Plymouth in B. Donn's *Devon* (1765). At a national level there were the skeletal plans embodied in the route maps of John Ogilby's *Britannia* (1675), and the more substantial surveys in William Stukeley's *Itinerarium Curiosum* (1724), and John Rocque's *A Collection of Plans of the Principal Cities of Great Britain and Ireland* (1764).[8]

Underpinning the development of urban cartography in the years after the Restoration was a shift away from the crude bird's-eye view towards the more detailed and accurate two-dimensional survey, which today would be recognized as a true map. As a consequence, this new generation of plans was far more reliable and informative than its predecessors. To assist the user some contained extensive keys: J. Chadwick's *Liverpool* (1725) had sixty items, W. and H. Doidge's *Canterbury* (1752) eighty-three, and Drake's *York* (1736) one hundred and nineteen, though the twenty-six in Samuel Winter's *Stratford on Avon* (1759) may have been more typical. Other maps benefited from valuable textual additions. In this respect the Bath productions were particularly well endowed: Gilmore's listed twenty-two local inns, and both Wood's survey and the *New and Correct Plan* were cased in a densely written margin, which constituted a mini-guide to the spa. Along with their practical uses, many maps were also

[6] J. E. Pritchard, 'A Hitherto Unknown Original Print of the Great Plan of Bristol by Jacobus Millerd, 1673', *Trans. of the Bristol and Gloucestershire Archaeological Soc.*, xliv (1922), 203-20; Pritchard, 'Plans and Views of Bristol', 334-40; R. M. Butler, 'A Late Seventeenth-Century Plan of York', *Antiquaries Jnl.*, ii, Part 2 (1972), 320-9; RCHM, *York*, iii, pp. xxxiv-xxxvi; R. Wright, 'The Early Plans of Bath', *Proceedings of the Somerset Archaeological and Natural History Soc., Bath and District Branch* (1929-33), 443-6.

[7] House Book, 3 Feb. 1701/2, 28 Jan. 1735/6, YCA; Drake, *Eboracum*, 330; Macmahon, *Beverley Corporation Minute-Books*, 13; Meyrick, *Time Measurement Instruments*, 43; J. Latimer, *The Annals of Bristol in the Seventeenth Century* (Bath, 1970), 248, 361-2.

[8] D. J. Butler, *The Town Plans of Chichester 1595-1898* (Chichester, 1972), 8-11; B. Donn, 'A Plan of the City and Suburbs of Exeter', sheet 42 in *A Map of the County of Devon* (1765), Devon and Cornwall Record Soc. (1965); Harley, *Maps for the Local Historian*, 12-13.

objects of display and ornament. Elevations of private houses and public buildings were frequently inserted, and a number of maps aspired, in their own fashion, to be works of art. Gilmore's plan was adorned by two cherubs wielding a surveyor's chain, John Cossins's *Leeds* contained a dedicatory cartouche supported by angelic trumpeters (see Fig. 1), and Wood's *Bath* was framed in an elegant oval border, and beautifully 'engraved by Mr Pine, after the manner of the celebrated plan of Paris'.[9]

In addition to drawings of buildings, a number of surveys, such as Millerd's *Bristol* (1673 edition) and Noble and Butlin's *Northampton* (1746), also sported miniature panoramas of their respective towns. This reflected the early days of mapping in which there was often little distinction between the plan and the prospect. Only with the evolution of the two-dimensional map did the two mediums begin to diverge, and an independent tradition of urban views develop. Three elements in this can be easily distinguished: reproductions of individual buildings and antiquities, drawings of larger-scale urban forms (like streets and squares), and the genuine prospect encompassing a whole portion of a town. The latter is particularly interesting since it purported, as far as was possible in a pre-aeronautic age, to capture a town in its entirety.

The earliest significant printed prospect of any British town was Hoefnagel's drawing of Oxford, published in the second volume of Braun and Hogenberg's *Civitates* (1575). During the early phase of its development the prospect trade, even more than that of mapping, was in the hands of foreigners who understandably focused their attention on London. Only after the Restoration, and particularly after 1700, does a truly indigenous and nation-wide commitment emerge, with the volume and variety of output mounting rapidly.[10] At least seven views of York were produced in the century after 1660, most of which were published, and four prospects of Leeds were printed between 1715 and 1767. The title-pages of several early newspapers, such as the *Ipswich Journal*, the *Northampton Mercury*, the *Norwich Gazette*, the *Preston Journal*, and the *Worcester Journal*, were headed by a view of their host town. Though these were rarely more than

[9] For full references to the individual maps see the Bibliography. The final quotation is from an advertisement at the end of J. Wood, *A Description of the Exchange of Bristol*, 1745, repr. (Bath, 1969).

[10] R. Hyde, *Gilded Scenes and Shining Prospects: Panoramic Views of British Towns 1575-1900* (New Haven, Conn., 1985), 11-27, 36-127.

crude impressions (the *Northampton Mercury* rose above this level), they served to bring the urban panorama to a wide audience.[11]

As in the case of plans, town prospects were occasionally published collectively. Among the earliest compilations were those printed by Peter Stent and John Overton in the mid-seventeenth century, issued either as a small group of broadsheets, or as a border to a map of the nation. These views were tiny in scale and poor in quality. Overton's *Several Prospects of the Chief Cities and Towns* (*c*.1665) crowded thirty-six views, most of which were reconstructed from the picture-maps of Braun and Hogenberg and of Speed, on to two sheets.[12] During the eighteenth century more substantial compendiums became available, the earliest of which, the *Nouveau Théâtre de la Grande Bretagne* (1707–early 1720s), contained a number of urban panoramas mixed in among illustrations of the more important country seats.

By far the most important collection of prospects was that prepared by the brothers Samuel and Nathaniel Buck. Working between the late 1710s and early 1750s, they produced eighty-nine different town views, which were originally published on a subscription basis and 'sold in separate numbers'. Later the majority of these were drawn together to form volume three of *Buck's Antiquities* (1774), under the title of 'Bucks's Perspective Views of near One Hundred Cities and Chief Towns in England and Wales'. The claim was a little exaggerated since only seventy towns were represented, of which sixty-three were in the English provinces. However, these included about three-quarters of the regional centres and provincial capitals. The drawings were generally of a high calibre and full of accurate detail, and each had a useful key which contained on average twenty items. A powerful theme in the Bucks' work was antiquarianism. The introduction to the *Antiquities* described the collection as a 'design . . . to rescue from the irresistible hand of time, and convey to futurity, those venerable piles of ancient grandeur', and this was fully reflected in the prospects of places such as Bury St Edmunds, Durham, and Norwich. However, the impact of rapid urban change, which made the recording of the

[11] RCHM, *York*, iii, pp. xxxii–xxxiii, and plates 2–3; K. J. Bonser and H. Nichols, 'Printed Maps and Plans of Leeds 1711–1900', *Publications of the Thoresby Soc.*, xlvii, No. 106 (1958), 1–5; R. M. Wiles, *Freshest Advices: Early Provincial Newspapers in England* (Columbus, Ohio, 1965), 2, 94, 188; J. B. Williams, 'Henry Cross-Grove, Jacobite, Journalist, and Printer', *Library*, 3rd ser., v (1914), 217; *Preston Weekly Jnl.*, No. 16, 9–16 Jan. 1740/1.

[12] E. J. Priestley, 'All the Cities of England', *Local Historian*, x. No. 3 (1972), 139–41.

past such a pressing necessity, was by no means ignored. Many new buildings and facilities were shown, and trade was fully represented with views of the crowded quays at Exeter, Newcastle, and Yarmouth, the river wharfs at Gloucester, Derby, and Maidstone, and the wet dock (opened in 1715) at Liverpool. Nor did the panoramas ignore the manifestations of industrial expansion. Among the items in the key for Birmingham can be found a 'steel works' and 'brass works', for Bristol the 'Baptist Mills Brass Works' (see Fig. 6), for Derby the famous 'silk mills', for Exeter a 'serge drying house' and 'lime works', and for Liverpool a 'copperas house', 'glasshouse', and 'sugar house'. In these engravings the old and the new mixed freely together, as the Bucks formulated the first truly comprehensive visual record of urban England.

2. PLANNING

The swelling volume of urban maps and prospects suggests a growing public interest in the townscape. Moreover, since they sought to recreate a complete picture of a settlement, they point to a novel awareness of the totality of the urban form. This transformation in visual perception laid the foundations for a new commitment to town planning. The will and capacity to arrange or reorganize large blocks of the landscape require an imaginative model of the area to be treated. In this respect good maps were a valuable tool, since they showed precisely how the separate parts of the built environment related to each other, and suggested how they might be advantageously reordered. This association between the mental and practical worlds of planning is demonstrated by the career of John Wood, who was not only engaged in the design and development of the new city at Bath, but also produced a fine plan and a history of the spa, which was full of architectural descriptions and illustrated with drawings and maps.

The early history of town planning in England is a disjointed and ambivalent one. After the first phase of development under the Romans there were few signs of new initiatives until the eighth or ninth centuries. The most fruitful phase of medieval activity occurred between the Norman Conquest and the Black Death, when at least 160 new towns were founded: in addition, many villages were promoted to join their ranks, and existing urban centres substantially

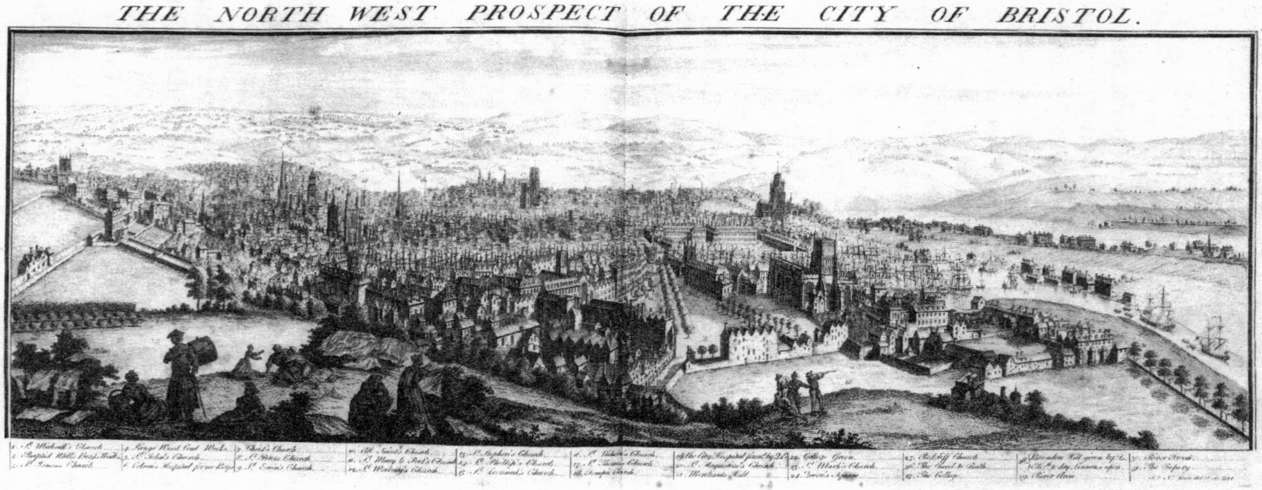

THE NORTH WEST PROSPECT OF THE CITY OF BRISTOL.

Fig. 6. The North-West Prospect of the City of Bristol, drawn and engraved by S. and N. Buck 1734

extended. All these types of settlements might display evidence of planning, especially through the application of a gridiron framework to the layout of their streets and lanes.[13] However, only a small proportion of new towns were truly rectilinear in form. Many that appear so were probably developed in a series of quite distinct phases rather than as one original scheme. Moreover, gridirons in themselves represent only the minimum of spatial organization, and might be nothing more than an easy method of establishing plot values.[14]

After the mid-fourteenth century urban planning virtually collapsed, and for the next three centuries remained a dormant force. Only a trickle of new towns were founded, and with the exception of a small portion of early Stuart London, there was little planned extension of existing settlements.[15] While Renaissance Europe forged ahead with sophisticated urban schemes, England remained rooted in the dark ages of planning. The turning-point came in the aftermath of the Fire of London (1666). A huge area of the City required reconstructing, and at least seven different projects were prepared, including Wren's ambitious classical design. Though none of these were to be implemented, they reveal the emergence of a new interest in urban planning. Furthermore, simple but important regulations were introduced to govern the rebuilding, which were to prove enormously influential both in the long-term growth of the metropolis and of provincial towns.[16]

In addition to Wren, another major baroque architect to take an interest in urban development was Hawksmoor. In the early eighteenth century he prepared a range of schemes for remodelling

[13] Aston and Bond, *Landscape of Towns*, chaps. 3–5; M. W. Barley (ed.), *The Plans and Topography of Medieval Towns in England and Wales*, Council for British Archaeology, Research Report, xiv (1976), 19–48; Beresford, *New Towns in the Middle Ages*, 146–54, and *passim*.

[14] Beresford, *New Towns in the Middle Ages*, 330; M. R. G. Conzen, 'The Use of Town Plans in the Study of Urban History', in H. J. Dyos (ed.), *The Study of Urban History* (London, 1976), 120–7; Lobel, 'Topographical Development', 154–5. For further discussion of the limited nature of medieval town planning see T. F. Tout, *Medieval Town Planning* (Manchester, 1934), 31–2; H. M. Colvin, 'Domestic Architecture and Town Planning', in A. L. Poole (ed.), *Medieval England* (Oxford, 1958), i. 64; Reynolds, *Medieval Towns*, 192–4.

[15] C. and R. Bell, *City Fathers: The Early History of Town Planning in Britain* (Harmondsworth, 1972), 59–68; Beresford, *New Towns in the Middle Ages*, 327–31; Aston and Bond, *Landscape of Towns*, 79–81, 109, 112–14.

[16] T. F. Reddaway, *The Rebuilding of London after the Great Fire* (London, 1951), 53; M. Whinney, *Wren* (London, 1971), 36–40; Cruickshank and Wyld, *Art of Georgian Building*, 22–33.

large parts of Cambridge, Oxford, and Greenwich.[17] Like that of his illustrious predecessor, Hawksmoor's plans came to nothing. Such failure was indicative of the considerable difficulties that faced anyone in this period who ventured into the realm of planning. Six major problems can be identified. First, England was so well endowed with medieval towns that there was little need to establish fresh settlements. Therefore, any new urban development was generally located in or on the edge of existing towns, where the scope for large-scale planning could be severely restricted. Second, there was no surviving domestic tradition of town planning, so that each project was something of a leap in the dark. The third problem, and perhaps the most intractable, related to landholding. A potential site for development, especially if it lay within an old town, might be controlled by a plethora of individuals: not only petty landowners, but also lessees and sub-lessees. Obtaining the agreement of all these parties could prove very difficult. Even where a single landlord exercised unchallenged authority over a promising area, much would depend upon his own predilections. At Whitehaven Sir John Lowther consciously strove to create a planned town, but at Deal the Archbishop of Canterbury permitted growth to progress in a haphazard fashion.[18] Corporate landlords, who frequently owned a good deal of inner-city property, seem to have taken a conservative approach to planning, perhaps because the interests of so many councillors had to be reconciled.

A fourth difficulty was that urban reconstruction and expansion could provoke strong resistance if it posed a threat to the economic livelihood and power of local residents. Widening or altering the position of an established street might endanger the commercial viability of businesses located there, and extramural development could draw trade away from the old town and reduce the influence of those who ruled it. Fifth, there was the diffuse nature of the contemporary building process. In a largish project there would often be three independent parties involved: the landowner or owners, the developer, and the speculative builders, the last sometimes varying from house to house.[19] In such circumstances it was difficult to ensure that a scheme was executed as originally intended. Even where covenants were introduced into the building leases to control development, these might be ignored. A final obstacle to planning was the disruptive

[17] K. Downes, *Hawksmoor* (London, 1969), 85-101.
[18] Chalklin, 'New Towns', 239-43.
[19] Chalklin, *Provincial Towns*, Parts 2 and 3.

hand of time. A substantial project could take decades to complete, during which time landowners and developers might die and fashions change, causing a scheme to be altered or even abandoned. These various problems form an essential backdrop to the emergence of town planning in the century after the Restoration. Judged by the standards of later generations the achievements of these years may appear unremarkable, but in the context of the times they were impressive, and were to prove of real long-term significance.

Though there existed no effective native planning tradition to draw upon, there were plenty of European precedents. In the late seventeenth century one of the most influential of these was the example of Versailles. From the late 1660s Louis XIV began developing the site of his country seat outside Paris as an alternative centre for the royal court and administration. The scheme involved a huge programme of building works that linked together town, house, and park on a* dramatic scale to form an awesome expression of the crown's authority.[20] In England the whole idea must have appealed enormously to Charles II. Not only was he a great admirer of the French king, but after the tense years of the Exclusion Crisis (1679–81) he had every reason to withdraw his court from its vulnerable location in the metropolis. Moreover, the crippling financial problems of the earlier years of his reign were easing by the 1680s, allowing some scope for renewed expenditure on building.[21] Charles's chosen 'retreat' was to be the ancient royal capital of Winchester. The project was to include a grand palace designed by Wren and modelled on Versailles, a formal avenue running directly from the house to the west end of the cathedral and flanked by courtiers' residences, and an extensive ornamental park to the south and west of the mansion. Work began probably in early 1683 and continued rapidly until Charles's death two years later. James, however, showed little interest in completing the scheme, and construction came to an abrupt halt, leaving the gaunt shell of the house to remind visitors of what might have been England's Versailles.[22]

[20] L. Benevolo, *The Architecture of the Renaissance* (London, 1978), ii. 737–41, 745–55, 769–83.

[21] C. D. Chandaman, *The English Public Revenue 1660–1688* (Oxford, 1975), 249–55.

[22] Rosen, 'Winchester', 180–1; H. M. Colvin (ed.), *The History of the King's Works*, Vol. V: *1660–1782* (London, 1976), 304–13; M. S. Briggs, *Wren the Incomparable* (London, 1953), 161–4; J. Evelyn, *The Diary of John Evelyn*, ed. E. S. De Beer (London, 1959), 755, 824; Defoe, *Tour*, i. 185–6; Powys, *Diaries*, 80–1; HMC, *Portland MSS*, vi. 174.

The French notion of schematically associating town, palace, and park, spread beyond the crown. Lord Bathurst's new residence (1714–18) at Cirencester, though hidden from citizens' eyes by a gigantic yew hedge, was aligned with the town's church tower and contained gardens whose principal avenue (which stretched for almost five miles) was linked directly with the urban street network.[23] The most important example of seigneurial planning in our period, and the subject that stimulated the writing of this study, is to be found at Warwick.[24] The context, if not the cause of the replanning, was the fire of 1694. As described earlier, its impact was devastating. About 150 properties located in ten streets were wholly or partially damaged, and the losses in buildings and goods amounted to around £40,000.[25] The blaze was concentrated in the most prestigious commercial, residential, and administrative district of the town,[26] making the area a prime site for redevelopment. What turned the potential of the situation into reality was the interest of the county gentry in *their* shire town, and above all the awesome presence of the castle. The latter deeply influenced the political and economic life of Warwick, and was the centre of a landed empire that stretched across several counties.[27] The fire provided its owner, Lord Brooke, with an ideal opportunity to refashion the town as an elegant antechamber to his baronial mansion and power house (see Map 1).

Though the general concept behind the remodelling of Warwick may have derived from Versailles, the immediate exemplar was London. The redevelopment of the City after the Great Fire and the expansion of the West End with its fine streets and squares transformed the nation's attitude to urban design. Men like Lord Brooke, who possessed a metropolitan residence, must have been especially affected. More particularly, the legislation draughted and the court appointed to govern the post-fire reconstruction of London provided provincial towns with a simple but effective blueprint for planning.[28] Warwick's fire act was closely modelled on the London ones, lifting whole paragraphs verbatim, and a body of commissioners was also

[23] *BE Gloucestershire: The Cotswolds* (Harmondsworth, 1970), 177–8, 184–7.

[24] This is discussed in detail in Borsay, 'Landscape and Leisure', 123–98; and also M. Turner, 'The Nature of Urban Renewal after Fires in Seven English Provincial Towns, *circa* 1675–1810', Ph.D. thesis (Exeter, 1985), especially 215–29, 272–84.

[25] Estimate; Borsay, 'Landscape and Leisure', 127–30, 195–8.

[26] Estimate; Warwickshire CRO, QS/11/3, 5, 7, 50 (Hearth Tax Returns 1662–74).

[27] Warwick Castle MSS, Castle Accounts, 1695–8, Warwickshire CRO.

[28] 18 & 19 Car. II, c. 7, 8.

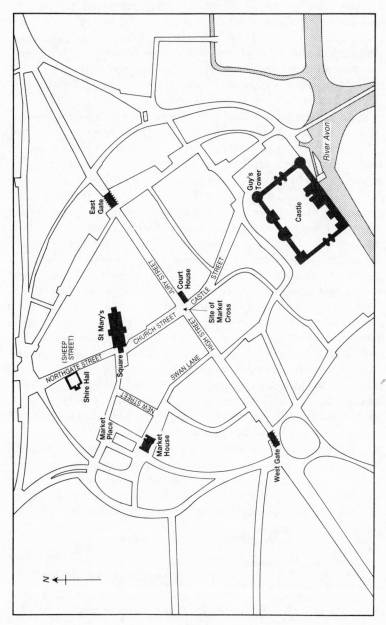

Map 1. Warwick in the early eighteenth century

established to control the rebuilding. The commission was packed with county notables rather than ordinary townsmen, emphasizing the gentry's influence over Warwick. It is significant that Brooke attended fifty of the eighty-six recorded sessions of the court (the fifth highest for any individual), and his son Francis, twenty-nine.[29] Though much of the commission's work dealt only with minutiae, Brooke clearly intended to retain a firm grip on its proceedings.

In the pre-fire landscape at Warwick there was no formal association between town and castle, with the two simply merging into each other. Any attempt to alter this during the rebuilding was severely hampered by two factors. First, the area immediately around the castle was unaffected by the conflagration, and second, in the damaged zone itself there existed a remarkably diffuse pattern of landownership and occupancy, which made a major reorganization of the ground-plan almost impossible. To complicate matters further, Brooke himself did not own any of the burnt properties.[30] However, it was feasible to execute limited changes in the town's layout. Several streets were widened,[31] though even this measure caused some friction. The scheme to broaden the southern end of Swan Lane provoked a bout of petitioning and counter-petitioning from local tradesmen, who felt that the proposals threatened the viability of their businesses.[32] None the less, the widening went ahead, and generally the commissioners appear to have been successful in introducing a greater sense of spaciousness into the town's thoroughfares.

If there was little scope for modifying the ground-plan of Warwick, its three-dimensional landscape proved more fertile territory. Here it was that the two major themes that underpinned the town's replanning —uniformity and hierarchy—were allowed to develop. The rebuilding act stipulated a fairly rigid model for the design of houses, which were to be of two storeys with garrets and cellars. Quoining was encouraged, and projections from the façade were either forbidden, as in the case of jettying, or severely restricted. Visual uniformity was further enhanced by requiring the use of stone, brick, or tile, and by proscribing

[29] Fire Act, 5; figures for attendance derived from Memorials.
[30] Estimate.
[31] Fire Act, 6–7; Memorials, 3, 6, 22, and 27 May, and 3 June 1695.
[32] Undated petition from the 'Mayor and corporation of the said borough [Warwick] and others the inhabitants of the High Street and places there adjacent'; undated petition from George Chinn *et al.*; undated petition from Thomas Roberts *et al.*, Warwickshire CRO, CR.1618, W.10 (Petitions to the Fire Court), bundle 2; Memorials, 13 May and 8 July 1695, 4 May 1696, 4 Apr. 1699.

traditional materials.[33] The theory of the legislation was turned into reality by the diligence of the fire court. It distributed the relief money, specified a 'scheme or draught . . . of the roofs of all houses to be rebuilt',[34] acted to safeguard the flow of the new building materials,[35] and in general rigorously policed the reconstruction process.[36] Such was the commissioners' vigilance, that when two citizens wished to extend their dwellings no more than two inches into the road, they were careful to seek the court's permission before proceeding.[37]

The impact of the pursuit of regularity can still be seen in the neat, red brick, quoined, and dormered houses that line the streets of Warwick today. But this was not the only aim of those responsible for the replanning. A properly arranged landscape, like a well-ordered society, was one that reflected the importance of hierarchy as well as uniformity. To meet this end, two areas of particular economic, social, and cultural significance in the town were treated in an architectural manner that highlighted their status. The first of these was the traditional centre of Warwick, where Jury Street, High Street, Church Street, and Castle Street intersected. This was the location of the market cross and the council house, and the heart of the town's most fashionable shopping area. The court ordered the three damaged corner houses that occupied the site to be rebuilt to three instead of two storeys and adorned with extra-large cornices, and permitted their façades to be decorated with giant projecting pilasters (see Fig. 7). The prestige of the area was further enhanced in the late 1720s, when the corporation's meeting-place, a converted inn which was only slightly burned in the fire, was demolished and replaced by a grand baroque town hall.[38] The second area to receive special attention was that centred on the great medieval church of St Mary's. Badly damaged by the fire, the church's reconstruction, with a commanding tower and spacious nave, was the high spot of the whole rebuilding programme, absorbing about two-thirds of the relief money.[39] A decision was made

---

[33] Fire Act, 7-11.

[34] Memorials, 1 July 1695.

[35] Ibid. 20 Oct. and 11 Nov. 1695, 15 June 1696.

[36] Ibid. 12 Aug. 1695, 17 Jan. 1697/8, 25 June 1698, 2 Aug. 1699.

[37] Ibid. 7 Oct. 1695, 4 May 1696.

[38] Estimate; Fire Act, 9; Memorials, 13 May, and 5 and 12 Aug. 1695, 22 June 1696; T. Kemp, *History of Warwick and its People* (Warwick, 1905), 173-7.

[39] P. B. Chatwin, 'The Rebuilding of St Mary's Church, Warwick', *TBAS*, lxv (1943-4), 1-40; P. B. Chatwin, 'The Great Fire of Warwick 1694', *TBAS*, lxvii (1947-8), 38-41.

Fig. 7. The three corner houses (rebuilt after the fire of 1694), at the crossing of Church Street, Jury Street, Castle Street, and High Street, Warwick

to lay out a square at its west end. This was to prove the only substantial alteration made to the town's ground-plan, and was possible only because the bulk of the property involved was either administered by the corporation, or owned by one of Lord Brooke's staff. The space enclosed was only tiny, but it ranks among the first provincial squares built in England.[40]

Circumstances made it impossible at Warwick to closely integrate town and house as at Versailles. But it was feasible to transform the town into an ordered and fashionable vestibule to the great mansion. Moreover, the two areas that received special treatment lay on a rough, if curved axis with the castle. Today this is difficult to visualize, since in the late eighteenth century a major piece of relandscaping threw a high wall across the middle of Castle Street, and dramatically isolated town and house.[41] But originally the rebuilding of the 1690s would have created a fine avenue that stretched along Church Street and Castle Street, and was closed at either end by the awesome masses of St Mary's and Guy's towers.[42] In this way Warwick and its castle would have been linked together in as intimate and impressive a manner as was practicable.

Whereas the potential for remodelling Warwick was seriously restricted by the presence of an already established urban landscape, a freshly created settlement could start with a relatively clean sheet. However, there were few genuinely new towns in post-Restoration England, and by no means all of these were properly planned.[43] Those that were invariably formed part of a speculative venture on the part of a substantial landowner, designed to exploit his own mineral assets or a profitable sea-based trade. Ambitious schemes were prepared in the 1720s for new ports at Bucklers Hard on the Beaulieu estate in Hampshire, to be used for the import of sugar, and Seaton Sluice on the Delaval estate in Northumberland, for the export of coal. The former was to be called Montaguetown, and a surviving plan shows that a sophisticated design was proposed, with two main boulevards, one running down to the quay and the other aligned at right angles to

---

[40] Estimate; Fire Act, 6; Memorials, 8 and 30 July 1695, 7 Sept. 1696, 25 Oct. 1697, 30 Mar. and 21 Sept. 1704. I am indebted to Michael Farr for drawing to my attention the fact that one of the largest property owners in this area was also an employee of Brooke.

[41] *VCH Warwickshire*, viii. 463.

[42] J. Fish and C. Bridgeman, Plan of Warwick (*c.* 1711), Warwickshire CRO, CR.217.

[43] Chalklin, 'New Towns', 229-51.

it, both meeting in a centrally placed square and merging into tree-lined avenues on the outskirts of the town. Houses were to be constructed of brick to encourage uniformity, considerable incentives were given to those who chose to build and settle there, and provision was to be made for a bath-house, chapel, and inn.[44]

Both the Beaulieu and Delaval projects appear to have been realized to only a very limited degree. Far more important was the case of Whitehaven. It was originally developed as a port to service the adjacent coal mines, but later tobacco also came to play a prominent part in the town's trade, especially in the 1730s and 1740s. Responsibility for the development of the port lay with three generations of the Lowther family, who owned the mines and property on which the new town was built: Sir Christopher (who came into possession of the estate from his father in 1637, and died in 1644), Sir John (1642–1706), and Sir James (1673–1755). Sir Christopher Lowther founded the town, laying out the first streets (beyond the old fishing village) on a rough gridiron pattern, but his son, Sir John, was undoubtedly the key figure in the planning of Whitehaven. During the 1680s he embarked on a major extension to the established community, displaying a keen paternalistic, even autocratic interest in its ordered growth.

A simple rectilinear layout was adopted for the port, with streets about ten yards wide. Inserted into this was a spacious avenue (Lowther Street) of around sixteen yards breadth, running from the waterfront to Sir John's new residence (Flat Hall) on the edge of the town. This echoed the Versailles model of planning, and was clearly intended to symbolize the relationship between the port and its overlord. In 1693 Lowther's agent wrote to his master stressing that 'the ornament of the street leading to your house is important', and three years later noted,

I have your directions formerly to make a greater allowance of ground in Lowther Street to such as would build above the ordinary. Mr Blaiklock has accordingly built a very fine and large house. Mr Gregs has built another which I intend for the standard of all the houses that shall hereafter be built in that street, and hope by this means to draw the better sort of inhabitants thither, which will . . . make a good street to your house. . . .

Throughout the town, houses were intended to be uniform in appearance, and builders were required to observe covenants governing the

[44] G. Darley, *Villages of Vision* (London, 1978), 125–7; *BE Hampshire and the Isle of Wight* (Harmondsworth, 1973), 147, 149.

dimensions and form of doors, windows, and other ornaments, which the Lowthers were prepared to enforce through legal proceedings. Sir John, eager to establish the town in its early stages, was willing to lend capital for house construction, to lease 'great quantities of ground sometimes for little rent to encourage builders', and he tried to attract Celtic settlers by having some of the thoroughfares 'known by the name of the Scotch Street and the Irish Street'. Planning also extended to the provision of public amenities, with the Lowthers providing land or financial support for building the town's school, colliers' almshouses, Presbyterian chapel, and three new churches. Though Whitehaven's local government was to be inadequately provided for, physically it emerged as one of the finest planned towns of the period.[45]

New towns may have been rare, but there were several cases where existing centres were substantially extended, thereby providing an opportunity for planning. Occasionally the additions were so extensive as to constitute new settlements. Some of the most striking examples were the naval dockyard towns, expanding rapidly under the impact of the wars against France. As early as 1698 Fiennes noted that Dock, developed to the west of Plymouth, 'looks a little town the buildings are so many', and Defoe later described how it emerged house by house, 'until at length there appeared a very handsome street, spacious and large, and as well inhabited, and so many houses are since added, that it is become a considerable town'. He found Portsea, which was located on the edge of Portsmouth and saw serious growth from about 1702, 'a kind of a suburb, or rather a new town . . . which is so well built, and seems to increase so fast, that in time it threatens to outdo for number of inhabitants, and beauty of buildings, even the town [of Portsmouth] itself'. In both these cases it is difficult to establish any evidence of formal planning. At Portsea a multiplicity of landowners and developers were involved, who do not appear to have used building covenants to control house design or to have provided any public facilities. It is argued that the settlement's regular street pattern simply reflects the fact that the agricultural land used for development had been previously divided into roughly parallel strips.

[45] Lowther, *Correspondence*, pp. xx–xxi, 87, 261, 497, and *passim*; Chalklin, 'New Towns', 231–2, 239–42; Millward, 'Cumbrian Town', 216–19; J. V. Beckett, *Coal and Tobacco: The Lowthers and the Economic Development of West Cumberland 1660–1760* (Cambridge, 1981), 179–200; W. Barnett *et al.*, *Whitehaven: A New Structure for a Restoration Town* (n.p., n.d.); draft typescript of the Introduction and chaps. 1 and 2, of the RCHM forthcoming vol. on Whitehaven.

However, the appearance of Dock and Portsea suggests that implicit if not explicit architectural conventions were operating, and that these helped to create an ordered landscape.[46]

With their potential for rapid urban growth, ports and industrial centres were also the sites of major urban extensions. After the Restoration development began at Liverpool to the south and east of the old town, on the estates of Sir Edward Moore and Lord Molyneux, the latter's estate leased to the corporation in 1672. Though later commentators were to complain about the inadequacy of the street plan, it is clear from Moore's 'survey' of his property that he paid considerable attention to how his estate was to be developed, and Defoe was so impressed with the general results that he claimed 'they have built more than another Liverpool that way in new streets, and fine large houses for their merchants'.[47] Much of the expansion of Bristol, like that of the West End of London, was based around residential squares, which appear to have been the nucleus of larger planning units: for example, Prince Street, which runs parallel with the west side of Queen Square, was developed simultaneously with it, and like the Square was subject to building covenants to ensure that houses were 'uniform and regular'.[48] In Birmingham, the Square was the centre-piece of a much wider area of prestigious development situated in the upper part of the town and bounded by Bull Street, Steelhouse Lane, Stafford Street, and Dale End. The land was purchased in around 1700 by John Pemberton, a Quaker ironmonger, and at least a portion of it was subject to lease controls to guarantee the construction of high-quality houses. The result was a fashionable residential district that in 1755 was said, 'like St James's' in London, to contain 'a number of new regular streets and a handsome square, all well built'.[49]

Somerset was the location of two smaller developments. In the early 1720s the Duke of Chandos purchased the manor and lordship of

[46] Fiennes, *Journeys*, 253; Defoe, *Tour*, i. 138-9, 230-1; Buck, *Antiquities*, iii, Plymouth, Portsmouth; Hoskins, *Devon*, 114-15, 456; Chalklin, 'New Towns', 234-9; Chalklin, *Provincial Towns*, 122-8.

[47] Chalklin, *Provincial Towns*, 98-102; Enfield, *Liverpool*, 21; Moore, *Liverpool*, *passim*; Defoe, *Tour*, ii. 69; J. Chadwick, *The Map of all the Streets, Lanes, and Alleys within the Town of Liverpool* (1725).

[48] Ison, *Bristol*, 21-2, 161-4.

[49] *VCH Warwickshire*, vii. 8; visitor from London quoted in Hill and Dent, *Old Square*, 24; W. Westley, *The Plan of Birmingham, Surveyed in the Year 1731*; W. Westley, *The East Prospect of Birmingham* (1732), reproduced in *VCH Warwickshire*, vii, facing p. 6.

Bridgwater with the purpose of commercially exploiting it. One aspect of the enterprise was various schemes for the addition of a square and interconnected streets. The whole venture proved rather a fiasco, though some building did occur. A fine Georgian terraced street (Castle Street) was constructed, described in 1767 as 'quite regular and uniform on both sides, built with brick, and having quite the air of London', which by the late eighteenth century fed into a pleasant square (King Square).[50] In the late seventeenth century Frome, something of a textile boom town at the time, saw the appearance of an industrial housing estate to the north-west of the old centre, in the present-day Trinity area. It was erected over a period of sixty to seventy years on property controlled by three principal landowners. The streets were arranged in an orderly fashion and the houses displayed a broadly uniform appearance that was at least partly due to the use of building covenants. Recently rescued from total demolition, the area now represents one of the 'earliest surviving planned urban developments for a semi-industrial population'.[51]

In the extended urban settlements the case for formal planning is far more difficult to establish than at Warwick or Whitehaven. This may be due to the paucity of research on the growth of these towns. But it might also reflect the reality of the situation: that a multiplicity of landlords, developers, and craftsmen were involved, and that, by twentieth-century standards, explicit building controls were very limited. However, as contemporary travellers and artists make clear, what emerged in these places often *looked* ordered and uniform, especially in the better-class residential areas. This suggests that despite the absence of formal controls, it was possible for a planned landscape to evolve on a piecemeal basis. Central to this informal and incremental process was a shared building tradition which stressed the value of regularity. Thus an independent developer would construct a street in a similar style to that of an adjacent one, not because he was required to do so, but because it was the fashionable practice. In these circumstances planning did not require the explicit direction of a powerful landlord or master planner, since it could be achieved by the implicit pressures of architectural tradition and social convention.

---

[50] C. H. Collins and M. I. Baker, *The Life and Circumstances of James Brydges, First Duke of Chandos* (Oxford, 1949), chap. 10; Penrose, *Letters*, 164; *BE South and West Somerset* (Harmondsworth, 1958), 100.

[51] Defoe, *Tour*, i. 280; R. Leech, *Early Industrial Housing: The Trinity Area of Frome*, RCHM, Supplementary Ser., 3 (London, 1981), 1–18, and back cover.

The most striking example of informal planning in Britain can be seen in the building of Georgian Bath.[52] Major development occurred from about the mid-1720s, and over the following century produced what is widely recognized as one of the finest examples of urban planning in Europe.[53] Underpinning the city's physical coherence is a general uniformity of building style, allied to the widespread practice of constructing individual dwellings as part of a larger architectural form, such as a street, square, or crescent. However, it is clear that these units are themselves often related to each other, and in one of three ways. The most obvious unity was created by a 'grand scheme': the Queen Square, Circus, and Royal Crescent group (1728–74), the components of which are linked together physically by streets and aesthetically by complementary spatial experiences, is a case in point. The later eighteenth-century developments at Bathwick and in Bath Street also fit into this schematic category (see Map 2). Second, many units are tied together simply by being designed in a similar fashion and lying contiguous with each other: for example, Bladud Buildings (1755) and the Paragon (1769–71) form one continuous line of building flanking the London Road. Third, there is linkage by association. The palatial façade became the key motif in unit development in eighteenth-century Bath and was applied to the whole range of squares, crescents, 'buildings', and parades that sprang up over the city. Though these blocks may be separated by some distance, their shared architectural theme helps to bind them together. The case of Lansdown Crescent takes the process of association even further. It was largely built between 1789 and 1793 on the upper slopes of Lansdown Hill, and sits roughly on an axis with the Royal Crescent completed two decades earlier, uncannily echoing its predecessor's elliptical form.

The creation of such a unified townscape would seem to imply the presence of a single powerful landlord assisted by an architect-planner. But this was not the case. Though there were a number of largish extramural estates, during the eighteenth century these were owned by a variety of parties whose attitude to development was by no means a consistently favourable one. In addition, the corporation took a very

[52] The key works on the subject are Wood, *Bath*; Ison, *Bath*; Neale, *Bath: A Social History*; Chalklin, *Provincial Towns*, 74–80; McIntyre, 'Rise of a Resort Town', 198–249; Summerson, 'English Town-Planning Tradition', 87–110. For further development of the arguments in this section see Borsay, 'Landscape and Leisure', 199–248.

[53] *BE North Somerset and Bristol* (Harmondsworth, 1958), 94; H. Rosenau, *The Ideal City* (London, 1959), 108; L. Mumford, *The City in History* (Harmondsworth, 1975), notes to plate 37.

cautious line about releasing its own considerable and strategically important property for new building. It is frequently suggested that the unity of Georgian Bath arose from the architectural vision of John Wood the elder, an impression which is cultivated by his own influential history of the city. However, important as Wood's contribution undoubtedly was, his role in the building of the spa needs a good deal of qualifying. There are no signs that the youthful and impractical plans he claims to have draughted in the 1720s were ever implemented, and his professional career in Bath was a tangled story of idealism, failure, opportunism, and compromise. The scheme most associated with his name, the Queen Square, Circus, and Royal Crescent complex, was assembled in bits and pieces over almost fifty years, and could not have been conceived in its original terms. Its *coup de grâce*, the Crescent, was built long after his death, as was most of classical Bath. In practice, the city's new landscape was the product of a host of decisions made by thousands of independent developers and craftsmen working throughout the century. And yet Bath is self-evidently a planned city. Given the absence of some overriding authority, this was only possible because a powerful architectural tradition emerged, which informally conditioned the way individual builders operated. It was a tradition that drew on the inherent ordering forces in classical architecture and the models for planning pioneered in post-Restoration London. But it was one that matured in the specific environmental and social context of Bath, where the unit building, with its capacity to accommodate status-conscious visitors behind a palatial façade, and the crescent, able to exploit the romantic views from the surrounding hills, were ideally suited to the needs of the city. By the early 1770s this tradition was fully developed, and for the next half century it exerted an aesthetic dominance that was to secure the homogeneity of the townscape.

3. PUBLIC BUILDINGS

The emergence of planning, on a formal or informal basis, helped create a more integrated and impressive urban landscape. This trend was strengthened by a rising tide of investment in public buildings and artefacts. These structures were of critical importance in establishing the overall image of the town. Not only did they constitute natural focal points among the mass of buildings, but, given their

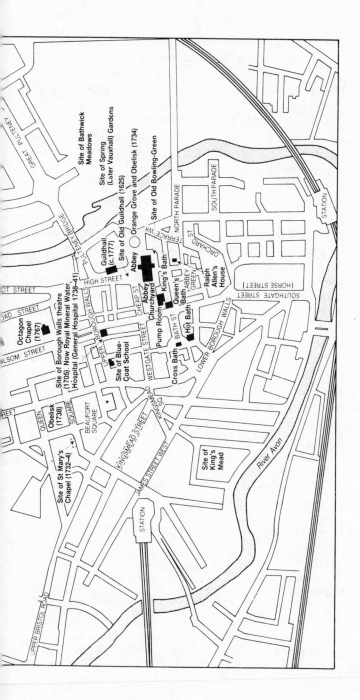

Map 2. Georgian Bath

public nature, they were also seen to symbolize the prosperity, humanity, and prestige of the whole community.

The greater medieval towns must have presented a striking spectacle, with their abundance of fine cathedrals, abbeys, parish churches, guildhalls, and fortifications. Between the Reformation and the Restoration this public fabric took a heavy beating as a consequence of religious change, economic decline, and warfare. Nor was there much to compensate for the losses that resulted. Only a handful of new town churches was erected,[54] while civic investment concentrated on constructing generally modest market-cum-town halls and individual benefactions on a number of schools and almshouses.[55] By the 1650s many of the leading English towns must have possessed a rather careworn and undistinguished public profile. However, from the late seventeenth century their image began to improve markedly, as a new phase of expenditure on civic works unfolded.[56] The West Riding towns have been the subject of a fine, detailed study which reveals the extent of this movement. Whereas in 1600 there were about fifty public buildings in the twelve towns examined, by 1700 the number had risen to ninety, and by 1800 to two hundred and forty. This was accompanied by growing levels of investment in such structures: in the first decade of the eighteenth century £2,800 was spent, by the 1740s this had reached almost £10,000, and by the 1760s it had climbed to £15,000. Though these sums were only a fraction of the figures reached by the early nineteenth century, they represented a major advance on the sparse years that preceded them.[57]

The new wave of public building affected five main areas of urban life: administration, commerce, welfare, religion, and culture. An understandable priority, because of its symbolic significance, was the town hall. Appendix 2 lists almost forty examples of halls constructed, rebuilt, or substantially modified in the century or so after the

[54] Summerson, *Architecture in Britain*, 171-4; Aston and Bond, *Landscape of Towns*, 122-3. For a rather different view see Airs, *Tudor and Jacobean*, 111-18.

[55] R. Tittler, 'The Building of Civic Halls in Dorset, *c*.1560-1640', *Bulletin of the Institute of Historical Research*, lviii (1985), 37-45; Everitt, 'Market Towns', 180-4; Airs, *Tudor and Jacobean*, 103-10; *VCH Wiltshire*, vi. 87; *VCH Oxfordshire*, x. 24; Wood, *Bath*, 213-14; Rudder, *Gloucestershire*, 89; Gillett and Macmahon, *Hull*, 133; Tupling, 'Lancashire Markets', 4-7; M. B. Weinstock, 'Blandford in Elizabethan and Stuart Times', *Somerset and Dorset Notes and Queries*, xxx (1975), 119; Lobel, *Atlas*, i, Hereford, 9-10, and Gloucester, 13; Hillaby, *Ledbury*, 105-6.

[56] Clark, *Provincial Towns*, 41; Aston and Bond, *Landscape of Towns*, 122-4, 169-73; R. Morrice, *The Buildings of Britain: Stuart and Baroque* (London, 1982), 75-118.

[57] Grady, 'Public Buildings in the West Riding', 28-32, 95.

Restoration, many of which still survive today. Architecturally they were of two types. The majority followed the traditional pattern of a large room or rooms raised on columns above an open arcade. Often these occupied island sites in the centre of the town. A smaller but more advanced group was built solidly across both storeys and was usually located outside the open street. From the reign of Elizabeth onwards a considerable number of small civic halls had been erected, but what characterized the post-Restoration contribution in this field was the scale of some of the enterprises and the sophistication of the architecture employed. At Abingdon (1678–*c*.1682) the homely room-on-pillars model was transformed into a classically designed civic *palazzo*, costing almost £3,000 (see Fig. 8). Similarly, grandeur and expense were a feature of the newer type of non-arcaded halls: that at Worcester (1721–3) stretched across fifteen bays, and was crowned by an enormous segmental pediment carried on giant corinthian pilasters, and the fine buildings at Warwick (*c*.1724–30) and

Fig. 8. The County or Town Hall (1678–*c*.1682), Abingdon

Fig. 9.   The Court House (*c*.1724–30), Warwick

Doncaster (1745–8) consumed over £2,000 and £8,000 respectively
(see Figs. 9, 10).[58] The provincial capitals of Newcastle-upon-Tyne
(*c*.1691) and York (1725–30) also created and furnished impressive
mayoral residences in which the city's leader could entertain guests,
especially from among the local gentry (see Fig. 11).[59] County centres
usually accommodated a range of buildings to handle shire business,
and these equally benefited from the new phase of public investment.
In the last three decades of the seventeenth century the county halls at
York (1673), Warwick (1676), Northampton (1676–8), Lincoln
(*c*.1688), Leicester (*c*.1690s), and Chester (*c*.1698) were either rebuilt
or considerably altered. That at Warwick was replaced eighty years
later (1753–8), at a cost escalating to around £4,000, with the present
elegant establishment, which provided a centre for the legal and social
life of the shire.[60]

[58] R. Gilyard-Beer, *The County Hall, Abingdon* (London, 1956); V. Green, *The History and Antiquities of the City and Suburbs of Worcester* (London, 1796), ii. 6–11; *BE Worcestershire*, 323; Kemp, *History of Warwick*, 173–7; Grady, 'Public Buildings in the West Riding', Gazetteer.

[59] Bourne, *Newcastle*, 127; Brand, *Newcastle*, i. 56; *VCH York*, 543–4.

[60] Drake, *Eboracum*, 287; A. C. Wood *The Rebuilding of the Shire Hall, Warwick*.

Fig. 10.   The Guildhall (1721–3), central bays, Worcester

The open area beneath the traditional type of town hall was invariably used as a market, neatly combining two of the major functions of public buildings at this time. With the general expansion in trade and the rapid demographic growth of several towns, the demand for commercial facilities proliferated. Allied to this was a trend to remove marketing from the open thoroughfares and to develop more specialized trading premises. Many, probably most towns, built, rebuilt, or substantially repaired their market houses, produce crosses, and shambles, sometimes to a classical design, as at

in the Mid Eighteenth Century (Warwick, 1983); W. Field, *An Historical and Descriptive Account of the Town and Castle of Warwick*, 1815, repr. (East Ardsley, 1969), 79–80; *VCH Northamptonshire*, iii. 35; Hill, *Stuart Lincoln*, 202; Fiennes, *Journeys*, 163, 178.

Fig. 11. The Mansion House (1725–30), York

Warwick (1670) and in the Thursday Market (1705) and Pavement (early 1700s?), York.[61] A number of cloth centres developed specialized facilities for the measuring, sealing, and sale of textiles. This was taken to its furthest point in the West Riding, where cloth halls were erected at Halifax (c.1700), Wakefield (1710), Huddersfield (1766), and Leeds, the last boasting separate establishments for unfinished (1710–11, and a new building 1755–6) and dyed textiles (1758).[62] In the ports the construction of a new customs-house provided an opportunity for public display, as in the fine classical edifices at King's Lynn (originally designed as a merchants' exchange, 1683), Bristol (1710–11), Liverpool (1721–2), and Lancaster (1764).[63] The most impressive of the new commercial structures were the

[61] *VCH Warwickshire*, viii. 427–8; Drake, *Eboracum*, 292–3, 323–4.

[62] Fiennes, *Journeys*, 142, 148, 227, 245; Cunnington, *Devizes*, 159–60, 208; Rudder, *Gloucestershire*, 468; Grady, 'Public Buildings in the West Riding', Gazetteer.

[63] Parker, *King's Lynn*, 152–4; Ison, *Bristol*, 146; Enfield, *Liverpool*, 59; *BE North Lancashire* (Harmondsworth, 1969), 159.

Fig. 12.   The Exchange (1741–3), north front, Bristol

merchants' exchanges, based on the influential model of the Royal
Exchange (completed 1671) in London, and intended to act both as a
business centre for the trading community and a celebration of the
trading ethic. The finest examples were the two built by Wood for
Bristol (1741–3) and Liverpool (1749–54), which were arranged
around a central courtyard and fronted by a monumental Palladian
façade decorated with symbols of commerce (see Fig. 12).[64]

Welfare institutions were powerful emblems of the corporate nature
of urban life. In the century after the Restoration few towns failed to
receive at least one benefaction to build an almshouse, and many were
blessed by several such gifts. During these years Newbury, Sheffield,
and Leeds each enjoyed four new foundations. At Abingdon not only
was the medieval Long Alley group of houses repaired and possibly
improved, but to these were added Twitty's (1707), the houses in
Brick Alley (1718), and Tomkins's (1733). The last three achieved
minor architectural distinction by the use of features such as gauged
and diapered brickwork, pediments, shaped gables, and carved balls

[64] Wood, *Exchange of Bristol*; Enfield, *Liverpool*, 58–9.

and vases.[65] Almshouses were occasionally known as hospitals, such as Jesus Hospital in Newcastle-upon-Tyne (built 1681) and Berkeley Hospital in Worcester (founded 1697, built 1703),[66] but true medical establishments only reached the provinces with the development of infirmaries from the late 1730s. These were generally based in county centres, though other important cities also benefited. The earliest were founded at Winchester (1736), Bristol (1737), Bath (built 1738–41, opened 1742), York (1740, new façade 1745), Exeter (1743), Northampton (1743, enlarged 1753), Gloucester (1745), Shrewsbury (1745), Liverpool (built 1745–8, opened 1749), Worcester (1746, built at a cost of over £6,000), and Newcastle-upon-Tyne (built 1751–2).[67] Such institutions largely catered for the less well-to-do, as of course did workhouses, whose numbers appear to have grown from the 1690s, as a more efficient and exemplary way of treating urban poverty. The workhouse at Birmingham was erected in 1733 at a cost of over £1,000, and in 1766 a further £400 was spent in adding an infirmary to it.[68] The poor were also the focus of the charity or blue-coat school movement, which swept the country in the early eighteenth century leaving its physical mark on town after town. The school at Bath, for example, was founded in 1711 to instruct fifty boys and fifty girls, and in 1722 acquired purpose-built accommodation costing about £1,000.[69]

For contemporaries welfare and religion were allied forces, and the secular wealth and spiritual energy directed towards charity also stimulated the first serious wave of urban ecclesiastical building since

[65] G. G. Astill, *Historic Towns in Berkshire: An Archaeological Appraisal*, Berkshire Archaeological Committee, Publication No. 2 (Reading, 1978), 51; Grady, 'Public Buildings in the West Riding', Gazetteer; A. Oswald, *Old Towns Revisited* (London, 1952), 25–32; and also W. H. Godfrey, *The English Almshouse* (London, 1955), 63–76, 80–6.

[66] Brand, *Newcastle*, i. 352–4; Fiennes, *Journeys*, 212; BE *Worcestershire*, 332.

[67] Everitt, 'County and Town', 98; Wood, *Bath*, 274–303; *VCH York*, 467; *VCH Northamptonshire*, iii. 38–9; Enfield, *Liverpool*, 50–1; T. Nash, *Collections for the History of Worcestershire* (London, 1781–2), Supplement (1799), 94–6; Brand, *Newcastle*, i. 412–16.

[68] G. Taylor, *The Problem of Poverty 1660-1834* (London, 1969), 30–1; Hutton, *History of Birmingham*, 214.

[69] Wood, *Bath*, 321; M. G. Jones, *The Charity School Movement: A Study of Eighteenth-Century Puritanism in Action* (Cambridge, 1938), 15–27, 69–72; G. S. Holmes, *Augustan England: Professions, State, and Society 1680-1730* (London, 1982), 53–5; *VCH York*, 253; Brown, 'Colchester in the Eighteenth Century', 153; Picton, *Liverpool Municipal Archives*, 75–6; Bourne, *Newcastle*, 136; Hutton, *History of Birmingham*, 213–14; Cunnington, *Devizes*, 206; Lobel, *Atlas*, i, Hereford, 11; Grady, 'Public Buildings in the West Riding', Gazetteer, Leeds, Sheffield, and Wakefield.

the Reformation. The number of towns which acquired fine new churches in the first sixty years of the eighteenth century is quite remarkable, given the preceding dearth of activity. In the North these included Congleton, Knutsford, Leeds, Liverpool (two cases), Manchester, Maryport, Sheffield, and Whitehaven (two); in the Midlands, Birmingham (three), Burton-upon-Trent, Castle Bromwich, Daventry, Derby, Shrewsbury, Stone, Warwick, Whitchurch, and Wolverhampton; in the East, Colchester, Gainsborough, Lincoln, and Yarmouth; in the South, Chichester, Deal, and Guildford; and in the West, Bath, Blandford Forum, Bristol, Gloucester, Stourbridge, Tiverton, and Worcester.[70] Some of these were constructed on a magisterial scale, such as Archer's St Philip's at Birmingham (1709–15, tower completed 1725) (see Fig. 4), and Gibbs's All Saints in Derby (1723–5, costing £4,500), both of which deservedly ascended to cathedral status in the twentieth century.[71] In addition to full-scale churches, there were many new Anglican chapels and dissenting meeting-houses, the latter constructed in the wake of the Toleration Act of 1689. Although the majority of these were small and unpretentious, several displayed some architectural distinction, like the proprietary chapels of St Mary's (1732–4) and the Octagon (1767) in Bath, or the still surviving Unitarian meeting-house at Ipswich (1699–1700), and the Presbyterian chapel at Bury St Edmunds (1711–12).[72] Secular culture was catered for by a range of new buildings associated with the growth in urban leisure, and these will be examined in detail later in the book.

Though this section has concentrated on new construction work, the impact of repairs, improvements, and refurbishing on established buildings should not be forgotten. Many an old friend received a modern face-lift. At Preston the timber-framed town hall was repaired and 'beautified' on four occasions between 1705 and 1719, on the last by the addition of a fashionable cupola, to be 'painted, finished, and perfected with a gilt ball on the top, or something in the representation of the town's arms'. In 1727 it was further agreed that 'the town hall be bricked about the next summer', sixteen years later that three new

[70] Many, though not all of these can be found in M. Whiffen, *Stuart and Georgian Churches* (London, 1947–8); Clarke, *Eighteenth-Century Church*; and C. W. Chalklin, 'The Financing of Church Building in the Provincial Towns of Eighteenth-Century England', in Clark, *Provincial Towns*, 284–310.

[71] Whiffen, *Stuart and Georgian Churches*, 23–5, 31–3.

[72] Chalklin, 'Financing of Church Building', 285–6; Wood, *Bath*, 312–15; Ison, *Bath*, 72–3; *BE Suffolk*, 2nd edn. (Harmondsworth, 1974), 145–6, 296–7.

windows be added on the west side 'to make the same uniform', and in 1761 the south end was ordered to be rebuilt to bring it into line with the new guildhall.[73] Few medieval churches would have escaped at least a dash of 'georgianizing', with the insertion of galleries, pews, organs, monuments, paintings, and altar-pieces. Some were substantially altered, as at Bideford, where it was reported in 1755 that 'a great part' of the church 'has been lately new built; the whole has been repaired and beautified, and new seats have been made'.[74]

The upsurge in the construction and improvement of public edifices displayed several broad characteristics. Projects tended to become larger and more expensive, and greater attention was paid to architectural appearance. New types of structures emerged, such as infirmaries or assembly rooms, and the basic categories became both more distinct from each other, and differentiated within themselves. Administration and marketing were increasingly separated, and commercial buildings displayed a greater emphasis on specialization. All this reflected the growing complexity and sophistication of urban public life. Generally speaking the towns which invested most in their public fabric were those which also displayed a concern for their landscape as a whole. Public buildings, because they were understood to represent the civic community *in toto*, were the final step in a broad process aimed at enhancing the physical coherence and image of the town. Like decorative bosses in a church roof, they drew together the various strands in the urban fabric, and celebrated the existence of the whole.

The second part of this book has explored the effect of the Urban Renaissance on the physical form of the town. Starting with the smallest building block, the house, and progressing through the street and square to the largest, the town itself, it has attempted to show how the appearance, and to some extent the coherence of the landscape was transformed in the century after the Restoration. The central features of this process were a fundamental shift in the prevailing architectural tradition, from vernacular to classical, and a new consciousness of and approach to urban design. Though the impact of change was rarely dramatic, and varied both within and

[73] Council Minutes, 3 Dec. 1705, 4 July 1709, 27 July and 13 Aug. 1716, 26 June and 31 July 1718, 31 Mar. and 9 July 1719, 6 Feb. 1726/7, 10 May 1728, 29 Jan. 1728/9, 23 June 1743, PCMSS; White Book, 23 Apr. 1761, PCMSS.

[74] *Gentleman's Magazine*, xxv (1755), 446; and also Thoresby, *Ducatus Leodiensis*, 40; Gillett and Macmahon, *Hull*, 208-9.

between communities, its long-term effects were impressive. This was particularly so given the old-fashioned and even decaying nature of substantial parts of the built environment in the mid-seventeenth century. The trend towards upgrading the town's image, to which the regeneration of its fabric contributed so much, was reinforced by changes in other spheres of urban culture, and it is to these that we now turn.

democracy
nationalism
"elite"
old → new
change
enlightenment

III
LEISURE

5
The Arts

As a result of their architectural renaissance, provincial towns came to appear visually more attractive and sophisticated. This created an appropriate physical setting for a parallel transformation in their social life. From the late seventeenth century, England experienced an explosion in the demand for, and provision of publicly available, high-status leisure.[1] The impact on towns was considerable, since they were the traditional gathering points and service centres of society. The communities most affected by these changes were those nearer the top of the urban hierarchy. The manner in which their cultural life was enriched will be explored in this and the following two chapters. The present one will examine the broad field of the arts, separately considering those pastimes involving some element of performance, and those predominantly concerned with cultivating the intellect, before placing both in their context of time and place. The next chapter will investigate the new facilities for personal display, and the third one, sports.

1. THE PERFORMING ARTS

Provincial theatre in Tudor and early Stuart England had been subject to a series of debilitating blows. The initial one arose from the disintegration of the rich ceremony and ritual, of which drama was an integral part, that characterized many of the larger medieval towns. Street processions were often attended by mystery plays or moral tableaux, as during the great guild pageants at Corpus Christi and Whitsuntide.[2] From the Reformation onwards these forms of religious

---

[1] J. H. Plumb, *The Commercialization of Leisure in Eighteenth-Century England* (Reading, 1973); J. H. Plumb, *Georgian Delights* (London, 1980); McKendrick *et al.*, *Birth of a Consumer Society*.

[2] A. P. Rossiter, *English Drama from Early Times to the Elizabethans* (London, 1969), 68; Palliser, *Tudor York*, 232; Clark and Slack, *Towns in Transition*, 143, 145; Fox, *Stratford-upon-Avon*, 92; C. Phythian-Adams, 'Ceremony and the Citizen: The Communal Year at Coventry 1450-1550', in Clark and Slack, *Crisis and Order*, 77.

drama came under mounting pressure, and during the reign of
Elizabeth many plays were either suppressed or simply abandoned.[3]
Some compensation was found in the growth of itinerant theatre and
puppetry. From as early as the 1530s Leicester and Bristol were hosting
travelling bands of actors, as were towns like Shrewsbury, Chester,
York, Stratford-upon-Avon, Norwich, and Worcester by Elizabeth's
reign.[4] However, many of these companies were based in London.
Only two that were centred in provincial towns obtained licences to
perform: one in Bristol in 1618, which appears to have survived for
only a short period, the other in York, where the licence was never
actually used. Strolling players might have developed stronger ties
with provincial society were it not for the campaign mounted against
them by civic authorities in the early seventeenth century. Fear for
public order, allied to puritan tendencies, drove several corporations
either into open conflict with touring companies, or to the diplomatic
expedient of paying them not to perform. By the 1630s visits had
begun to diminish markedly. The decline of provincial drama was
finally capped by attack from the centre, with the parliamentary
ordinances and army theatre raids of the 1640s and 1650s.[5]

At the Restoration provincial urban drama must have seemed
distinctly beleaguered, yet within a century it had undergone a
remarkable revival. A rich network of companies criss-crossed the
country, with the more important towns usually boasting a lengthy
season of performances, and even the small centres enjoying at least a
few days of Thespian delights each year.[6] The development of the

[3] H. C. Gardiner, *Mysteries' End: An Investigation of the Last Days of the Medieval
Religious Stage* (n.p., 1967), 29–93; G. Wickham, *Early English Stages 1300–1600*
(London, 1959–81), ii, Part 1, 96, 99; Palliser, *Tudor York*, 279–80; Phythian-Adams,
'Ceremony and the Citizen', 79; Phythian-Adams, 'Urban Decay', 177–8.

[4] J. Simmons, *Leicester Past and Present*, Vol. 1: *Ancient Borough to 1860* (London,
1974), 51, 84; G. T. Watts, *Theatrical Bristol* (Bristol, 1915), 7–11; K. Barker, *Bristol at
Play: Five Centuries of Live Entertainment* (Bradford-on-Avon, 1976), 2; Wickham,
Early English Stages, i. 269–70; Fox, *Stratford-upon-Avon*, 140; T. W. Craik (ed.), *The
Revels History of English Drama*, Vol. 3: *1576–1613* (London, 1975), 24; Dyer,
Worcester in the Sixteenth Century, 249–50; G. Speaight, *The History of the English
Puppet Theatre* (London, 1955), chap. 4.

[5] Wickham, *Early English Stages*, ii, Part 1, 141–8; Barker, *Bristol at Play*, 3–4; Fox,
Stratford-upon-Avon, 143–4; Gillett and Macmahon, *Hull*, 121; Simmons, *Leicester*,
84; T. L. G. Burley, *Playhouses and Players of East Anglia* (Norwich, 1928), 165–6;
MacCaffrey, *Exeter*, 271; J.-C. Agnew, *Worlds Apart: The Market and the Theatre in
Anglo-American Thought 1550–1750* (Cambridge, 1986), 125–48; D. Brailsford, *Sport
and Society* (London, 1969), 138; L. Hotson, *The Commonwealth and Restoration
Stage* (New York, 1962), 3–59.

[6] S. Rosenfeld, *Strolling Players and Drama in the Provinces 1660–1765*

theatre during the intervening period was far from uniform. There was probably rapid growth in the early eighteenth century, followed by a short-term crisis in 1737 due to the introduction of potentially harsh legislation. Not only did this provide for rigorous censorship, but it also appeared to outlaw provincial drama altogether and to expose itinerant performers to the full force of the vagrancy laws.[7] In practice, fashionable theatre seems to have escaped relatively unscathed.[8] On the one hand, the implementation of the act depended upon the co-operation of local justices who had little interest in curtailing a pleasure enjoyed by themselves and their peers. On the other hand, managers responded prudently and resourcefully. Some attempted to evade the terms of the act by billing their plays as concerts punctuated by dramatic interludes, while others cultivated a respectable profile by organizing benefit performances for, or making direct contributions to local charities.[9] By the 1750s any lingering doubts about the legitimacy or health of the theatre were vanishing, as the first major wave of investment in purpose-built auditoriums occurred.

The expansion in provincial drama was built around three types of company: that on summer tour from London, that of a genuinely itinerant nature, and that based in a particular town.[10] By the early eighteenth century the impact of the metropolitan companies was greatest in the Home Counties and resorts. In the country as a whole their influence was more restricted. The rising national demand for drama, frequently at times that clashed with the London season, required an increasing supply of talent, which the metropolitan stage was unable to satisfy. One alternative was the provincial strolling company. This could vary from a small band of actors specially

(Cambridge, 1939); Burley, *Players of East Anglia, passim*; G. Hare, *The Georgian Theatre in Wessex* (London, 1958), chaps. 1-4; J. L. Hodgkinson and R. Pogson, *The Early Manchester Theatre* (London, 1960), 3-72; H. Sargeant, *A History of Portsmouth Theatres*, Portsmouth Papers No. 13 (1971), 1-7; Barker, *Bristol at Play*,chaps. 1-2; L. Fitzsimmons, 'The Theatre Royal, York', *York History*, iv (n.d.), 169-76.

[7] 10 Geo. II, c. 28; P. Hartnoll, 'The Theatre and the Licensing Act of 1737', in A. Natan (ed.), *Silver Renaissance: Essays in Eighteenth-Century History* (London, 1961), 165-86; J. Loftis, *The Politics of Drama in Augustan England* (Oxford, 1963), 128-53; T. W. Craik (ed.), *The Revels History of English Drama*, Vol. 5: *1660-1750* (London, 1976), chap. 3.

[8] Rosenfeld, *Strolling Players*, 7-9, Barker, *Bristol at Play*, 7; Fitzsimmons, 'Theatre Royal, York', 170.

[9] Burley, *Players of East Anglia*, 4-7; Hodgkinson and Pogson, *Early Manchester Theatre*, 19-20, 25-6, 29; T. Fawcett, *Music in Eighteenth-Century Norwich and Norfolk* (Norwich, 1979), 22; *Bath Advertiser*, No. 1, 18 Oct. 1755.

[10] Rosenfeld, *Strolling Players*, 5; Fitzsimmons, 'Theatre Royal, York', 170.

assembled for a limited tour, weaving its way from village to town, to a more permanent group, following a well-trodden circuit of substantial engagements. The line between the established travelling companies and the town-based players is rather blurred, since all the urban groups operated regional circuits. What distinguished them from the truly itinerant companies was a major commitment to their host town, invariably performing a lengthy season before embarking on tour.

By the late 1720s there had emerged at least three town companies: those at Norwich, York, and Bath. Their development was interlinked, since the Bath and York groups originated in Norwich, and for a time operated both there and in their future homes, before finally leaving the Norfolk capital under the pressure of competition. In this way touring players were propelled along the urban system as they were forced out of old markets and compelled to explore new ones. During the majority of our period it is unlikely that many bands of performers made the full transformation from a strolling to an urban-based troupe. However, by the mid-eighteenth century more and more town companies were forming, including ones at Birmingham (operating in the 1750s), Plymouth (established *c*.1758), and Salisbury (established 1765).[11] The rise of such groups reflects the growing organization and urban focus of provincial drama. The large towns developed as the nodal points of the system, offering an extensive programme of drama themselves, as well as servicing a circuit of satellite venues. It was a trend that suited both guest and host. Players enjoyed the monetary rewards, convenience, and stability that a major centre could offer; towns benefited from possessing a valuable and reliable recreational facility with which to enhance their image and attract visitors. These mutual interests were acknowledged at York in the early 1730s, when the promoter Thomas Keregan presented the city fathers with his proposals 'to build a playhouse, . . . requesting that some order might be made in his favour'. Recognizing the economic value of the project to York, the corporation responded by guaranteeing him a long-term performing monopoly. The epilogue, delivered on the opening night of the new theatre, encapsulated the transformation from strolling to town-based company:

---

[11] Rosenfeld, *Strolling Players*, chaps. 2–3, 6, 8; Money, *Experience and Identity*, 87; Hare, *Georgian Theatre*, 43, 49, 63–4.

But I vow I don't much like this transmigration;
Grant heaven we don't return to our first station,
Strolling, from place to place, about the nation.
.   .   .   .
But providence, we hope, designed this place
To be the players' refuge in distress;
That, when the winter comes, we may all flock hither,
As to a shed, to shield us from the weather.[12]

A vital ingredient of the theatrical scene was music, both to accompany songs and dances, and to provide interludes. Some companies, indeed, carried their own band of instrumentalists.[13] It is to the general subject of aural entertainment that we now turn. Late Stuart and early Georgian England was gripped by a passion for music, and this had a profound effect on its provision and performance.[14] In his 'Memoirs of Music' completed in 1728, Roger North pointed to the Restoration as a watershed in the history of the art, prefacing his section on this period with the comment, 'but now to observe the steps of the grand metamorphosis of music, whereby it hath mounted into those altitudes of esteem it now enjoys'. He declined to detail all the features of what he goes on to refer to as a 'revolution', partly because its sheer fertility and complexity defied description. 'What a work would it be', he argued, 'to enumerate the masters regnant, with their characters, and the number of consorts, sonatas, and concertos, besides solos innumerable, bred and born here or brought from abroad; the magnificences of the operas, the famous organs, organists, and builders; the various societies, and assemblies for music. . . .' Nor was this a passing craze. For one unsympathetic observer in the 1750s, the pastime had by then reached obsessive proportions. 'Music', he complained, 'never was intended by the great Author of Wisdom . . . in itself, to become the labour, principal attention, or great business of a people. Yet, how far, how scandalously it has of late prevailed . . . let the shameful number of concerts now subscribed for in this

[12] House Book, 29 Jan. 1732/3, YCA; epilogue reproduced in Rosenfeld, *Strolling Players*, 120.
[13] Fawcett, *Music in Eighteenth-Century Norwich*, 21-9; Rosenfeld, *Strolling Players*, 18.
[14] E. D. Mackerness, *A Social History of English Music* (London, 1964), chaps. 2-3; *The New Grove Dictionary of Music*, ed. S. Sadie (London, 1980), vi. 172-5; P. M. Young, *A History of British Music* (London, 1967), 312-14; J. Harley, *Music in Purcell's London* (London, 1968), especially 161-74; Plumb, *Commercialization of Leisure*, 14-16.

kingdom, declare'.[15] Central to North's 'grand metamorphosis' was the opening up of art music to what by early modern terms was a mass market. The pleasures of this refined entertainment were no longer to be confined to the closed circles of court, chapel, and country house, but became easily accessible to thousands of middle-ranking English citizens. This was reflected in a transformation of the organization, transmission, and content of music.

The most striking development in the organization of classical music was the growth in public performances. London with its huge potential market led the way with three major innovations. The first was the introduction of commercial concerts. A form of these had been widely available in tavern music-houses since at least the 1650s, but the first true series of concerts began in the 1670s, with the ventures promoted by John Banister (1672 or 1673) and Thomas Britton (1678). Second, there was the rise of the musical festival. The Corporation of the Sons of the Clergy, founded in 1655 and incorporated by charter in 1678, promoted a grand choral service every year, and from about the 1670s London celebrated the feast of the patroness of music with an annual St Cecilia's day concert. Third, the metropolitan stage pioneered the development of musical theatre in England, initially through what North called the 'semi-opera', or we might term musical, and later by the introduction of the full-scale Italian opera.[16] The spas were the first provincial centres to feel the impact of these innovations, because of their close connection with London society. Other towns were slower to respond, though by the mid-eighteenth century the musical revolution had reached a great many of them.[17] Appendix 4 shows that by the 1730s at least eight or nine centres had experimented with public concert series, which were normally held on a regular weekly, fortnightly, or monthly basis, and to which admission was by individual or season ticket.[18] By the 1760s

[15] J. Wilson (ed.), *Roger North on Music* (London, 1959), 349, 351, 359; *London Magazine* (Nov. 1754), 484.

[16] Wilson, *North on Music*, 302-14, 351-4; Harley, *Purcell's London*, 113-51; J. Strutt, *Glig-Gamena Angel-Deod, or the Sports and Pastimes of the People of England*, 2nd edn. (London, 1810), 254-5; R. McGuinness, 'The Music Business in Early Eighteenth-Century London', *Quarterly Jnl. of Social Affairs*, i, No. 3 (1985), 249-59.

[17] S. Sadie, 'Concert Life in Eighteenth-Century England', *Proceedings of the Royal Musical Association*, lxxxv (1958-9), 17-30; M. Tilmouth, 'The Beginnings of Provincial Concert Life in England', in C. Hogwood and R. Luckett (eds.), *Music in Eighteenth-Century England* (Cambridge, 1983), 1-17; Fawcett, *Music in Eighteenth-Century Norwich*.

[18] J. Looney, 'Advertising and Society in England 1720-1820: A Statistical Analysis of Yorkshire Newspaper Advertisements', Ph.D. thesis (Princeton, 1983), 166-7.

another dozen or so towns had hosted such series, and in all probability further research would reveal many more.

In addition to the regular concerts there was also a variety of one-off performances of instrumental pieces, songs, operas, and choral works. In the shire towns these usually clustered around the two climactic points in the annual social calendar, assize and race weeks. But in a number of centres the highpoint of the musical year occurred during a special festival. In the 1690s and early 1700s St Cecilia's day concerts were arranged at Oxford, Salisbury, Winchester, Wells, and probably Norwich. The one at Salisbury blossomed into a two-day event in 1748, and twenty years later a third day was added.[19] The charitable Corporation of the Sons of the Clergy, and later the Foundling Hospital (chartered in 1739, where from 1750 there were annual performances of Handel's *Messiah*), provided a further metropolitan prototype for the provincial festivals. A 'Sons of the Clergy' society was founded at Newcastle-upon-Tyne in 1710, and by at least 1722 it was mounting an annual choral service.[20] The most important offshoot of the London model was the Three Choirs Festival, founded in about 1718, and rotating annually between Gloucester, Worcester, and Hereford. Though originally devoid of any formal philanthropic associations, by 1724 a collection was being made for orphans of the poorer diocesan clergy and choir members, and five years later it was claimed that 'our present society is ambitious some way to be resembled' to the London society. Initially the performances were spread over two days, with religious choral works in the cathedral in the morning, and more secular compositions in the evening, but by the 1750s a third day had been added. Later, festivals were also introduced at Bristol (held annually between 1757 and 1760), Winchester (from 1760), Birmingham (1768, in support of the new General Hospital, and subsequently held on an occasional basis), and Norwich (from 1770).[21]

Much of this public music was organized by a proliferating body of

[19] Tilmouth, 'Provincial Concert Life', 9–11; *New Grove*, xvi. 421; xx. 446; E. Hobhouse (ed.), *The Diary of a West Country Physician* (London, 1934), 42 and *passim*.

[20] Ellis, 'Social Relations in Newcastle', 200; Young, *History of British Music*, 313.

[21] W. Shaw, *The Three Choirs Festival* (Worcester and London, 1954), 1–29; T. Bisse, *A Sermon Preached in the Cathedral Church of Hereford, at the Anniversary Meeting of the Three Choirs, Gloucester, Worcester, Hereford, September 3, 1729* (London, 1729), 18; Barry, 'Cultural Life of Bristol', 186; *New Grove*, vi. 175; xviii. 792–3; xx. 446; *Gloucester Jnl.*, xxxv, No. 1789, 7 Sept. 1756; J. S. Smith, *The Story of Music in Birmingham* (Birmingham, 1945), 23–7.

musical clubs and societies. The earliest were formed in London shortly after the Restoration, and these provided a blueprint for the provinces. In his *Musical Companion* of 1701 Henry Playford expressed the wish that 'the several cities, towns, corporations, etc. in the kingdoms of Great Britain and Ireland . . . will follow the example of well-wishers to vocal and instrumental music in this famous city [London], by establishing . . . weekly meetings', and he offered to direct those seeking to form a club to a supplier from whom they could obtain music books and a set of model rules.[22] It was probably about this date that the earliest provincial groups began to appear. 'The Society of Lovers of Music' at Salisbury was already in existence by 1700, arranging St Cecilia's day celebrations,[23] and Appendix 4 documents the emergence of another twenty or so societies over the next seven decades. Given the presence of places as small as Dedham, Spalding, Swaffham, and Wells in the list, this number must represent only a fraction of the true total. Though in theory all were private associations, it seems that membership and the entertainments arranged were usually open to all respectable lovers of music. The Wells club frequently hosted visitors; its ranks were augmented with 'strangers' during sessions week; and it promoted a well-attended open concert on St Cecilia's day. In the larger fashionable centres the societies were even more publicly and commercially oriented. The 'music assembly' at York seems to have been a scion of the new assembly rooms complex and mounted weekly subscription concerts during the winter season, as well as staging several morning entertainments during race week.[24]

The growing public character of music altered not only its organization, but also the human agencies through which it was transmitted. An expanding market generated greater career opportunities for the professional.[25] Though amateurs played a vital part in the operation of the clubs, societies, and festivals, even these

[22] H. Playford, *The Second Book of the Pleasant Musical Companion*, 4th edn. (London, 1701), Preface; Wilson, *North on Music*, 303-5.

[23] T. Naish, *The Diary of Thomas Naish*, ed. D. Slatter, Wiltshire Archaeological and Natural History Soc., Records Branch, xx (1964), 4, 42; *New Grove*, xvi. 421.

[24] Hobhouse, *Diary of a West Country Physician*, 39-43, 51-2, 56, 58-9, 64-5, 68, 71, 74, 82, 84, 113, 133-4; Assembly Rooms: Directors' Minute Book (1730-58), 24 Mar. 1732/3, 23 Apr. 1742, 6 Feb. 1744/5, 28 July 1752, 31 Dec. 1754, YCA, M.23/1; Fawcett, *Music in Eighteenth-Century Norwich*, 4-9.

[25] Holmes, *Augustan England*, 28-31; Harley, *Purcell's London*, 169; Tilmouth, 'Provincial Concert Life', 2; R. Campbell, *The London Tradesman*, 1747, repr. (Newton Abbot, 1969), 93.

often depended heavily upon the services of employed musicians. One reason for this was that a paying public demanded the standards and consistency that only full-time performers could offer. A sign of the expanding employment opportunities open to professionals was the influx of foreign artists. Between 1675 and 1750 there were more Italian composers resident in London than any other city except Vienna, and quite a number of their compatriots made their way onto the provincial circuit as performers.[26] Germans were similarly welcome, not only Handel, but also William Herschel (1738–1822), who after an early visit to England as an oboist in the Hanoverian guards, returned in 1757 to seek his fortune first in the North-East (including Leeds and Halifax), and from 1766 as composer, promoter, and resident organist at the fashionable Octagon Chapel in Bath.[27]

The new public music not only drew upon exotic foreign talent, but also exploited some very traditional English sources of professional or semi-professional performers. Town waits had been serving as watchmen and providing the music for civic ceremonial since at least the late medieval period. With their apparently antiquated duties, they may have been expected to be among the first casualties of the musical revolution. In reality they survived remarkably well, continuing to operate in late seventeenth- or eighteenth-century London, Norwich, Yarmouth, Bristol, Newcastle-upon-Tyne, York, Leicester, Bath, and Sheffield.[28] Their resilience was due partly to the continuing, perhaps enhanced importance of urban ritual; but it also reflected their value as a local reservoir of reliable performers to service the new forms of music. A Norwich bye-law of 1714 required the waits to hold a monthly music meeting, 'for the accommodation and diversion of the lovers of music in this city', and though there is no further evidence to confirm that such concerts took place, the waits certainly performed at the assemblies at Chapelfield House. In York they were the backbone of the city's musical life, accompanying the

[26] Harley, *Purcell's London*, 156–60; Wilson, *North on Music*, 307–11, 355–9; *New Grove*, vii. 223–6; Assembly Rooms Minute Book, 20 Dec. 1733, 4 and 10 Dec. 1736, 7 Feb. 1736/7, 16 Dec. 1737, 24 Jan. 1737/8, 19 Mar. 1752, YCA; Hodgkinson and Pogson, *Early Manchester Theatre*, 37.

[27] A. J. Turner, *Science and Music in Eighteenth-Century Bath* (Bath, 1977), 21–49.

[28] Harley, *Purcell's London*, 50–3; Fawcett, *Music in Eighteenth-Century Norwich*, 2–4, 33; Barry, 'Cultural Life of Bristol', 227; Wood, *Exchange of Bristol*, 30; Brand, *Newcastle*, ii. 353–4; *VCH York*, 233, 247; Simmons, *Leicester*, 84; Wood, *Bath*, 417; Council Minutes, 26 Mar. 1733, BCA; Chamberlain's Accounts, 1701/2, 1710/11, 1712/13, BCA; J. D. Leader, *The Records of the Burgery of Sheffield* (London, 1897), pp. xxxii–xxxvi.

regular Monday assemblies, assisting at the balls and concerts mounted in race week, and almost certainly performing at the music assembly's Friday subscription series. The corporation fully acknow-ledged their importance to York by paying them an annual salary, providing them with new liveries every six years, and taking some care over their training.[29]

Traditionally, the church had been the most important source of public music. It was a role the church was to reinforce rather than relinquish in the future, as it adapted with considerable flexibility to the new musical context. Such a process was perhaps most evident in the influential role played by organists in the musical revolution, many becoming in practice, if not in name, civic kapellmeisters. In town after town, musicians of high artistic and entrepreneurial calibre were appointed to the post: men such as Thomas Chilcot and William Herschel in Bath, Barnabas Gunn, John Eversman, and Richard Hobbs in Birmingham, Musgrave Heighington, John Christian Mantel, and William Mully in Yarmouth, Capel Bond in Coventry, Joseph Gibbs in Dedham, Charles Burney in King's Lynn, and Charles Avison in Newcastle-upon-Tyne. Frequently they were the mainstay of the whole musical scene in the town and surrounding area, organizing concerts, founding and promoting festivals and societies, teaching, composing, and writing. Avison (1709–70), whose father had been a Newcastle wait, was organist at St Nicholas's from 1736, and despite receiving many attractive offers from other cities, remained there until his death thirty-four years later. In 1738 he was appointed director of the subscription concerts in the town, and later helped promote a similar venture in Durham, as well as arranging informal musical evenings at the vicarage. In addition to teaching and writing on music, he was also a fine and productive composer, best known for his attractive concerti grossi for string orchestra.[30]

A final effect of the growth in public music-making was a change in the type of music that was performed. Larger audiences and greater

[29] Fawcett, *Music in Eighteenth-Century Norwich*, 3–4; G. A. Cranfield, *The Development of the Provincial Newspaper 1700–1760* (Oxford, 1962), 217; Assembly Rooms Minute Book, 21 Aug. 1732, 27 July 1733, 8 Aug. 1735, 19 July 1736, 12 May 1744, YCA: Assembly Rooms Ledger and Register of Subscribers (1732–47), *passim*, YCA, M.23/4/A; House Book, 23 Apr. and 30 Nov. 1705, 27 Apr. 1705, 13 Apr. and 31 Aug. 1711, 8 Feb. 1719/20, 28 Apr. 1742, 9 May 1746, YCA.

[30] *New Grove*, i. 748–51; ii. 286; iv. 227; xviii. 793; Smith, *Music in Birmingham*, 10–11, 14, 19, 21, 24; Fawcett, *Music in Eighteenth-Century Norwich*, 33–7; *VCH Warwickshire*, viii. 224; Sadie, 'Concert Life', 23; J. Barry, 'Religion in the Georgian Town', in *Life in the Georgian Town* (London, 1986), 39.

professionalism encouraged the presentation of more extrovert, showy, and brilliant compositions. Initially this was reflected in the craze for French and Italian music.[31] With their emphasis on large-scale dramatic contrasts, such pieces were eminently more suited to public performance than the comparatively intimate character of traditional English compositions. Moreover, the concertino element in the Italian concerto grosso and the form of Italian opera and song allowed individual artists to display their skills to the fullest, and encouraged the development of that phenomenon of the mass entertainment industry, the star system. In the short term, English church music was an understandable casualty of the vogue for virtuoso foreign compositions. In about 1718 Thomas Tudway commented on 'how it comes to pass, that church music only should be so little regarded, in an age when music in general is come to such a height of improvement . . . and the composers of secular music are become much greater masters, than ever was known before'.[32] But the influence of the church, and more broadly of religion in English music was too ingrained to be easily shaken off. In response to changing fashions a new type of church music was developed, more dramatic and attractive, and less devotional in nature than its predecessor. One form this took was the great choral set pieces of Purcell, Croft, Handel, and Boyce, often composed to accompany public ceremonies and celebrations, such as Handel's *Coronation Anthems* (1727) and his *Utrecht* (1713) and *Dettingen* (1743) *Te Deums*. However, the most successful of the new modes of religious music was the oratorio. Combining the flair and public appeal of musical theatre with the sentiments of the English choral tradition, and tapping a rising tide of moderate bourgeois evangelicalism, it broke the dominance of Italian opera from the late 1730s and triumphantly reaffirmed the influence of the sacred in musical life.[33]

2. THE INTELLECTUAL ARTS

The performing arts provided one focus around which urban cultural facilities developed. Another key area was that which sought to directly educate and succour the human mind. In this mission the

[31] Wilson, *North on Music*, 299–302, 307–14, 349–51, 355–9.

[32] C. Hogwood, 'Thomas Tudway's History of Music', in Hogwood and Luckett, *Music in Eighteenth-Century England*, 44.

[33] W. Dean, *The New Grove Handel* (London, 1982), 47–71.

printed word and its institutions held pride of place, but other
agencies, such as societies, lectures, and schools also had an important
part to play. The lapse of the Licensing Act in 1695 triggered a
sustained growth in the publishing industry, with books, pamphlets,
newspapers, and journals flowing from the presses at an unparalleled
rate. Only the 1640s and early 1650s could compare, and then over a
much narrower range of material and for a briefer period.[34] By far the
most important centres of publishing and serious printing were
London and to a lesser extent Oxford and Cambridge. However, the
contribution of the provincial trade should not be overlooked, a
particular danger given the ephemeral nature, and poor survival and
cataloguing of much of its output.[35]

Though the mainstay of the local presses was job-printing, and
much of their cultural output was devoted to ballad sheets,
chapbooks, and almanacs, a number of businesses produced items of
more sophisticated content. Chester, where the earliest known book to
be printed in the city appeared in 1688, was home to at least three
printers by about 1720. Two of them seem to have concentrated on
sermons and theological material, but the third printing office, run by
Roger Adams and his widow Elizabeth, produced works of such scope
as J. Grundy's *Philosophical and Mathematical Reasons* (no date), *The
Raree Show: Or, the Foxtrapt* (1740, an opera), and volume three of
Thomas Pennant's *The British Zoology* (1768–70, for a London
bookseller). Several non-metropolitan presses turned out work of a
high calibre. Benjamin Collins of Salisbury was joint publisher and
possibly printer of the first edition of Goldsmith's *Vicar of Wakefield*,
and the physical quality of his output was generally high. Henry
Bourne's *History of Newcastle-upon-Tyne* (1736) was printed in that
city by John White (local history was a field in which the provincial
presses made a particularly important contribution); and Ann Ward of
York probably produced the first two volumes of Sterne's *Tristram
Shandy* (1759). In the preface to his two-volume edition of the works
of Milton, published at his office in Birmingham in 1757, the
pioneering typographer John Baskerville (1706–75) outlined his
personal credo:

[34] J. H. Plumb, 'The Public, Literature, and the Arts in the Eighteenth Century', in
M. R. Marrus (ed.), *The Emergence of Leisure* (New York, 1974), 12–24.
[35] A. Sterenberg, 'The Spread of Printing in Suffolk in the Eighteenth Century',
in M. Crump and M. Harris (eds.), *Searching the Eighteenth Century* (London, 1983),
29–31.

Amongst the several mechanic arts that have engaged my attention, there is no one which I have pursued with so much steadiness and pleasure, as that of letter-founding. . . . It is not my desire to print many books; but such only, as are books of consequence, of intrinsic merit, or established reputation, and which the public may be pleased to see in an elegant dress, and to purchase at such a price, as will repay the extraordinary care and expense that must necessarily be bestowed upon them.[36]

The single most important contribution local printers made to urban culture was the foundation of the provincial newspaper. The earliest unofficial London papers were published on a regular basis from the 1690s, and in 1702 the first daily appeared on the streets of the metropolis. The leading provincial towns were quick to follow suit. The earliest to acquire a newspaper was probably Norwich in 1701, and before the end of the decade it had been joined by Bristol (1702), Exeter (1704), Shrewsbury (1705), Yarmouth (1708), and Worcester (1709). By 1760 around 150 publications had been introduced in over fifty towns, at least twenty-nine of which possessed an operating weekly paper at this date.[37] During these early years there were many individual failures, as newspaper proprietors competed for control of particular towns and regions: Manchester witnessed at least eight new starts, Bristol no less than sixteen. However, by the mid-eighteenth century the organization and operation of the provincial press was settling down, with distribution networks stabilizing at smaller but more manageable and efficient sizes, and proprietors displaying a greater maturity and expertise in their approach to the business.[38]

[36] J. Feather, *The Provincial Book Trade in Eighteenth-Century England* (Cambridge, 1985), 104–21; R. Stewart-Brown, 'The Stationers, Booksellers, and Printers of Chester to about 1800', *Trans. of the Historic Soc. of Lancashire and Cheshire*, lxxxiii (1932), 115–19, 123–4, 130–1; C. Y. Ferdinand, 'Benjamin Collins: Salisbury Printer', in Crump and Harris, *Searching the Eighteenth Century*, 74–92; *VCH York*, 250; Baskerville, in Denvir, *Eighteenth Century*, 228–9.

[37] Plumb, *Commercialization of Leisure*, 6–7; G. A. Cranfield, *A Handlist of English Provincial Newspapers and Periodicals 1700-1760*, Cambridge Bibliographical Soc. Monographs, No. 2 (Cambridge, 1952); G. A. Cranfield, 'A Handlist of English Provincial Newspapers and Periodicals 1700–1760: Additions and Corrections', *Trans. of the Cambridge Bibliographical Soc.*, ii, No. 3 (1956), 269–74; R. M. Wiles, 'Further Additions and Corrections to G. A. Cranfield's Handlist', *Trans. of the Cambridge Bibliographical Soc.*, ii, No. 5 (1958), 385–9; Wiles, *Freshest Advices*, 374–519. The dates for the first issue of a provincial newspaper are rather uncertain. For the dubious claim of the *Worcester Post-Man* to be the earliest provincial newspaper see I. Griffiths, *Berrow's Worcester Journal: An Examination of the Antiquity of Britain's Oldest Newspaper* (Worcester, 1941); Green, *History and Antiquities of Worcester*, ii. 25–6; Wiles, *Freshest Advices*, 506–7.

[38] Cranfield, *Development of Provincial Newspaper*, 204–6, 256–73; Looney, 'Advertising and Society', 49–51.

By today's standards these early newspapers might seem unsophist-
icated and derivative, with a crude printed format and editorial
organization. Though local input increased during the period, the
majority of news items and features were openly derived from the
London and continental press.[39] However, comparisons with our
present-day product are misleading. To the early eighteenth-century,
news-hungry provinces these first local newspapers were a valuable
innovation. As such, they had a cultural impact at three levels. First,
they helped to broaden the geographical and political horizons of their
readership with a digest of national and international news. Second,
they entertained and educated their purchasers. When Addison
claimed that 'there is no humour in my countrymen, which I am more
inclined to wonder at, than their general thirst after news', he was well
aware that this was largely due to the public's love of a ripping yarn,
full of curiosity, drama, and suspense. Warfare was particularly good
copy, providing a riveting, ongoing story, and stimulating a boom in
the trade. One editor readily acknowledged that 'my fellow authors
are all men of martial spirits, and have an ungovernable appetite for
blood and mortality. As if they were sextons of the camp, and their
papers the charnel-houses, they toll thousands daily to their long
home; a charitable office! but they are paid for it'.[40] Yet proprietors
offered more than blood-and-thunder journalism. Most carried some
type of improving literature, with poems, serialized fiction, literary
criticism, and features on history, geography, topography, biography,
science, gardening, religion, and morality. A number of local presses
also produced literary journals, though this was largely a London
preserve.[41] A third sphere of cultural influence arose through
advertising. Originally this had been relatively sparse, but from about

[39] *Keating's Stratford and Warwick Mercury: Or Cirencester, Shipston, and Alcester Weekly Journal*, iii, No. 114, 9 Mar. 1752; Cranfield, *Development of Provincial Newspaper*, 28-32; Wiles, *Freshest Advices*, 197-208, 249-58; T. N. Brushfield, 'Andrew Brice and the Early Exeter Newspaper Press', *Trans. of the Devonshire Association*, xx (1888), 166-7; S. F. Watson, 'Some Materials for a History of Printing and Publishing in Ipswich', *Proceedings of the Suffolk Institute of Archaeology and Natural History*, xxiv, Part 3 (1949), 204.

[40] *The Spectator*, No. 452, 8 Aug. 1712, in G. G. Smith (ed.), *The Spectator* (London, 1907), vi. 201; *Stratford, Shipston, and Alcester Jnl.*, i, No. 1, 5 Feb. 1749/50; Cranfield, *Development of Provincial Newspaper*, 65-7; Wiles, *Freshest Advices*, 217.

[41] Cranfield, *Development of Provincial Newspaper*, 99-116; Wiles, *Freshest Advices*, 303-38; Williams, 'Henry Cross-Grove', 215-17; Barry, 'Cultural Life of Bristol', 108-10.

the 1720s it began to play a major part in the format and financing of newspapers, by the mid-eighteenth century taking up, in many cases, a half or more of the available space. A substantial group of these advertisements acted as a channel of communication for the leisure industry, either by encouraging the sale of luxury consumer products, like books, and musical scores and instruments, or by promoting recreational events, such as plays, concerts, lectures, cricket matches, and race-meetings. Thus the development of pleasure and press in the provinces were bound together in a common economic nexus.[42]

Closely allied to the business of printing newspapers was that of selling books. Printers frequently retailed publications they were not themselves involved in producing, and booksellers often acted as agents for newspapers. The sophisticated network of supply and distribution developed by the local press in the early eighteenth century, and the opportunities newspapers offered for advertising were to prove a crucial stimulus to the provincial book trade. One recent estimate suggests that in 1700 there may have been about 200 booksellers operating in 50 different towns, figures which themselves could reflect considerable post-Restoration expansion. By the mid-1740s the list of subscription agents for *The Harleian Miscellany* reveals the existence of 381 traders in 174 urban centres.[43] This growth in the trade is reflected in the evidence from individual towns. Ten booksellers, printers, binders, or stationers have been traced in Chester between 1600 and 1699, and a further twenty in the years 1700 to 1759. During the latter period about thirty booksellers have been discovered in Norwich, though at any one moment the numbers were much smaller: six in 1701, and about nine in 1750. Chester and Norwich were provincial capitals and would expect to be well supplied with bookshops. But evidence from rather smaller centres suggests that vending facilities were a regular feature of all reasonably sized towns. Between 1700 and 1759, eight booksellers were working in Yarmouth and seven in King's Lynn, and Stratford-upon-Avon had at least five such traders between the 1680s and 1750s. In 1742 the Preston Guild Roll listed two printers, a bookbinder, and a bookseller among the in-burgesses, and the town's newspaper indicates several men retailing printed

---

[42] Cranfield, *Development of Provincial Newspaper*, 207-23; Wiles, *Freshest Advices*, 149-86; Looney, 'Advertising and Society', especially 157-203.

[43] Feather, *Book Trade*, 12-31; D. Davis, *A History of Shopping* (London, 1966), 171-7; H. Plomer *et al.*, *A Dictionary of Printers and Booksellers . . . in England, Scotland, and Ireland 1641-1775* (Oxford, 1968).

literature during the early 1740s. Nor was Preston free from
competition. An advertisement of 1742 shows that Lancaster,
Ormskirk, Wigan, Warrington, and Liverpool also enjoyed the services
of booksellers.[44] The agent at Ormskirk was later called 'bookseller
and ironmonger', suggesting that the number of shops vending publications may be much wider than has been suspected.[45] Multiple-
trading was one means by which smaller towns might have access to
printed matter; another was through the services of visiting sales-
men. In 1718 the bookseller George Barton's home base was in
Huntingdon, but he also maintained 'shops' in Peterborough, St Ives,
and St Neots, open 'every market day'; and in the early 1750s James
Keating, as well as owning 'the Printing Office, and bookseller's shop
opposite the Cross' in Stratford-upon-Avon, also kept 'shops' at the
neighbouring small market centres of Shipston-on-Stour and
Alcester.[46]

To assess the full impact of printed matter it is important to
examine not only the facilities for production and sale, but also those
for circulation. Individually purchased newspapers and books must
have been frequently passed on to family and friends, multiplying
their readership several-fold. Book auctions also encouraged the flow
of the existing stock of published material. A more formal engine of
circulation was the publicly accessible library. Cathedrals had long
possessed fine collections of books which were frequently open to the
general reader. Some of their holdings were quite large (Lichfield had
about 3,000 volumes on loan in the later eighteenth century), and
they seem to have been well maintained and housed.[47] Another type

[44] Stewart-Brown, 'Printers of Chester', 116–47; T. Fawcett, 'Eighteenth-Century
Norfolk Booksellers: A Survey and Register', *Trans. of the Cambridge Bibliographical
Soc.*, vi (1972–6), 12–18; P. Morgan, 'Early Booksellers, Printers, and Publishers in
Stratford-upon-Avon', *TBAS*, lxvii (1947–8), 55–9; Guild Roll 1742, PCMSS; *Preston
Jnl.*, No. 104, 17–21 Sept. 1742; No. 195, 15–22 June 1744; *True British Courant*,
No. 22, 7 June 1745; and also Barry, 'Cultural Life of Bristol', 69–76, 352.

[45] *British Courant*, No. 278, 1–8 June 1750; and also Fawcett, 'Norfolk Booksellers',
14–15, for James Carlos and Thomas Eldridge; Feather, *Book Trade*, 80–1.

[46] *St Ives Post-Boy*, No. 20, 28 Oct. 1718, reproduced in P. Kaufman, 'The
Community Library: A Chapter in English Social History', *Trans. of the American
Philosophical Soc.*, new ser., lvii, Part 7 (1967), 8; *Keating's Stratford and Warwick
Mercury*, iii, No. 114, 9 Mar. 1752; Feather, *Book Trade*, 13.

[47] P. Kaufman, *Libraries and their Users* (London, 1969), 76–89; P. Kaufman,
'Readers and their Reading in Eighteenth-Century Lichfield', *Library*, 5th ser., xxviii,
No. 2 (1973), 108; *Wells Cathedral Library*, 2nd edn. (Wells, 1978), 3–4; F. C. and
P. E. Morgan, *Hereford Cathedral Libraries and Muniments* (Hereford, 1970), 9–10;
Briggs, *Wren*, 217–18; Students Diary, fos. 34–5.

of religious foundation widely accessible to laymen was the parochial library. In the early eighteenth century there was a movement to revitalize these collections, which culminated in the Parochial Libraries Act of 1709. New libraries were founded at Bedford (1700), Reigate (1701), Warwick (refounded *c*.1701), Maldon (*c*.1704), Beccles (*c*.1705), Doncaster (1726), and St Philip's Birmingham (1733). In 1736 the collection at St Nicholas's Newcastle-upon-Tyne was rehoused in a new extension to the church, which by 1745 accommodated around 5,000 volumes.[48] Closely allied to these collections were the ones belonging to the civic community and to schools. The golden age for founding town libraries was in the eighty years preceding the Restoration, but their holdings continued to be supplemented by donations and were usually properly maintained.[49] Many school libraries were intended for public as well as private use. When a visitor passed through Manchester in 1725 he discovered that at the College 'any person, though he be a stranger, has liberty to come into this place, and peruse what books he pleases'; the gift of 1,200 books to the Nottingham Blue-coat School in 1744 was seen as the 'foundation of a public library for the use of' educated society 'living . . . in the . . . town or within . . . eight computed miles from it'; and the records of the Shrewsbury School collection show the vast majority of listed users came from the community at large.[50]

For the serious reading public, the traditional type of urban library represented a valuable literary resource. But given such libraries' religious and moral associations, and their reliance upon benefactions as a source for new books, the majority of their stock might well have been of a rather old-fashioned or theological nature, and therefore of limited general appeal. More dynamic and influential were the new forms of lending facilities emerging in the eighteenth century. Foremost among these were the commercial circulating libraries, which were generally developed by booksellers as an adjunct to their businesses. The earliest known provincial example dates from 1718, when the Huntingdon bookseller George Barton advertised 'plays, or

---

[48] Kaufman, 'Community Library', 41-3; P. Morgan, 'St Mary's Library, Warwick', *TBAS*, lxxix (1960-1), 36-60; M. Ellwood, 'Library Provision in a Small Market Town 1700-1929', *Library History*, v (1979), 48-50; Kaufman, *Libraries and their Users*, 93-101; Money, *Experience and Identity*, 126; Brand, *Newcastle*, i. 269-70.

[49] Kaufman, 'Community Library', 38-41; Bristol Common Council Proceedings, 17 Nov. 1690, 27 Feb. 1690/1, 1 Dec. 1691, Bristol AO; Ison, *Bristol*, 93-4.

[50] Students Diary, fos. 54-5; quoted in Kaufman, 'Community Library', 44; Kaufman, *Libraries and their Users*, 130.

any other books to be let out to read by the week'. By the 1720s
establishments were operating in Bristol, Birmingham, and possibly
Bath and Norwich. Altogether there were at least thirty-six different
libraries based in twenty-three provincial towns before 1770.[51] In 1757
Newcastle-upon-Tyne boasted at least two such outlets, which
between them claimed a circulating stock of over 3,000 volumes.
Developed on the cutting-edge of the market, these collections were
far more attuned to fashionable literary taste than those of the
traditional institutions. Secular works were much better represented,
including a substantial though varying amount of fiction. At Samuel
Clay's shop in Warwick, almost three-quarters of the titles borrowed
over a nineteen-month period (August 1770 to March 1772) were
novels.[52]

Circulating libraries were ideally suited to a public pursuing reading
as a recreation. Their stock was up-to-date, and for the cost of
purchasing one book access could be obtained to many, multiplying
the amount of leisure time obtained from a given expenditure. Such
establishments were especially popular in the resorts, where there was
plenty of spare time to be filled. In 1767 a visitor to Tunbridge Wells
noted that the bookshop permitted customers to 'have what books you
please home to your lodging to read, and there being a great and well
chosen variety, I find it particularly useful and agreeable to me in bad
weather'.[53] At Bath the libraries became places of resort in their own
right. Leake's famous shop on the Terrace Walk, 'a spacious room,
filled from the cornice to the skirting', was a natural venue for the
company to gather in and while away the day, as a poem of 1748
suggested:

> Now with a motley throng, resorts the fop,
> To kill an hour, to Leake's fine spacious shop.

[51] The figures are largely derived from Kaufman, 'Community Library', 6–25, 50–3,
with additions from Fawcett, 'Norfolk Booksellers', 8–9, and Cranfield, *Development
of Provincial Newspaper*, 216–17. Barton's 'library' is only counted once. See also
H. M. Hamlyn, 'Eighteenth-Century Circulating Libraries in England', *Library*, 5th ser.,
i (1946–7), 197–222.

[52] J. Knott, 'Circulating Libraries in Newcastle in the Eighteenth and Nineteenth
Centuries', *Library History*, ii, No. 6 (1972), 228–30; Kaufman, 'Community Library',
11–19; J. Fergus, 'Eighteenth-Century Readers in Provincial England: The Customers of
Samuel Clay's Circulating Library and Bookshop in Warwick 1770–72', *Papers of the
Bibliographical Soc. of America*, lxxviii (1984), 179–80.

[53] Quoted in M. Barton, *Tunbridge Wells* (London, 1937), 342–3; Burr, *Tunbridge
Wells*, 117.

CAPER, whose learning lies below his knees,
With curious eye a tract on dancing sees;
He takes it home; first bids Leake set it down,
And to be à la mode subscribes his crown.
ILLITERATUS Greek aloud demands,
Who common English hardly understands.
And many just pop in, and look about,
And read a paragraph, and then pop out.

Nearby in the Abbey Churchyard was 'the little fan-makers', which offered its customers 'a well chosen collection of books' available on subscription, together with 'a good warm parlour', where the newspapers could be perused 'from eight o'clock in the morning till three in the afternoon, and after that till ten at night'.[54]

More circumspect and exclusive than the commercial circulating shops were the private subscription societies or libraries, which began to appear from the mid-eighteenth century. By 1769 at least nine towns had such institutions.[55] These were an offshoot of the private book club, which emerged much earlier, and of which nineteen have been recorded for the years before 1770. Almost all were based in towns, though they were frequented by a mixed urban and rural clientele. The clubs bought publications on a group basis, circulated them among each other, and then sold them. It was an ideal way to keep abreast of the contemporary scene, a point reflected in their predominant areas of purchase: current reviews and annuals, politics, and topical affairs, followed by travel and geography, with notably small acquisitions of religious literature. Their members were largely drawn from the professions and gentry. One of the latter was Sir Roger Newdigate of Arbury in Warwickshire, who in the mid-eighteenth century was a diligent member of the nearby Atherstone club. In 1751 his diary records him attending the club on four occasions and borrowing sixteen items, at least one of which ran into four volumes. In June he brought home Smollett's recently published *Peregrine Pickle*, and also purchased for or from the club, 'Rabelais 5 vols. . . . Fielding's *Inquiry* . . . [and] Stevenham's *Garden*', a mixed collection

[54] E. C. Boyle (ed.), *The Orrery Papers* (London, 1903), i. 99–100; *Bath: A Poem* (London, Bath, and Bristol, 1748), 21–2; *Bath Advertiser*, No. 1, 18 Oct. 1755; and also Wood, *Bath*, 417–18, 439; M. Chandler, *A Description of Bath: A Poem* (London, 1734), 15.

[55] Kaufman, 'Community Library', 25–8.

of literature whose perusal must have afforded him a good deal of amusement.[56]

The importance of private subscription libraries and book clubs in spreading the printed word highlights the wider role that societies generally played in enhancing the facilities available for learning and pleasure. Contemporaries displayed a positive relish for founding and joining clubs, and some of these developed into national movements, like the Bucks and the Freemasons.[57] Though many of them had an underlying protective function, that of safeguarding their brethren against hard times by the practice of mutual benevolence, most were also committed to the cultural improvement of their members. This element naturally predominated in the so-called gentlemen's societies, where economic insurance was not a pressing need. One of the earliest of these associations, and in a way a prototype, was the Spalding Gentlemen's Society, founded in 1709 and formally established three years later. Maurice Johnson, its indefatigable secretary, deliberately kept a record of their meetings so as to encourage 'other gentlemen my acquaintance and friends in Lincoln City, Peterborough, Stamford, Boston, Oundle, Wisbech, and elsewhere, to institute and provide the like design, and hold correspondence with us. In some of these places this succeeded. . . .'[58]

The staple diet of the Spalding society was antiquarian studies, but members dabbled in a whole range of other intellectual pursuits, including history, music, medicine, botany, biology, ornithology, literature, and technology, as well as maintaining their own museum, library, and physic garden. Some of these specific areas engendered specialist clubs. The growing interest in the natural world, perhaps as a reaction to urbanization, encouraged the formation of gardening and related societies. At Norwich, where there had been an annual florists' 'feast' or competition since at least 1631, there were separate natural

[56] P. Kaufman, 'English Book Clubs and their Role in Social History', *Libri*, xiv, No. 1 (1964), 1-31; Lancashire RO, PR.2847, Miscell. (5), 4; Newdigate Diaries, 4 Jan. 1750/1, 21 June, 23 Aug., and 20 Sept. 1751.

[57] R. Porter, *English Society in the Eighteenth Century* (Harmondsworth, 1982), 172-3; J. Brewer, 'Commercialization and Politics', in McKendrick *et al.*, *Birth of a Consumer Society*, 217-24; J. Hamill, *The Craft: A History of Freemasonry* (n.p., 1986), chaps. 1-5; Money, *Experience and Identity*, chaps. 5-6.

[58] D. M. Owen (ed.), *The Minute-Books of the Spalding Gentlemen's Society 1712-1755*, Lincoln Record Soc., lxxiii (1981), p. ix; T. Fawcett, 'Measuring the Provincial Enlightenment: The Case of Norwich', *Eighteenth-Century Life*, new ser., xviii, Part 1 (1982), 15; T. Fawcett, 'Self-Improvement Societies: The Early "Lit. and Phils."', in *Life in the Georgian Town*, 16-17.

history and botanical societies by the mid-eighteenth century, and during the early Georgian period flower-shows and clubs styling themselves 'Sons of Flora' were a common feature of provincial towns.[59] For many contemporaries horticulture was closely allied to science. Developments in London, particularly the founding of the Royal Society in 1660, have dominated the history of scientific societies, but groups also met shortly after the Restoration in major provincial centres, such as Norwich, York, Exeter, and Oxford, a trend which continued in the following century. From about the 1710s these societies could call upon the services of professional itinerant lecturers, who by the middle of the century were carrying their knowledge around a wide circuit of provincial capitals, shire towns, and resorts. The close association between fashionable social centres and the dissemination of scientific ideas suggests that for most consumers the subject was not a serious academic discipline, but merely one constituent in a diverse package of polite cultural pursuits, intended as much to amuse as instruct. As Burr noted of the lectures available at Tunbridge Wells in the 1760s, they were 'superficial enough to entertain the imagination without fatiguing the understanding'.[60]

The role of lectures in spreading the fruits of learning raises the broader issue of educational provision as a whole. Traditionally, historians have taken a rather dim view of the post-Restoration record in this field, comparing it unfavourably with the achievements of the Tudors and early Stuarts.[61] However, recent research, focusing less on the larger educational institutions, has revealed a more positive

[59] K. Thomas, *Man and the Natural World* (Harmondsworth, 1984), 229; Priestley and Fenner, *Shops and Shopkeepers*, 28-30; Fawcett, 'Measuring the Provincial Enlightenment', 16; R. E. Duthie, 'English Florists' Societies and Feasts in the Seventeenth and First Half of the Eighteenth Centuries', *Garden History*, x (1982), 17-35; J. H. Plumb, 'The Acceptance of Modernity', in McKendrick *et al.*, *Birth of a Consumer Society*, 324-5; Everitt, 'Urban Inn', 117-18; Barry, 'Cultural Life of Bristol', 153-4; Looney, 'Advertising and Society', 176-7.

[60] M. Hunter, *Science and Society in Restoration England* (Cambridge, 1981), 66-74, 81-3, 191-2; A. E. Musson (ed.), *Science, Technology, and Economic Growth in the Eighteenth Century* (London, 1972), 60-1, 76-8, 136-47; R. Porter, 'Science, Provincial Culture, and Public Opinion in Enlightenment England', *British Jnl. for Eighteenth-Century Studies*, iii (1980), 20-46; Plumb, 'Acceptance of Modernity', 328-9; Barry, 'Cultural Life of Bristol', 262-5; Fawcett, 'Measuring the Provincial Enlightenment', 15-16; Turner, *Science and Music*, 84-5; Wood, *Bath*, 438-9; Burr, *Tunbridge Wells*, 124.

[61] L. Stone, 'The Educational Revolution in England 1560-1640', *Past and Present*, xxviii (1964), especially 73-5; L. Stone, 'Literacy and Education in England 1640-1900', *Past and Present*, xlii (1969), especially 85, 131-2, 137; Clark and Slack, *Towns in Transition*, 152-5.

picture. Far from declining, urban schooling was a growth industry, with a proliferation of small private academies. Syllabuses were acquiring an increasingly modern character, and the teaching body was becoming both larger and more professional.[62] Many of the subjects taught were of an overtly utilitarian kind, but there was also a surprisingly extensive range of institutions and individuals engaged in the business of education for leisure. Much of this was sandwiched into the broader school curriculum, though there also existed specialist agencies. Early eighteenth-century York possessed a riding school with its own premises, as did Manchester in the middle of the century, and from 1760 the theatre at the latter town hosted an academy run by Signor Fabiano, 'to teach young ladies and gentlemen a minuet or hornpipe, in the most elegant and genteelest taste'. From 1763 Birmingham had the services of a drawing school on Snow Hill, where, in addition, lessons on the German flute could be taken. Language instruction was widely available, and though of course this had a certain practical worth, it was also, as an advertisement in the *Norwich Mercury* makes clear, valued for the social cachet it conferred: 'a Norwich la langue Francoise est enseignee . . . par G. R. Hue . . . il ne doute pas, qu'il n'y ait des messieurs et des dames qui seront ravis d'une occasion si favourable [*sic*] sur tout le Francois etant et devenant en practique comme il faut aujourd'hui parmi les personnes de qualite. . . .' ('the French language is taught at Norwich . . . by G. R. Hue . . . he does not doubt that there are ladies and gentlemen who will be delighted to take advantage of such an opportunity, especially as French is, and is becoming in practice a social necessity today among people of quality. . . .')[63]

Education for leisure was particularly associated with aspiring young ladies, for whom the acquisition of the social graces was a serious business, since it was intimately related to their success in marriage and later life. Specialist gentlewomen's academies formed a sizeable sector of the education industry, and appear to have been concentrated in the shire towns and resorts. At Shrewsbury Fiennes found 'a

---

[62] J. H. Plumb, 'The New World of Children in Eighteenth-Century England', *Past and Present*, lxvii (1975), 71–80; Holmes, *Augustan England*, 43–80; Cranfield, *Development of Provincial Newspaper*, 215–16; Feather, *Book Trade*, 33–5.

[63] House Book, 2 Sept. 1727, YCA; Hodgkinson and Pogson, *Early Manchester Theatre*, 29–31, which includes the quotation from the *Manchester Mercury*; Money, *Experience and Identity*, 136; *Norwich Mercury*, 11 Aug. 1750, quoted in Cranfield, *Development of Provincial Newspaper*, 216. I am indebted to Sonia Spurdle for her translation of the last item.

very good school for young gentlewomen for learning work, and behaviour, and music', and Drake argued that one of the reasons that the gentry resided in York was because it was 'very well qualified for the education of their children, especially females, in all the necessary accomplishments belonging to that sex'. The instruction of the daughter of Wells physician Claver Morris began in her native town, where from 1705 she attended a day-school and took violin and singing lessons, until 1708 when she was moved to a dancing academy in Salisbury for about a year. When the Cornish vicar John Penrose visited Bath in 1766, he and his wife took the opportunity to survey the available educational facilities with the intention of placing their 14-year-old daughter in a suitable establishment. His wife visited and carefully scrutinized a boarding-school, where the extra costs included 'three pounds a year learning to dance . . . One ball in the year, at which is paid five shillings; and five shillings a year for a seat in the church.' Fashionable urban centres like Bath provided an ideal setting for finishing schools, partly because the parents frequently resided in or visited such places and were able to oversee their offspring's education, and partly because these towns enjoyed the full round of public recreations into which the young belles were to be initiated.[64]

3. TIME AND PLACE

The provision of fashionable leisure was not a random affair, but was organized within relatively well defined temporal and spatial contexts. There was a time and a place for everything. The basic framework was provided by two parallel (and largely annual) social cycles. In the first, events were sustained over a lengthy time-span or 'season', and in the second, they were confined to a brief period usually built around a traditional public occasion.

In the provincial capitals and shire towns the bulk of cultural activities were packed into the 'winter season'. The prototype of this emerged in London as early as Elizabethan times. Its impact was reinforced after the Glorious Revolution by the practice of holding regular and lengthy parliamentary sessions, which attracted substantial

[64] Fiennes, *Journeys*, 227; McInnes, *English Town*, 21; Drake, *Eboracum*, 240; Hobhouse, *Diary of a West Country Physician*, 31, 58; Penrose, *Letters*, 144, 146, 167, 171-2; and also Barry, 'Cultural Life of Bristol', 46-7, 192, 205.

numbers of the nobility, gentry, and their families to the capital.[65] No provincial town could hope to challenge the scale of the metropolitan season, but already by the late seventeenth century Norwich was beginning to imitate its example, and during the following century the more important social centres followed suit. At York the corporation in 1733 acknowledged the value of a permanent theatre as a means of encouraging the nobility and gentry 'to spend their winter seasons here', twelve years later Thomas Grimstone could write of how the city 'is extreme gay this winter, and very full of company', and in 1769 a visitor to the northern capital noted how 'there are . . . in winter all kinds of amusements to divert the company who resort here, as to London, from every part of the country round'.[66] The provision of music and drama was closely tied to this seasonal cycle. In mid-eighteenth-century York the Friday concerts were run between mid-October and mid-March, and later in the century the subscription series at Canterbury and Chichester were held on a fortnightly basis for six months during the winter.[67] The theatre season had a similar rhythm, though with greater emphasis on the phase after Christmas. The 1751-2 season at the Vine Theatre in Salisbury ran from December to the end of April, and at Norwich and York the first three or four months in the year also marked the boundaries of the main period of dramatic entertainment, the resident theatre companies treating this as their primary annual obligation before venturing out on circuit.[68]

Between late spring and early autumn fashionable society vacated London and the county centres to concentrate on the pleasures of their country estates, and to engage in outdoor pursuits such as horse-racing (which season ran largely from April to October) and cricket (from about May to September).[69] This left the metropolis, as one correspondent remarked in late August 1700, 'extreme empty', a view

[65] G. E. Mingay, *English Landed Society in the Eighteenth Century* (London, 1963), 156-8; Thomas, *Man and the Natural World*, 247; L. Stone, *An Open Élite? England 1540-1880* (Oxford, 1986), 160-2, 225-30; Stone, 'Residential Development', 174-5, 183.

[66] Corfield, 'Provincial Capital', 291; Everitt, 'Urban Inn', 117, 119; House Book, 29 Jan. 1732/3, YCA; HMC, *Grimstone MSS*, 49; HMC, *Verulam MSS*, 236.

[67] Drake, *Eboracum*, 240; Looney, 'Advertising and Society', 167-8; Sadie, 'Concert Life', 24-6.

[68] Hare, *Georgian Theatre*, 43-5, 60-1; Rosenfeld, *Strolling Players*, 51, 53, 61-2, 113, 118; Fawcett, *Music in Eighteenth Century Norwich*, 21.

[69] Borsay, 'Landscape and Leisure', 399; G. B. Buckley, *Fresh Light on 18th Century Cricket* (Birmingham, 1935), *passim*.

echoed by Lybbe Powys in July 1765, when she found 'the great city dull, dusty, and abandoned'. This diarist had visited York eight years earlier and discovered it wore a similar 'dull aspect', because, she was told, 'in summer all the principal inhabitants retire into the country'.[70] However, not all social centres were forsaken at this time of year: a number, indeed, had a critical role to play in the operation of the summer season.

When the gentry and citizens left London, one of the places they headed for was the resort. In July 1685 Laurence Clayton wrote from Tunbridge Wells, 'partly my pleasure has brought me hither, where all the good company that used to be in London are adjourned', and Defoe noted that the City businessmen took up family lodgings at Epsom during the summer.[71] The timing and duration of the season in particular spas varied according to their importance and the competition they faced from rivals. In early seventeenth-century Tunbridge Wells it ran from May to October, in eighteenth-century Bristol Hotwells from late April to about the end of September, while in the 1770s the height of activity at Cheltenham was between July and September, and at Matlock during July and August. Such places hibernated out of season. Defoe noted that at Epsom 'as it is full of mirth and gaiety in the summer, so the prospect in the winter presents you with little but good houses shut up, and windows fastened; the furniture taken down, the families removed, the walks out of repair, the leaves off of the trees, and the people out of the town'.[72] The cycle at Bath was more complex. Up until the Restoration, and perhaps for some time afterwards, the spa ran two seasons, one in spring and the other in autumn. Though later this was replaced by a single summer season, reflecting the normal arrangement in the resorts, by the early 1720s Bath had reverted to its traditional spring/autumn axis, and it was this pattern that held sway during the middle decades of the eighteenth century.[73] However, as Bath emerged as a long-term

[70] Warwickshire CRO, CR.1368, i, fo. 71; Powys, *Diaries*, 16, 85.

[71] HMC, *Egmont MSS*, ii. 159; Defoe, *Tour*, i. 161.

[72] Burr, *Tunbridge Wells*, 22; Little, 'Gloucestershire Spas', 175; Rudder, *Gloucestershire*, 335; Suffolk RO, E2/44/1, fo. 299; Defoe, *Tour*, i. 162.

[73] Lennard, 'Watering-Places', 25-6, 47-8; P. S. Brown, 'The Vendors of Medicines Advertised in Eighteenth-Century Bath Newspapers', *Medical History*, xix (1975), 355-6; Misson, *Memoirs*, 14; Wood, *Bath*, 85, 220, 437; *A Journey to Bath: An Heroic-Comic-Historic-, and Geographical Poem* (London, [1717]), 3, 19; *The Pleasures of Bath: With the First and Second Part of the Tipling Philosophers* (Bristol, 1721); *England Illustrated or, a Compendium of the Natural History, Geography,*

residential centre the seasonal factor began to decline in importance. In mid-June 1767 John Penrose noted that 'there is a deal of company now in Bath, though the season is out'; during the late 1750s and early 1760s George Lucy regularly resided in the spa over the winter months; and by 1780 the city's guides show that the most expensive period for hiring lodgings lasted the full nine months from September to May.[74]

The existence of a seasonal cycle of leisure resulted from a combination of practical and psychological forces. During the winter the countryside was inhospitable, outdoor recreations were often difficult to practise, and mobility could be severely restricted. Wood noted that in about the 1690s people 'seldom' came to Bath 'but in the summer time, when the roads were dry and passable', and in a similar vein Defoe remarked that in the winter 'the ordinary roads both to' Epsom 'and near it, except only on the side of the Downs, are deep, stiff, full of sloughs, and, in a word, unpassable'.[75] In such circumstances it was natural that during the inclement months of the year members of fashionable society should put down roots in a large, comfortable, and easily accessible town, where they could enjoy a sustained round of leisure. Though the provincial capitals and shire towns happily met these requirements in the winter, they appeared less attractive as warmer days arrived. Not only were the constraints on travel and country pleasures now relaxed, but the larger towns became notoriously dusty, dirty, and unhealthy.[76]

The character of the seasonal leisure cycle also reflected a considerable cultural input. Changes between winter and summer injected variety into the round of polite recreations, regularly compelling the beau monde to disband and reorganize into different social groups, meeting at different locations, and engaging in different pastimes. Thus leisured life was saved from the endemic threat of becoming intolerably boring. The close parallel between the leisure seasons and the natural divisions of the year also reinforced educated society's

Topography, and Antiquities Ecclesiastical and Civil, of England and Wales (London, 1764), ii. 212; Defoe, *Moll Flanders*, 1722, repr. (London, 1971), 108–10; Penrose, *Letters*, 138, 142, 149, 189; J. Hervey, *Letter-Books of John Hervey, First Earl of Bristol*, ed. S. H. A. H. (Wells, 1894), ii. 161, 176, 266, 268, 313, 328.

[74] Penrose, *Letters*, 201; Warwickshire CRO, L6/1451-71; McIntyre, 'Rise of a Resort Town', 208.

[75] Wood, *Bath*, 220; Defoe, *Tour*, i. 162.

[76] Wrigley and Schofield, *Population History*, 295.

developing myth of nature, particularly since the summer portion of the cycle overtly celebrated the outdoors and the countryside.

The recreational use of towns during the summer was due not only to the presence of the resorts, but also to the existence of a second cycle of fashionable leisure. Its events largely fell between spring and autumn, were often associated with an established public occasion, lasted for a relatively brief period of time, and generally recurred on an annual basis. One exception to the annual rule was the Preston Guild, which was held every twenty years. This was formally concerned with the registration of burgesses and the general governance of the town, but by the eighteenth century, if not before, the Guild had also become a huge festival of pleasure, directed particularly towards fêting the county and town élite.[77] Annual fairs, which were becoming increasingly recreationally rather than economically oriented, could also attract polite entertainments. In 1688 Colonel Thomas Bellingham attended at least three plays during the eight days of the August fair at Preston, and the fair at Salisbury in mid-March 1744 also attracted the services of a travelling theatre company. The most celebrated of the fairs patronized by the well-to-do was the one at Bury St Edmunds, which Macky described as lasting a fortnight and drawing 'all the neighbouring nobility and gentry . . . every afternoon, where they divert themselves in raffling till it is time to go to the comedy, which is acted here every night'.[78]

Due to their openness and plebeian clientele, fairs played only a small and declining role in the occasional cycle of fashionable leisure. Far more important were the assizes, held in the shire towns once or twice a year, usually during lent and summer. Because of their importance and prestige, these events attracted a substantial proportion of the county élite and their families, and naturally developed into a major feature of the provincial gentry's social calendar. The royal justices were always welcomed into town with great ceremony, and this set the tone for several days in which the melodrama in the court room was only one part of a wider package of entertainments. Fictional as

[77] Guild Rolls 1662–1762, PCMSS; [Kuerden], *Preston*, 47–89; *The Guild Merchant of Preston, with an Extract of the Original Charter* (Preston, [1762]), especially 14–17; W. A. Abram, *Memorials of the Preston Guilds* (Preston, 1882); R. D. Parker, 'The Changing Character of Preston Guild Merchant 1762–1862', *Northern History*, xx (1984), 108–26.

[78] T. Bellingham, *Diary of Thomas Bellingham*, ed. A. Hewitson (Preston, 1908), 4–7; Hare, *Georgian Theatre*, 37; M. P. Statham, 'The Bury Fairs', *Suffolk Review*, iv (1974), 131–2; Macky, *Journey*, i. 6.

opposed to real theatre was frequently provided. In early eighteenth-century York the managers Thomas Ager and Thomas Keregan leased premises for 'six weeks at Lent Assize and six weeks at Lammas Assize' to accommodate plays, and at Norwich the town's drama company regularly broke its summer circuit to appear at the city's sessions week. Concerts were also often specially mounted. The other major event in polite society's occasional recreational cycle was race week, which will be examined in a later chapter. Towards the mid-eighteenth century it was evident that the races, rather than the assizes, were becoming the climax of the social year. In 1736 Drake could write of York,

twice in the year the assizes . . . are held here. On which occasion, besides the men of business, did formerly resort a great number of our northern gentry to partake of the diversions that were usually set up in the city for that time. Of late years this is altered; and the grand meeting of the nobility and gentry of the North, and other parts of England, is now at York in or about the month of August; drawn thither by the hopes of being agreeably entertained, for a week, in horse-racing, balls, assemblies, etc.[79]

Just as *when* fashionable leisure activities occurred was determined by cyclical conventions of time, so *where* they took place followed a predictable, if not rigid pattern. During the early phase of its development, polite urban culture had to make do with facilities that already existed rather than enjoying the benefits of purpose-built accommodation. The most important of these generalized venues were inns and coffee-houses. The former stood at the apex of the victualling hierarchy, and grew remarkably in number between the reigns of Elizabeth and George III. With their ready provision of food, accommodation, stabling, and large public chambers, and their association with the more affluent, it was natural that they should adapt to service the growth in polite leisure.[80] Plays were frequently performed either inside one of the capacious rooms of a leading hostelry, or in a booth erected adjacent to it. Until 1758 the chief theatre in Norwich was at the White Swan, though the Angel, the Red Lion, and the King's

---

[79] Rosenfeld, *Strolling Players*, 54-5, 57, 59, 61, 109, 111, 176-7; Tilmouth, 'Provincial Concert Life', 10; Fawcett, *Music in Eighteenth-Century Norwich*, frontispiece; Hobhouse, *Diary of a West Country Physician*, 84; Drake, *Eboracum*, 241.

[80] Everitt, 'Urban Inn', 91-137; T. M. James, 'The Inns of Croydon 1640-1840', *Surrey Archaeological Collections*, lxviii (1971), 109-29; P. Clark, *The English Alehouse: A Social History 1200-1830* (London, 1983), 6-10.

Arms were also used during the early eighteenth century.[81] The more important inns also regularly hosted music-making. In the mid-1760s one of the venues for concerts at Banbury was 'Mr Barker's room' at the Three Tuns and when in 1726 the Wells music club was forced to leave the Close Hall, 'We all agreed, except the vicars, to have a club every Tuesday night (as before) at the Mitre, and when we had hands to have music.'[82] Inns might additionally cater for more cerebral pastimes. The book club at Huntingdon met at the George, that at Ely and Atherstone at the Red Lion in their respective towns, and in 1760 the Angel at Yeovil housed an antiquarian museum containing 'curiosities of every sort its owner can collect—as china, pictures, shells, antiques, etc., all ranged in order. There is two dishes of Roman earth', and a lamp said to have been 'dug out of the ruins of Herculaneum'.[83]

The real seat of intellectual delights was the coffee-house. The earliest known example opened in Oxford in 1650, and though it was in London that the coffee-house really developed and proliferated, the provinces also shared in the trend. Bristol, where coffee-houses were to be especially popular, had perhaps four as early as 1666, Ipswich possessed two in 1696, Northampton two in 1722, and Macky records two each in Newmarket and Bury St Edmunds, as well as discovering at Shrewsbury 'the most coffee-houses round it that ever I saw in any town: but when you come into them, they are but alehouses, only they think that the name of coffee-house gives a better air'.[84] Such establishments were primarily information centres and talk-shops. In 1719 the French traveller Misson found them to be 'extremely convenient. You have all the manner of news there; you have a good fire, which you may sit by as long as you please; you have a dish of

---

[81] Rosenfeld, *Strolling Players*, 21-2, 64-6, 116, 163, 173, 176, 180-1; Burley, *Players of East Anglia*, 1-4; and also Hare, *Georgian Theatre*, 21, 38; *VCH Oxfordshire*, x. 14.

[82] J. S. W. Gibson, 'The Three Tuns in the Eighteenth Century', *Cake and Cockhorse*, viii (1979), 5; Hobhouse, *Diary of a West Country Physician*, 42, 133-4; and also Brown, 'Colchester in the Eighteenth Century', 163; Fawcett, *Music in Eighteenth-Century Norwich*, 5, 21-2, 37; Looney, 'Advertising and Society', 174.

[83] Kaufman, 'English Book Clubs', 5, 9; Newdigate Diaries, 15 May 1752; Powys, *Diaries*, 78-9.

[84] A. Ellis, *The Penny Universities: A History of the Coffee-Houses* (London, 1956), especially 192-222; Barry, 'Cultural Life of Bristol', 100-2; B. Lillywhite, *London Coffee-Houses* (London, 1963); Macky, *Journey*, i. 5, 128; ii. 140. For other provincial coffee-houses see *VCH York*, 199, 246; *VCH Wiltshire*, vi. 141; Bellingham, *Diary*, 27, 39, 44, 105; T. Kemp, 'Warwick Registers', *TBAS*, xlv (1919), 14.

coffee; you meet your friends for the transaction of business, and all
for a penny, if you don't care to spend more.'[85] Most carried a wide
range of newspapers and many offered writing facilities.[86] These
provisions were particularly important in the spas, since good
communications were of critical importance to the visitors. At
Tunbridge Wells, where a plan of 1739 shows three coffee-houses on
the Walks, a gentleman subscribed 'a crown or more' to his favoured
venue, entitling 'him to the use of pens, ink, paper, etc.'. In mid-
eighteenth-century Bath the most fashionable rendezvous for coffee
was Morgan's, whose clientele were nicely caricatured in a poem of
1748:

> CHREMES sits scheming on affairs of state,
> And on his shoulders bears all Europe's weight:
> He cannot drink his coffee with a *goût*,
> 'Till he has read the papers thro and thro:
>
> .   .   .   .
>
> RATTLE, joined by a whole unthinking crowd,
> At least once ev'ry day calls out, aloud,
> Boy, does the London post go out? I pray:[87]

Coffee rooms were frequently used by clubs and discussion groups.
The early meetings of the Spalding Gentlemen's Society were held at
'Mr Younger's coffee-house', and at Bath in 1730 the informal intellectual circle of which Viscount Percival was a member met at one of
the spa's establishments to consider historical problems such as the
Reformation, the antiquity of Parliament, and 'Queen Elizabeth's
reign, and her putting Mary, Queen of Scots, to death'.[88]

Beyond the comfortable accommodation of an inn or coffee-house,
polite leisure had to seek out the best facilities it could. Adequate
space was a critical requirement, particularly in the case of theatre,
where plays were not infrequently performed in barns and stables. At
Bath in about the 1690s 'a stable by the Abbey Gate was appropriated
for a theatre', and when Edward Pigott visited Cheltenham in 1776,
he recorded that 'a troop of comedians acts twice a week . . . they don't

[85] Misson, *Memoirs*, 39–40.

[86] Cranfield, *Development of Provincial Newspaper*, 11–12, 182–3, 200; Hobhouse,
Diary of a West Country Physician, 18, 52.

[87] Ellis, *Penny Universities*, 213–14; Burr, *Tunbridge Wells*, 115; Macky, *Journey*, i.
89; *Bath: A Poem*, 20; Wood, *Bath*, 417, 438; Penrose, *Letters*, 139; Students Diary,
fos. 42, 118.

[88] Owen, *Spalding Gentlemen's Society*, p. x; HMC, *Egmont MSS*, Diary i. 108–13,
117–18.

act so very bad, but the barn is inconvenient, cold, and dirty, nevertheless I have seen worse'.[89] Public buildings must have represented rather more salubrious venues, and town, guild, and market halls were among the most regularly used premises for drama and music. During the seventeenth century the room over the Guildhall at Bath doubled as a theatre, and in early eighteenth-century York plays were performed at the Merchant Taylors' Hall, St Anthony's Hall, and the Thursday Market House.[90] The Three Choirs Festival mounted some of its meetings in the Guildhall at Worcester, the Booth Hall at Gloucester, and schoolrooms at both Worcester and Hereford.[91] However, the festival was primarily conducted in the cities' three great cathedrals, and this was indicative of the wide use of churches and religious buildings for musical entertainments, especially those of a sacred character. Secular music was a staple fare of pleasure gardens and assembly rooms,[92] and the latter might also be used for drama. Both the early rooms in Bath appear to have possessed theatres: at Harrison's the auditorium was located in the basement, although puppet performances were also mounted upstairs.[93]

During this early period of growth most polite leisure activities had to be housed in generalized accommodation. Specialized music rooms appear to be unknown outside London, with the exception of the Holywell Music Room (built *c*.1742-8) Oxford, and possibly a concert room advertised at Bath in 1755.[94] Libraries enjoyed a space of their

[89] Wood, *Bath*, 220; Pigott Diary, i, article 457; Hutton, *History of Birmingham*, 125; Rosenfeld, *Strolling Players*, 21-2; Hare, *Georgian Theatre*, 59.

[90] Wood, *Bath*, 214; Barbeau, *Bath*, 19 n. 7; Drake, *Eboracum*, 315-16; Rosenfeld, *Strolling Players*, 66, 107, 110-11, 127; and also *Suffolk Mercury or St Edmund's Bury Post*, xvi, No. 4, 24 May 1725; Brown, 'Colchester in the Eighteenth Century', 163; Hare, *Georgian Theatre*, 59; Simmons, *Leicester*, 119; Hodgkinson and Pogson, *Early Manchester Theatre*, 6.

[91] *Gloucester Jnl.*, xxxv, No. 1789, 7 Sept. 1756; Shaw, *Three Choirs Festival*, 12; and also Barker, *Bristol at Play*, 8; Money, *Experience and Identity*, 81.

[92] S. Sydenham, *Bath Pleasure Gardens of the 18th Century, Issuing Metal Admission Tickets* (Bath, 1969), 4-6; Fawcett, *Music in Eighteenth-Century Norwich*, 29-32; Smith, *Music in Birmingham*, 10-11; Brand, *Newcastle*, ii. 538; *VCH Warwickshire*, viii. 224; Margaret Luttrell to Henry Luttrell, 23 May 1759, Somerset RO, DD/L (Luttrell MSS); Assembly Rooms Minute Book, 24 Mar. 1732/3, YCA; Hill and Dent, *Old Square*, 84-5; Wood, *Bath*, 438-9; Barker, *Bristol at Play*, 9; Young, *History of British Music*, 312; *New Grove*, xvi. 421.

[93] Wood, *Bath*, 443-4; Wood, *Plan of Bath*, items 34, 35; Hervey, *Letter-Books*, ii. 278; Hare, *Georgian Theatre*, 62.

[94] Harley, *Purcell's London*, 147-9; J. H. Mee, *The Oldest Music Room in Europe: A Record of Eighteenth-Century Enterprise at Oxford* (London and New York, 1911), 7-8; *Bath Advertiser*, No. 1, 18 Oct. 1755.

own, almost by definition, though this was invariably attached to some larger institution like a church, school, or, in the case of commercial circulating libraries, a bookshop. A splendid exception was the city library in King Street Bristol, completely rebuilt to a Palladian design between about 1738 and 1740 at a cost of £1,300.[95] One area of leisure where specialized accommodation managed to make significant progress before the end of our period, was that of drama. This was understandable given the considerable spatial and technological demands of theatre, and the necessity for the audience to have a clear view of the actors. Public buildings often required adaptation to take performances, and this could be troublesome and potentially damaging. One solution adopted was to construct a temporary booth, or in the case of puppeteers to transport their own portable stage (no doubt one of their attractions).[96] But the only satisfactory long-term answer was to provide specially constructed or converted theatres. Appendix 3 lists twenty-six towns where such premises probably existed before 1770.

Some of the earliest auditoriums date back to the very beginning of the eighteenth century, such as those built in Bath in 1705 and in Bristol the following year, but the great bulk of theatre construction seems to have occurred from the mid-1740s. Many of these premises were built on a limited budget and were probably small and primitive inside. However, a number involved a considerable outlay and were capacious centres of entertainment. The Borough Walls Theatre in Bath (opened 1705) cost £1,300 to build, the Jacob's Wells (1729) and the King Street (1766) Theatres Bristol both around £5,000, and the Theatre Royal Liverpool (1772) £6,000; the theatre at Colchester (1764) held an audience of 200, the rebuilt playhouse in the Mint Yard at York (1765) about 550, and that in Northgate Street Sheffield (1762) 800. The York establishment was described in the local newspaper as 'by far the most spacious in Great Britain, Drury Lane and Covent Garden excepted, and for convenience and elegance it is thought to be equal, if not superior, to either of them', and the *Norwich Gazette* welcomed the city's new theatre in 1758 with the claim that it 'is allowed by all connoisseurs and judges to be the most perfect and complete structure of the kind in this kingdom. It is most

---

[95] Ison, *Bristol*, 93-4.
[96] Rosenfeld, *Strolling Players*, 111; *Guild Merchant of Preston*, 16; Hare, *Georgian Theatre*, 59; McIntyre, 'Health and Pleasure Resorts', 199; Speaight, *Puppet Theatre*, 150.

admirably constructed for seeing and hearing'.[97] Only one other recreation matched drama's investment in purpose-built accommodation, the assemblies. It is to this subject that we turn in the next chapter.

[97] C. W. Chalklin, 'Capital Expenditure on Building for Cultural Purposes in Provincial England 1730-1830', *Business History*, xxii (1980), 52-4; *York Courant*, 8 Jan. 1765, quoted in Fitzsimmons, 'Theatre Royal, York', 172; *Norwich Gazette*, 28 Jan. 1758, quoted in Rosenfeld, *Strolling Players*, 91.

6

Arenas of Display

Of all the new leisure facilities that developed in the post-Restoration town, perhaps those which most reflected the elegance of Georgian urban culture were the public assemblies and walks. Dancing and walking might be superficially viewed as a form of exercise. Yet it is clear that recreation was of only minor importance to the participants when compared with the opportunities these pastimes provided for undiluted socializing and personal display. Other activities, such as visits to the theatre or races, also met this purpose, but assemblies and walks concentrated on it almost exclusively. Without an actor or a horse to divert their attention, the company were propelled into contact with each other to gossip and flirt, to see and be seen.

1. ASSEMBLIES

Defoe claimed that 'the keeping up assemblies among the younger gentry was first set up' in York, and it has been suggested that they already operated in the city before the Civil War.[1] After the Restoration there was open-air dancing on the bowling-greens at Bath and Tunbridge Wells, and the latter may have had assembly rooms as early as the 1650s or 1660s, and Buckingham from about 1670.[2] But the rise of assemblies as a country-wide phenomenon dates from the turn of the century. Macky, writing in the early 1700s, claimed that they existed 'in all the great towns of the nation', and that 'formerly the country ladies were stewed up in their fathers' old mansion houses, and seldom saw company, but at an assize, a horse-race, or a fair'. Defoe similarly suggested their modernity in his *Tour*, published

[1] Defoe, *Tour*, ii. 230; R. Wittkower, *History of York Assembly Rooms* (York, 1951), 2.
[2] Barbeau, *Bath*, 19 n. 5; A. Hamilton, *Count Grammont at the Court of Charles II*, ed. and trans. N. Deakin (London, 1965), 154; Burr, *Tunbridge Wells*, 38, 44-5; Clark and Slack, *Crisis and Order*, 15.

between 1724 and 1726, when he criticized 'the new mode of forming assemblies, so much, and so fatally now in vogue'.[3] By the mid-eighteenth century the novelty of an earlier generation had become part of the established urban scene. Appendix 5 lists over sixty towns and spas which by 1770 had experimented with assemblies or assembly rooms, and there must have been many more. It shows that such facilities were a regular feature of the resorts, regional centres, and provincial capitals, not to mention a number of ordinary market towns.

The history of the assemblies in York and Bath amply demonstrates the development of the new institution. Despite earlier signs of activity, there is little evidence of regular meetings in York until the 1710s. Originally housed in the King's Manor, formerly the home of the Council in the North, the entertainments were later transferred to a private house in Minster Yard, and here they were observed by Macky.[4] This makeshift accommodation continued until the new Blake Street rooms, designed by Lord Burlington, provided the assemblies with a new and lavish home. Proposals for building the establishment were published in March 1730, the foundation stone was laid exactly a year later, and the rooms were opened for August race week 1732, though work on the fabric continued for some time after this date (see Fig. 13).[5] And more down-market facilities were also operated: In 1732 'the assembly house in Ogleforth' offered a series of cut-price balls, so 'that all persons of every rank and degree may not complain of being excluded from any part of the town diversions, during the races'.[6]

Developments in Bath pressed ahead rather more rapidly. By the end of the seventeenth century the bowling-green had given way as a venue for the assemblies to more commodious surroundings. In 1696 a visitor noted that there were 'balls every night in the town hall', and two years later Fiennes commended the 'very fine hall which is set on

---

[3] Macky, *Journey*, ii. 41; Defoe, *Tour*, i. 115.

[4] Drake, *Eboracum*, 240; *VCH York*, 245; McInnes, *English Town*, 21; Macky, *Journey*, ii. 211.

[5] Printed 'Proposals for Building, by Subscription, Assembly Rooms, in the City of York', YCA, M.23/3; Assembly Rooms Minute Book, *passim*, YCA; *Leeds Mercury*, No. 300, 9–16 Mar. 1730/1; G. S. Thomson (ed.), *Letters of a Grandmother 1732–1735* (London, 1943), 58; *VCH York*, 531. I owe the reference in the *Leeds Mercury* to John Quinn.

[6] *Yorkshire Herald*, 7 Aug. 1732, quoted in J. Fairfax-Blakeborough, *Northern Turf History* (London, n.d.), iii. 51.

Fig. 13.   The Great Room, Assembly Rooms (1731–*c*.1733), Blake Street, York

pillars which they use for the balls and dancing'.[7] Within a decade the spa obtained its first purpose-built establishment, when Thomas Harrison opened his commercial rooms in 1708. A large new ballroom was added twelve years later, and in 1749 the facilities were further remodelled and enlarged. After 1730 they faced competition from Lindsey's (itself improved in 1748), which was erected on the opposite side of the Terrace Walk (see Fig. 14).[8] The physical expansion of Bath provided the impetus for change. The building of Lindsey's coincided with the first of the major extramural developments to the west of the city, and when (during the 1740s) Wood was engaged in the construction of the Parades, he included in his plans a new assembly house. This was designed on an extraordinarily grand scale (the ballroom was two and a half times the size of either Harrison's or Lindsey's), and it self-consciously aspired to emulate the new rooms in York.[9] Though the Parades went ahead the assembly scheme proved abortive, and Bath had to wait another thirty years for new facilities. The stimulus

   [7] HMC, *Hastings MSS*, ii. 279; Fiennes, *Journeys*, 236; and also Wood, *Bath*, 220.
   [8] Wood, *Bath*, 225, 242, 245, 250, 319–20; Ison, *Bath*, 49–50.
   [9] Printed 'Proposals for Erecting by Subscription an Assembly House in the City of Bath', Bristol AO, 04479(2); Wood, *Bath*, 320.

Fig. 14. The Grand or North Parade (1740–8), Bath, *c*.1777. On the right is Harrison's old assembly house (1708, extended 1720 and 1749), and in the distance the Terrace Walk (1728)

on this occasion came from the mid-century building developments on the lower part of Lansdown Hill (including the Circus and the Royal Crescent), which altered the residential orientation of the city and left the old rooms stranded. To fill the gap, as well as to cater for the spa's rising population, the splendid Upper Rooms were built (1769–71) just to the east of the Circus (see Map 2). The lower rooms inevitably declined after this. Lindsey's was converted into a warehouse, though Harrison's continued to operate until a fire in 1820.[10]

The assemblies mounted in York, Bath, and elsewhere can be divided into two types, which roughly correspond to the two leisure cycles described in the previous chapter. On the one hand, there were the meetings of a regular nature sustained over a lengthy period, and on the other, there were those associated with some special and relatively brief occasion. The regular assemblies were the staple of the provincial town's social round. Frequently they met on a weekly basis, as at Salisbury, Winchester, Shrewsbury, Northampton, and Manchester,

[10] Ison, *Bath*, 49–54; *Bath Assembly Rooms*, National Trust Guide (1979); Pigott Diary, i, article 477; J. Collinson, *The History and Antiquities of the County of Somerset* (Bath, 1791), i. 51–2.

though monthly cycles also occurred.[11] Fashionable residents and neighbouring gentry often became subscribers, purchasing a ticket that admitted them to a defined series of balls. In York a fee of half a crown (a common rate) was charged for a 'quarter' of ten Monday meetings. The operation of the regular assemblies in the northern capital, as in most county centres, reflected the influence of a pronounced winter season. The average ticket issue for the forty-seven quarters between 1732 and 1747 was 200, but for the sessions beginning in January or February this rose to between 260 and 280.[12] In the winter, York's assemblies were held on a consecutive weekly basis, but during the summer they were staged only irregularly. Of the 470 meetings held between 1732 and 1747, 84 per cent were packed into the seven months from October to April, and a mere 16 per cent into the five months from May to September. June was particularly barren, having only six balls during the period.

The regular assemblies in the resorts were run on a rather different basis than those in the shire towns. Not only were they generally concentrated in the summer 'holiday' season, but also, because they were catering for visitors whose time was largely devoted to recreation, they had to provide a more intensive level of service. Cheltenham, Bristol Hot Wells, Bath, and Tunbridge Wells offered twice-weekly assemblies in mid-century, the latter two allocating different nights to each of their rooms. Earlier in the century Macky reported that balls were held four times a week at Tunbridge, and visitors to Scarborough in 1733 and Matlock in 1768 recorded dancing every evening.[13] Burr suggests that admission to the Tunbridge balls was by individual ticket, 'half a crown each for the gentlemen, and one shilling each for the ladies', whereas Wood implies that the Bath assemblies were organized on a subscription basis, the head of a family contributing 'two guineas at the assembly houses towards the balls, and music in the Pump House, for which he is entitled to three tickets every ball night'.[14]

[11] Macky, *Journey*, ii. 41–2, 140–1; Everitt, 'Urban Inn', 117; Aikin, *Manchester*, 187; *Gentleman's Magazine*, xxv (1755), 163; Gibson, 'Three Tuns', 5; Brown, 'Colchester in the Eighteenth Century', 163.

[12] This excludes tickets issued in the tenth week of the previous quarter, which could be used for the succeeding quarter. The evidence is drawn from Assembly Rooms Ledger, YCA. The figures might be slightly affected by a gap in the records Mar.–Sept. 1738.

[13] Hart, *Cheltenham*, 127; Powys, *Diaries*, 49; Wood, *Bath*, 443; Burr, *Tunbridge Wells*, 120; Macky, *Journey*, i. 91; A. Rowntree (ed.), *The History of Scarborough* (London and Toronto, 1931), 257; HMC, *Verulam MSS*, 233.

[14] Burr, *Tunbridge Wells*, 121; Wood, *Bath*, 417, 443; and also Whyman, 'Margate before the Railway', 142.

Alongside the regular assemblies ran the occasional ones. Several of these were staged to highlight events of local and national importance. In 1747 Preston corporation agreed to mount a public ball to mark the fact that their patron, Lord Strange, had 'lately brought his lady to town', and many urban centres arranged balls to celebrate coronations and royal birthdays.[15] These were of course cyclical events, and this was the time scheme for most occasional assemblies. Preston Guild, held only every twenty years, compensated for its infrequency by offering a surfeit of balls. During the month it met in 1762 there were no less than five every week: two Grand Balls on Monday and Friday, 'to which every person who went properly dressed was admitted', the Ladies' Assemblies on Tuesday and Thursday, and the Trade Assembly on Wednesday. Occasional assemblies were more commonly associated with annual events. At Bury St Edmunds' fair the balls were probably the most important of the entertainments on offer, and the Three Choirs Festival was normally enlivened by the presence of evening dances.[16]

Assemblies were invariably the social high spot of sessions and race weeks. When in March 1734 the regular Monday assembly's meeting at York coincided with the assizes, it was ordered that the assembly rooms' grand hall, which was normally closed during the winter (and a smaller adjoining room used), 'be fitted and cleaned out . . . and the lustres all got up and illuminated', so as to accommodate the expected crowds. Five years later the directors agreed to an application from 'several ladies' to 'give leave to Mr Haughton to have the use of the rooms for his ball . . . in the ensuing assize week'. In 1763 a correspondent reported on the 'two exceeding good balls' at the Salisbury assizes, finding 'no fault but that the sheriff being in high spirits at being so well attended . . . he made us drink much higher than I approved of . . . the sheriff côuld not get to his lodgings [without] some supporters, and Lord Seymour Webb . . . walked into the dirtiest ditch . . . and came out the most dismal figure . . . for he had been in the sewers'. When three years later John Mordaunt was touring the North East, he visited both Durham and Newcastle during the assizes, at the former being pressed to 'throw aside our travelling dress, curls,

[15] Council Minutes, 8 Aug. 1747, PCMSS; Suffolk RO, E2/25 (Hanson Letters)/1, fo. 134A; Hervey, *Letter-Books*, ii. 303; Penrose, *Letters*, 198; Macmahon, *Beverley Corporation Minute-Books*, 42; Hodgkinson and Pogson, *Early Manchester Theatre*, 6.
[16] *Guild Merchant of Preston*, 16; Macky, *Journey*, i. 6; Defoe, *Tour*, i. 52; HMC, *Portland MSS*, vi. 150; Suffolk RO, E2/25/2, fos. 87, 153; Shaw, *Three Choirs Festival*, 13-14; *Gloucester Jnl.*, xxxv, No. 1789, 7 Sept. 1756.

and powder, and go to the ball', and at the latter accepting an invitation to attend 'the ball, a most crowded one, with chiefly the inhabitants of the town, which is full of wealthy people'. [17]

The assemblies arranged to mark special occasions were often brilliant spectacles, stage-managed to create a ritual splendour. During the Preston Guild of 1762 the stateroom of the new Guildhall, 'and the adjoining town hall (a spacious chamber) were, every assembly and ball night, illuminated by some hundreds of wax tapers, in several grand chandeliers, girandoles, and sconces. . . . These two rooms, being united, were capable of containing near one thousand people: which number, it was conjectured by many, appeared therein each ball night.' The entertainments arranged at Bath in 1738 to celebrate the Princess of Wales's birthday, and held in Harrison's old rooms, were an even grander affair:

A most magnificent ball was subscribed for . . . and the tickets that were delivered on that occasion are computed at about 1,500. The throng of people of all ranks was so great, that the doors, which were ordered not to be opened till six, were forced to be opened before four. There was such a brilliant appearance of the ladies that it was impossible the richness of their dress, every one endeavouring to outvie the other both in dress and jewels; and it's believed so rich a ball has not been seen here.

Not that all assemblies reached these dazzling heights, particularly at the smaller social centres. When Edward Pigott visited Cowbridge (Glamorgan) races in 1777, he dined at an ordinary at which 'all the ladies clogged at the top of the table and the gentlemen at the other end', before progressing to the ballroom, which was 'lighted with little glass lamps, placed on unpainted deal boards: the oil, they say, was half water so that half of them went out, and in their place a dozen tallow candles were stuck up'. Parsimonious the Welsh may have been, but they undoubtedly enjoyed themselves. Two years earlier, Sir John Cullum had ventured to the very limits of urban civilization, and visited St David's (Pembrokeshire) during the annual audit of the chapter. In the evening he attended 'the only dance which the Menevian misses have in the whole year', mounted in a granary lit by farthing candles stuck in balls of clay on the wall, at which the

<hr/>

[17] Assembly Rooms Minute Book, 9 Mar. 1733/4, 7 Mar. 1738/9, YCA; unidentified correspondent to Dolly Long, 29 July 1763, Wiltshire RO, 947 (Long MSS); Warwickshire CRO, CR.1368, v, fo. 36; and also Suffolk RO, E2/25/1, fos. 67, 71, 93.

revellers danced 'with more glee than can be met with in the most elegant rooms filled with the genteelest company'.[18]

Though assemblies rarely had to resort to the use of agricultural buildings, they were accommodated in a wide variety of premises. Inns were understandably a popular venue: Appendix 5 lists fourteen towns where hostelries were used. Some landlords saw a considerable commercial potential in the occasions, and converted a part of their premises into, or added on to them an elegant ballroom; the White Lion in Eye (Suffolk) and the Lion at Shrewsbury are still embellished with fine examples of this (see Fig. 15).[19] Another favourite location was the public building, such as guildhall, market house, and school; a number of new town halls were undoubtedly designed with assemblies in mind.[20] The halls built at Worcester and Warwick in the 1720s, and Doncaster in the 1740s contain fine ballrooms on their upper floors, as did the Exchange at Liverpool, which was opened in 1754 'with a splendid ball, graced by the presence of three hundred and forty ladies'.[21]

The inclusion of a capacious ballroom in the design of new civic buildings was symptomatic of a wider trend towards the acquisition of more specialized accommodation. In some cases this involved modifying existing premises, usually those already possessed of a large room that could be adapted for dancing. The theatre on St Augustine's Back, Bristol, and a school in the Square at Birmingham, were converted to this end.[22] Purpose-built establishments were of course preferable, and considerable progress had been made in obtaining these by 1770. Pioneering their development were the resorts, where there was a high level of demand and often a scarcity of facilities.[23]

---

[18] *Guild Merchant of Preston*, 17; *Lancashire Jnl.*, No. 23, 4 Dec. 1738; Pigott Diary, i, article 551; Suffolk RO, E2/20 (Cullum Correspondence)/1B, fo. 140.

[19] Keverne, *Old Inns*, 52, 125.

[20] Council Minutes, 20 Sept. 1728, PCMSS; *VCH Lancashire*, vii (London, 1912), 78; *VCH Warwickshire*, viii. 224; *VCH Yorkshire: East Riding*, i (London, 1969), 209; Hodgkinson and Pogson, *Early Manchester Theatre*, 6; C. Gill, *History of Birmingham*, Vol. 1: *Manor and Borough to 1865* (London, 1952), 68; Simmons, *Leicester*, 119; M. Walton, *Sheffield: Its Story and its Achievements*, 3rd edn. (Sheffield, 1952), 104; Grady, 'Public Buildings in the West Riding', Gazetteer, Barnsley and Rotherham; *Suffolk Mercury*, xxiv, No. 71, 7 May 1733; *Post-Boy*, No. 2415, 2–4 Nov. 1710. I owe this last reference to Geoffrey Holmes.

[21] *BE Worcestershire*, 323; *VCH Warwickshire*, viii. 431–2; Fairfax-Blakeborough, *Northern Turf History*, iii. 198–9; E. Baines, *History, Directory, and Gazetteer of the County Palatine of Lancaster*, 1824, repr. (Newton Abbot, 1968), i. 164.

[22] Barker, *Bristol at Play*, 9; Hill and Dent, *Old Square*, 84.

[23] Chalklin, 'Building for Cultural Purposes', 54–5.

Fig. 15.   The Ballroom, White Lion Hotel, Broad Street, Eye, Suffolk

Epsom had acquired two rooms by about 1710, the Long Room at
Bristol Hot Wells was built in 1722 (a second one opened in 1768)
and that at Scarborough by 1725 (a new assembly house was
constructed in about 1760), the rooms at Matlock were erected in
1734, Tunbridge Wells and Cheltenham each had two rooms by the
middle of the century, and an establishment was opened at Margate in
1769. Other provincial towns were slower to build specialized
premises, but by the middle of the century there are signs of widespread activity in this field. To the celebrated example of York (largely
completed by 1732), can be added Leeds (completed before 1726),
Wakefield (1727), Stamford (c.1727), Bungay (1736), Norwich
(1754), Bristol (1755), Sheffield (1762), Beverley (1763), Derby
(1764), Southampton (1767), and no doubt several other towns.[24] The
investment required for many of these projects must have been
substantial. The theatre and assembly house at Sheffield cost over
£3,000, a subscription of £3,600 was established for building the
Prince Street rooms in Bristol, Wood proposed raising £4,200 for his

[24] See Appendix 5.

abortive project on the Parades at Bath, the York rooms cost over £5,000, those at Newcastle-upon-Tyne (built 1774–6) about £6,700, and the bill for the Upper Rooms at Bath (1769–71) came to around £20,000.[25]

Visiting the assemblies was an elegant and prestigious pastime, and ✓ those attending expected to be surrounded by the most fashionable architecture and furnishings. Even inns expended some effort in this field, occasionally creating hidden gems of design. The ballroom added to the Lion at Shrewsbury in the 1770s contains tall arched windows with fine mouldings, two ornamental fireplaces and oval mirrors, a saucer dome in the centre of the ceiling, delicate stucco decoration on the walls and ceiling, and delightful paintings of dancers on the entrance door and the balustrade of the minstrels' gallery. A musician's gallery is also a feature that can be found at the White Lion in Eye (see Fig. 15), the George at St Neots, the Court House in Warwick, and on a more elaborate scale at Derby and Bath (Upper Rooms).[26]

The grandest establishments had considerable attention lavished on their design. The York rooms are one of the major creations of the English Palladian movement, and its famous 'Egyptian Hall' has been judged 'perhaps the most classical building of the early 18th century in Europe'. Contemporaries were fully aware of its architectural splendours. In 1757 Lybbe Powys noted that it was 'called the completest ballroom in England', a sentiment repeated by a visitor eleven years later, who described the hall as 'of its kind, the most magnificent in England . . . it is 120 feet in length, 40 feet in height, and same in breadth, supported by 44 corinthian columns of York stone, and illuminated by 44 large chandeliers' (see Fig. 13). If Wood's project for the Parades at Bath had materialized it would have rivalled this. His main room was to be larger than that at York, and was to be surrounded by an impressive gallery lined with thirty corinthian columns.[27] The ballroom was not the only feature of these palaces of pleasure. The establishments at York, Bristol (Prince

[25] Grady, 'Public Buildings in the West Riding', Gazetteer; Ison, *Bristol*, 109; Bristol AO, 04479(2); Assembly Rooms Minute Book, 7 Jan. 1731/2, YCA; Brand, *Newcastle*, i. 122; Ison, *Bath*, 51.

[26] Keverne, *Old Inns*, 52, 125; *BE Shropshire* (Harmondsworth, 1974), 284; C. T. Tebbutt, *St Neots* (Chichester, 1978), 125–6, 244–5; *BE Derbyshire* (London, 1953), plate 60b; Ison, *Bath*, 51.

[27] Wittkower, *York Assembly Rooms*, 19; Powys, *Diaries*, 17; HMC, *Verulam MSS*, 236; Bristol AO, 04479(2).

Street), Norwich, and Bath (Harrison's, Lindsey's, the Upper Rooms, and Wood's Parades proposal) contained whole suites of finely decorated rooms which could be used for activities other than dancing. When all these areas were opened on the night of a grand ball, they provided a labyrinth of spaces through which the company could circulate, and in which they could flirt, gossip, and intrigue.[28]

The administration of the assembly houses varied according to the type of establishment involved. Many were run on a purely commercial basis, with a proprietor handling all the arrangements. But there were also several semi-public rooms owned by a body of shareholders, such as the Prince Street rooms Bristol, the Upper Rooms Bath, and the Blake Street rooms York. There is some surviving evidence about the organization of the Blake Street rooms. The original shareholders numbered about 200.[29] They elected twelve directors at the annual general meeting, and these men, with the help of a secretary/steward, effectively ran the establishment. In the early years most of their time was absorbed in overseeing the construction work, but from about 1734 a routine pattern of administration began to emerge. Securing the financial viability of the rooms was obviously an important concern. However, this did not present any serious problems, since many shareholders appear not to have claimed their annual dividends: by 1754 the accumulated uncollected payments (covering 1736 to 1753) amounted to over £500, or about two years full interest.[30] Much of the income from the sale of tickets and letting of the rooms was used on maintenance and improvements. The chandeliers, with their delicate glass parts and pulley ropes (if the latter deteriorated the potential risk was great), were a constant source of attention.[31] During the early 1750s the facilities were substantially upgraded. Six stoves were purchased for the 'Great Room' so that it could be used during the winter, 'three pissing places, two without doors, and one within' were ordered to be added, and it was also agreed to allow the directors to spend almost £300 'to buy such furniture or make such improvements as they shall think convenient and necessary for the use or ornament of the rooms'.[32] The steward

[28] M. Girouard, *Life in the English Country House* (Harmondsworth, 1980), 191-8.
[29] Assembly Rooms Minute Book, fos. 3-5, YCA; 'Proposals for . . . Assembly Rooms', YCA.
[30] Assembly Rooms Minute Book, 20 Oct. 1757, YCA.
[31] Ibid. 26 May and 2 June 1732, 21 Mar. 1733/4, 28 June 1734, 19 June 1735, 23 Oct. 1736, 9 July 1737, 12 May 1744, 16 June 1748.
[32] Ibid. 20 Nov. 1753, 20 Feb. and 21 Oct. 1754.

and his assistants were responsible for public order in the rooms, though policy in this area was drafted by the directors. In other establishments the behaviour of the company and the organization of the dancing was controlled by a formal master of ceremonies.[33]

One of the further duties of the directors at York was that of vetting applications from outsiders, such as impresarios and genteel societies, who wished to use the rooms.[34] This was indicative of the way in which assembly houses usually accommodated a wide range of entertainments other than balls. Considerable capital had often been invested in their construction, and it made economic sense to exploit the facilities as extensively as possible. Many, therefore, developed into an early form of leisure centre. As noted in the previous chapter, assembly rooms frequently housed plays and concerts, particularly the latter. The Prince Street rooms in Bristol were also known as 'the New Music Room', and opened in 1756 with Handel's *Messiah*.[35] Most establishments made some provision for card-playing: the assembly house at Wakefield, the Prince Street rooms Bristol, the Exchange at Liverpool, and the three houses at Bath allocated specific rooms for this. At York, where card-tables were available during the regular Monday assemblies, it was agreed in 1737 to also open the rooms 'every Wednesday night for carding without music or dancing', and in the mid-eighteenth century 'card assemblies' were held four times a week at Cheltenham, and every evening in alternate establishments at Tunbridge Wells.[36] The rooms in the spas, most of which were run on tight commercial budgets, were used particularly intensively. Those at Bath hosted, in addition to the dancing assemblies, public breakfasts and dinners, concerts and concert breakfasts, theatre, puppetry, lectures, cards, gaming, and tea drinking.[37] However, there were limits to the recreational demands that could be safely made on this type of venue. In 1745 the directors at York were forced to reassert their authority over the use of the facilities, when they discovered 'that several gentlemen and ladies have met in these rooms to play at

[33] Ibid. 26 Oct. 1734, 4 Aug. 1750; Burr, *Tunbridge Wells*, 121–2; Wood, *Bath*, 415.

[34] Assembly Rooms Minute Book, 24 Apr. 1751, 10 Apr. 1755, YCA.

[35] Quoted in Ison, *Bristol*, 109.

[36] Grady, 'Public Buildings in the West Riding', Gazetteer; Ison, *Bristol*, 110; HMC, *Verulam MSS*, 270; Wood, *Bath*, 319–20; Collinson, *Somerset*, i. 52; Ison, *Bath*, 54; Assembly Rooms Minute Book, 26 Jan. 1735/6, 7 Nov. 1737, YCA; Hart, *Cheltenham*, 127; Barton, *Tunbridge Wells*, 342.

[37] Wood, *Bath*, 438–9, 442–4; HMC, *Egmont MSS*, Diary i. 113; Warwickshire CRO, L6/1454–5, 1472, 1474; Students Diary, fo. 118; Hervey, *Letter-Books*, ii. 278.

shuttlecock, whereby some of the branches of the lustres have been broken'.[38]

2. WALKS AND GARDENS

Important as assembly rooms were in hosting the generality of polite entertainments, their principal function was to stage dances and balls, and therefore to act as an arena for overt personal display. Out of doors this was a role that fell to public walks and gardens. Most medieval and early modern towns possessed communal open-air spaces, where traditional games, festivals, and military training could be accommodated. No doubt inhabitants also regularly strolled in these areas. But the formal practice of public promenading and the construction of specialized facilities to service this appear to have emerged only in the seventeenth century. London set the pace, initially through the introduction of landscaped walks at Moorfields and the Inns of Court, and later with the impressive tree-lined avenues in St James's Park, and the development of the sophisticated commercial pleasure gardens that sprang up on the edge of the capital.[39] Among the earliest of the provincial town walks were those at Tunbridge Wells (constructed in 1638, and forming the core of the later Pantiles), Exeter (laid out before the Civil War on Northernhay), and the Oxbridge Colleges (planted during the seventeenth century).[40] However, it was not until about the 1690s that the provincial promenade was developed on a wide scale. Appendix 6 lists thirty towns and spas which by 1770 had public walks or gardens; by this period there could have been few important urban centres that were unable to offer their citizens or visitors the use of such facilities.

The timing and manner in which these early town parades were introduced can best be illustrated by examining a number of case-studies. Preston's role as a fashionable county centre required it to include a formal promenade among its recreational attractions. An

[38] Assembly Rooms Minute Book, 6 Feb. 1744/5.

[39] Brett-James, *Stuart London*, 444-73; S. E. Rasmussen, *London the Unique City* (Harmondsworth, 1960), 72-92; Wroth, *London Pleasure Gardens*. For the general subject of walks see M. Girouard, 'The Georgian Promenade', in *Life in the Georgian Town*, 26-33.

[40] Burr, *Tunbridge Wells*, 32; D. and S. Lysons, *Magna Britannia: Being a Concise Topographical Account of the Several Counties of Great Britain* (London, 1806-22), vi. 185, 191; Thomas, *Man and the Natural World*, 205.

ideal site for this was provided by a strip of ground that projected from the steeply sloping south side of the town, rather like a land-based pier. Already by the late 1680s polite society was frequenting an area to the north of this called Avenham Garden, but the first reference to the walk of the same name comes in the following decade, when a corporation committee was ordered to negotiate 'for the ground upon Avenham now and heretofore used as a walk, and that the same be afterwards planted with trees and made into a gravel walk'.[41] After this initial investment the town fathers were diligent in maintaining and safeguarding their new asset: in 1710 and 1736 seats were repaired, and in 1733 it was agreed to take legal action against an adjoining landholder who had demolished 'a considerable part of the quickset hedge along' the walk's east side. During the late 1730s a scheme was introduced, jointly financed by a public contribution and corporate funds, for 'enlarging, repairing, and beautifying' the walk, which included the addition of a neighbouring close. The town's esplanade is clearly visible in the Bucks' 'South Prospect of Preston' (drawn in 1728), and thirty years later a visitor portrayed the upgraded facilities as a 'delightful terrace walk', a description still apposite today.[42]

York, because it was a provincial capital, required more extensive and sophisticated walks than those at Preston. The earliest purpose-built promenade was probably that called the 'Lord Mayor's Walk', which was situated north of the Minster adjacent to the city walls. Precisely when it was constructed is unclear, but in 1719 the mayor was given permission to 'order such a number of trees as he shall judge necessary and convenient to be planted . . . as an ornament to' the walk. The result clearly failed to meet the city's requirements, for only six years later one visitor was complaining that fashionable society was forced to exercise in the main aisle of the Minster 'after evening service in the summer time, for want of a convenience of a park or gardens'.[43] This gap was filled in the early 1730s with the laying out of the 'New' or 'Long Walk', a tree-lined avenue that ran south from the town walls for about a mile along the east bank of the Ouse. Access was obtained at the city end through 'a handsome iron palisade . . . in

[41] Bellingham, *Diary*, 4–6; corporation order quoted in Hewitson, *History of Preston*, 320; Small Order Book, 23 May and 7 Nov. 1698, PCMSS.

[42] Council Minutes, 20 Mar. 1709/10, 3 Apr. 1733, 6 Apr. 1736, 28 Jan. and 18 Feb. 1736/7, PCMSS; Buck, *Antiquities*, iii; Crofts, 'Lakeland Journey', 289.

[43] Drake, *Eboracum*, 254; House Book, 31 Dec. 1719, YCA; HMC, *Portland MSS*, vi. 93. I owe the last reference to Geoffrey Holmes.

Fig. 16. The New or Long Walk, York. Engraving by C. Grignion, after a painting of 1756 by N. Drake

a stone arch', while towards the far end a bridge was built to cross the point where the Foss entered the Ouse. Both the gate and the bridge were closed every evening at times varying according to the season of the year. In 1739–40 the walk was enlarged and relandscaped at a cost of about £300, and gardeners were employed to 'clip the hedges . . . plant trees', and control public use of the space.[44] The middle decades of the century saw further improvements, with the purchase of new seats, the addition of one or more elaborate garden follies, and the erection of 'a handsome bridge with one arch built of stone' over the Foss (see Fig. 16).[45]

Walks were a fundamental part of a resort's facilities, and Bath, as the country's leading spa, naturally came to possess the most impressive group of provincial parades. When Fiennes visited the city, probably in the late 1680s, she was most impressed with the walks to the west of the walls (on King's Mead), although the main area of future development lay to the east, close to the Abbey. South of the great church was

[44] Drake, *Eboracum*, 249, and map opposite 244; House Book, 9 Mar. 1731/2, 7 Dec. 1732, 16 Oct. and 29 Nov. 1739, 28 Feb. 1739/40, 12 Sept. 1740, 28 Apr. and 14 July 1742, YCA.
[45] House Book, 15 July 1751, YCA; Allen, *County of York*, ii. 323–4; *VCH York*, 208; HMC, *Verulam MSS*, 236.

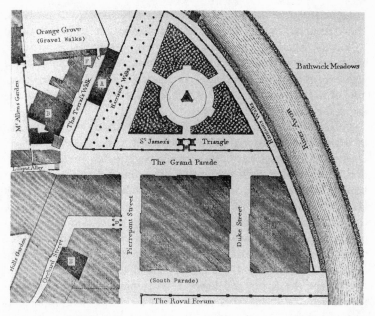

A. Harrison's Assembly Rooms

B. Lindsey's Assembly Rooms

C. St Peter's Gate

D. St James's Porticoe

E. Theatre

F. Mr Leake's Book Shop

Fig. 17. The south-east corner of Bath, adapted from John Wood's plan of *c*.1749

situated the Abbey Garden and Abbey Green, and to the south-east, the Old Bowling Green. In 1693 the town authorities agreed that the paths in the Bowling Green 'be gravelled the next spring', and their accounts for 1693/4 reveal payments for levelling ground, laying gravel and turf, replanting trees, and cutting grass on 'the green'.[46] But the focal point of the corporation's interest was an area immediately to the east of the Abbey, known as the Gravel Walks (see Fig. 17). These are already clearly marked in Gilmore's survey of the early 1690s, but it was not until the early 1700s that a broad pavement

---

[46] Fiennes, *Journeys*, 20–1, 23; Council Minutes, 11 Dec. 1693, BCA; Chamberlain's Accounts, 1693/4, BCA.

was added to their south side, and colonized by commercial premises. This effectively divided the area into two halves: the upper, 'a paved walk of two hundred feet in length, and twenty-seven feet in breadth', which was 'spacious and well shaded, planted round with shops filled with everything that contributes to pleasure', and the lower, 'three rows of tall sycamore trees . . . which were spread with gravel, for the use of the common sort of people'.[47]

Almost adjacent to the Gravel Walks, but outside the town walls, lay Harrison's commercial gardens (attached to his assembly house). Developed contemporaneously with the city's walks, the two were in direct competition with each other, and this led to some conflict between entrepreneur and corporation.[48] Immediately to the west of Harrison's was situated the Terrace Walk, whose construction began in late 1728, and included a further assembly house (Lindsey's). This represented an additional threat to the Gravel Walks and prompted the city fathers to embark on a major improvement scheme for their facilities. In the early 1730s it was agreed to merge together and relandscape the upper and lower walks, replacing the tall old syca- mores with new young trees, and in 1734 the project was rounded off when an obelisk was erected to commemorate the 'happy restoration of the health of the Prince of Orange' during a visit to Bath. After this the area became known generally as the Orange Grove.[49] During the next decade the splendid Grand and South Parades were constructed by Wood at right angles to the Terrace Walk, and the Grand Parade, with its impressive views over the Avon, soon became 'the principal place of public resort in the city' (see Figs. 14, 18). Also about this time the Spring Gardens were opened on the opposite side of the river in Bathwick Meadows, access to which, until the opening of Pulteney Bridge in 1774, was obtained by ferry from the Orange Grove (see Map 2).[50] By the mid-eighteenth century Bath possessed a wide range of interlinked walks and gardens, lined with luxury shops, assembly rooms, and prestigious residential accommodation, all conveniently packed into a compact site in the eastern corner of the city. Taken

[47] Council Minutes, 29 Dec. 1701, 30 Mar. and 28 Dec. 1702, 26 Mar. and 1 Oct. 1705, 1 July and 30 Sept. 1706, 17 Feb. 1706/7, 31 Mar. 1707, BCA; Wood, *Bath*, 224, 343; Macky, *Journey*, ii. 128.

[48] Wood, *Bath*, 225; Council Minutes, 7 May 1711, BCA.

[49] Wood, *Bath*, 243–6, 342–3; Council Minutes, 28 Dec. 1730, 20 Nov. 1732, BCA.

[50] Wood, *Bath*, 349–51; Sydenham, *Bath Pleasure Gardens*, 2–11; Council Minutes, 30 June 1760, BCA; Penrose, *Letters*, 70.

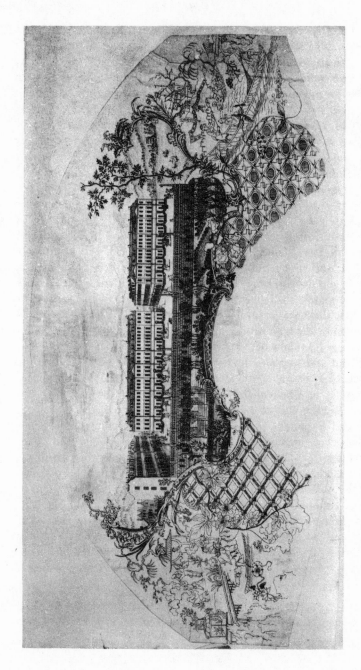

Fig. 18. The Grand or North Parade (1740–8), Bath, from a design for a fan mount by Speren

together, they constituted the most sophisticated complex of leisure facilities to be found in the provinces.

The situation and form of the walks and gardens at Preston, York, and Bath were typical of many other places. Invariably they were located on the town's periphery, frequently following the line of the city walls (as at Bath, Chester, Chichester, Dorchester, Exeter, Hereford, Newcastle-upon-Tyne, Norwich, Shrewsbury, and York), or running along the banks of a river (as at Bath, Bristol, Exeter, Leeds, Maidstone, Norwich, Shrewsbury, and York). In the spas they needed to be close to the watering facilities, since walking and drinking were seen as associated regimes.[51] To secure the footing, and safeguard the footwear of strollers from mud and dirt, many of these parades were laid with gravel or paved with stone and brick.[52] A measure of protection from wind, rain, and sun was provided by a corridor of hedges or trees. Limes, sycamores, elms, and firs were commonly planted, and they required regular maintenance because of ageing, disease, and damage from the elements. In 1733 it was agreed at York that the mayor 'shall give directions to a gardener to take care to cut and pen the trees in my Lord Mayor's Walk . . . which are much shattered by the high winds', and seven years later that he may 'order what trees he thinks necessary be planted in the room of those that were hurt and wounded by the ice upon the new walk'. During the winters of 1739 and 1740 Henry Skillicorne planted 133 elms on his new walks at Cheltenham: in the droughts of the following two summers seventy-six of them died and had to be replaced.[53]

Several important promenades became focal points for superior residential accommodation and sophisticated consumer and recreational services. This was particularly so in the resorts where there was considerable scope for new development. It has already been shown how the walks in Bath followed this model, and a similar pattern of growth occurred on the Pantiles at Tunbridge Wells (see Fig. 19). From about 1676 the Lord of the Manor was promoting the erection of shops and houses on the walks, and though these were 'entirely consumed' during a fire in 1687, they were soon rebuilt 'more regularly planned, and better contrived'. When Fiennes visited a

[51] Lennard, 'Watering-Places', 15, 54.
[52] Fiennes, *Journeys*, 31, 134; Burr, *Tunbridge Wells*, 56-9; Penrose, *Letters*, 137-8.
[53] House Book, 21 Dec. 1733, 28 Jan. 1740/1, YCA; Hart, *Cheltenham*, 126.

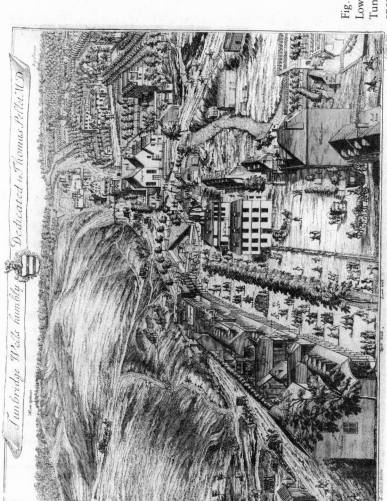

Fig. 19. The Upper and Lower Walks (the Pantiles), Tunbridge Wells, c.1714, engraved by J. Kip

decade later she found a flourishing market on one side, and on the other,

> shops full of all sorts of toys, silver, china, milliners, and all sorts of curious wooden ware, which this place is noted for . . . besides which there are two large coffee-houses for tea, chocolate, etc., and two rooms for the lottery and hazard board: these are all built with an arch or penthouse beyond the shops, some of which are supported by pillars like a piazza, which is paved with brick and stone for the dry walking of the company in rain.

In the 1760s Burr described a similar scene: 'on the right hand of the paved walk . . . is the assembly room, the coffee-houses, and the shops for silversmiths, jewellers, milliners, booksellers, Tunbridge-ware, etc. . . . From thence a portico is extended the whole length of the parade, supported by tuscan pillars, for the company to walk under occasionally.'[54] With their gaming-houses and souvenir shops the Pantiles were a precursor, albeit a refined one, of Blackpool's 'Golden Mile' (see Fig. 20).

In addition to the specialized promenade, the post-Restoration town enjoyed a wide range of other walking facilities. Visitors to early eighteenth-century Tunbridge Wells had the choice of three groves in which to saunter: Southborough, Queen's, and that on Mount Sion. Queen's Grove was a triple row of birch trees planted on Bishop's Down Common to celebrate Anne's accession, and the grove at Mount Sion contained four acres of oaks and beeches.[55] Public gardens could also be found in some towns. The Abbey Gardens at Shrewsbury were particularly lavish, as Fiennes's description of 1698 shows. They were laid out,

> with gravel walks set full of all sorts of greens, orange, and lemon trees . . . there was also firs, myrtles, and hollies of all sorts, and a greenhouse full of all sorts of curiosities of flowers and greens, there was the aloe plant: out of this went another garden, much larger, with several fine grass walks kept exactly cut and rolled for company to walk in: every Wednesday most of the town, the ladies and gentlemen, walk there as in St James's Park.[56]

By the mid-eighteenth century commercial pleasure gardens had also been opened at Bath, Birmingham, Bristol, Coventry, Newcastle-upon-Tyne, Norwich, and possibly Leeds. These were much more than

---

[54] Burr, *Tunbridge Wells*, 50-1, 55-6, 101; Fiennes, *Journeys*, 133-4; and also Hamilton, *Count Grammont*, 153-4; Macky, *Journey*, i. 89.
[55] Barton, *Tunbridge Wells*, 117; Savidge, *Tunbridge Wells*, 50.
[56] Fiennes, *Journeys*, 227.

Fig. 20. The Upper Walks (the Pantiles), Tunbridge Wells, from a drawing of 1748 by Loggon

centres of horticultural delights. Several of them accommodated concerts, and the Spring (later Vauxhall) Gardens at Bath was a leisure park in its own right, possessing not only walks and gardens, but also facilities for breakfasting, dancing, and bowling.[57]

Quite apart from the provision of formal walking areas, many towns also saw considerable growth in generalized perambulating space as a consequence of the physical renewal of their landscapes. Streets in the higher-class areas of towns were lined with elegant architecture, and were becoming more spacious, and better cleansed, paved, and lighted. Squares and crescents were built, the former often containing gardens. These developments created a series of pseudo-promenades in which the company could exercise themselves, without running the risk, as they might in Tudor and early Stuart thoroughfares, of dirtying their clothes and shoes, offending their noses, or being threatened by criminals. A visitor to Scarborough noted in 1733 how Long Room Street had been 'lately paved with broad stones, and set with posts, and may be called the Pall Mall of Scarborough', and forty years later Edward Pigott remarked how at Bath, 'when it is rather cold, the company' vacated the formal Parades and headed for the sheltered surroundings of the Royal Crescent.[58] Just as walking could be practised in virtually any respectable area, so the art of personal display was not confined to assemblies and promenades. Sporting occasions and arenas provided an obvious alternative, and these form the subject of the next chapter.

[57] See Appendix 6 for pleasure gardens; Sydenham, *Bath Pleasure Gardens*, 2–11; Penrose, *Letters*, 70, 96; Margaret Luttrell to Henry Luttrell, [?] 1759, Somerset RO, DD/L.
[58] *Journey from London to Scarborough*, 42; Pigott Diary, i, article 488.

7

Sport

Stuart and Georgian Englishmen were devoted to sport. Horses and hounds occupied a place in many a gentleman's affections that was scarcely less important than that of his wife and family, at least to judge from contemporary art where animals were lovingly portrayed, and sporting painting was a buoyant and lucrative genre.[1] No description of cultural activities could therefore be complete without some consideration of the physical recreations. Though these had traditionally been associated with the countryside, post-Restoration towns were extraordinarily resourceful in establishing a substantial and secure foothold in the world of sport. This chapter will begin by briefly examining a variety of sporting recreations, before embarking on a more detailed study of horse-racing, where the impact of change and the influence of the town can be seen at their most powerful.

1. BAT AND BALL SPORTS

One of the most popular of gentlemanly sports under the Stuarts, and one that left a clear imprint on the urban landscape, was that of bowling.[2] The Bucks' prospects of the early Georgian years show greens at Bridgnorth, Chester, Ipswich, Lancaster, Leicester, Lichfield, Liverpool, Newcastle-upon-Tyne, Sheffield, Winchester, Worcester, and Yarmouth, and eighteenth-century town plans reveal one in Leeds (1725) (see Fig. 1), two in Exeter (1765), and three in Worcester (*c*.1780).[3] In the early nineteenth century Strutt claimed that greens were to be found 'in most country towns of any note', though it is

---

[1] E. Waterhouse, *Painting in Britain 1530 to 1790*, 4th edn. (Harmondsworth, 1978), 297-314; *British Sporting Painting 1650-1850*, Arts Council of Great Britain (London, 1974).

[2] Brailsford, *Sport and Society*, 116-17, 212-13.

[3] Buck, *Antiquities*, iii; Cossins, *Plan of Leeds*; Donn, 'Plan of Exeter'; Nash, *Worcestershire*, ii, 'Plan of Worcester'.

clear that places of social resort were particularly well provisioned: these included county centres like Buckingham, Shrewsbury, Winchester (with two greens in the late seventeenth century), and York, and spas such as Bath (two in the early 1690s), Epsom (at least two by 1711), Scarborough, and Tunbridge Wells (four in 1697).[4] The facilities were frequented not only by townsmen and holiday-makers, but also by local rural society. The green at Bedford attracted both 'town and country gentlemen, of which many resort to it, especially the market-days', and in the mid-eighteenth century Sir Roger Newdigate of Arbury regularly bowled at the neighbouring Warwickshire town of Atherstone.[5]

Most greens would have possessed at least rudimentary accommodation for players and spectators. The ground at Bedford was 'well kept with seats and summer-houses in it', and the Bucks' view of Liverpool shows a substantial two-storey structure on the periphery of the playing area, called the 'bowling-green house'. A building known by the same name was situated on Preston Marsh, and was probably used in 1690 when Colonel Bellingham recorded that he and 'several of the gentlemen had a very good dinner at the Marsh, and bowled in the afternoon'. The facilities at Newcastle-upon-Tyne were particularly elaborate. In the 1650s a green was laid out and a house built for its keeper on the Forth, a traditional spot for recreational activities located on the western edge of the city. Three decades later the corporation considerably improved the site, ordering a wall to be erected, trees planted, and the 'Firth-house' to be made 'suitable for entertainment, with a cellar convenient, and a handsome room, etc.'. When Fiennes visited in 1698 she found the playing area the centre of a network of walks and gardens (which are clearly marked on Bourne's map of the 1730s):

There is a very pleasant bowling-green a litle walk out of the town with a large gravel walk round it, with two rows of trees on each side making it very shady; there is a fine entertaining house that makes up the fourth side, before which is a paved walk under piazzas of brick; there is a pretty garden by the side

[4] Strutt, *Sports and Pastimes*, 236; Clark and Slack, *Crisis and Order*, 15; *A Prospect of the Town of Shrewsbury Taken as it Appear'd in the Great Frost 1739*, reproduced in Hyde, *Gilded Scenes*, 78-9; Rosen, 'Winchester', 180; Drake, *Eboracum*, 258; Gilmore, *Map of Bath*; [J. Toland], *The Description of Epsom with the Humours and Politics of the Place* (London, 1711), 11; Clark, 'Epsom Spa', 19, 23-4; McIntyre, 'Health and Pleasure Resorts', 198; Fiennes, *Journeys*, 134-5.

[5] Fiennes, *Journeys*, 340; Newdigate Diaries, *passim*.

shady walk, it's a sort of Spring Garden where the gentlemen and ladies walk in the evening; there is a greenhouse in the garden.[6]

Facilities for eating and drinking must have been available at many greens, particularly since a number were attached to inns, such as the Three Tuns (referred to in 1677) and the Reindeer (1706) in Banbury, the Salutation (1720) in Topsham, the Plough (1739) in Cheltenham, the Hen and Chickens (1741) in Birmingham, and a hostelry in Preston, where in 1700 the landlord obtained permission 'to get sods on' the Moor 'for laying a bowling-green on the back of the Old Antler'.[7]

Bowling was at the peak of its popularity during the seventeenth and early eighteenth centuries. Under the Georgians its appeal began to fade a little, and by the early 1800s Strutt felt that none of the country town greens were 'now so generally frequented as they were accustomed to be formerly'. Several were sold to provide much wanted urban building land, such as the two at Bath, which had been lost to property development by the late 1720s.[8] If bowling was declining, cricket was one of the up-and-coming recreations of the period. Little systematic research has been completed on the origins of the modern sport, but it appears that the years after the Restoration saw the critical transition from a folk game to a regulated, commercialized, and above all fashionable pastime.[9] The forcing-house for change was London and the Home Counties, particularly Kent and Sussex, though the new type of cricket had spread beyond the metropolitan region before the mid-eighteenth century. Towns were closely involved in the development of the sport. Newspaper notices suggest that a high proportion of Kentish towns possessed teams, and point to the existence of many other urban-based sides throughout the country. In 1760 the Society of Cricket Players of Birmingham

---

[6] Fiennes, *Journeys*, 211, 340; Buck, *Antiquities*, iii; Bellingham, *Diary*, 51, 116; Brand, *Newcastle*, i. 418-19; Bourne, *Newcastle*, for his plan of the city.

[7] *VCH Oxfordshire*, x. 15, 32; Hoskins, *Devon*, 498; Hart, *Cheltenham*, 127; Wise, 'Birmingham and its Trade Relations', 75; Small Order Book, 8 Feb. 1699/1700, PCMSS.

[8] Strutt, *Sports and Pastimes*, 237; Brailsford, *Sport and Society*, 212-13; Wood, *Bath*, 227, 244.

[9] H. S. Altham and E. W. Swanton, *A History of Cricket*, 2nd edn. (London, 1938), 15-40; J. Ford, *Cricket: A Social History 1700-1835* (Newton Abbot, 1975); C. Brookes, *English Cricket: The Game and its Players through the Ages* (Newton Abbot, 1978), 9-66; R. W. Malcolmson, *Popular Recreations in English Society 1700-1850* (Cambridge, 1973), 40-2.

advertised their willingness to play two matches on a return basis with any town up to thirty miles away, and in the same year the Gentlemen Cricket Players at Leeds gave notice of what appears to be an annual meeting and dinner. Eight years earlier eleven Bristol gentlemen had gathered on the city Downs to compete against a side from London. From the mid-eighteenth century cricket became increasingly popular in Colchester, where the sport was often connected with local hostelries. Indeed, it was a widespread practice for landlords to promote the game, sometimes providing a ground to play on or prizes to compete for, and always feeding and lubricating the players and spectators. In many, perhaps most matches, there was a reward of cash or kind (hats or pairs of gloves were a common accolade of victory), and the sport was deeply permeated by gambling, a key factor behind the growing success of cricket, which by the end of our period had blossomed into a major recreation.[10] In 1767 it was reported from Godalming that 'cricket is very much followed in this part, there being scarce a week but there is a considerable match about this town and Guildford', and in the following year it was reported that 600 to 700 spectators gathered to watch a game between Bury St Edmunds and neighbouring Langham (held on Langham Heath).[11]

2. ANIMAL SPORTS

In several sports the critical piece of equipment was not an inert artefact but a live animal, with which a close relationship could be established, and through which competition could be vicariously pursued. To modern Englishmen cock-fighting appears little short of barbarous, but most of their Stuart and Georgian predecessors considered it a perfectly acceptable, even laudable diversion. As one admittedly committed commentator wrote in 1709, 'amongst all the pleasures and delights this lower sphere affords to mortals here on earth, there is nothing more taking with the heroic, and truly generous soul, than the noble and princely pastime of cock-fighting'.[12] The

[10] G. B. Buckley, *Fresh Light on Pre-Victorian Cricket* (Birmingham, 1937), *passim*; Buckley, *18th Century Cricket*, *passim*; Looney, 'Advertising and Society', 180; Barry, 'Cultural Life of Bristol', 157; Brown, 'Colchester in the Eighteenth Century', 164; Brookes, *English Cricket*, 50.

[11] *Whitehall Evening Post*, 23 July 1767, quoted in Buckley, *18th Century Cricket*, 46; Suffolk RO, E2/25/1, fo. 67.

[12] R. H. Howlett, *The Royal Pastime of Cock-Fighting*, 1709, repr. (Liss, 1973), 1.

recreation can be traced back at least to the twelfth century, but it appears to have only become established as a widespread national amusement during the reign of Elizabeth, from when, according to its historian, it 'reigned as Britain's premier sport' for the next two centuries.[13]

Macky described a cockpit as 'the very model of an amphitheatre of the ancients. The cocks fight in the area, as the beasts did formerly among the Romans; and round the circle above sit the spectators in their several rows'. Many towns displayed examples of this gladiatorial architecture. The Earl of Derby endowed Chester with a pit in 1619, Gilmore's survey of Bath (1694) shows one on Timber Green near to the West Gate, Whitehaven had one by 1706, thirty years later Drake referred to a 'handsome cockpit' in the Bootham area of York, and Chapman's 1787 plan of Newmarket (the metropolis of the sport) shows a substantial pit at the far end of High Street. In the early 1750s a new cockpit was erected at the top of Deansgate in Manchester, which was the centre of a leisure complex containing not only the fighting arena and 'upwards of 200 pens, two good feeding rooms, and rooms for laying of straw', but also an assembly room above the pit, and an adjacent bowling-green and 'public house'.[14] Urban inns were closely associated with the sport. In 1737 it was reported that 'a main of cocks' was to be 'fought at . . . the George Inn in Swaffham every morning during the races'; fifteen years later the Talbot in Halifax was advertised as the venue for an early 'Roses' match between a Yorkshire and a Lancashire gentleman, 'for ten guineas a battle, and one hundred the main'; while the Bushell Inn at Newmarket accommodated a pit in its cellar, and according to an inventory of 1773, the splendid Duke's Head at King's Lynn contained a special room with 'deal furniture for fighting cocks'.[15]

For many the aggression and competitiveness of animal contests, which was heightened by the stakes and heavy betting involved,

[13] G. R. Scott, *The History of Cock-Fighting* (London, 1957), 99; Thomas, *Man and the Natural World*, 144–5.

[14] Macky, *Journey*, i. 129; F. H. Crossley, *Cheshire* (London, 1949), 73; Wood, *Bath*, 220; Beckett, *Coal and Tobacco*, 188; Drake, *Eboracum*, 258; May, *Newmarket*, 27–8, 63; Hodgkinson and Pogson, *Early Manchester Theatre*, 21–4.

[15] *Suffolk Mercury*, xxiv, No. 275, 13 June 1737; *Orion Adam's Weekly Journal; or the Manchester Advertiser*, 11 Feb. 1752, quoted in R. M. Wiles, 'Crowd-Pleasing Spectacles in Eighteenth-Century England', *Jnl. of Popular Culture*, i (1967), 92; May, *Newmarket*, 28; Parker, *King's Lynn*, 128–9; and also Clark, *English Alehouse*, 234; Malcolmson, *Popular Recreations*, 49.

proved a compulsive pleasure. The frequent references to cock-fighting in Preston, terse as they may be, in Colonel Bellingham's diary of 1688–90, suggest the commitment both he and his companions had to the sport:

Great cock-fighting. Sr. Tho. Stanley lost every battle . . . Cocking continues . . . Great cocking at the Marsh . . . I was at the Marsh, and saw several matches at cock-fighting . . . There were some few cock matches . . . Several cock matches . . . I din'd there [Penworthan], and saw a battle raged between 4 cocks . . . Great cocking at Graystocks . . . I went to the Marsh a cocking.

However, like bowling, there are signs that the pastime's appeal within fashionable society was beginning to wane a little by the mid-eighteenth century. The cockpit in the Wednesday Market at Beverley was dismantled in about 1730, and Bath maps and guides from the 1730s onwards make no mention of the Timber Green pit. Vulnerable to attack as an uncivilized activity, and amid a widespread denunciation of the plebeian diversion of cock-throwing, it seems probable that among the élite cock-fighting became increasingly the preserve of a hard core of sporting gentry.[16]

　　Rarely were cocks the subjects of serious animal painting. The stars of this genre were undoubtedly horses and hounds, reflecting their individual prestige and that of the recreations with which they were associated, racing, riding, and hunting. During our period towns developed a surprisingly close relationship with hunting, either directly by supporting their own hunts, or indirectly by servicing rural meetings. Macky noted of Lewes that 'several gentlemen here keep packs of dogs', and a number of towns, such as Preston, York, Leeds (from at least 1740), Liverpool (1746), Beverley (1753), and probably Bristol (1755) maintained their own hounds, often with corporation support. The Preston hunt can be traced back to 1698, when the council granted one of its own members a lease on 'a plot of ground at the end of Peel Moor . . . whereon to build the house to keep the hounds in, and for a court and garden to it'. How long this remained the home of the pack is unclear, though in 1746 the 'gentlemen hunters residing in the town' successfully petitioned the corporation for 'a vacant piece of ground on Syke Hill near the Poor House . . . to

[16] Bellingham, *Diary*, 50–1, 65, 105, 113, 117; Macmahon, *Beverley Corporation Minute-Books*, 14–15; J. Brand, *Observations on Popular Antiquities* (Newcastle-upon-Tyne, 1777), 234, 377–9; Strutt, *Sports and Pastimes*, 248–51; *VCH York*, 246; Malcolmson, *Popular Recreations*, 119–22, 135; Thomas, *Man and the Natural World*, 159–60.

erect a dog kennel upon, for the keeping up of their hounds in the hunting seasons'. The pack was run on a subscription basis, and in 1770 there were about fifty contributors, two of whom filled the offices of 'master of the hounds' and 'dog lad'. The hunt at York goes back to at least 1719. It was under strong corporation patronage and influence, with the town paying an annual salary of £10 to the huntsman and an equal sum 'towards providing him a horse and keeping the dogs'. In return he was expected to arrange meetings twice a week, which were open not only to residents, but also to gentlemen attending the city's great social events.[17]

The relationship between towns and rural hunts rested firmly on the wide range of services urban centres could offer the sport. In 1762 Leicester staged the county's hunt ball, with a sumptuous supper of sixty-two dishes on each table 'dressed by Mr Meynell's man-cook, who keeps the hounds seven miles off'. Further north, it was advertised in 1752 that 'the gentlemen of Cheshire, Staffordshire, and Shropshire will meet at Tho. Pursall's at the sign of the Black Lion in the market-place, Congleton, to take the diversion of fox-hunting on Monday, Tuesday, and Wednesday. . . . On Tuesday evening there will be a ball for the ladies, and it is expected to be a very splendid appearance'. During the eighteenth century, particularly in the later decades, the pattern of hunting was undergoing a transformation. Foxes replaced stags and hares as the quarry, the operation of the sport became more dynamic and sophisticated, and its social context became more public and fashionable.[18] This last factor must have enhanced the role of towns as service centres for the rural packs. In the 1780s Loughborough was the social capital of the recreation in Leicestershire, the home of the new type of hunting, and by the turn of the century Melton Mowbray was rapidly emerging as 'the hunting metropolis of all England'.[19]

---

[17] Macky, *Journey*, i. 95; R. G. Wilson, *Gentlemen Merchants: The Merchant Community in Leeds 1700-1830* (Manchester, 1971), 232; Picton, *Liverpool Municipal Archives*, 129; Macmahon, *Beverley Corporation Minute-Books*, 33; Barry, 'Cultural Life of Bristol', 157; Small Order Book, 11 and 21 July 1698, PCMSS; Council Minutes, 4 Nov. 1746, 18 Apr. 1748, PCMSS; Subscriptions to the Union Hunt in Preston 1770, Lancashire RO, DDX/146/2; House Book, 13 Apr. 1719, 8 and 23 Dec. 1720, 6 Aug. and 1 Dec. 1731, 19 Sept. and 12 Dec. 1735, 16 Oct. 1739, 23 Oct. 1754, YCA; Fairfax-Blakeborough, *Northern Turf History*, iii. 45-6.

[18] Suffolk RO, E2/20/1A, fo. 10; advertisement quoted in Crossley, *Cheshire*, 75-6; R. Carr, *English Fox-Hunting: A History* (London, 1976), 21-64.

[19] D. C. Itzkowitz, *Peculiar Privilege: A Social History of English Fox-Hunting 1753-1885* (Hassocks, 1977), 7-9.

The rough and tumble of the chase would not have been to everyone's taste. However, a gentle outing on horseback or in a coach would be a pleasant diversion for even the most fragile soul. Hyde Park in London accommodated a prototype of the sort of facilities that might be provided, with its famous 'ring railed in, round which [runs] a gravel way that would admit of twelve if not more rows of coaches, which the gentry to take the air and see each other, comes and drives round and round'. The resorts, with their population of invalids and socialites, were quick to copy this model. Fiennes noted how at Epsom 'on the hill where is the race posts, they have made a ring as in Hyde Park, and they come in coaches and drive round', and in 1711 Toland reported from the spa that 'the great number of gentlemen and ladies, that take the air every evening and morning on horseback . . . is a most entertaining object. You can never miss of it on the fine grounds of the new orbicular race, which may well be termed a rural cirque.' As early as 1699 the city fathers at Bath agreed 'that part of the common shall be set out for gentlemen's coaches or horses to take the air', and it is probably the product of this investment that Wood described as 'a small ring in imitation of the Ring in Hyde Park, near London: it is six hundred yards in circumference, almost upon a level, upon a gravelly soil, highly situated, defended from the winds, is part of the town common, and the field out of which it is taken is called Hyde Park'. Wood also singled out three other places 'for taking the air and exercise, in coaches or on horseback' about Bath: Lansdown Hill, the London Road (where 'the toll imposed for amending the roads don't extend so far as to affect people in Bath, who travel for air or recreation, provided they return to the city the same day'), and Claverton Down.[20] The latter was also the home of the spa's racecourse, and it is horse-racing that will occupy our attention for the remainder of this chapter.

3. THE DEVELOPMENT OF HORSE-RACING

If horses were the élite among sporting animals, then racehorses were the aristocrats of their species. Stubbs's glowing portraits of early heroes of the turf, such as 'Eclipse' and 'Gimcrack', reveal the esteem

---

[20] Fiennes, *Journeys*, 293, 350; [Toland], *Description of Epsom*, 28; Council Minutes, 4 Sept. 1699, BCA; Wood, *Bath*, 225, 362, 364-5, 439-40.

in which thoroughbreds were held. This was itself indicative of the general prestige of the sport in which they were the key constituent. Horse-racing was the most rapidly developing and commercially oriented of eighteenth-century physical recreations, and deserves rather more detailed attention than the pastimes already discussed. This examination will begin by briefly exploring the sport's chronological development, before investigating what is of central concern to this book, the close bond that emerged between town and turf.

Englishmen have engaged in equine competition for hundreds and perhaps thousands of years. But horse-racing as it is understood today, that is regular meetings with established prizes open to a wide range of competitors, seems to date from the Tudor period.[21] A number of meetings can be traced back to the first half of the sixteenth century, including Chester (1511), Gatherley Moor, and York (1530). However, the first major phase of growth occurred during the reigns of Elizabeth and of her Stuart successor. Strutt claimed that 'in the reign of James the First public races were established in many parts of the kingdom',[22] and the statistical evidence available bears out his emphasis on this period. Appendix 7 lists 308 meetings operating in England before 1771. I have traced only six of these to before 1575, a further six to between 1575 and 1599, but twenty-one to the first quarter of the seventeenth century.[23] An important factor stimulating this early growth of the sport was government policy, which sought to encourage the breeding and nurturing of horses, especially within the ranks of the gentry, to supply the nation's military requirements. This promoted a developing interest among the social élite in the whole art of horse breeding and training, which naturally spilled over into competitive racing.[24]

The middle decades of the seventeenth century were difficult years for the turf. The earliest references to only eleven meetings can be

[21] The early history of horse-racing has received little academic attention. W. Vamplew, *The Turf: A Social and Economic History of Horse-Racing* (London, 1976), deals largely with nineteenth-century Britain, while R. Longrigg, *The History of Horse-Racing* (London, 1972), is an international history of the sport. The arguments presented here are necessarily of an exploratory nature.

[22] Strutt, *Sports and Pastimes*, 42; J. Rice, *History of the British Turf* (London, 1879), i. 5; M. Vale, *The Gentleman's Recreations* (Cambridge, 1977), 20; Brailsford, *Sport and Society*, 110–12.

[23] A further two meetings have their earliest references in the sixteenth century as a whole, and one in the seventeenth century.

[24] J. Thirsk, *Horses in Early Modern England: For Service, for Pleasure, for Power* (Reading, 1978).

traced to the two quarters 1625 to 1674, suggesting that few courses were established in this period. During the Interregnum racing was put under considerable pressure (though never completely banned) by the puritan authorities: Newmarket was hit particularly severely.[25] But more influential than any formal suppression was the changing tenor of élite life, which made large gatherings of mounted gentlemen engaging in competitive recreations both socially inappropriate and politically dangerous. From about the 1680s recovery set in, and racing entered upon its second major phase of development, only on this occasion growth was on an altogether grander scale. The precise chronology of this boom, which lasted until the 1730s, is difficult to establish because of the nature of the sources. But when the *Racing Calendar* was first published in 1727 it already listed 112 courses; by 1739 the number had risen to 138, which among them accommodated over 400 prizes and matches valued at about £13,500. Such was the rate of growth during these years that Drake was prompted to observe in 1736, 'It is surprising to think to what a height this spirit of horse-racing is now arrived in this kingdom, when there is scarce a village so mean that has not a bit of plate raised once a year for this purpose.'[26]

The development of racing during this period was not just a matter of the numerical growth in venues. Existing meetings were qualitatively upgraded by enhancing their facilities and programmes of events. At York these improvements came in two phases. The first, in the early years of the eighteenth century, concentrated on extending the duration and raising the prize money and prestige of the meeting. In 1708 the corporation agreed to make an annual contribution of £15 'towards a plate to encourage and bring about a horse-race . . . and to invite the gentry to run their horses for the same, and to make such further additions to the said plate as they please', and in the following year 'a collection was made through the city for purchasing five plates'. Two years later Queen Anne donated a gold cup of a hundred guineas, which became a permanent feature among the prizes, and an important status symbol for the course. During these years a full week of events was quickly established: from three days racing in 1709 and 1710, the meeting grew to at least five days in 1712, and six in 1713. Seven years later Nicholas Blundell described in his diary the rich

[25] May, *Newmarket*, 15; *VCH Cambridgeshire*, v (London, 1973), 279; Brailsford, *Sport and Society*, 138.

[26] Figure for 1727 from T. A. Cook, *A History of the English Turf*, Vol. 1, Division 1 (London, 1901), 199; *Racing Calendar* (1739); Drake, *Eboracum*, 241.

variety of prizes available: the 'King's Golden Cup' of 100 guineas, 'a
silver soup dish of £30 value', the 'Ladies' Gold Cup', a '6 guineas
purse', and 'a silver cup and cover' of £20.[27]

The second phase of improvements at York came in the early 1730s.
The old course at Clifton Ings lay on the banks of the Ouse. The
serious threat from flooding and a 'misunderstanding with the owner'
of the Ings caused the meeting to be moved to the city common called
Knavesmire, where it still flourishes today. The new course was
skilfully landscaped by John Telford, a professional gardener, and the
results were highly commended. Drake wrote that,

> though the ground be a dead flat, and in many places very moist, yet by
> building arches, and drainage where it was proper, the course was made as
> convenient for this diversion as is requisite. The form of the race being like a
> horseshoe, the company in the midst and on the scaffolds, can never lose sight
> of the horses: for all which reasons this piece of ground has acquired the
> reputation of being one of the best horse-courses in England.

In 1738 the corporation displayed its gratitude to Telford, when it
granted him 'the profits of the admittance of horses at the Knavesmire
for one year next after the debt now owing by the ward shall be paid,
in consideration of the great pains, care, and trouble he has been at'.[28]
Hand in hand with raising the quality of the racing facilities went
improvements in the meeting's social infrastructure, and it is
significant that the men pressing the corporation to move the course to
Knavesmire in 1730 were also those directing the construction of the
splendid new assembly rooms, which were to accommodate many of
the entertainments associated with race week.[29]

The period from about 1680 to 1740 was one of the most influential
in the history of the turf, witnessing the establishment of a rich
network of meetings throughout the nation. However, saturation
point was approached by the mid-1730s. There is little growth in the
recorded number of meetings after 1736, or in total winnings
throughout the 1730s. What finally brought the boom to an abrupt
halt and dramatically reversed the progress of the previous decades was
the introduction of legislation in 1740 'to restrain and prevent the

---

[27] House Book, 1 Nov. 1708, YCA; Fairfax-Blakeborough, *Northern Turf History*,
iii. 20–4; Drake, *Eboracum*, 241; Blundell, *Diurnal*, iii. 20.

[28] Fairfax-Blakeborough, *Northern Turf History*, iii. 30–1, 36; Drake, *Eboracum*,
241, 398; House Book, 24 Jan. 1737/8, YCA.

[29] Assembly Rooms Minute Book, 17 Nov. 1730, YCA.

excessive increase of horse-races'.[30] The principal feature of the act was a stipulation that all prizes and matches, with a few exceptions, should be of at least £50 in value. Such a demand was little short of Draconian, since in 1739 almost nine in every ten races recorded in the *Calendar* fell below this level, and two-thirds were valued at or below twenty guineas. The legislation appears to have been rigorously observed, at least to judge from the details in the *Calendars*. The act came into operation on 24 June, and only one race of below £50 is recorded for the remainder of the year. By 1745, when any weaknesses in the law should have been exposed, only eight of the 155 races where a value is specified failed to meet the minimum requirement, and several of these would have been officially exempted. The inevitable consequence of the act was to plunge racing into a serious crisis. Table 7.1 shows that by the end of the 1740s the level of recorded winnings had fallen by about a third (from £13,500 to £8,500), and the number

Table 7.1. *The English Turf 1730-1770*

Date	Courses	Race days[i]	Prizes and matches[ii]	Total winnings[iii] (£)
1730	124	316	353	13,983
1739	138	—	406	13,496
1740	84	221	227	9,279
1745	53	—	159	9,587
1749	47	132	140	8,634
1760	70	221	310	33,486
1770	89	298	—	—

Note: The figures in this, and subsequent tables based on the *Calendars*, should be taken as a guide rather than a precise indication of winnings, since there are considerable difficulties in calculating the totals involved.

[i] This is defined as a separate day of racing held at any individual meeting.

[ii] This includes a number of forfeited matches, and prizes advertised but not run for.

[iii] This excludes a number of races where the value is not given, where it is impossible to compute, or where the match was forfeited.

Source: Racing Calendar.

[30] 13 Geo. II, c. 19; and also *The History and Proceedings of the House of Commons*, xi (London, 1743), 282, 296, 317-18, 327; *Gentleman's Magazine*, x (1740), 257.

of courses and races by around two-thirds (from 138 courses to 47, and 406 prizes and matches to 140) of their 1739 level.

The recession lasted until about 1750, after which the sport entered the third key phase of its development. By 1760 there were clear signs of recovery, with the number of recorded courses rising to seventy, and races to 310, though this was still well below the pre-act levels. However, of far greater significance was the remarkable escalation in the volume of recorded winnings, which by 1760 had climbed to £33,500, or two and a half times the amount in 1739. All this points to the emergence of a more rationalized and commercialized recreation. The crisis of the 1740s effectively pruned back the weaker courses (many of which had sprung into existence during the heady days of the preceding phase), leaving only the larger, more resilient meetings. When wealth flowed back into the business on an unprecedented scale, it was the latter which reaped the benefits; thus a more compact and healthier racing industry developed. Rationalization also brought with it a greater degree of urban influence, and it is the relationship between the town and the sport which will now be explored.

4. TOWN AND TURF

Though racing is often perceived as a rural pastime, the majority of courses were located in or on the edge of towns, and frequently played an important part in their economic and social life. Of the meetings traced between 1500 and 1770, 70 per cent were based on market towns. The *Calendars*, though they omit a number of rural courses, suggest that by the mid-eighteenth century the proportion was even higher: in the 1730s between 74 and 80 per cent, and by 1770, after the impact of rationalization had been felt, almost 90 per cent (see Table 7.2). Even allowing for difficulties in defining an urban settlement, or doubts about the comprehensiveness of the *Calendars*, this still points to an intimate relationship between town and turf. There were practical reasons why this should be the case. A race-course based on an urban centre was able to exploit the advantages of an established meeting-place, with its own defined catchment area, to provide a core of support. It could also call upon a range of services, such as stabling, smith work, saddlery, food, drink, accommodation, and entertainment, which were concentrated in towns and were essential to the operation of the sport.

Table 7.2. *The Location of English Racecourses 1500–1770*

Date	Total	Market towns		County towns	
		No.	%	No.	%
1500–1770	308	216	70	—	—
1730	124	98	79	21	17
1736	130	96	74	23	18
1739	138	110	80	25	18
1745	53	44	83	17	32
1749	47	38	81	15	32
1755	90	76	84	23	26
1760	70	62	86	23	33
1770	89	78	88	25	28

Sources: Racing Calendar; Miège, *New State of England*, for list of market and county towns; Appendix 7.

The urban meetings can be ordered into a rough hierarchy. At the very top of the league, in a division all of its own, reigned Newmarket. According to the *Calendars*, which may exaggerate the position a little, a substantial slice of all prize and match money was won and lost on Newmarket Heath. In the 1730s this amounted to about one-third of the national total, and though during the crisis of the 1740s it dropped to a fifth, the course was to be the principal beneficiary of the subsequent inrush of wealth into the industry, so that by 1760 the proportion had risen to over a half. To accommodate such a huge share of the sport's monetary rewards, the town developed a far more extended calendar of events than was to be found elsewhere. This was reflected both in the large number of racing days held on the Heath, and in the tradition of mounting several meetings a year, a practice consistently followed only at Newmarket. A programme of spring and autumn events may have emerged as early as the 1620s, and this became a regular feature of racing in the town.[31] Even in the dismal year of 1740, when the number of racing days dropped to eight (there had been twenty-two in 1730), two gatherings still took place. By 1770, with the course's dominance if anything growing, there were five annual meetings, though these were still built largely around the

[31] F. Siltzer, *Newmarket: Its Sport and Personalities* (London, 1923), 21; *VCH Cambridgeshire*, v. 279.

spring/autumn axis. The year opened with the 'First Spring Meeting' in April, followed by the 'Second Spring Meeting' in May, the 'July Meeting', the 'First October Meeting', the 'Second October Meeting', and finished with the 'Houghton Meeting' in November.[32] The town's pre-eminence was reflected in its relations with the wider world of racing: from the early 1730s there is evidence of other courses referring disputed races 'to the judgement of Newmarket'.[33]

The dominant position of the course flowed from the prestigious patronage that it attracted. In the early seventeenth century James I established Newmarket as a recreational retreat for the Court, and from then on it received regular and often lavish support from Stuart monarchs. James himself spent over £20,000 on royal buildings in the town (an original palace, finished in 1610, collapsed three years later and was replaced with one designed by Inigo Jones), and in 1668 Charles II purchased and extended two properties in High Street to form a new royal residence.[34] At some point in the late seventeenth or early eighteenth century royal favour was replaced by that of an élite coterie of aristocrats. Of the twelve owners running horses in the twenty-eight races listed in Muir's *The Old New-Markitt Calendar* (which covered the latter part of 1718), only two were commoners. In 1771 it was reported from Newmarket that 'many of the nobility and gentry have here built themselves houses for their occasional residence', and at the end of the century large stables were maintained in the town by noblemen such as the Dukes of Bolton, Cumberland, Devonshire, Grafton, Northumberland, and Queensbury, and Lords Abingdon, Clermont, Egremont, and Grosvenor.[35] During the 1750s the course's aristocratic circle coalesced into a more formal body that became known as the Jockey Club.[36]

Newmarket's unique status was not inevitable. The crown's patronage, the initial stimulus behind the course's success, had occasionally wavered in other directions. The royal home at Windsor provided an alternative focus for racing. Charles II attended events at Datchet Ferry close to the castle, and during Anne's reign the nearby meeting at

[32] *Racing Calendar* (1740 and 1770).

[33] Longrigg, *Horse-Racing*, 89; *Racing Calendar* (1740), Bridgnorth.

[34] May, *Newmarket*, 3–5, 23–9, 43; J. Harris, *The Palladians* (London, 1981), 44; Evelyn, *Diary*, 542; R. Onslow, *The Heath and the Turf: A History of Newmarket* (London, 1971), 19–24; Siltzer, *Newmarket*, 49, 63; Longrigg, *Horse-Racing*, 39, 46–7.

[35] May, *Newmarket*, 62–4; Suffolk RO, E2/44/1, fo. 359; Mingay, *Landed Society*, 151; and also *VCH Cambridgeshire*, v. 281; Hervey, *Letter-Books*, i, *passim*.

[36] R. Mortimer, *The Jockey Club* (London, 1958), 10–34.

Ascot was established.[37] Charles II's allegiance to Newmarket appears to have been wearing thin during the latter part of his reign. In 1681, under the influence of the Oxford Parliament, he moved his horses from the Heath to Burford, and urged his friends to do likewise. During his very last years, as part of his plan to transform Winchester into an English Versailles, he encouraged the development of the city's racing facilities.[38] Though none of these twists and turns in royal favour were ever to create a serious rival to Newmarket, they gave to the chosen courses a certain kudos, that in the case of Ascot was to be fully realized at a much later date.

Below Newmarket came the first general category of courses, the county meetings. All of these were located in county centres, though these need not necessarily be formal shire towns. In Lancashire and Staffordshire the focal points of county social life were Preston and Lichfield, rather than Lancaster and Stafford, and this is reflected in the pattern of racing at these places. Lichfield is mentioned in all seventeen of a sample of years drawn from the *Calendars* between 1730 and 1770, Stafford in only one; Preston in ten of the years, Lancaster in five.[39] Yorkshire, because of its size and great racing tradition, possessed several county meetings, not only at York, but also at Beverley and Doncaster.[40] After 1740 it is clear, even using the formal shire town as a crude marker of the county meeting, that this sector grew considerably in importance, and at the expense of the smaller racing centres. Whereas in 1739 less than one in five courses were located in shire towns, by 1760 the proportion had risen to one in three. The county meeting's capacity both to survive and capitalize on the years of crisis was partly due to the valuable short-term financial support that their host communities, which were relatively large and wealthy, were able to offer. In June 1740, a week before the racing legislation came into operation and two months before the city's race week, York corporation was informed that 'it hath been thought proper to advertise that the races for the future will be continued annually for

[37] J. Gill, *Racecourses of Great Britain* (London, 1975), 221–2; Longrigg, *Horse-Racing*, 55.

[38] Longrigg, *Horse-Racing*, 47; Defoe, *Tour*, i. 185; Evelyn, *Diary*, 755; Rosen, 'Winchester', 180.

[39] The sample years are 1730, 1735–40, 1745–6, 1749, 1755–60, and 1770. For the importance of the Lichfield races see A. J. Kettle, 'Lichfield Races', *Trans. of the Lichfield and South Staffordshire Archaeological Soc.*, vi (1964–5), 39–44.

[40] Beverley appears in all seventeen of the sample years and Doncaster in sixteen. For the Doncaster meeting see Fairfax-Blakeborough, *Northern Turf History*, iii. 193–203.

four days successively, for prizes not less than fifty pounds'. The town fathers agreed to guarantee this by underwriting the cost of the four prizes, as well as continuing their 'usual allowance' of £15. Other centres pursued a similar policy.[41] At a more general level, the county meeting's resilience and success derived from three principal characteristics: the size and nature of the region it serviced, the high status of those who attended it, and the sophisticated facilities that evolved around it.

It was essential that the county meeting draw its patronage not simply from the immediate locality, in the way a smaller course might do, but from a wide region. This need not conform precisely to county boundaries. In the early 1700s Nicholas Blundell and his cousin attended not only their native Lancashire meetings, but also occasionally crossed the Pennines to York, and in the mid-eighteenth century Sir Roger Newdigate, who lived close to the Staffordshire border in north Warwickshire, regularly visited both the Warwick and Lichfield races.[42] None the less, a county meeting had to have a specific shire, or portion of one, on whose backing it could depend. In drawing upon this core of support it was able to exploit a particularly lucrative and loyal source of demand. During the early modern period the county emerged as a vitally important administrative and political unit, one which provided a focus around which the ruling élite could organize themselves in the localities and develop a sense of social cohesion.[43] Subscription to a plate or prize and attendance at the races and the concomitant entertainments were a sign of one's allegiance to shire society, and an opportunity to reaffirm the bonds that held it together.

The second feature of the county meeting, its wealth and prestige, flowed naturally from the first. Contemporaries often commented on the numbers and quality of the 'company' who visited the county events. In 1733 one correspondent enthusiastically reported how 'my sister Delves, Dolly, and myself went to Lichfield races . . . where we met all the world, indeed, I never saw so much good company together in any place before', and Defoe could write of Nottingham, 'it is a glorious show they have here when the running season begins,

---

[41] House Book, 17 June 1740, YCA; Fairfax-Blakeborough, *Northern Turf History*, iii. 196; Brand, *Newcastle*, i. 434.

[42] Blundell, *Diurnal*, iii. 19–21, 218; Newdigate Diaries, 7–8 and 27–8 Aug. 1751, 11–12 and 25–6 Aug. 1752.

[43] Everitt, 'County and Town', 88–9.

for here is such an assembly of gentlemen of quality, that not Banstead Down, or Newmarket Heath, produces better company'.[44] This impression of the high status of those frequenting county meetings is confirmed by the evidence from subscription lists for gentlemen's race prizes. Three such lists survive for mid-eighteenth-century Warwick (1744, 1745, and 1754) and one for Stratford-upon-Avon (1755).[45] Those for Warwick reveal that perhaps 30 per cent of the subscribers held the title of knight or above, and that about 15 per cent could be included among the aristocracy. The single list for Stratford provides a useful comparison. Though 13 per cent of the contributors were aristocrats, the overall proportion of the subscribers with the title of knight or above is only 20 per cent. This suggests that there was a significant difference between the status of a shire meeting, like that at Warwick, and an important market town course, such as that of neighbouring Stratford.

The county meeting's third characteristic was its sophisticated social infrastructure. Much of this focused upon the provision of food and refreshments, which could give rise to some bumper feasts or 'ordinaries'. At Lichfield in 1733 'there was a hundred and fifty gentlemen dined at one ordinary, beside what dined at another inn in town and private houses', and in 1751 '174 dined in garden, and in house in all 200'. It was reported from Worcester in 1759 that 'Upwards of five hundred persons were at the public breakfast at Digley bowling-green on the Thursday morning, and about three hundred on Friday morning.' Inns were at the forefront in catering for these occasions, and in 1755 four of Worcester's hostelries took it in turn to provide an ordinary on each day of the meeting.[46] Inns, together with booths on the course,[47] also purveyed alcoholic beverages, which for a number of racegoers appear to have been the *raison d'être* of the whole event. Among those attending the Salisbury races in 1766 was 'Lord Starorsdale, who got most exceedingly drunk the last day', and in 1731 Thomas Smales recorded in his diary, 'June 12, to Newcastle races.

[44] HMC, *Hastings MSS*, iii. 18; Defoe, *Tour*, ii. 143.

[45] Subscribers to the Warwick Plate 1744 and 1745, Warwickshire CRO, CR.136 (Newdigate MSS)/2523; Articles and Subscription List, Warwick Races 1754, CR.229 (Shirley MSS), Box 2/2; Subscription Lists, Stratford-upon-Avon Races 1755 and 1758, Shakespeare Birthplace Trust, ER.2/188.

[46] HMC, *Hastings MSS*, iii. 18; Newdigate Diaries, 27 Aug. 1751; *Berrow's Worcester Jnl.*, 1759, quoted in Gill, *Racecourses*, 230.

[47] For booths see *VCH Shropshire*, ii (London, 1973), 178; Macmahon, *Beverley Corporation Minute-Books*, 14, 24; *Bath Advertiser*, No. 49, 18 Sept. 1756.

Very drunk. June 13, Sunday. At do. Drinking day and night. June 14, won the plate. Drinking day and night. . . . June 17, at home very ill.' For the Sussex grocer Thomas Turner, the Lewes races were often the excuse for painful overindulgence:

Sat. 5 Aug. [1758] I came home [from the races] . . . about ten; but, to my shame do I say it, very much in liquor.
Thurs. 23 Aug. [1764] . . . Came home about 9.30, but happy should I be could I say sober. Oh my unhappy—nay, I may say, unfortunate—disposition, that am so irresolute and cannot refrain from what my soul detests. . . . Saw several London riders upon the downs, with whom I drank a glass or two [of] punch.[48]

Food and drink, as well as providing sustenance, were also part of a wider nexus of facilities designed to offer entertainment and promote social contact. Cock-fighting frequently accompanied the racing,[49] and the *Calendars* had a specific section advertising matches, often between rival counties. Hunts were occasionally arranged to coincide with the races. In 1753 it was reported that at Doncaster 'a number of stables are taken up for hunters by gentlemen who intend to take the diversion of stag- and fox-hunting during the race week and week after', and two years earlier it had been claimed that over 4,000 mounted noblemen, squires, and yeomen met the Marquis of Granby's staghounds on the town moor.[50] For the less robust there were often the services of a travelling theatre group or band of musicians. In 1723 'Mr Tollett, with his company of comedians', advertised his intention 'to entertain the public with some celebrated pieces of dramatic performance' at the Bury St Edmunds' meeting. Two years later 'Tollett's company of comedians' was again on hand for the occasion, although this time it faced the competition of 'Powell's puppet-show from the Bath . . . designing to divert the quality and gentry with new entertainments every evening during the horse-race'.[51] The Guildhall at Shrewsbury accommodated a concert during

[48] Dorothy Long to her brother, 26 Aug. 1766, Wiltshire RO, 947; Smales diary quoted in Gill, *Racecourses*, 143; T. Turner, *The Diary of Thomas Turner*, ed. D. Vaisey (Oxford, 1984), 160, 300–1.

[49] Scott, *History of Cock-Fighting*, 107; printed Bills for Stratford-upon-Avon and Warwick Races (1769), Shakespeare Birthplace Trust, PR.64; Fairfax-Blakeborough, *Northern Turf History*, ii. 4, 35, 37, 73, 86, 125–6, 195–6, 238, 260; Rice, *British Turf*, ii. 34; Kettle, 'Lichfield Races', 43; Bellingham, *Diary*, 113.

[50] Fairfax-Blakeborough, *Northern Turf History*, iii. 197, 201.

[51] *Suffolk Mercury*, x, No. 9, 19 Aug. 1723; xvi, No. 4, 24 May 1725; and also Rosenfeld, *Strolling Players*, 6, 111, 117, 176.

the race week of 1729, and forty years later 'the company' at Lichfield 'was entertained at the public breakfasts by a fine band of music from London', whose expenses were so great that they plunged the meeting's accounts into deficit.[52] The most impressive and prestigious of the entertainments mounted were the evening assemblies. In 1757 Thomas Turner, not himself a member of the charmed county circle, arrived at the Lewes meeting 'just as the people came from the hill. We went in to see the ball, which, in my opinion, was an extreme pretty sight.' In the same year Lybbe Powys, visiting Chesterfield during race week, recorded how 'on the Wednesday . . . about ten we went to the assembly room, where the Duke of Devonshire always presided as master of the ceremonies . . . on the third day again went to the course . . . that evening's ball was equally brilliant as the first night, and both gave us strangers a high idea of these annual assemblies'.[53]

The social infrastructure was to be seen at its most sophisticated at York, the racing capital of the North. For a week in late summer the city buzzed with activity, as the gentry and nobility gathered in their hundreds to enjoy a feast of leisure pursuits.[54] In 1730 Simon Scrope could write with pleasurable anticipation,

Tomorrow we set out for York . . . to join the great doings of the week, the like of which no town or city can compare with for gaiety, sports, and company all of one mind. Every year there be more noble lords, gentle dames, and commoners of high and low degree at York for the races, the cockings, assemblies, and meetings of horse-coursers and hunters.[55]

Off the course, the focal point of activity was the assembly rooms. One of the principal reasons for building the magnificent new premises opened during the York meeting of 1732 was to accommodate the lavish entertainments of race week. During the morning these included daily concerts and recitals given by the music assembly and visiting artistes, assisted by the city waits and other hired performers.[56]

---

[52] *VCH Shropshire*, ii. 178; *Aris's Birmingham Gazette*, quoted in M. A. Hopkins, *Dr Johnson's Lichfield* (London, 1956), 53; Kettle, 'Lichfield Races', 42.

[53] Turner, *Diary*, 108; Powys, *Diaries*, 24–5.

[54] Drake, *Eboracum*, 241; Fairfax-Blakeborough, *Northern Turf History*, iii. 26, 65; Thomson, *Letters of a Grandmother*, 57.

[55] Diary quoted in Fairfax-Blakeborough, *Northern Turf History*, iii. 31.

[56] Assembly Rooms Minute Book, 24 Mar. 1732/3, 27 July and 2 Aug. 1733, 27 July 1739, 19 July 1736, 5 Sept. 1737, 12 May 1744, 28 July 1752, 26 May 1753, YCA; Thomson, *Letters of a Grandmother*, 58.

In the evening the rooms housed the grand assemblies. Though we cannot be sure how many attended these special balls, several hundreds may have packed into the building at any one time. Normally between 200 and 300 subscribers' tickets were printed for race week, though this could rise considerably higher: in 1755, 600 were produced, and in the following year, 400. Not all these were necessarily purchased, but there are reports of 314 subscribers in 1752 (oddly above the volume of tickets printed in that year), and 449 people attending the assemblies in 1768.[57] Refreshments and recreational accessories within the rooms were provided by a number of approved tradesmen. During race week 1736 Mrs Wilson sold tea, coffee, chocolate, orange chips, queen-cakes, gloves, and packs of cards; Philemon Marsh dealt in more heady beverages, offering 'arrack made into punch', 'mountain wine in a negus', French white wine, French claret, red and white port, Burgundy, and Champagne; and Mr Joy was given permission to 'keep a basset-table'.[58] The race balls, crowded with the élite of northern society, and embellished by the very acme of architectural and sartorial elegance, must have presented a stunning spectacle. In 1736 Drake wrote of these occasions,

here it is that York shines indeed, when, by the light of several elegant lustres, a concourse of four or five hundred of both sexes, out of the best families in the kingdom, are met together. In short, the politeness of the gentlemen, the richness of the dress, and remarkable beauty of the ladies, and, of late, the magnificence of the room they meet in, cannot be equalled, throughout, in any part of Europe (see Fig. 13).[59]

Below the grand county meetings came a rather amorphous group of market town courses. These drew their clientele from a much narrower geographical area; consequently the status of those who attended was generally lower and the social facilities proportionately less developed. Not that social facilities were entirely missing. Swaffham and Bungay both mounted race assemblies in 1737, and in 1725 Beccles was to be visited during its meeting by a jeweller from Bury St Edmunds selling 'all sorts of silverware, of the newest fashion, and china, and Tunbridge ware'.[60] At various times Swaffham,

[57] Assembly Rooms Minute Book, 3 Aug. 1752, 26 July 1755, 13 Aug. 1756, YCA; Fairfax-Blakeborough, *Northern Turf History*, iii. 55, 67.

[58] Assembly Rooms Minute Book, 12 and 26 July 1736, YCA.

[59] Drake, *Eboracum*, 241.

[60] *Suffolk Mercury*, xvi, No. 6, 7 June 1725; xxiv, No. 274, 6 June 1737; xxiv, No. 280, 18 July 1737.

Stratford-upon-Avon, Barnsley, and Rugby laid on ordinaries, though not on the scale of the county meetings: at the Rugby races in 1752 Sir Roger Newdigate counted only fifteen couples dining on the first day, and fifty-four gentlemen on the second.[61]

Somewhat different in character from the market town courses were those located in the resorts. Able to draw on the support of wealthy visitors, these meetings enjoyed a cosmopolitan and prestigious image. This quality was alluded to in 1727, when it was reported of Bath that 'the neighbouring hills afford the most pleasant down imaginable, where it is incredible what a number of coaches and horses appear there at a race'.[62] That symbol of status, tne coach, was also to be found on Banstead Downs near Epsom, which Defoe observed 'on the public race days . . . are covered with coaches and ladies, and an innumerable company of horsemen, as well gentlemen as citizens, attending the sport'. Epsom was in fact one of the great courses of the land. Though the principal event was in May, there were at various times two and even three meetings a year, and by 1770 a biannual policy seems to have been firmly settled. Epsom's importance rested squarely on its position as a resort located only a short distance from the metropolis, and as early as 1663 Pepys recorded that on race days the road from London was 'full of citizens going and coming toward Epsom'.[63]

One further way in which several of the resort courses differed from the market town meetings was in their setting. Neither Epsom or Tunbridge Wells were normally listed as market towns, and both seem to have cultivated a semi-rural image to enhance their appeal to Londoners. In this sense they belonged to a whole category of rural meetings, which contained its own internal hierarchy. At the top were those courses staging prestigious events, such as Wallasey in Cheshire and Hambleton in Yorkshire, the former used by a circle of wealthy aristocrats in the North-West, the latter supported by large numbers of the Yorkshire gentry.[64] Socially on a par with this type of course,

[61] Ibid. xxiv, No. 274, 6 June 1737; printed Bill for Stratford-upon-Avon Races (1769), Shakespeare Birthplace Trust, PR.64; Fairfax-Blakeborough, *Northern Turf History*, ii. 27; Newdigate Diaries, 23 June 1752.

[62] Cox, *Magna Britannia*, iv. 734.

[63] Defoe, *Tour*, i. 159; *Racing Calendar* (1730, 1740, 1749, 1760, and 1770); D. Hunn, *Epsom Racecourse: Its Story and its People* (London, 1973), 27–48; Pepys, *Diary*, iv. 245.

[64] Fairfax-Blakeborough, *Northern Turf History*, i, chap. 1; ii. 263–4; Defoe, *Tour*, ii. 235.

but of less wide significance, were the park meetings situated in the grounds of a country house, as at Lynsted Park (Kent), Bramham (Yorkshire), Knowsley (Lancashire), and Whittlebury (Northampton-shire). Very much at the bottom of the ladder came the village meet-ing, which catered largely for plebeian society. A particular form of this was to be found in the plethora of small courses that grew up on the fringe of London to serve its huge working population. The rural meetings never appear to have played more than a minority role in the world of racing, though there may have been many that never reached the pages of contemporary newspapers and yearbooks. They comprise less than a third of the pre-1771 courses traced, and an even lower proportion of those for any individual year in the *Calendars*. Many were seriously damaged by the legislation of 1740, which was deliberately cast to destroy such meetings. Even high-status courses like Wallasey and Hambleton were to be critically weakened in the long-term by their lack of the social infrastructure that a town could offer. Significantly, both were swallowed up by two of the urban racing giants: during the eighteenth century the valuable Wallasey Stakes was moved to Newmarket and the Hambleton Gold Cup transferred to nearby York.[65]

The period between about 1680 and 1760 laid the foundations of modern horse-racing. Though steeple-chasing was yet to be introduced, a present day devotee of the flat would find much to recognize in the world of racing at George III's accession. One immediately intelligible feature would be the close, almost symbiotic relationship between town and turf. From the beginning of the sport most courses had developed in urban centres. The crisis of the 1740s, with its attendant rationalization, simply accentuated this pattern. But the links between towns and racing were much deeper than ones of mere geography. Both shared a common economic and social interest. On the one hand, many towns during this period, as we have seen, were developing a novel and lucrative role as centres of fashionable pastimes and services, and were constantly seeking to improve the quality and range of those they possessed. On the other hand, racing itself was becoming more and more a social occasion, and not just a sporting one, that required the extensive lodging, leisure, and consumer facilities which only a town, and preferably a large one, could offer. It was a merging of interests, though on a lesser scale, that

[65] *VCH Cambridgeshire*, v. 281; Longrigg, *Horse-Racing*, 88.

can be discerned in several of the recreations examined in this chapter, not least cricket and hunting. During the eighteenth century the world of the town and that of sport was becoming increasingly bound together in a marriage of mutual convenience.

In this section the spotlight has been turned on high-status leisure. All the signs point to a remarkable degree of development in this field, either through the introduction of new pastimes and facilities (such as coffee-houses, the provincial press, circulating libraries, assemblies, and public walks), or through the transformation of old ones (like drama, music, cricket, and horse-racing). Much of this growth was focused on provincial towns, injecting a new degree of refinement into their social life and raising their cultural image from the depressed level of the pre-Restoration years, so that by the reign of George III many were in the vanguard of fashion. The following section will explore why this transformation occurred, and what were its social implications.

IV
SOCIETY

8

The Economic Foundations

Sections Two and Three of this study sought to establish the material forms of the Urban Renaissance. But why did such a movement emerge, and how did it affect the social psychology and behaviour of those drawn into its sphere of influence? These are the questions addressed in this fourth section of the book. An initial chapter examines the socio-economic foundations of the Urban Renaissance, while the next two show how it was driven by the very different but complementary forces of competition and idealism as manifested in the pursuit of status, civility, and sociability. The final chapter explores how the impact of the movement spread beyond the élite to generate cultural differences and tensions in society as a whole, which prefigured the class divisions of a later period.

The foundations of the Urban Renaissance were first and foremost economic ones. Somebody had to purchase and somebody had to produce the goods and services that constituted the cultural revival. Given this, then two interrelated factors require investigation: the flow of wealth or demand, and the means of production or supply. But the urban dimension of the process must also be accounted for, to explain how it was that the town came to be a focal point for the consumption and manufacture of culture.

1. DEMAND

One of the most striking features of post-Restoration England was its economic buoyancy. Commerce, agriculture, and industry flourished in a manner that contrasted sharply with the 'lean years' of the early seventeenth century, and placed the nation's economy in a quite new context.[1] Such prosperity generated powerful new flows of wealth,

[1] Wilson, *England's Apprenticeship*, calls 1603-60 'The Lean Years', and 1660-1700' 'The Turning Tide'; Coleman, *Economy of England*, writes of 'The New Context' in the English economy in the century after 1650.

which in their turn were to reshape the whole pattern of cultural consumption.

The products and facilities of the Urban Renaissance were self-evidently of a luxury nature. As such they would have only a secondary call on a family's income, purchasable only after the basic necessities of life had been satisfied. The demand for high-status cultural goods, therefore, depended upon the volume of what may be called *surplus wealth*. This was critically affected both by the level of the national income, and by its social distribution. Not only was England's total wealth growing considerably after 1660, but it was also being distributed in a fashion that encouraged the expansion of non-essential personal disposable income. Two factors encouraged the second of these processes. First, demographic stagnation ensured that the substantial increase in wealth seen in the period led to a significant rise in average per capita real income. During the later Tudor and early Stuart years quite the opposite had happened, as population growth had outstripped that of the economy as a whole, depressing the incomes of the majority, and driving many into serious poverty.[2] Second, it is clear that the benefits of later Stuart and early Georgian prosperity were not evenly distributed, but went disproportionately to those occupying the higher rungs of the social ladder, including not only the traditional ruling élite, but also the rapidly expanding middling ranks. These were precisely the groups that enjoyed the highest ratio of surplus to basic wealth and had the greatest tendency to direct any additional income towards luxury expenditure. It was they who provided the bulk of demand for the products of the Urban Renaissance, and whose economic fortunes must therefore be explored in greater detail.

Individually, the most well-heeled of all consumers were the landed élite, among whom a superfluity of wealth (real or apparent) was almost a defining characteristic. In many respects the golden age of the country gentry pre-dated the Urban Renaissance.[3] Able to exploit escalating food prices, improving rent-rolls, and a land bonanza, during the sixteenth and seventeenth centuries their numbers and

[2] Wrigley and Schofield, *Population History*, 208-9; K. Wrightson, *English Society 1580-1680* (London, 1982), 121-48.

[3] G. E. Mingay, *The Gentry: The Rise and Fall of a Ruling Class* (London, 1976), 39-73; F. M. L. Thompson, 'The Social Distribution of Landed Property in England since the Sixteenth Century', *EcHR*, 2nd ser., xix, No. 3 (1966), 514-15; J. P. Cooper, 'The Social Distribution of Land and Men in England 1436-1700', *EcHR*, 2nd ser., xx, No. 3 (1967), 419-40.

personal wealth increased substantially. One estimate suggests that the body of the lesser gentry grew threefold in the period, and another that between the early fifteenth century and about 1700 the gentry (excluding the greatest landowners) increased their ownership of English and Welsh property from around a quarter to a half of the total acreage.[4] It is argued that after 1650 this age of prosperity was already beginning to wane. Civil war debts, and later, falling agricultural prices. stagnant or declining rent-rolls, spiralling living costs, and from the 1690s an astringent land tax, all conspired to undermine the well-being of at least the smaller landowners. However, the accumulated wealth of the landed élite remained a major force in consumer demand in the century after the Restoration. The aristocracy and greater county gentry enjoyed continuing, and probably mounting affluence during this period, their large capital resources allowing them to exploit the rich economic opportunities available. Moreover, the pressures on the smaller gentry may have been exaggerated. The land tax was not as ferocious as it appeared, since it was only levied at its full rate in East Anglia and areas close to London, and the burden of payment was not infrequently passed on to tenants. The fall in grain prices was positively beneficial for landlords in pastoral regions, since it reduced the cost of animal foodstuffs and permitted them to raise their rentals. For the more enterprising gentry, even given limited resources, there were ever widening opportunities for investment in agricultural improvement, industrial ventures, trade, and the securities market. If some of the parish gentry failed, as they did in all periods, there was always a pool of new recruits, several with their fortunes made in city and town, to take their privileged place.[5]

The most critical factor in stimulating consumer demand among the landed élite, and one that potentially affected all of its members, was their almost reckless tendency to spend up to the limit of their income, and beyond. This was due not so much to any hedonistic inclination

[4] L. Stone, 'Social Mobility in England 1500-1700', *Past and Present*, xxxiii (1966), 23-4; Mingay, *Gentry*, 59.

[5] H. J. Habakkuk, 'English Landownership 1680-1740', *EcHR*, x (1939-40), 2-17; B. A. Holderness, 'The English Land Market in the Eighteenth Century: The Case of Lincolnshire', *EcHR*, 2nd ser., xxvii, No. 4 (1974), 557-76; J. V. Beckett, 'English Landownership in the Later Seventeenth and Eighteenth Centuries: The Debate and the Problems', *EcHR*, 2nd ser., xxx, No. 4 (1977), 567-81; J. V. Beckett, 'Land Tax Administration at the Local Level', in M. Turner and D. Mills (eds.), *Land and Property: The English Land Tax 1692-1832* (Gloucester, 1986), 165-72; Jenkins, *Ruling Class*, 44-72; W. A. Speck, *Stability and Strife: England 1714-1760* (London, 1977), 70-3.

towards extravagance, as to the extraordinary pressures on them to engage in conspicuous consumption merely to maintain, let alone improve their status.[6] Given that these pressures had escalated to a quite new level, as will be argued, there is every reason to believe that the gentry and aristocracy were directing a greater proportion of their resources into luxury expenditure than ever before. They were encouraged in this by the expanding opportunities for borrowing, particularly through mortgaging their properties. Such practices permitted them to raise their spending power, at least in the short term, considerably beyond that of their normal annual income.

The most telling sign of the landed élite's contribution to the Urban Renaissance, and a suggestive indication of their prosperity as a social group, lies in contemporary evidence of their impact on town life. Innumerable letters, diaries, visitors' lists, and travellers' descriptions leave no doubt as to their influence on the development of the major spas. Less spectacular, but of greater general significance, was their contribution to the evolution of the county centres. The nearby estates of the landed gentry were of considerable value to such towns. Defoe observed this to be the case at Lewes when he wrote 'that which adds to the character of this town, is that both the town and the country adjacent is full of gentlemen of good families and fortunes'; the same was true at Winchester where an 'abundance of gentry being in the neighbourhood, it adds to the sociableness of the place' and at Maidstone where the surrounding country was 'spangled with . . . delicious seats of the nobility and gentry; . . . this neighbourhood of persons of figure and quality, makes' the town 'a very agreeable place to live in'.[7]

The rural gentry's demand for luxury crafts, services, and entertainments in the shire towns can be traced in their personal and estate records. The list of subscribers to the Warwick races of 1754 reads like a roll-call of the county's gentry, with figures like Lord Brooke of Warwick Castle, Sir Roger Newdigate of Arbury, Sir Charles Mordaunt of Walton, and George Lucy of Charlecote. The Mordaunt and Lucy families, living only six to eight miles from Warwick, regularly

---

[6] N. McKendrick, 'The Commercialization of Fashion', in McKendrick *et al.*, *Birth of a Consumer Society*, 55; and for examples of high expenditure and indebtedness see Jenkins, *Ruling Class*, 67, 196–9; J. V. Beckett, 'The Lowthers at Holker: Marriage, Inheritance, and Debt in the Fortunes of an Eighteenth-Century Landowning Family', *Trans. of the Historic Soc. of Lancashire and Cheshire*, cxxvii (1978), 47–64.

[7] Defoe, *Tour*, i. 114–15, 129, 186; and also Macky, *Journey*, i. 88.

patronized the town's services and trades. During the 1690s and early
1700s Sir John Mordaunt made payments to John Bradshaw the
apothecary (for medicine and home visits), George Tongue the bookseller, and a number of mercers and tailors working in the town. Dr
William Lucy's account book of 1723 records that he spent £2.11s. at
the Warwick races (excluding a contribution of a guinea to the plate),
and that during the year he settled bills with several of the town's
mercers and haberdashers, a wine merchant, chandler, brazier, and
'Mr Smith, master builder', the renowned Francis Smith whose yard in
Warwick was the nerve-centre of a major provincial building firm.
George Lucy's housekeeper's accounts of the mid-eighteenth century
reveal the purchase of textiles and china in the town, including '3 pair
of fine holland sheets . . . and 3 pair of pillow-cases marked G.L.',
and 'a dozen of blue and white china tea cups and saucers, 6 chocolate
cups and saucers, [and] 6 coffee mugs with handles'. They also show
that in 1763 'Mr Hiorn's men began to alter the great parlour', a
reference to another important architectural practice based in
Warwick, which in the 1750s was responsible for 'gothicising' Sir
Roger Newdigate's library at Arbury.[8]

The landed élite's impact on county centres was not confined to the
role of visitor and external consumer. Several maintained permanent
urban residences, secondary to their main estates, which they could
use as a base from which to engage in the social and political activities
of the town. Such archetypal Georgian streets as Micklegate in York
and Broad Street in Ludlow, with their fine classical façades and
interiors, owe a good deal to this practice.[9] A number of major
landowners also had their principal residences in, or adjacent to a
town: figures like the Lowthers at Whitehaven, the Brookes at
Warwick, the Dukes of Somerset at Petworth, and the Earl of Bathurst
at Cirencester. The economic impact of these seigneurial families on
their hosts must have been enormous. During the rebuilding of
Petworth House in the late 1680s and 1690s, upwards of £1,000 a year
was being paid to local men in wages alone. In 1695 Lord Brooke's
'stewards of the house' dispensed about £4,000, just over a quarter of
which was used during family visits to London and Bath, leaving the

[8] Warwickshire CRO, CR.229, Box 2/2; CR.1368, i, fo. 17; iv, fos. 42, 44-5, 72;
Personal Account Book of Dr William Lucy 2 Jan. 1722/3-1 Feb. 1723/4, L6/1257;
Household Book of Mrs Hayes 1755-71, L6/1476; Colvin, *Dictionary*.

[9] RCHM, *York*, iii. 68 and *passim*; Lloyd, *Broad Street*, 19-20; Hall, *Beverley*, 3,
53-4; Lobel, *Atlas*, i, Gloucester, 14; HMC, *Portland MSS*, vi. 190.

remainder to be distributed among a profusion of servants, tradesmen, and craftsmen, the majority of whom appear to have been based
in Warwick.[10]

The geographical proximity of these landed grandees and their
towns was in a way accidental. But this was not the case for a large
group of gentry who chose to reside permanently in urban centres. In
1709 Calamy described Preston as having an 'abundance of gentry in
it'; Defoe observed that at Salisbury 'there are many good families
. . . besides the citizens', and that at York an 'abundance of good
families live here'; in the 1760s Burr wrote of Tonbridge that 'a great
many good houses have lately been erected in it by gentlemen who
have fixed upon this town as their place of residence'; and later in the
century Nash claimed that at Worcester a 'great concourse of polite
strangers . . . come here to reside from every quarter'.[11] Such people
were part of a novel social stratum, the so-called town or pseudo-
gentry, and it has been estimated that by the second half of the
eighteenth century they comprised about 4 per cent of a county
centre's population. In such numbers, and with their wealth and
cultural aspirations, they played a central role in the revival of these
communities. Some of their number were *émigré* country gentlemen,
but the majority were primarily townspeople who lived an essentially
leisured existence, succoured not by any occupation but by the
lucrative returns on inherited capital. Their swelling ranks owed much
to the considerable number of small fortunes accumulated and
bequeathed in post-Restoration England, and to the widening
opportunities to secure a regular income from money-lending and
investment in urban property and the stock-market.[12]

If the gentry and pseudo-gentry provided a solid foundation of
support for the Urban Renaissance, it was the expanding middling
ranks whose wealth was the dynamic and decisive force behind it. Even
prior to the Restoration, but at an accelerating rate after it, these
groups were coming to form a substantial section in English society.[13]

[10] Kenyon, 'Petworth Town and Trades', 95; Castle Accounts, 1695-8, Warwickshire
CRO, Warwick Castle MSS.

[11] E. Calamy, *An Historical Account of My Own Life*, ed. J. T. Rutt (London, 1829),
ii. 221; Defoe, *Tour*, i. 189; ii. 230; Burr, *Tunbridge Wells*, 223-4; Nash,
Worcestershire, ii, p. cxv.

[12] A. Everitt, 'Social Mobility in Early Modern England', *Past and Present*, xxxiii
(1966), 70-2; Everitt, 'County and Town', 95-6; A. Henstock, 'Group Projects in Local
History: Buildings and Society in a Georgian Market Town', *Bulletin of Local History:
East Midlands Region*, xiii (1978), 4-5.

[13] Stone, 'Social Mobility', 24-6; Stone, *Open Élite*, 290-1; Porter, *English Society*,
85-99.

Though not as well off individually as most of the landed élite, together they generated a total demand that may have rivalled, and even eclipsed that of their superiors. Spearheading the contribution of the urban bourgeoisie were the professions. It is argued that the years 1680 to 1730 are among the most influential in the development of this occupational group. Under the influence of an increasingly complex economy and society, of rising standards of material prosperity, and of the expansion of the state to meet the exigencies of war, the number of those employed in the professions increased by almost 70 per cent to between 55,000 and 60,000 individuals.[14] In town after town their size and influence grew during the seventeenth century, particularly after 1660,[15] and many were able to command rising fees and salaries. Several of the new intellectual institutions established in towns owed their existence to professional people. Of the original nineteen founders of the Huntingdon book club in 1742, there were eight clergymen, six attorneys, as well as a surgeon, a physician, an apothecary, and two unidentified members. Two years later the Revd Dr William Standfast left over a thousand volumes to the Nottingham Blue-coat School to establish a public library to be utilized by 'clergy, lawyers, physicians, and other persons of a liberal and learned education'. The founder and leading light of the Spalding Gentlemen's Society was Maurice Johnson, a counsellor-at-law, who in his history of the society noted that 'all the presidents, almost, were men of professions'.[16] The intellectual influence of such men is also revealed by the key role they played, from the later Stuart period onwards, in the compiling of town histories.[17]

The impact of the professions can be traced most vividly in their contribution to the urban architectural revival. Lawyers, who were concentrated especially in assize, duchy, and palatinate towns, spent

[14] Holmes, *Augustan England*, especially 12, 16.

[15] A. Everitt, *Change in the Provinces: The Seventeenth Century* (Leicester, 1969), 43-6; Everitt, *Ways and Means*, 36, 38; Clark, *Country Towns*, 23-4; Clark, *Provincial Towns*, 32-4; Clark, 'Civic Leaders', 324; McInnes, *English Town*, 25-6; Borsay, 'Provincial Urban Culture', 584-5; Brown, 'Colchester in the Eighteenth Century', 158-9, 161; Parker, *King's Lynn*, 14-16; May, *Newmarket*, 70-2; Reed, 'Seventeenth-Century Ipswich', 102-3, 110-14; Rosen, 'Winchester', 177-9; McIntyre, 'Rise of a Resort Town', 221, 228; Phillips, 'Economic Change in Kendal', 104; Ellis, 'Social Relations in Newcastle', 194.

[16] Kaufman, 'English Book Clubs', 16, 24; quoted in Kaufman, 'Community Library', 44; Owen, *Spalding Gentlemen's Society*, pp. viii-ix. For the importance of the professions in the cultural life of Bristol see Barry, 'Cultural Life of Bristol', 94-5, 99, 206.

[17] P. Clark, 'Visions of the Urban Community; Antiquarians and the English City before 1800', in Fraser and Sutcliffe, *Urban History*, 115-17.

minor fortunes in erecting and decorating their dwellings. When Fiennes visited Preston, home of the Duchy of Lancaster courts and a place well populated by 'attorneys, proctors, and notaries', she noted at the entrance to the town the fashionable home of a local legal family the Pattens: 'a very good house . . . all stone work, 5 windows in the front, and high built according to the eastern building near London, the ascent to the house was 14 or 15 stone steps, large and handsome court with open iron palisades'. She discovered at Launceston '2 or 3 good houses built after the London form by some lawyers', and observed in the Newarke at Leicester 'several good houses, some of stone and brick, in which some lawyers live frank'. Though the Preston mansion of the Pattens was dismantled in 1835, the grandiloquent classical town houses of the legal princes of the period still adorn the streets of several towns.[18]

A number of the lawyers' new houses belonged to men working in the ecclesiastical courts,[19] which suggests another group among the professions that added to the town's physical embellishment, the clergy. Particularly important was the 'privileged pyramid' of their upper ranks, at this time boosted by increasing recruitment from among the gentry and by the availability of substantial incomes. Cathedral centres, where they generally resided, witnessed a surge in clerical building activity after the Restoration, which produced smart town houses that were frequently clustered together around a close.[20] Macky found 'the best houses in Winchester are the Dean and prebends' houses in the Close', and Defoe confirmed that 'the clergy here live . . . very handsomely', there 'are very good houses, and very handsomely built, for the prebendaries, canons, and other dignitaries of this church'.[21]

Medicine was among the most dynamic of the professions in Augustan England, as the numbers and status of physicians, and espe-

---

[18] Fiennes, *Journeys*, 163, 187, 269; Defoe, *Tour*, ii. 268; *VCH Lancashire*, vii. 77 n. 65; *BE Oxfordshire*, 508-9; *BE Wiltshire*, 2nd edn. (Harmondsworth, 1975), 172, 429; Holmes, *Augustan England*, 161; G. Acton and D. Lloyd, *Ludlow Walks* (n.p. [1983]); *BE Shropshire*, 187-8; Lloyd, *Broad Street*, 37; *BE Northamptonshire*, 366; J. L. Cartwright, 'Oundle in the Eighteenth Century through the Eyes of John Clifton', *Northamptonshire Past and Present*, v, Part 4 (1976), 340; D. Dodd, *Mompesson House, Salisbury*, National Trust Guide (1984).

[19] Fiennes, *Journeys*, 202; Drake, *Eboracum*, 319.

[20] Holmes, Augustan England, 87-94; Fiennes, *Journeys*, 5-6; Macky, *Journey*, ii. 38; Defoe, *Tour*, i. 117-18, 227; ii. 80; *VCH Wiltshire*, vi. 78; *BE Wiltshire*, 422-34.

[21] Macky, *Journey*, ii. 14; Defoe, *Tour*, i. 184; Rosen, 'Winchester', 182; *BE Hampshire*, 687-90.

cially apothecaries and surgeons, rose substantially. In major towns they came to form a sizeable community. The Preston in-burgesses' roll of 1742 records two physicians, five apothecaries, a druggist, and two surgeons, not to mention thirty-three barbers who may have purveyed some medical services; and Bristol in 1758 boasted five physicians, twenty-nine apothecaries, nineteen surgeons, and thirteen barber-surgeons.[22] The development of the profession on this scale, whilst itself reflecting the general growth in disposable income (as more and more people were able to afford the luxury of specialist therapeutic treatment), also contributed directly to the stock of surplus wealth. Many a successful medical practitioner invested his earnings in a handsome town dwelling, several of which still survive. The tall Cupola House in Bury St Edmunds, aptly named after its crowning feature, was built in 1693 by the apothecary Thomas Macro, and was described by Fiennes shortly after its construction as 'in the new mode of building, 4 rooms of a floor pretty sizeable and high, well furnished, a drawing-room, and a chamber full of china, and a damask bed embroidered'. A year before Macro erected his new home, the Warwick physician William Johnston (*c*.1643-1725) celebrated his successful career (he had arrived in the town in about 1675 with an overseas qualification, and ten years later was admitted a fellow of the Royal College of Physicians) by building a fine residence just outside the East Gate. Constructed of brick with stone dressing, composed of five bays and two storeys with attics, lighted by sash-windows, and decorated with a fine modillion cornice, it was to prove something of a model for post-fire houses in the town. Seven years later the prosperous physician Claver Morris (1659-1727) laid out £800 on the construction of his new home in the East Liberty at Wells. In the early 1720s he embellished the roofline with ten hugely pretentious but modish classical vases, 'the urn fluted, with leafage in the body; the cover fluted and guddornd [*sic*], and flame at the top', each no less than three feet high.[23]

[22] Holmes, *Augustan England*, chaps. 6-7, especially pp. 191-2, 223-32; Guild Roll 1742, PCMSS; T. D. Whittet, 'The Apothecary in Provincial Guilds', *Medical History*, viii, No. 3 (1964), 249.

[23] Fiennes, *Journeys*, 152; *BE Suffolk*, 149; R. A. Cohen, 'Documents Concerning Dr William Johnston, Physician, of Warwick', *TBAS*, lxxviii (1962), 55-9; *VCH Warwickshire*, viii. 443; Landor House: Articles of Agreement and Proposed Elevation, Warwickshire CRO, CR.1618, WA.6/116 (Ann Johnston's Charity); Hobhouse, *Diary of a West Country Physician*, 13, 37-8, 122, 124, 127-9, 131. For other surviving houses of the medical profession see *BE Oxfordshire*, 519-20; *VCH York*, 249; Hutchinson and

Among the middling ranks the contribution of the professions to the Urban Renaissance was almost equalled by that of commerce and business. The expansion of internal and external trade after the Restoration, and the growth of industry, particularly textiles and metalwares, increased the size and lined the pockets of the merchant and manufacturing communities. Material signs of their prosperity abounded. The handsome Bridgeland Street constructed alongside the quay at Bideford (*c*.1690–1700) was, according to Defoe, 'well inhabited with considerable and wealthy merchants'.[24] On the east coast Defoe found the quay at Yarmouth even more impressive: 'in this pleasant and agreeable range of houses are some very magnificent buildings, and among the rest . . . some merchants' houses, which look like little palaces rather than dwelling-houses of private men'. One of these, six bays wide and three storeys high (still surviving today) was built in about 1720 for John Andrews, renowned as 'the greatest herring merchant in Europe'.[25] On the south coast at Chichester one of the main imports was wine. Wealth procured in this trade probably allowed Henry Peckham to construct his ambitious house (1713) in the North Pallant, with its exquisite brickwork and outrageous stone ostriches (the family crest) perched on the gatepiers, which have earned it the local name of the Dodo House. Internally it was also built to impress, since the hall, stairs, and landing consume a full third of its interior space, squeezing the domestic accommodation into disproportionately small rooms (see Fig. 21).[26]

In the West Riding of Yorkshire the expanding woollen-cloth industry supported the wealthy gentlemen merchants of Leeds. John Cossins's map of the town in 1725 is surrounded by cameos of fifteen of the most fashionable houses there, all but one of which belonged to merchants (see Fig. 1).[27] The prosperity of the Wiltshire clothiers of the early eighteenth century has left the towns on the western border

Palliser, *York*, 159; RCHM, *Dorset*, iii, Part 1, 26; Everitt, *Urban History*, 9; Lloyd, *Broad Street*, 12.

[24] Hoskins, *Devon*, 336; Defoe, *Tour*, i. 260; *Gentleman's Magazine*, xxv (1755), 445.

[25] Defoe, *Tour*, i. 65–6; description of Andrews quoted in BE *North-East Norfolk and Norwich* (Harmondsworth, 1962), 151.

[26] Andrews, 'Port of Chichester', 104–5; BE *Sussex*, 183; *Pallant House Gallery, Chichester* (Chichester, 1982). For other merchants' houses see Parker, *King's Lynn*, 89–90; H. M. Colvin and L. M. Wodehouse, 'Henry Bell of King's Lynn', *Architectural History*, iv (1961), 53; Fiennes, *Journeys*, 148.

[27] Cossins, *Plan of Leeds*; Wilson, *Gentlemen Merchants*, 195.

Fig. 21.   Pallant House (1713), North Pallant, Chichester

of the county studded with fine classical dwellings of this period, fashioned in the superb oolitic limestone of the area.[28] In 1768 it was reported of Birmingham that 'in the upper parts [are] many good houses belonging to the principal inhabitants', among whose ranks were the town's metalware merchants. By 1719, nine of the sixteen properties in the new square were owned by ironmongers, and in 1762 the elegant buildings of the nearby Temple Row were described as being 'inhabited by people of fortune, who are great wholesale dealers in the manufactures of this town' (see Fig. 4).[29]

[28] Defoe, *Tour*, i. 280-1; Rogers, 'Trowbridge Clothiers', 138-62; *VCH Wiltshire*, viii. 94, 110-11; *BE Wiltshire*, Bradford-on-Avon, Trowbridge, and Warminster.

[29] HMC, *Verulam MSS*, 240; Rowlands, *Masters and Men*, 116-17; Hill and Dent, *Old Square, passim*; W. Toldervy, *England and Wales Described in a Series of Letters* (London, 1762), 349; B. Walker, 'Some Eighteenth-Century Birmingham Houses, and the Men Who Lived in Them', *TBAS*, lvi (1932), 1-11.

The wealth made by business men was not only directed towards private aggrandizement. In 1718 Robert Downes a Sheffield gold-smith offered £1,000 towards building the town's new St Paul's; eight years later a Stourbridge clothier left £300 for a new church; and Christ Church (1775–6) in Macclesfield was the gift of Charles Roe a silk manufacturer in the town. Cultural enterprises also received support. The catalogue (1760) of Liverpool's subscription library, founded in 1758, lists a membership of 140, 103 of whom are assigned a status or occupation. Of those whose trades or professions can be deciphered, over fifty are merchants, a following shared by two-thirds of the original subscriber-shareholders of the port's new theatre (opened in 1772).[30]

The lower echelons of commerce and manufacture, though rarely able to command the incomes of their superiors, must also have played a part in the Urban Renaissance. The prosperity enjoyed by skilled craftsmen and luxury retailers, partly as a result of the growth of surplus wealth, allowed many of them to accumulate enough extra capital to rebuild their homes, or at least to refront them in a fashionable style.[31] Probably the most spectacular examples of trades-men's wealth were to be found among the élite of the innkeeping fraternity, flourishing as a result of the expansion in personal mobility and internal trade. The particular gift of these men to the town's architectural revival was their great inns, whose physical grandeur (with tall, broad frontages stretching across many bays, frequently pierced by an impressive entrance arch) aroused much comment among travellers. Clerk found at Penrith 'several public inns, particularly three very large ones about three or four storeys high and of hewn stone'; Defoe reported that the George at Northampton 'looks more like a palace than an inn, and cost above 2,000 l. building'; and Macky discovered the Bull at Stamford to be 'a fine square of free-stone, sash-windows, and would pass in Italy for a palace'.[32] Many of these princely hostelries still survive, such as the

[30] Clarke, *Eighteenth-Century Church*, 56, 86, 88; Walton, *Sheffield*, 99–101; Kaufman, 'Community Library', 27, 30; Chalklin, 'Building for Cultural Purposes', 63.
[31] Borsay, 'Landscape and Leisure', 166–8; Clark, *Country Towns*, 24; Harris, 'Architecture of Stamford', 83.
[32] Everitt, 'Urban Inn', especially 100–4, 123–7; J. Clerk, 'A Journie to Carlyle and Penrith in 1731', ed. W. A. J. Prevost, *Trans. of the Cumberland and Westmorland Antiquarian and Archaeological Soc.*, new ser., lxi (1961), 216; Defoe, *Tour*, ii. 86; Macky, *Journey*, ii. 205.

Fig. 22.   The Rose and Crown Hotel (front *c*.1700), Market Place, Saffron
Walden

Red Lion at Blandford Forum (built *c*.1732, though no longer an inn),
the Bath Arms at Warminster (*c*.1732), the Rose and Crown at Saffron
Walden (front *c*.1700) (see Fig. 22), the Duke's Head at King's Lynn
(facade *c*.1700), the King's Head at Richmond (early 1700s) (see Fig.
23), and the Bear at Woodstock (central block *c*.1700): they are the
true *palazzi* of the English Augustan town.[33]

It is scarcely possible to measure quantitatively the rising volume of
surplus wealth in society, or its widening distribution. None the less,
there can be little doubt that these were among the key factors in
creating the Urban Renaissance. However, the process of change was a
complex one. The number of those possessing significant levels of
disposable income was probably expanding for at least a century
before the Civil War. What so decisively altered the situation after the
Restoration was both a rapid acceleration in this long-term trend, and

[33] RCHM, *Dorset*, iii, Part 1, 32; *VCH Wiltshire*, viii. 94; *BE Essex* (Harmondsworth,
1954), 307; Parker, *King's Lynn*, 128-9; *BE Yorkshire: The North Riding*
(Harmondsworth, 1966), 296; *BE Oxfordshire*, 858.

Fig. 23. The King's Head Hotel (early 1700s), Market Place, Richmond, Yorkshire

the crossing of that critical consumer threshold, where the market became large enough to make its commercial exploitation viable. Here we turn from the demand to the supply side of the equation, from consumption to production. For whatever the nature of the demand that existed, there could be no Urban Renaissance without the emergence of an 'industry' to service, shape, and expand that demand. The entry of leisure and luxury into the commercial arena, on a scale hitherto unparalleled, was therefore a necessary part of the process of cultural change.[34]

2. SUPPLY

The emergence of a leisure and luxury industry depended upon the willingness of individuals and institutions to sink their time and capital in this area, and upon the entrepreneurial skills which they displayed in exploiting their investment. The aristocracy and landed gentry were inevitably involved, because they owned much of the

[34] Plumb, *Commercialization of Leisure*.

property on which fashionable building development occurred and on which valuable natural assets, such as springs, were located.[35] But one of the most striking features of the town's cultural revival was the wide range of business talent that it attracted, including ambitious men of a relatively low social background. Of the triumvirate of Georgian Bath, John Wood (poor enough to be educated at the town's blue-coat school) was the son of a local builder, Richard Nash's father was a custom collector and partner in a Swansea glass-works, and Ralph Allen's origins, though rather indeterminate, appear to be that of a shopkeeping/innkeeping family in Cornwall.[36] One of the sponsors of the musical entertainments at the Duddeston Hall Gardens in mid-eighteenth-century Birmingham was an organist and postmaster, and the town's rival Apollo Gardens were opened by a house-painter. The two men who purchased the lease of the Bristol Hot Wells in 1695 were a soap-boiler and draper; the builder and manager of the assembly rooms at Stamford had formerly run a boarding-school; and the proprietor of the Orchard Street theatre in Bath was a brewer and tallow-chandler.[37]

Perhaps because the recruitment net was spread so wide, cultural entrepreneurs frequently displayed considerable enterprise, endurance, and shrewdness. These were vital qualities for the development of what were often novel and high-risk areas of business activity. Wood at Bath had an almost manic ability to visualize his utopian city and dream up endless projects to achieve this; on the other hand, he was perceptive enough to see the economic potential of the spa, hard-headed enough to handle complex building schemes and financial transactions, flexible enough to modify cherished plans to meet opportunities as they arose, and astute enough to publicize his achievements.[38] Many of his fellows shared his shrewd commercial sense. James Keating introduced the first newspaper to be printed in Stratford-upon-Avon when a potential competitor in the region, the

[35] Defoe, *Tour*, ii. 167; Heape, *Buxton*, 19-41; Burr, *Tunbridge Wells*, 40-4, 50-1; Neale, *Bath: A Social History*, 115-53, 226-42.

[36] Colvin, *Dictionary*; Penrose, *Letters*, 82-3; W. Connely, *Beau Nash* (London, 1955), 2-3; Boyce, *Ralph Allen*, 1-3.

[37] Smith, *Music in Birmingham*, 10-11; Little, 'Gloucestershire Spas', 172; RCHM, *Stamford*, 49-50; McIntyre, 'Rise of a Resort Town', 219, 228.

[38] Wood's career can best be traced in Colvin, *Dictionary*; Ison, *Bath*, 2nd edn. (Bath, 1980), appendices 5-9; Summerson, 'English Town-Planning Tradition', 87-110; Neale, *Bath: A Social History*, 116-225; and Wood's own publications, especially his history of *Bath*.

Oxford Flying Weekly Journal and Cirencester Gazette, closed down.[39] Traders often revealed a good deal of skill in analysing the needs of the market, and were careful to offer their customers a wide range of services and inducements. Owners of circulating libraries permitted country clients to borrow additional volumes to compensate for their restricted access to the stock, and provided facilities to deliver books to the surrounding villages.[40] Newspaper proprietors developed wide-ranging networks of agents and newsmen to distribute their papers, collect advertisements, and vend other products in which they traded. In 1725 the *Gloucester Journal* was distributed in twelve English and Welsh counties, and in 1756 advertisements were accepted by offices as far apart as London, Salisbury, Bristol, Hereford, Brecon, and Carmarthen. In 1743 the *York Courant* had agents in over forty-three towns in an area ranging from Scarborough to Manchester.[41] Keating sought to boost the sales of his Stratford paper by occasionally distributing with it a free copy of a moral news-sheet (such supplements were a common inducement), and by giving 'our customers four papers a year that we are not paid for'.[42]

Among the entrepreneurs of leisure, two groups deserve a special accolade: urban innkeepers and town councils. Earlier chapters have documented the way in which they sponsored or accommodated virtually all the developing forms of urban leisure. Their role was particularly important in the early years of the Urban Renaissance, before the emergence of specialist promoters and purpose-built premises. Horse-racing provides a good example of the value of their patronage. Hostelries were not only heavily involved in financing prizes, but also provided more general support for the recreation. In the early eighteenth century a group of innholders at Yarmouth leased land from the corporation on which to establish a race-track, and at Barnsley and Beverley they acted as clerks of the course, fulfilling what may have been a common duty.[43] It was normal for the town

[39] *Stratford, Shipston, and Alcester Jnl.*, i, No. 1, 5 Feb. 1749/50; Cranfield, *Handlist* (1952), 18.

[40] Kaufman, 'Community Library', 19; Knott, 'Circulating Libraries in Newcastle', 230.

[41] Wiles, *Freshest Advices*, 113–42, 367–72; *Gloucester Jnl.*, xxxv, No. 1789, 7 Sept. 1756; Cranfield, *Development of Provincial Newspaper*, 190–206; and also Sterenberg, 'Spread of Printing in Suffolk', 38–40; Feather, *Book Trade*, 17.

[42] *Keating's Stratford and Warwick Mercury*, iii, No. 114, 9 Mar. 1752; iv, No. 210, 12 Nov. 1753; Wiles, *Freshest Advices*, 110–12.

[43] Fairfax-Blakeborough, *Northern Turf History*, ii. 27; iii. 21; Gill, *Racecourses*, 33, 231.

authorities to donate a sizeable sum towards the race prizes: evidence for this exists at Chester, Doncaster, Leicester, Lichfield, Liverpool, Newcastle-upon-Tyne, Norwich, Nottingham, Preston, Stockton-on-Tees, Winchester, and York.[44] These contributions not only assisted in attracting competitors, but also encouraged private subscribers to come forward. Moreover, since civic payments were often guaranteed for several years ahead, they helped to assure the long-term future of a meeting. A number of councils, such as those at Bath, Newcastle-upon-Tyne, Preston, and York, also made a valuable contribution to the sport by maintaining and improving the racing facilities. At Bath, for example, a permanent home for the spa's course was secured in 1723, when the corporation took a lease of Claverton Down for twenty-one years at an annual rent of £20, and then shrewdly subleased it for £45 a year for all but the period of the meeting.[45]

An impressive range of individuals and institutions were attracted into the cultural business sector. Such a movement of talent and capital could never have occurred, nor the leisure industry developed to the extent that it did, had not substantial commercial incentives existed. Some entrepreneurs reaped considerable personal rewards. The puppet impresario Martin Powell was said in 1713 to have 'gathered such wealth as is ten times sufficient to buy all the poets in England . . . he seldom goes out without a chair'. At her death Dame Lindsey, a proprietor of one of the assembly rooms in Bath, was reputed to have 'in a few years, amassed . . . at least 8,000 pounds', a similar sum to that accumulated by the manager of the Theatre Royal in Liverpool by the time of his death in 1771.[46]

One area of leisure where considerable, sometimes spectacular gains could be made was racing. The sport's expansion from the late seventeenth century must have boosted the earnings available to

[44] Longrigg, *Horse-Racing*, 29–30, 39–40; Gill, *Racecourses*, 59, 123, 163–4, 199; Fairfax-Blakeborough, *Northern Turf History*, iii. 196; Kettle, 'Lichfield Races', 39; Picton, *Liverpool Municipal Archives*, 83; Brand, *Newcastle*, i. 434; Corfield, 'A Provincial Capital', 292; Council Minutes, 10 Mar. 1725/6, 3 Apr. 1733, PCMSS; Rosen, 'Winchester', 180; House Book, 1 Nov. 1708, 26 Aug. 1713, 17 June 1740, 11 Dec. 1750, 9 July 1752, YCA.

[45] Council Minutes, 7 Aug. 1722, 28 Feb. 1722/3, 25 Mar. 1723, BCA; Wood, *Bath*, 440; Brand, *Newcastle*, i. 434–5; Council Minutes, 6 May 1726, 3 Apr. 1733, PCMSS; House Book, 7 Dec. 1730, 24 Jan. 1737/8, 7 Dec. 1753, 27 Jan. 1755, 18 Oct. 1756, YCA.

[46] *Les Soupirs de la Grand Bretaigne, or the Groans of Great Britain* (1713), quoted in Speaight, *Puppet Theatre*, 101; Wood, *Bath*, 319; Chalklin, 'Building for Cultural Purposes', 62.

owners, though to measure this quantitatively is impossible given the inadequacy of the sources. None the less, huge sums, occasionally as much as several thousand pounds, were staked on early eighteenth-century matches, especially those run at Newmarket.[47] The arrival of the *Racing Calendar* in 1727 provides the first evidence, despite its limitations, of the national situation. Table 8.1 shows that during the 1730s annual winnings appear to have reached a plateau of around £13,000 to £14,000. Though the troubled years of the 1740s saw a serious decline, by 1752 earnings had recovered to the level attained before ·the Racing Act. There then followed a remarkable surge forward, primarily under the influence of a rise in match money, so that by the late 1750s and early 1760s total winnings were fluctuating between £33,000 and £51,000.

Table 8.1. *Winnings on the English Turf 1730–1762*

Date	Prize Money	Match Money	Total Winnings
	(£/s)	(£/s)	(£/s)
1730	8,076.12	5,906.05	13,982.17
1739	9,416.18	4,079.05	13,496.03
1740	7,279.03	2,000.06	9,279.09
1745	7,623.01	1,963.10	9,586.11
1749	6,770.07	1,863.10	8,633.17
1751	9,663.09	2,918.05	12,581.14
1752	11,456.15	2,096.10	13,553.05
1753	12,666.06	3,786.00	16,452.06
1754	12,991.06	5,817.15	18,809.01
1755	13,519.12	9,477.09	22,997.01
1756	13,272.06	16,069.10	29,341.16
1757	13,292.16	20,973.05	34,266.01
1758	12,318.06	20,736.10	33,054.16
1759	11,283.06	39,778.05	51,061.11
1760	10,864.06	22,622.00	33,486.06
1762	11,861.16	34,998.05	46,860.01

Note: See notes to Table 7.1.
Sources: The figures for 1730, 1739, 1740, 1745, 1749, and 1760 are calculated from the *Racing Calendar* for those years. The figures for 1751–9 and 1762 are totals listed in the *Racing Calendars* of 1760 and 1763.

[47] Defoe, *Tour*, i. 75–6; Cook, *English Turf*, 185–6.

The growth in prize and match money was accompanied by important changes in the organization of racing, which permitted owners more effectively to maximize their returns from the sport. Geographical rationalization allowed them to concentrate their efforts on fewer meetings, and avoid dissipating their energies on a crowded circuit of small events. The dominance of Newmarket, by 1760 handling half of the recorded winnings on the English turf, meant that the racing fraternity need hardly stray from the Heath to make a handsome profit. None the less, mobility was important for those who wished to take advantage of the richer prizes and sweepstakes available at the major meetings, and who sought to establish the reputation of their animals with an eye to their future value in the breeding industry. The widespread turnpiking of trunk roads may have improved the speed and comfort with which horses could be moved. A number certainly travelled considerable distances. In 1738 'Black Chase' won prestigious King's Plates at Lincoln, Lewes, Guildford, Winchester, and Salisbury, and started at Newmarket.[48] For those in the sport to exploit efficiently the national network of meetings and plan their annual campaigns, knowledge was required about the location and time of races, the value of prizes, entry qualifications, registration procedures, and fees. Formal information channels soon developed to meet these needs. The initial stimulus came with the growth in the metropolitan and provincial press, which frequently carried advertisements for meetings. More comprehensive was the *Racing Calendar*, annually published from 1727 and attracting around a thousand subscribers. Though the details it contained were retrospective, it provided a national picture and an approximate schedule of the events of the coming year. However, its most valuable service was as a guide to form, listing the winner of each race, and the place of each runner in every heat.

Changes in the format of racing, though only slowly introduced and focused particularly on Newmarket, were also improving the commercial potential of the sport. The age at which horses were introduced to the turf was gradually reduced, allowing a quicker return on capital and lengthening the earning life of the animal.[49] There was a decline in bizarre races, and at Newmarket a decrease in the number and length

[48] Fairfax-Blakeborough, *Northern Turf History*, i. 51, 176, 183; Cook, *English Turf*, 139-40.

[49] Longrigg, *Horse-Racing*, 85; *VCH Cambridgeshire*, v. 282; Mortimer, *Jockey Club*, 15-17.

of heats, both of which reduced the risk of physical damage to the horse and helped protect a valuable asset.[50] Perhaps the most significant development was the rise of the sweepstake, a form of race with which at least a dozen meetings were experimenting by 1760. Unlike the traditional two-horse match, the sweepstake permitted several competitors to stake money against each other, and therefore offered the possibility of substantial winnings from a relatively small wagered sum.[51]

Some of the most lucrative returns in racing were to be found not on the course (though this was an essential testing ground), but on the stud-farm and in the market-place. Horses were big business, and the breeding industry had developed rapidly during the early modern period. Racehorses stood at the apex of the trade. In the early eighteenth century their principal breeding area was the Vale of York, and their most important provincial market was that held in the Staffordshire town of Penkridge, where hundreds of guineas could change hands for a fine horse. But this was only a fraction of the sums that might be earned once an animal had proved itself. In 1768 the famous 'Eclipse' was sold for 1,750 guineas, and it was said that his new owner subsequently received £25,000 in stud fees.[52]

The benefits to be reaped by investment in urban entertainments were often of an indirect nature, though no less substantial for that. Innkeeping and corporate sponsorship were essentially sprats to catch a mackerel. Victuallers saw leisure principally as a means of attracting customers to use their stabling, lodging, drinking, and feeding facilities. Several race prizes required competitors to accommodate their horses at contributing inns, and the right to sell liquor on the course would sometimes be limited to subscribers.[53] Town authorities were equally aware of the economic value of recreational events. The York corporation granted Keregan his theatre monopoly in 1733, because they felt that the playhouse he had agreed to build 'may very much conduce to the entertainment of the nobility and gentry

[50] *Racing Calendar* (1760 and 1770); Fairfax-Blakeborough, *Northern Turf History*, iii. 57; *VCH Cambridgeshire*, v. 282; Mortimer, *Jockey Club*, 30.
[51] Longrigg, *Horse-Racing*, 74; *VCH Cambridgeshire*, v. 281; *Racing Calendar* (1760).
[52] Thirsk, *Horses in Early Modern England*, 21-8; Plumb, 'Acceptance of Modernity', 318-20; Defoe, *Tour*, ii. 78-9, 219, 221-2; *British Sporting Painting*, 51; Longrigg, *Horse-Racing*, 80.
[53] Warwickshire CRO, CR.229, Box 2/2; *Suffolk Mercury*, xxiv, No. 272, 23 May 1737; *Bath Advertiser*, No. 49, 18 Sept. 1756.

resorting to this city . . . encouraging them to spend their winter seasons here', and the council's decision in 1739 to 'contribute to the musical entertainments . . . next winter' was motivated by the view that 'it conduces to bring company to the city who spend money and advance trade'. York's sponsorship of racing was also commercially oriented. In 1708 the corporation claimed that 'the making of a yearly horse-race . . . may be of advantage and profit to the . . . city', a view confirmed in 1740 when it was stated that 'the horse-races are found to have been of great service to this city'. A few years earlier Drake had almost ventured to put a figure to the 'profit', when he argued that the races are 'certainly of great benefit to the city and citizens, by being the occasion that some thousands of pounds are annually spent in it in a week's time'.[54] Town authorities handled their racing investments very carefully, manipulating their contributions to maximize the number of prizes, which in turn determined the length of the meeting and the resort of visitors to the town's services.[55]

The commercial potential of cultural investment helped attract entrepreneurs into the field and therefore to turn consumer demand into material reality. Not that producers only played a reactive role, for they were continuously engaged in expanding the boundaries of the market. One aspect of this process was the cultivation of new consumer expectations through advertising or by the publication of guidebooks and architectural manuals. Another aspect, perhaps the most critical of all, was that of finding ways to lower the price of fashionable culture to make it accessible to a wider market. A commonly adopted device for achieving this was the subscription system, which spread the cost of investment or consumption among a number of parties rather than concentrating it on one person. It was a method that represented a transitional phase between the expensive world of individual patronage, and the cut-price culture of the mass market.[56]

The most widespread use of the system was to be found in the resorts. Respectable visitors inaugurated their stay by contributing to a range of facilities that provided a full package of entertainments and services to fill the vacant weeks ahead. A traveller to Scarborough in

---

[54] House Book, 1 Nov. 1708, 29 Jan. 1732/3, 22 Sept. 1739, 17 June 1740, YCA; Drake, *Eboracum*, 241.

[55] Council Minutes, 10 Mar. 1725/6, PCMSS; Fairfax-Blakeborough, *Northern Turf History*, iii. 196, 202.

[56] Plumb, *Commercialization of Leisure*, 17–18; Brewer, 'Commercialization and Politics', 198, 224–7.

1725 found that 'Subscriptions here are five shillings to the long room, two shillings and sixpence to the coffee-house for the use of pen, ink, paper, and news, two shillings and sixpence to the women at the spa, and five shillings to Dicky for the use of a necessary house.' In mid-eighteenth-century Tunbridge Wells the list was even longer:

Here your first business is to go to the well . . . and pay the customary fee . . . you then proceed to the other public places, and there subscribe according to your rank—at the assembly room, a crown or more each person; at the coffee-house, the same . . . again at the bookseller's the subscription is the same . . . the music will next address you in expectation of half a guinea . . . Thus subscriptions are ended till the clergyman's book is opened, and you may now freely engage in all the amusements of the place.

At Cheltenham in 1776 Edward Pigott discovered that 'you must, to do things elegantly, subscribe to the following articles: 5 shillings for the room at the well, the same for the other; 5 shillings for the music, 2 and sixpence for the newspaper, and something for the walk; if you drink the water you give about half a guinea when you go away'. The total payment might have been a little daunting to the newly arrived visitor, but the nature of the system ensured that this represented value for money. As Pigott recorded after describing the subscription payable in the assembly rooms at Bath, 'a person that is fond of public places will be very much pleased here and at a very cheap rate'.[57]

Other towns also used subscriptions to support cultural activities and projects. The York winter season was financed in this fashion, Drake noting in 1736 that 'a quarter of a year's polite entertainment' may be 'had at a most moderate expense, Monday assembly being half a crown, music a crown, and plays . . . fifteen shillings, which added together makes but one pound two shillings and sixpence'. The assembly ticket covered a generous ten meetings, and the theatre subscription (in 1734, when prices were a little higher) provided admission to a full season of twenty-six twice-weekly plays.[58] The book trade and reading facilities were particularly dependent upon the system. Many eighteenth-century volumes are prefaced by a lengthy list of subscribers, and printers frequently advertised in advance their plans for a new book to encourage potential purchasers to come

[57] Students Diary, fo. 42; Burr, *Tunbridge Wells*, 115–16; Pigott Diary, i, articles 457, 477.

[58] Drake, *Eboracum*, 241; Assembly Rooms Ledger, YCA; Rosenfeld, *Strolling Players*, 118.

forward, sometimes offering them special pre-publication rates. Circulating and institutional libraries were often run on a subscription basis, and book clubs were principally a means of sharing the costs of acquisition among a circle of like-minded bibliophiles. As Doddridge said of the Kibworth club in 1725, 'It is my happiness to be a member of a society, in which, for little more than a crown a year, I have the reading of all that are purchased by the common stock, amounting to sixteen pounds yearly.'[59] The race prizes, which were the staple diet of the majority of meetings, were generally raised by subscription. Since the contributors were rarely competitors in the events, their payments were essentially a method of sharing the costs of mounting a spectator sport. Subscriptions were also used to raise capital for the building of entertainment facilities, such as theatres, assembly rooms, and libraries. Though superficially an investment, the comparatively small size of many shareholdings, and the user-rights associated with them, suggests that many contributors thought primarily in terms of consumption.[60]

A further factor which conspired to hold down prices was competition. For newspaper proprietors this represented a continuous pressure. In a larger centre there might be several rival publications: at least three each in Norwich in about 1707, Bristol in the late 1740s, and Bath in the early 1760s.[61] Even for a smaller one-newspaper town there was the challenge posed by other local journals, not to mention the London press. Theatre companies could be ruthlessly competitive. In 1723 Tollett informed the readers of the *Norwich Gazette*, 'that my adversaries have raised malicious falsehoods of me in order to promote their own ends and . . . they report, that my company will not be in Norwich this Christmas season: this is to satisfy the public, that I have hired a vessel for that purpose, and hope to be at Norwich in a few days'.[62] The major spas usually enjoyed a range of rival facilities. In early eighteenth-century Epsom there were two sets of wells, and two, possibly three bowling-greens.[63] Tunbridge Wells possessed at least five lodging centres or hamlets, most of which at some time had a

[59] Feather, *Book Trade*, 51-3, 114-15; P. Doddridge, *The Correspondence and Diary of Philip Doddridge*, ed. J. Doddridge Humphreys (London, 1829), ii. 57.

[60] Chalklin, 'Building for Cultural Purposes', 61-6; Grady, 'Public Buildings in the West Riding', 167.

[61] Cranfield, *Handlist*, 1-3, 16.

[62] *Norwich Gazette*, 30 Nov.-3 Dec. 1723, quoted in Rosenfeld, *Strolling Players*, 53.

[63] Clark, 'Epsom Spa', 1-41; Fiennes, *Journeys*, 337-8, 349-50.

bowling-green with an adjacent room for dancing.[64] At points
between 1730 and 1750 Bath was serviced by two sets of independent
ballrooms and commercial gardens, and three theatres.[65] Competition
was therefore an endemic feature of the leisure industry, and must
have exerted a significant downward pressure on prices.

3. THE URBAN FACTOR

This chapter has explored how new flows of wealth and novel entrepreneurial initiatives combined to create the economic context in
which the Urban Renaissance occurred. It was the meeting and interaction of the forces of demand and supply that was the engine of
change. But how was it that these forces came to focus on the town?
Why was there an *urban* renaissance? Answers to these questions have
been approached earlier, but it may be useful here to summarize the
main reasons. Of central importance was the fact that the middling
ranks and prosperous tradesmen, whose growing numbers and surplus
wealth were such a dynamic factor in generating demand for cultural
products, were very often townspeople. It is true that some rich
citizens turned their backs on urban living and bought their way into
the county gentry, and that land markets operating in the hinterland
of the growing ports and industrial centres were particularly active
ones. But this did not represent a serious migration of the town's
leaders and their wealth. The numbers who purchased estates large
enough to elevate them to full membership of the landed élite were
relatively small, not least because this was such an expensive procedure. Moreover, many citizens who invested in rural property
retained their businesses and primary residences in their home communities, and those who did leave often moved only to a smallish
estate or villa on the fringe of the town, continuing to maintain the
predominantly urban focus of their lives.[66]

[64] Fiennes, *Journeys*, 134-5; Burr, *Tunbridge Wells*, 45-6, 102-7.
[65] Wood, *Bath*, 225, 245, 319, 443; Wood, *Plan of Bath*, items 34-6; Sydenham,
Bath Pleasure Gardens, 1-2; Rosenfeld, *Strolling Players*, chaps. 8-9.
[66] Clark and Slack, *Towns in Transition*, 117-18; Beckett, 'English Landownership',
579; Holderness, 'English Land Market', 561, 574-5; Wilson, *Gentlemen Merchants*,
220-30; Stone, *Open Élite*, 132-41, 286-8; N. Rogers, 'Money, Land, and Lineage:
The Big Bourgeoisie of Hanoverian London', *Social History*, iv (1979), 452-3; Burley,
'Economic Development of Essex', 16-18, 347-51; Defoe, *Tour*, i. 158-69; Morant,
Essex, i. 1; Wood, *Bath*, 91, 96; HMC, *Verulam MSS*, 270, 273.

More than counteracting any flow of people and wealth from town to country was the increasing tendency of the aristocracy and gentry to patronize urban centres. This stemmed in part from political changes, as the struggle to control borough seats intensified in the post-Restoration years. The direct impact of politics on the urban landscape can be seen in the generous contributions made by patrons and Members of Parliament to public buildings and works, in order to enhance their political reputation.[67] But of much greater general importance was the burgeoning appetite of the gentry for an urban life-style and culture. London played a vital early role in stimulating and satisfying this need, but by the latter decades of the seventeenth century its impact was extending into the provincial towns. This was not only because the metropolis could no longer cope with the expansion in the level and geographical distribution of demand, but also because society's leaders developed a need for specialist cultural centres, like the resorts, divorced from the bustle and social heterogeneity of the capital, and because provincial society itself was growing stronger and wealthier, increasingly able and willing to assert its own identity.

The landed élite's passion for urban culture resulted primarily from changing social attitudes, and these will be explored in the following two chapters. However, of more than minor significance were the practical attractions of towns. Not least among these were the relatively low cost of living and the easy access to an abundance of high quality foodstuffs. Fiennes found Tunbridge Wells to be 'furnished with great plenty of all sorts, flesh, fowl, and fish . . . the markets well stored and provision cheap'; Defoe praised Ipswich for the 'wonderful plenty of all manner of provisions, whether flesh or fish, and very good of the kind . . . The provisions very cheap'; and Macky suggested that at York, 'The plenty and cheapness of this city brings abundance of strangers hither for the conveniency of boarding, which is very cheap, and the apartments and diet good.'[68] Though fashionable provincial towns were hardly centres of monastic frugality, it was far more economical to live there than to run a country house and estate. Nor

---

[67] Council Minutes, 16 May 1718, 3 Feb. 1734/5, 31 Dec. 1744, BCA; HMC, *Verulam MSS*, 229, 243; P. Styles, 'The Corporation of Warwick 1660–1835', *TBAS*, lix (1935), 70; Tupling, 'Lancashire Markets', 7 n. 1; Hill, *Stuart Lincoln*, 211; Kemp, *History of Warwick*, 109 n. 190; Cunnington, *Devizes*, 213; *VCH Wiltshire*, vi. 110, 112; Spershott, *Memoirs*, 17; McIntyre, 'Health and Pleasure Resorts', 243; McIntyre, 'Rise of a Resort Town', 231.

[68] Fiennes, *Journeys*, 133; Defoe, *Tour*, i. 46; Macky, *Journey*, ii. 211; and also Drake, *Eboracum*, 240; Styles, 'Corporation of Warwick', 86.

did provincial towns offer the range of expensive temptations to be found in London. For a rural gentleman facing serious financial pressures, such as Jane Austen's Sir Walter Elliot, a period of urban exile was a prudent but not painful solution; and, as in the case of Sir Walter, a provincial town rather than the metropolis was a sensible choice, since 'it was much safer for a gentleman in his predicament'. The Elliot family settled on Bath as their urban retreat, though as a centre for financial retrenchment the spa could not rival Totnes, which Defoe discovered to be 'very cheap', and 'a very good place to live in, especially for such as have large families and but small estates, and many such are said to come into these parts on purpose for saving money, and to live in proportion to their income'.[69]

The country gentry were not the only ones drawn to the provincial town by the low cost of living. It also understandably attracted those with enough income to live comfortably, but not enough to make investment in a landed estate a viable consideration, such as the pseudo-gentry or retired and half-pay officers. On the more positive side, fashionable social centres provided an increasingly pleasant and commodious environment to reside in, with rising architectural standards, cleaner and better lighted streets, and improving water supplies. They also furnished a much wider range of consumer and recreational opportunities than could possibly be found in the countryside, and in general provided a ready-tailored civilized society into which all with wealth and the appropriate social accomplishments could be easily assimilated. The resorts and county towns did not reach this level of sophistication overnight, but in the long term they were carried forward on a self-sustaining spiral of growth: the more people they attracted, the more they offered and the more attractive they became.

[69] J. Austen, *Persuasion*, ed. D. W. Harding (Harmondsworth, 1971), 44; Defoe, *Tour*, i. 225.

9

The Pursuit of Status

In the previous chapter it was suggested that one of the principal economic supports of the Urban Renaissance was the rapidly growing stock of surplus wealth, which helped raise the demand for polite culture to a quite new plane. Arguments were put forward to explain *where* this wealth came from, but they left unanswered the questions of *why* it was directed into culture, and specifically into fashionable pastimes and products. The following two chapters will try to answer these questions.

For those who possessed significant levels of disposable income, a central concern was the use of it to enhance social position. Then, as now, pride was a compulsive passion, and the achievement of a measure of superiority over one's fellow beings was a delectable human pleasure. Mandeville claimed in *The Fable of the Bees* (1714), his brutal paean to social emulation, that 'the wordly minded, voluptuous, and ambitious man . . . covets precedence everywhere, and desires to be dignified above his betters', and argued that flattery 'this bewitching engine . . . must be the most powerful argument that could be used to human creatures'.[1] This chapter will focus on the pursuit of status. It will begin by investigating the development of more liberal attitudes to gentility, before exploring the various devices and contexts with and within which social kudos could be competed for and acquired.

1. CULTURE AND GENTILITY

In early modern England the most influential model of status among the wealthy and powerful and those who aspired to join their ranks was that of gentility. Though commentators stressed the gulf that existed between those who conformed to this model and the rest of mankind,

[1] B. Mandeville, *The Fable of the Bees*, ed. P. Harth (Harmondsworth, 1970), 82, 170.

they were often rather vague as to the precise attributes of a
gentleman.[2] The most objective test was one of birth; as Miège stated,
'gentlemen are properly such as are descended of a good family,
bearing a coat of arms'.[3] Hence the Tudor and Stuart fascination with
genealogy. Membership of the higher echelons of the royal service and
the professions similarly conferred gentility. None of these qualifications allowed the newly prosperous much opportunity for social
advancement. However, it was also recognized, as William Harrison
explained in 1577, that any man who 'can live without manual
labour, and thereto is able and will bear the port, charge, and
countenance of a gentleman, he shall for money have a coat of arms
bestowed upon his family by the heralds . . . and [be] reputed for a
gentleman ever after'.[4] A person could therefore become a gentleman,
regardless of his parental background, as long as he looked and
behaved like one. Since the capacity to do this depended upon the
possession of certain cultural objects and attributes, most of which
could be openly purchased, then this was the channel by which wealth
could be freely transferred into status. It is unclear what weight this
cultural rather than genetic definition of gentility carried in Tudor and
early Stuart England, or to what extent it was exploited to achieve
social mobility. Business and trade remained somewhat dubious
occupations, which were not altogether free from the taint of 'manual
labour', and the financial resources to purchase the cultural trappings
of a gentleman were heavily concentrated, at least outside London,
among the more substantial landowners. In mid-seventeenth-century
Britain birth was probably still the principal factor in defining a
gentleman, and the ownership of a rural estate the most common
method of sustaining this honour.

In the years after the Restoration this traditional model of gentility
was seriously eroded. Though ancestry remained an important qualification and land a valuable support, the critical definition of a
gentleman increasingly became a cultural one. In the 1699 edition of
his *New State of England*, Miège acknowledged that 'anyone that
without a coat of arms, has either a liberal, or genteel education, that
looks gentleman-like (whether he be so or not), and has wherewithal

[2] P. Laslett, *The World We Have Lost* (London, 1965), 22–43; Mingay, *The Gentry*,
2–3; B. Coward, *The Stuart Age: A History of England 1603-1714* (London, 1980), 38-
40; Wrightson, *English Society*, 18–30.

[3] Miège, *New State of England*, 149.

[4] F. J. Furnivall (ed.), 'Harrison's Description of England in Shakespeare's Youth',
New Shakespere Soc., ser. 6, i (London, 1877), 128–9.

to live freely and handsomely, is by the courtesy of England usually called a gentleman'.[5] By the 1748 edition of his *Present State of Great Britain*, the sartorial and behavioural characteristics of gentility were even more explicitly stated: 'In short, the title of gentleman is commonly given in England to all that distinguish themselves from the common sort of people, by a genteel dress and carriage, good education, learning, or an independent station.'[6] Much now rested merely upon appearance. Defoe found that on the walks at Tunbridge Wells 'anything that looks like a gentleman, has an address agreeable, and behaves with decency and good manners, may single out whom he pleases', and a contributor to the *Preston Journal* of 1750 noted that

> A butcher of a good estate,
> Commenced a gentleman of late,
> So would you think him by his stride,
> And furniture o'th' outer side.[7]

Though costume may not in itself have been enough, cultural attributes as a whole had become a prerequisite of gentility. In the late 1720s Defoe argued 'that virtue, learning, a liberal education, and a degree of natural and acquired knowledge, are necessary to finish the born gentleman . . . without them the entitled heir will be but the shadow of a gentleman', and in 1731 the *Weekly Register* declared 'that no one can be properly styled a gentleman, who does not take every opportunity to enrich his own capacity, and settle the elements of taste'.[8]

Behind the rise to pre-eminence of the cultural definition of gentility lay the proliferation of non-landed sources of wealth, and the growing numbers and surplus income of the middling ranks.[9] These developments forced a reordering of the traditional qualifications for a gentleman, placing the emphasis on acquired rather than inherited attributes, since only the former permitted wealth to be freely converted into status. The demise of the old model of gentility is evident in the growing futility of the post-Restoration heraldic

[5] Miège, *New State of England*, 149.

[6] G. Miège, *Present State of Great Britain*, 11th edn. (London, 1748), 157.

[7] Defoe, *Tour*, i. 126; *True British Courant*, No. 287, 3 Aug. 1750.

[8] D. Defoe, *The Compleat English Gentleman*, ed. K. D. Bülbring (London, 1890), 5; *Weekly Register*, 6 Feb. 1731, in Denvir, *Eighteenth Century*, 63.

[9] Stone, *Open Élite*, 132–41, 290–5, though arguing there was no substantial movement of the middling sort into the landed élite (as he defines it), shows that the 'cult of gentility spread astonishingly far down the social scale' to encompass the middle ranks.

visitations. These were executed on a county basis, and their main function was to establish those who had the right to possess arms, and, by implication, those who could be truly considered gentlemen. Because of the cumbersome procedures and archaic rules of the visitations (including an obsession with pedigrees), and because of the reality of a rapidly changing social structure, a credibility gap emerged in the work of the heralds. During the Warwickshire visitation of 1682-3 scarcely more than half of those summoned to register their claims responded, and there was a considerable disparity between those who were called gentlemen in general usage, including official records, and those whom the heralds finally entered in their books. In these circumstances it was understandable that after the Revolution William III should refuse to continue the outmoded procedure.[10]

With the new approach to gentility, more and more of the middling groups acquired the right to be addressed as a gentleman, though often only by grasping the very bottom rung of the titular ladder, that carrying the marginal assignation of 'Mr'. The membership of the professions as a whole, and not just their leading lights, now securely enjoyed the courtesy of gentility. In poll books, attorneys' and solicitors' occupations are frequently omitted in favour of the more elegant 'Mr' or 'gent', and the rise of their social standing is embodied in the name of their first professional organization, formed in the late 1730s, 'The Society of Gentlemen Practisers'.[11] Even the newer, borderline professions could offer a passport to social recognition. Provincial theatre managers such as Thomas Keregan and Thomas Ager, builder-architects like Francis Smith or John Wood, or an engineer such as George Sorocold, would readily be called 'Mr', 'gent', or even 'esq'.[12] In 1752 the engraver Grignion and the painters Devis and Hoare were recommended as 'gentlemen' of 'good moral characters', and it was felt 'that you could hardly find a man in the kingdom more desirable than Mr Hoare with regard to your son's education as a gentleman, a man of sense and virtue'.[13] Commerce

---

[10] P. Styles, 'The Heralds' Visitation of Warwickshire 1682-3', *TBAS*, lxxi (1955), especially 121-2, 126.

[11] Holmes, *Augustan England*, 9, 117-18, 154-5.

[12] Rosenfeld, *Strolling Players*, chap. 6; House Book, 29 Jan. 1732/3, YCA; H. M. Colvin, 'Francis Smith of Warwick 1672-1738', *Warwickshire History*, ii, No. 2 (1972/3), 6, 10; Wood, *Plan of Bath*; Ison, *Bath*, 2nd edn., 235; F. Williamson, 'George Sorocold, of Derby: A Pioneer of Water Supply', *Jnl. of the Derbyshire Archaeological and Natural History Soc.*, new ser., x, No. 57 (1936), 51, 54, 87.

[13] Letter quoted in E. Hughes, *North Country Life in the Eighteenth Century* (London, 1952, 1965), ii. 94.

also became a legitimate sphere for a gentleman to occupy. Whereas in 1669 Chamberlayne could state that 'tradesmen in all ages and nations have been reputed ignoble', thirty years later Miège felt that 'whereas trading formerly rendered a gentleman ignoble, now an ignoble person makes himself by merchandising as good as a gentleman', and Defoe asserted in the 1720s that 'trade is so far from being inconsistent with a gentleman, that, in short, trade in England makes gentlemen, and has peopled the nation with gentlemen'.[14]

Towns pioneered a more liberal approach to status, not least because their own citizens had most to gain from it. Throughout the early modern period the rulers of the major cities probably enjoyed the title and reputation of gentlemen within their own communities. From the 1490s the aldermen and recorder of York began to designate themselves 'master', and towards the end of the sixteenth century elevated this to 'esq', as the former title percolated down to the wider body of councillors, the Twenty-Four. In York and London exceptional citizens might even acquire a knighthood.[15] Whether such practices stretched to the generality of Tudor towns is doubtful. However, during the seventeenth century, gentrified epithets appear to have been acquiring widespread currency among the principal figures in urban communities. Later Stuart tax records from Kineton Hundred in Warwickshire consistently point to a large body of 'gentlemen' living in the town of Warwick: twenty-five, or a fifth of those listed as gentlemen in the Hundred returns for the Free and Voluntary Gift of 1661, and forty-five, or a third of those in later Hearth Tax lists. Only a handful of these men would have possessed a landed estate or the genealogical qualifications to justify the use of their titles, the majority being members of the professions and trading classes resident in Warwick. In the late seventeenth-century records of towns such as Preston and Bath, councillors were normally styled 'Mr' or 'gent', and by the 1720s the mayor of the former town was beginning to use the title of 'esq'.[16]

---

[14] Chamberlayne quoted in Stone, 'Social Mobility', 18; Miège, *New State of England*, 151; Defoe, *Tradesman*, 246; however, see also D. T. Andrew, 'Aldermen and Big Bourgeoisie of London Reconsidered', *Social History*, vi (1981), 363–4.

[15] Palliser, *Tudor York*, 100–1; *VCH York*, 180; R. G. Lang, 'Social Origins and Social Aspirations of Jacobean London Merchants', *EcHR*, 2nd ser., xxvii, No. 1 (1974), 40–7.

[16] Clark and Slack, *Towns in Transition*, 120–1; P. Styles, 'The Social Structure of Kineton Hundred in the Reign of Charles II', *TBAS*, lxxviii (1962), 98, 106; White Book and Council Minutes, *passim*, PCMSS; Council Minutes, *passim*, BCA.

It could be argued that town and country operated parallel but independent status systems, and that the urban 'inflation of honours' was an insular affair that had little validity within wider society.[17] Though there may be an element of truth in this, the inextricable economic, social, and political ties that linked town and country made it difficult for the two systems of privilege to operate in isolation. Three factors especially militated against this. First was the rise of the urban pseudo-gentry, who enjoyed a cultivated life-style that imitated that of the rural élite with whom they often had close associations. Second, there was the increasing tendency of country gentlemen to place their younger sons in urban occupations. The growth of the town-based professions, with their comparatively high status and incomes, was tailor-made to accommodate the gentry's surplus progeny. Trade also had its attractions. In 1699 Miège could write of 'merchandising' that 'many gentlemen born (some of them younger sons of noblemen) take upon them this profession, without any prejudice or blemish to their birth', and in the same year a bill introduced into the House of Commons for the creation of a new parish in Liverpool drew attention to the 'many gentlemen's sons of the counties of Lancaster, Yorkshire, Derbyshire, Staffordshire, Cheshire, and North Wales . . . put apprentice in this town'.[18]

The third factor that helped weld together the twin status systems, and one encouraged by the urban recruitment of younger sons, was the degree of social intercourse between town and rural gentry. Contemporary diaries, such as that of the army officer Thomas Bellingham, or those of the country gentlemen Nicholas Blundell and Sir Roger Newdigate, leave little doubt about the frequency or quality of this type of contact. Newdigate had close connections with Coventry and Birmingham society in the mid-eighteenth century. At the former town he had a particular friend in Dr Burgh, not only calling on his medical skills, but also frequently dining and breakfasting at his home. Sir Roger mixed with the other leading citizens of Coventry at

[17] Reed, 'Seventeenth-Century Ipswich', 114.

[18] G. S. Holmes, 'The Achievement of Stability: The Social Context of Politics from the 1680s to the Age of Walpole', in J. Cannon (ed.), *The Whig Ascendancy* (London, 1981), 14–17; Miège, *New State of England*, 151; bill quoted in B. L. Poole, 'Liverpool's Trade in the Reign of Queen Anne', M.A. thesis (Liverpool, 1960), 31; and also Wilson, *Gentlemen Merchants*, 24–5, 231; Stone, 'Social Mobility', 53; Stone, *Open Élite*, 148–54, takes a less sanguine view about the movement of the younger sons of the 'landed élite' into the professions and trade.

the annual Drapers' feast, whose company he had joined in 1753.[19] In Birmingham he was an active member of the town's Bean Club, a loyalist association in which the local bourgeoisie and rural gentry hobnobbed freely together, under the relaxing influence of food, drink, and entertainment. During the club's anniversary meeting in 1752 Newdigate recorded that '140 gent dined in booth in the garden of the Swan. Laid at Hen and Chickens. Players from London at theatre', and two years later noted, 'Dined 158 in the booth. Tea at inn and play the *Provoked Husband*—supped at inn.'[20] Contacts of this type were stimulated not only by the growing recreational opportunities to be found in towns, but also by common participation in charitable projects and by the lavish extent to which corporations wined and dined the rural élite.[21]

The ascendancy of cultural factors in the acquisition of status provided the swelling middle tier of society with a means of entering the privileged sphere of gentility. This, together with the growing fraternization between the leaders of urban and rural society, led to the emergence of a broader social élite, and with it an inevitable escalation in the competition for status. No one could escape the pressures generated by this, not even the traditional country squire, who was now compelled to justify his social standing by the continuous purchase and display of cultural products. Such were the forces unleashed by these changes that observers felt that society had become imprisoned in a spiral of social emulation. Mandeville noted how 'We all look above ourselves, and as fast as we can, strive to imitate those that some way or other are superior to us.' Fielding lamented that 'while the nobleman will emulate the grandeur of a prince, and the gentleman will aspire to the proper state of a nobleman, the tradesman steps from behind his counter into the vacant place of the gentleman. Nor doth the confusion end here: it reaches the very dregs of the people', sentiments echoed by Defoe when he complained that 'the poor will be like the rich, and the rich like the great, and the great like the greatest, and thus the world runs onto a kind of distraction at

[19] Newdigate Diaries, 6 Jan., 11 and 30 June, 5–6 Oct., and 16–17 and 21–2 Dec. 1752; 1 Jan., 14 Apr., and 31 Dec. 1753; and also Wilson, *Gentlemen Merchants*, 230–2.
[20] Newdigate Diaries, 17 July 1752, 29 July 1754; Money, *Experience and Identity*, 99–102.
[21] Wood, *Bath*, 301–3; Money, *Experience and Identity*, 9–11.

this time'.[22] Though such remarks exaggerated the degree to which society as a whole had been drawn into this vortex of competition, there is no ignoring the real fears that prompted their perturbed and even frenzied tone. The Urban Renaissance, for all its elegance, was the progeny of an unappetizing struggle for personal precedence. The remainder of this chapter will investigate the various ways in which urban culture serviced the demand for status, by examining the role of the house, personal accoutrements, resorts, marriage markets, games, publications and public works, and the civic domain.

2. THE HOUSE

One of the main agents through which a person established social position was the home. A house, and particularly its façade, spoke volumes about the way owners and occupants saw themselves and wished to be seen by others. The urban transition to classical architecture brought the aesthetic standards of town and country élite into alignment, and gave them a common language of status. Thus for a townsman to build in the new style was in itself a sign of gentility. However, classicism, because of its linguistic richness and social tradition, could also be used to express wide variations of status. An early recognition of this potential in the urban context was embodied in the London Rebuilding Act of 1667, which laid down the specifications of four types of dwellings: 'the first and least sort of houses fronting by-lanes, the second sort . . . fronting streets and lanes of note, the third sort . . . fronting high and principal streets, the fourth and largest sort of mansion houses for citizens or other persons of extraordinary quality'. The idea of socially determined categories of dwellings proved highly influential, affecting the drafting of subsequent legislation and the content of architectural manuals, which even in the 1820s were still composing their model elevations and plans according to the four 'rates'. In his study of Bath, John Wood recognized six categories of residences, at the apex of which lay the town house of Ralph Allen, consisting 'of a basement storey sustaining a double storey under the crowning; and this is surmounted by an

[22] Mandeville, *Fable*, 153; H. Fielding, 'An Enquiry into the Causes of the Late Increase in Robbers', in *The Works of Henry Fielding*, ed. J. P. Browne (London, 1871), x. 360; Defoe, *Tradesman*, 73–4; and also H. J. Perkin, 'The Social Causes of the Industrial Revolution', *TRHS*, 5th ser., xviii (1968), 140.

attic, which created a sixth rate house, and a sample for the greatest magnificence that was ever proposed by me for our city houses'. Pattern-books were highly sensitive to the need to match the form of a house to the rank of its occupant. Ware directed that new dwellings were 'to be suited either to the condition of the person who is to inhabit' them, or where this was not known, 'according to the place where' they were to stand, adding that 'he would be mad who should build a shed in Grosvenor Square, or a palace in Hedge Lane'.[23]

The most important element in the classical language for transmitting status was decoration. Freed of any substantial functional role, it was a form of unalloyed conspicuous consumption and a sign of a house owner's elevation above the necessities of life. The use of ornamental features was governed by a mixture of traditional rules and the whims of fashion. Both of these could be discovered through the purchase of a pattern-book, and one of the great attractions of these publications was that they revealed to the uninitiated the status signals embodied in architecture. Up until about the 1720s in London, and for a good deal longer in the provinces, there was much to be said for a liberal application of decorative devices. Many such houses survive today, which were clearly meant to draw the admiration of passers-by through their sheer exuberance.

Some ornamental features conveyed particular prestige. In the later Stuart period a cupola, such as that on Thomas Macro's house at Bury St Edmunds, or Alderman Atkinson's mansion in Leeds, imparted a real touch of grandeur, imitating as it did the practice of country houses like Coleshill, Ashdown, and Belton.[24] By the mid-eighteenth century the acme of fashion was the triple-lighted Venetian window, introduced into England in the 1720s, which Ware described as of 'a kind calculated for show, and very pompous in their nature: and, when executed with judgement, of extreme elegance'. One of these windows might form the centre-piece of the first floor or *piano nobile*. However, on Broad Street Ludlow, pride got the better part of judgement, when the owner of number thirty-nine crowded not one but eight such windows onto the three storeys of his façade (see Fig. 2).[25]

[23] 18 & 19 Car. II, c. 8; Cruickshank and Wyld, *Art of Georgian Building*, 22–34; Wood, *Bath*, 241, 243, 245; Ware, *Body of Architecture*, 291.

[24] *BE Suffolk*, 149; Thoresby, *Ducatus Leodiensis*, 76; Morrice, *Stuart and Baroque*, 28–33.

[25] Ware, *Body of Architecture*, 467; Summerson, *Architecture in Britain*, 336; Cruickshank, *Guide*, 40–2; Cruickshank and Wyld, *Art of Georgian Building*, 154–9; Ison, *Bath*, 154, 156, 160.

Fig. 24. The Circus (1754-8), Bath. Drawing by J. R. Cozens for an aquatint, pub. 1773

Throughout the period the use of the classical orders, and particularly of pilasters and columns, was an unmistakable mark of distinction. In the early years of the eighteenth century giant pilasters, stretching across several storeys, were a favourite device for injecting grandeur into a facade: for example, in the houses at the crossing area in Warwick (*c*.1695) (see Fig. 7), General Wade's house in the Abbey Churchyard Bath (*c*.1720), and the Red Lion at Blandford Forum (*c*.1732).[26] One of the noblest gestures was to lay the different orders on top of each other. This was done to stunning effect by Wood in the Circus at Bath, where Penrose noted that 'each storey has over it a grand cornice, supported by pillars of different orders: the lowest pillars of (I believe) the tuscan order; the middle ones, of the ionic; the highest of the corinthian. The whole pile of building, truly magnificent' (see Fig. 24). Half a century earlier the same principle had been applied on a more incongruous domestic scale to number twenty-nine Queen Square Bristol, to create a façade of cluttered but delightful pretentiousness (see Fig. 25).[27]

[26] *BE Warwickshire* (Harmondsworth, 1966), 461, 463; Ison, *Bath*, 121; RCHM, *Dorset*, iii, Part 1, 32; and also *BE Oxfordshire*, 509, 516; Gomme *et al.*, *Bristol*, 126-9; Cruickshank, *Guide*, 36-7.

[27] Penrose, *Letters*, 67; Ison, *Bristol*, 148-9.

Fig. 25. No. 29 (1709–11), Queen Square, Bristol

As Palladianism took root from about the 1720s, flamboyant decoration became increasingly *passé*. This development will be examined in a later chapter, but for the moment the significant point is that the social language of architecture changed, so that restraint rather than exuberance became the mark of prestige. This emphasis on simplicity potentially reduced the scope for the expression of status. However, one feature in the façade, the door-case, continued to act as a focus for ornamental treatment and permitted even the most uniform house to distinguish itself. Here it was that the English townsman excelled himself. Ware complained, 'how often do we see in London doors which appear not to belong to the house, but to be joined to it against nature; that seem to be stuck on, not raised with the building. . . . This is the error of those who mean to be magnificent'. Despite such exhortations—and Ware's aim was to improve rather than remove the decoration of door-cases—citizens continued to raise their own triumphal portals, whose extraordinary ingenuity and variety of design helped relieve the inherent blandness of later street terracing.[28]

For the status-conscious townsman one of the advantages of classical as opposed to vernacular architecture was that even the plainest dwelling had a family association, however tenuous, with the fine palaces and country houses of the period. This was a theme the Woods were to exploit brilliantly at Bath. In Queen Square (1728-36) John Wood the elder pioneered a method by which individual dwellings were combined into one grand structure with a palatial facade. This might be royalty on the cheap (a typical eighteenth-century solution, which spread the cost of cultural consumption), but few could deny that the north side of Queen Square, with its twenty-three bays and stately architecture, rivalled the front of the finest mansions of the time (see Fig. 5). Wood repeated the idea in the Parades (1740-48) and developed it even further in the Circus (1754-8). Architect and public were only too aware of the social pretensions of these edifices. Wood himself described how the north side of Queen Square 'soars above other buildings with a sprightliness, which gives it the elegance and grandeur of the body of a stately palace'. It was noted of the Parades that they were built 'to have the appearance of but one house, though it was to have been divided into several. . . . This building from the neighbouring hills looks like one grand palace' (see Fig. 18), and Penrose called the lodgings in Queen Square and the Circus 'pompous enough for palaces for great princes'. The multi-unit dwelling with its stately façade proved enormously popular in Georgian Bath. Parades and crescents sprang up all over the city, pandering to the inflated aspirations of visitors and residents. The idea reached its climax in Wood the younger's Royal Crescent (1769-74), in which thirty houses were combined into a sweeping linear edifice

[28] Ware, *Body of Architecture*, 438. For the importance of door-cases see Cruickshank and Wyld, *Art of Georgian Building*, 82-153; and for examples of door-cases see Ison, *Bath*, plates 111-16; Ison, *Bristol*, plates 54-6; C. Amery (ed.), *Period Houses and their Details* (London, 1978), plates 33-95; I. and E. Hall, *Georgian Hull* (York, 1978/9), plates 67-75; RCHM, *York*, iii, plates 62-5; RCHM, *Stamford*, pp. lxxvi-lxxvii, and plate 124.

with a major axis of 538 feet and 114 giant ionic columns separating 105 bays. Though it was all pure façade, since nothing substantial lay to the rear, here was a public front that no English country mansion could match.[29]

The palatial façade was the most audacious of the architectural devices used to enhance status. But the principle upon which it was based, the merging of individual residences into a single impressive structure, was one widely exploited, not only in the planning of squares and street terraces, but also in the design of smaller groups of dwellings. *The Modern Builder's Assistant* includes a pattern 'for three town houses' to be constructed as one building, and in post-fire Blandford Forum John Bastard built 26 Market-Place / 75 East Street as one grandiose baroque house, though in fact it contained his own and two other separate homes leased to a brazier and an apothecary. In West Stockwell Street Colchester, a pair of houses of about 1750 pool their resources to share the distinction of a projecting three bay centre-piece, which contains a Venetian window and is surmounted by a triangular pediment.[30] Underpinning all these exercises in amalgamation was the belief that big was beautiful and that a larger building would reflect its grandeur on the occupants, however many there were.

3. PERSONAL ACCOUTREMENTS

Personal appearance was central to the pursuit of status. A well-shaped body provided a useful foundation, particularly in the case of a woman, but of far greater importance were the garments and access-ories adorning it. As Mandeville observed, 'fine feathers make fine birds, and people where they are not known, are generally honoured according to their clothes and other accoutrements they have about them: from the richness of them we judge of their wealth, and by their ordering of them we guess at their understanding'. This was a point emphasized by Mr Wilson in Fielding's *Joseph Andrews*, who recounted how in his youth, 'The character I was ambitious of attaining was that of a fine gentleman, the first requisites to which I apprehended were to be supplied by a tailor, a periwig-maker, and

---

[29] Wood, *Bath*, 346; *England Illustrated*, ii. 212; Penrose, *Letters*, 67–8; Ison, *Bath*, 127–33, 145–8, 154–6.

[30] Halfpenny *et al.*, *Builder's Assistant*, 36–7, and plate 44; RCHM, *Dorset*, iii, Part 1, 31, and plate 108; Cruickshank, *Guide*, 34–6.

some few more tradesmen, who deal in furnishing out the human body.'[31]

Contemporary descriptions of fashionable urban life are full of references to clothing. Burr noted how after dinner at Tunbridge Wells, 'morning dress is laid aside, and all appear in full and splendid attire', a sight observed by Defoe, who found the 'walks covered with ladies completely dressed and gay to profusion, where rich clothes, jewels, and beauty . . . dazzles the eyes from one end of the range to the other' (see Fig. 20).[32] Sartorial descriptions fill the correspondence of visitors to Bath, among whom 'mutton dressed as lamb' was a theme frequently rehearsed. In 1766 Penrose reported that 'ladies without teeth, without eyes, with a foot and half in the grave, ape youth, and dress themselves forth with the fantastic pride of eighteen or twenty', and two years earlier Elizabeth Montagu had noted how 'The Rooms were prodigiously crowded with very uncouth figures most wonderfully dressed: those who nature designed to be homely art rendered hideous, and many, who education made awkward, mantua-makers, tailors, friseurs, and milliners made monstrous.'[33] Such caricatures reflected a widespread fascination with clothes among the spa's devotees. In 1759 Margaret Luttrell wrote to her husband about their son, at that moment attending a ball, 'I did wish for mother to have seen Harry today with his hair dressed and powdered . . . I lent him my stone buckles, and we tacked on some lace to his shirt by way of ruffles, so he is quite a beau'. Next year she reported of herself, 'last night I assure you I cut a figure at the ball, with all the finery your goodness bestowed upon me, and a new negligee which I found myself obliged to purchase'.[34]

Certain accoutrements endowed their owners with especial prestige. Observers frequently commented on the presence of jewellery. It was reported that during the Warwick races of 1728, 'Mrs Archer and Mrs Bromley of Cambridgeshire were loaded with jewels', and that at a ball in Bath in 1761, 'there was . . . above four hundred persons and Mrs Clive outshone them all, I mean in jewels only, as she is not the most beautiful'. In 1714 it was said that one of the great attractions of dice to the ladies visiting Bath was 'the opportunity it gives to display

[31] Mandeville, *Fable*, 152; H. Fielding, *Joseph Andrews*, ed. A. R. Humphreys (London, 1973), 155.

[32] Burr, *Tunbridge Wells*, 119; Defoe, *Tour*, i. 126.

[33] Penrose, *Letters*, 29; HMC, *Bath MSS*, i. 334.

[34] Margaret Luttrell to Henry Luttrell, [?]1759; Margaret Luttrell to Henry Luttrell, 12 Mar. 1760, Somerset RO, DD/L.

the well-turned arm, and to scatter to advantage the rays of the diamond'.[35] The impact of precious stones derived in part from their arresting physical qualities (greatly enhanced by candle-light), which were guaranteed to attract public notice. But more important was jewelry's role, a product of its high economic value and low practical utility, as a symbol of lavish wealth.

An article of attire which drew particular comment was hair. Wigs and other ornamental accessories were often used to decorate the pate, sometimes to spectacular, if risible effect. In 1764 Elizabeth Montagu noted that in the Rooms at Bath 'some of the misses seem to be adorned with the scalps of Indian warriors', and thirteen years later Edward Pigott was so impressed by the hair-dos on view, as to record details and drawings of them in his diary:

these two head-dresses were the most fashionable last winter at Bath . . . the height of hair was above the length of the face, the height of the cap another length, and the feathers another length . . . these head-dresses were not in the least remarkable for their height, there being many much higher . . . it is ridiculous to see the ladies dressed thus, in a coach, hanging their heads forward, and then, even when the cushion of the seat is taken away, they can hardly place themselves, so as not to discompose the elegant edifice.

Such appendages were an excellent method of capturing attention. As a poem of 1748 remarked of a rakish old woman at Bath,

> She jigs, and turns with an uncommon air;
> A feather flaunting in her cap or hair,
> That she may be conspicuous in our sight.

Hair and its accessories became a sort of flag hoisted by a woman to declare her presence, and especially important in a crowded theatre or ballroom, where individual figures might be difficult to discern at a distance.[36]

The importance of clothing stemmed from the emphasis placed on a person's external image in establishing status. This was particularly the case in the resorts, where visitors might be unknown to each other. At Tunbridge it was said that 'the chief diversion of the wells is to stare one at another, and he or she that is best dressed, is the greatest

[35] Warwickshire CRO, CR.1368, ii, fo. 12; Warwickshire CRO, L6/1463; 'A Description of the Bath', in *The Tunbridge and Bath Miscellany for the Year 1714* (London, 1714), 22.
[36] HMC, *Bath MSS*, i. 334; Pigott Diary, i, article 502; *Bath: A Poem*, 27.

subject of the morning's tittle-tattle',[37] and ladies just arrived at Bath were careful not to 'appear in public', or at least any 'fashionable place', until their baggage had arrived with their best clothes.[38] Penrose, who found it 'very disagreeable to be all day dressed in form', implied that at Bath the display of costumal finery was the real motive behind the heavy programme of house calls: 'visitors here . . . make very short visits; they bounce into the room, and show themselves, and away; and being generally well-dressed, they make me compare them to Jupiter, when he came in his glory to Semela; they are glorious in their apparel, make a noise like thunder, and are gone again quick as lightning'.[39]

The effectiveness of dress in conveying prestige was largely due to the mediating offices of fashion, which helped ascribe inherently worthless pieces of attire with a recognizable social value. Fashion, because of its protean nature, also facilitated freer access to status. Changes in style ensured that the social worth of particular accoutrements was constantly altering. In 1698 Sir John Mordaunt wrote to his wife, 'probably when the King returns some new fashion may appear, and therefore [I] would defer making my clothes as long as I could'; in 1767 John Penrose was unable to match a piece of silk sent him from the country because 'the pattern is too old for Bath. . . . The mercers here . . . are supplied only with silks of one, two, or three years old patterns'; and in 1781 William Hutton wrote that the buckle, 'this offspring of fancy, like the clouds, is ever changing. The fashion of today, is thrown into the casting pot tomorrow'.[40] Such gyrations in taste permitted newcomers to compete for status on equal terms with the already privileged, since the latter would be forced to engage in regular bouts of consumption merely to maintain social position. Fashion was thus a social grading machine, constantly helping to realign wealth and status. Finally, it should be noted that image-building was not just a question of decorating the body; of equal importance was the adornment of the mind and the refinement of behaviour. Consequently, the expansion in the provision of fashionable educational facilities and the explosion in the informal channels

[37] 'A Letter from Tunbridge to a Friend in London', in *Tunbridge and Bath Miscellany . . . 1714*.

[38] *Step to the Bath*, 155; Penrose, *Letters*, 29.

[39] Penrose, *Letters*, 88.

[40] Warwickshire CRO, CR.1368, i, fo. 4; Penrose, *Letters*, 198; Hutton, *History of Birmingham*, 77.

of learning (both of which were surveyed earlier) also played a crucial part in the quest for gentility.

4. RESORTS

In the acquisition of status the construction of a favourable image went hand in hand with the need to display that persona in the most advantageous social context. All the cosmetic treatment imaginable would win little recognition if exhibited in the wrong place. Social centres (particularly the resorts) were especially well-adapted to servicing this need, since they provided settings carefully modelled to accommodate the pursuit of prestige.

The simple act of visiting a holiday centre could carry with it a good deal of prestige, so care had to be taken in selecting the correct venue. Defoe found 'the company who frequent Tunbridge, seem to be a degree or two above the society of' Epsom and Hampstead, and claimed that 'as the nobility and gentry go to Tunbridge, the merchants and rich citizens to Epsom, so the common people go chiefly to Dulwich and Streatham'.[41] The queen of the spas was undoubtedly Bath. Its reputation owed much to the way it assiduously cultivated royal patronage and associations. The reflected glory of the monarchy was an irresistible attraction, and its presence in the spa was guaranteed to draw in visitors. Queen Anne's stays in Bath in 1702 and 1703 'brought such a concourse of people to the city . . . that the drinking pumps could not supply them: all the neighbouring villages were filled with people of rank and fortune . . . lodgings were then so scarce, that many were obliged to pay a guinea a night for their beds'.[42] Bath went to great lengths to celebrate and publicize a royal sojourn, so that the memory of the occasion would linger long after the principal actors had departed.[43] One method of doing this was to immortalize the event in monumental form. After the visits by the Prince of Orange in 1734 and the Prince and Princess of Wales in 1738, ostentatious obelisks were erected in the Gravel Walks and

[41] Defoe, *Tour*, i. 128, 157.
[42] Wood, *Bath*, 221.
[43] See the description of the ceremonies and festivities during the Prince and Princess of Wales's visit in 1738, in the *Lancashire Jnl.*, No. 17, 23 Oct. 1738; No. 19, 6 Nov. 1738; No. 20, 13 Nov. 1738; No. 23, 4 Dec. 1738; and for other royal visits see Wood, *Bath*, 324–5.

Queen Square to commemorate the occasions.[44] The Somerset spa took its sovereign pretensions even further, appropriating the highest titles for its finest buildings and facilities, such as the King's Bath, the Queen's Bath, Queen Square, the King's Circus, and the Royal Crescent. It even enjoyed its own royal foundation myth, amply expounded in Wood's history, which claimed that the city had been established by the philosopher-king Bladud, and had been originally called Caerbren, or, city of the king.[45]

Within Bath and other fashionable urban centres existed a wide range of arenas (assemblies, walks, theatres, concerts, clubs, and churches) in which to pursue status. Mere admission to these facilities would often bestow prestige, since the cost of a ticket and the appropriate clothing would generally guarantee their exclusive nature. One commentator warned potential visitors to early eighteenth-century Tunbridge Wells, 'let your pockets be well furnished', and another, 'without money a man is nobody at Tunbridge . . . when any man finds his pockets low, he has nothing left to think of, but to be gone'.[46] Such financial qualifications pertained to places of worship as well as to those of pleasure, in death as well as in life. The proprietary chapels of Bath, of which the best known were St Mary's Queen Square (opened 1734) and the Octagon in Milsom Street (1767), were designed to be select establishments, and Penrose noted that at the former 'a stranger cannot get a sitting under half a crown a time, or a guinea for the season'. Death, far from being the great leveller, reinforced exclusivity and status. It was reported from Bath that 'the fees for breaking ground in churches [are] monstrous high, ten pounds at the Abbey. So all the poor and middling people, nay all except the rich and great, are carried, when dead, to . . . two neighbouring parishes the other side the river Avon, which is crossed in a ferry boat'. The present walls of the Abbey, encrusted with Stuart and Georgian urns, busts, cartouches, and tablets, suggest that many were willing to make this final investment in self-esteem.[47]

Within these arenas differences of status were understood and acknowledged. Balls in the lower rooms at Bath were 'commonly opened with a minuet danced by two persons of the highest distinction', while the rules required that 'no chair or bench can be called on

[44] Wood, *Bath*, 342–3, 347–8; *Lancashire Jnl.*, No. 22, 27 Nov. 1738.
[45] Wood, *Bath*, 7–40, 43; R. J. Stewart, *The Myth of King Bladud* (Bath, 1980).
[46] 'Letter from Tunbridge'; Defoe, *Tour*, i. 127.
[47] Ison, *Bath*, 72–3; Penrose, *Letters*, 81; *BE North Somerset and Bristol*, 103–5.

ball nights for any person, who does not rank as a peer or peeress', and at the Bennett Street rooms 'the first row of benches at the upper end of the rooms' was retained 'for the peeresses'.[48] When in 1731 the recently elevated Earl of Orrery entered the Pump Rooms at Bath, he discovered that 'as soon as the circling whisper had taken air that the Earl of Orrery was present, all eyes were fixed upon me. . . . Some months ago I should have been as little regarded as my own natural shyness could desire. But now I had seats, salutes, and innumerable civilities offered to me from every quarter.' Later he visited Leake's bookshop, and found the proprietor 'looks upon every man, distinguished by any title, not only as his friend, but his companion, and treats him accordingly; but he disposes of his favours and regards as methodically as Nash takes out the ladies to dance, and therefore speaks not to a marquess whilst a duke is in the room'. One reason people deferred so readily to superiors was that it enhanced their own image to do so. Status by association was an inexhaustible pleasure as a poet of 1748 succinctly wrote,

> All seek acquaintance, for of that they boast,
> And those are happiest, who gain the most.

George Lucy's letters from Bath leave no doubt as to the satisfaction that he derived, though himself a substantial country gentleman, from mixing with the great:

[27 March 1751] The Duke of B—— hath done me the honour to speak to me since I wrote last, and last night I attacked the Duchess with great fury, till the want of conversation occasioned my best bow and retired.
[20 March 1763] L——d Cholmondeley . . . becomes our intimate this evening, so that we shall soon cut a figure, and look as big as some others.
[14 April 1765] Yesterday I made the greatest figure I have done since I came here, I had the honour in the morning of conducting Lady Northampton . . . to our musical academy. . . .[49]

5. MARRIAGE MARKETS

It would be misleading to dwell too much on the importance of title. The cultural definition of gentility, together with other powerful

[48] Wood, *Bath*, 443; Penrose, *Letters*, 136; Pigott Diary, i, article 478.
[49] Boyle, *Orrery Papers*, i. 99; *Bath: A Poem*, 27; Warwickshire CRO, L6/1426, 1470, 1473.

forces to be discussed in the next chapter, helped restrict the impact of
formal distinctions. This encouraged free social competition, and
allowed urban cultural arenas to operate as markets in which wealth
could be exchanged for status. Nowhere was this bartering process
more obvious than in the case of marriage. This was one of the most
critical economic and social decisions facing individuals and their
parents, particularly among the middling and upper ranks. A successful alliance could bring with it substantial wealth and influential
connections; an ill-judged match might dissipate a family's valuable
material and social assets. Marriage was therefore a crucial mechanism
in the distribution and redistribution of wealth, power, and status.[50]

Mandeville noted that 'among the fashionable part of mankind, the
people of birth and fortune, it is expected that matrimony should
never be entered upon without a curious regard to family, estate, and
reputation'.[51] In such circumstances the context in which partner
selection occurred was of the greatest importance. Though there was
some argument for keeping the procedure as tightly controlled and
secretive as possible to minimize the risk of any blunders, the most
influential pressures in the late seventeenth century tended towards a
more liberal approach. There were several reasons for this. First, a
larger and more open market extended the range of choice and
enhanced the chances of striking a successful, even spectacular
bargain. Second, the growth in the wealth and numbers of the
middling groups inevitably increased the demand for and supply of
marriage partners 'among the fashionable part of mankind', and
necessitated the development of more expansive marketing arrangements. Third, the mounting financial and social pressures on many
country gentlemen encouraged them to look further afield, both geographically and socially, to procure a lucrative and prestigious alliance.
Finally, it appears that because greater emphasis was being placed on
emotional compatibility in marital relationships, children were
permitted a greater say in their choice of a husband or wife.[52] As a
consequence, there was a move to widen the pool of prospective
partners. The outcome of these four developments was that the

[50] Mingay, *Landed Society*, 28–36; Stone, *Open Élite*, 73–9; Jenkins, *Ruling Class*,
40–1; Beckett, 'Lowthers at Holker', 59; M. Slater, 'The Weightiest Business: Marriage
in an Upper-Gentry Family in Seventeenth-Century England', *Past and Present*, lxxii
(1976), 25–54.
[51] Mandeville, *Fable*, 166–7.
[52] L. Stone, *The Family, Sex, and Marriage in England 1500–1800* (Harmondsworth,
1979), chaps. 7–8.

bartering of brides and bridegrooms could no longer be effectively transacted through the narrow channels traditionally employed, and that larger, more cosmopolitan, and better appointed markets were now required.

The prosperity of the provincial resorts and social centres was due in no small part to their success in meeting this demand.[53] In 1732 it was noted that the fair at Bury St Edmunds was 'much frequented by the ladies that live in the counties adjacent, to show themselves and make their market', and Macky claimed that 'it is more a market for ladies than merchandises'.[54] Defoe found the assemblies at Winchester 'pleasant and agreeable to the young people, and sometimes fatal to them', but defended the reputation of York, arguing 'nor has there been so many young fortunes carried off here by half-pay men, as has been said to be in other towns, of merry fame, westward and south-ward'.[55] Race-meetings were frequently venues for matchmaking. In 1732 the Duchess of Marlborough complained that 'these races that are now got almost all over England do a great deal of mischief . . . all the young women lay out more than they can spare in hopes to get good husbands', and in 1754 a disappointed Viscount Stormont grumbled about the York meeting, 'I . . . went through the drudgery of pleasure there very well, but had not the honour of being taken in any shape . . . I never saw more pretty women anywhere'.[56] The equine competition on these occasions seems to have sharpened the bargaining instincts of the spectators. After the Warwick meeting of 1728 Sir Charles Mordaunt, whose wife had died two years earlier, wrote to his mother, 'though there were some very agreeable young women, I would not engage myself to any till I had seen what Hampshire would afford'.[57]

The most active marriage marts were to be found in the resorts. Macky argued that 'there is no place in the world better to begin an intrigue in than' Tunbridge Wells, and Burr recommended the spa for 'the commerce of love and gallantry'. In the 1740s Edward Young reported from Tunbridge, 'here is a great fortune which is followed by a pack of noble beagles', and Elizabeth Montagu related, 'I have not

[53] R. Williams, *The Country and the City* (London, 1973), 51-4; Stone, *Family, Sex, and Marriage*, 213.

[54] HMC, *Portland MSS*, vi. 150; Macky, *Journey*, i. 6; and also Defoe, *Tour*, i. 51-2, 216-17; Suffolk RO, E2/25/1, fo. 294.

[55] Defoe, *Tour*, i. 186; ii. 231; and also Macky, *Journey*, ii. 41-2.

[56] Thomson, *Letters of a Grandmother*, 58; HMC, *Hastings MSS*, iii. 88.

[57] Warwickshire CRO, CR.1368, ii, fo. 12.

seen our friend. . . . I hear he is disconsolate for the loss of the widow
. . . the conqueror, Mr Grove, has carried her to Bath'.[58] The
Somerset resort was the most prestigious of these markets. In 1754
Pococke claimed 'that there is no place in the world so fit for the
necessary and honourable business of making alliances'.[59] This may be
the reason George Lucy spent so much time at Bath. Since the 1740s,
when he inherited his Warwickshire estate, he had been under
pressure from his relatives and housekeeper to find a wife.[60] His letters
home reveal not only his own (abortive) efforts, but also the extraordinary degree of intrigue in the city:

[6 January 1754] Col——— Pyot's widow is here and extremely young and
pretty. Excepting a few gay widows, I think there is a set of the most disagreeable women that was ever huddled together in one case. . . .

[29 December 1758] One evening I played at cards . . . in Gay Street . . .
there was a lady there much cried up, by name, Miss Hyat, who is supposed a
large fortune and a beauty. . . .

[10 January 1759] Sir Charles Hardy took a wife with him from hence on
Saturday last, and [I] hear many more are upon the same plan. . . . The
famous Miss Hyat will have difficulty, I believe, to get clear off, she is much
admired and deemed good for her sum.

[22 February 1761] The account I sent you in my last of a certain negotiation is
now pretty plain, I believe, to most people here. We now appear together in
public at concerts and at the rooms, and played on Friday night last at cribbage
publicly there. However, you'll let nothing transpire, I flatter myself, till you
have my consent.

[17 April 1763] Upon asking Jenny when she was to enter the holy state, her
answer was, when she thought proper. I imagine about a fortnight will
complete the affair. . . .[61]

The facilities at Bath were carefully organized to promote the
market's smooth operation. At the assemblies, 'elder ladies and
children' were required to 'be contented with a second bench . . . as
being past or not come to perfection', and 'gentlemen' were
'requested not to stand between the ladies sitting down and the
country dancers', presumably to permit a full appraisal.[62] All the spa's
cultural resources could be pressed into service for the business of

[58] Macky, *Journey*, i. 91; Burr, *Tunbridge Wells*, 126; HMC, *Bath MSS*, i. 263, 331.
[59] R. Pococke, *The Travels through England*, Camden Soc., 2nd ser. (1888-9), ii. 32;
and also Neale, *Bath*, 19-21.
[60] Warwickshire CRO, L6/1371, 1373, 1377, 1385, 1396-8.
[61] Ibid. L6/1432, 1451-2, 1471.
[62] Wood, *Bath*, 249; Penrose, *Letters*, 136.

matchmaking. In 1700 it was remarked of the Abbey that 'it is crowded during divine service, as much as St Paul's: in which time there is more billet-doux conveyed to the ladies, than notes to desire the prayers of the congregation at B——'s meeting-house . . . the ladies were the only saints several came to adore'. Bath was also well equipped to put the finishing touches to any transaction. Wood recorded that 'suits of wedding clothes for the ladies, from far and near', are 'constantly making in the shops of the city', and in 1755 it was reported that Lord Dartmouth was 'married at Queen Square church. . . . First came in Lord Dartmouth in a white cloth coat and satin waistcoat trimmed with silver . . . [a] quarter of an hour after, the bride in [a] white satin negligee, etc.'.[63]

The economic value of the goods on offer was of central importance to those employing the urban marriage markets. Among the company at Buxton in 1744 could be found a Mrs Jessop, 'worth £16,000, and was last year here to be cured of a frenzy, wherein she is succeeded. That good success brought her here again this year. She is now very orderly behaved and has got a lover.' George Lucy reported from Bath, 'they tell me I have a twenty-thousand-pounder my next neighbour, and only parted by one thin partition', and it was claimed of Tunbridge Wells in 1714, 'here are a great many gold mines to be found under the petticoat, where an able workman may line his pocket at the trouble of digging'.[64] Financial attractions could compensate for physical faults. One poet noted in *The Tunbridge and Bath Miscellany* of 1714,

> With scorn Cloudalia's haughty face we view,
> The deadened aspect, and the sordid hue,
> Her wealth discovered gives her features lies,
> And we find charms to reconcile our eyes.

Thirty years later a visitor to Buxton recorded in his diary, 'Mr Watts . . . came from Leeds. . . . He brought with him his sister, a fortune of £20,000, and so she needs be, being blind, ugly, and crooked.'[65]

---

[63] *Step to the Bath*, 166; Wood, *Bath*, 436; HMC, *Hastings MSS*, iii. 94.
[64] HMC, *Egmont MSS*, Diary iii. 297–8; Warwickshire CRO, L6/1451; 'Letter from Tunbridge'.
[65] 'An Epistle to a Friend', in *Tunbridge and Bath Miscellany . . . 1714*, 12; HMC, *Egmont MSS*, Diary iii. 298; and also *The Spectator*, No. 155, 28 Aug. 1711, in A. Ross (ed.), *Selections from The Tatler and The Spectator of Steele and Addison* (Harmondsworth, 1982), 291–2; 'On a Young Gentleman's Marrying an Old Lady for her Riches', in *The Lover's Miscellany: Or, Poems on Several Occasions, Amorous and Gallant* (London, 1719), 33.

The crude monetary worth of alliances should not obscure the real motives behind such transactions. Wealth was the high road to status and power. If it came in the form of cash or securities it could be converted into prestige and influence through cultural consumption or the purchase of land; if it came in property, then it would normally automatically confer these benefits. Playing the marriage market was therefore a means to sustain or improve one's social position. Financial difficulties could be eased and social demotion avoided by a favourable match. At Buxton in 1744 Sir Archibald Grant, whose estate had been sequestered following his 'mismanagement in the charitable corporation of which he was a director . . . made love to Mrs Jessop to mend his private affairs', and in *The Tatler* Steele relates the case of Will Vafer, who 'has lately lost . . . half the income . . . his estate will bring in within seven years', and 'proposes to marry to set all right'.[66] Matrimony could also provide a successful middle ranking family with an opportunity to convert their wealth into status, by wedding their suitably endowed daughters to a landed gentleman, or even aristocrat. Miège claimed in 1699 that 'now it is common for gentlemen's and merchants' sons and daughters to intermarry', and Defoe suggested 'that when a noble family is loaded with titles and honour rather than fortune, they come down into the city and choose wives among the merchants' and tradesmen's daughters'.[67] But, given the competitive nature of the market, *caveat emptor*. Those frequenting Tunbridge Wells were warned that it was 'a rare place for a beau to be jilted in a wife: for many set up to be great fortunes, who feed their mouths with their tails, and cover their backs with bellies'.[68]

6. GAMES

The atmosphere of competition that so manifested itself in the marriage market infused many aspects of cultural life in the urban social centres. One area where it surfaced openly was sports and games, particularly cock-fighting, horse-racing, and gambling. These pas-

[66] HMC, *Egmont MSS*, Diary iii. 297–8; *The Tatler*, No. 56, 16–18 Aug. 1709, in Ross, *Tatler and Spectator*, 108.

[67] Miège, *New State of England*, 151; Defoe, *Tradesman*, 226; W. A. Speck, 'Conflict in Society', in Holmes, *Glorious Revolution*, 145–7; Rogers, 'Bourgeoisie of Hanoverian London', 444–6.

[68] 'Letter from Tunbridge'.

times, though apparently divorced from the realities of life, generated an extraordinary degree of commitment and passion among their adherents. The gentry and nobility poured thousands of pounds into horse-racing and breeding, and Defoe complained of how the sportsmen at Newmarket 'were all so intent, so eager, so busy upon the sharping part of the sport, their wagers and bets, that to me they seemed just as so many horse-coursers in Smithfield, descending (the greatest of them) from their high dignity and quality, to picking one another's pockets, and biting one another as much as possible'.[69] Goldsmith could only account for the strange eagerness with which 'the healthy could ever consent to follow the sick' to the spas by the fact that 'the gaming-table was properly the salutary fount to which such numbers flocked'. Women particularly succumbed to gambling. One diarist reported that 'in Bath it is very customary for ladies to play at hazard, at Harrison's and other coffee-houses', something which the hero of 'Cupid Defeated at Bath' lamented when he declaimed,

> Adieu . . . ye giddy fair,
> I will no longer stay;
> Those hearts deserve from me no care,
> That are usurped by play.[70]

Heavy involvement in gaming induced a quite special and intense state of concentration. At Tunbridge Wells Burr found 'the parties engaged in play are too deeply interested in the success of their game, to attend to anything around them'. Lady Bristol reported on her own gambling activities at Bath that 'here is very deep play', and George Lucy wrote home from the spa, 'the only set I should choose to play with, play so deep that I don't choose to meddle'.[71] The large sums of money wagered on such occasions and the acute level of concentration displayed by the participants suggest that during 'deep play' cherished ambitions were at stake. Foremost among them was surely the acquisition of status, a point hinted at in a poem of 1740:

---

[69] Defoe, *Tour*, i. 75. For the heavy involvement of the Earl of Bristol in racing and betting, see Hervey, *Letter-Books*, i. *passim*.

[70] O. Goldsmith, 'The Life of Richard Nash', in *Collected Works of Oliver Goldsmith*, ed. A. Friedman (Oxford, 1966), iii. 299; Students Diary, fo. 118; 'Cupid Defeated', quoted in W. Tyte, *Bath in the Eighteenth Century* (Bath, 1903), 53; and also Penrose, *Letters*, 119; Wood, *Bath*, 446–53.

[71] Burr, *Tunbridge Wells*, 120; Hervey, *Letter-Books*, ii. 203; Warwickshire CRO, L6/1453.

How true those cards life represent!
'Tis all in tricks, and honours spent:

. . . .

The ace, the king, the queen, the knave,
Command the board, and privilege crave;
The rest from single ten, to duce, and tray
Humble obedience to the higher pay.[72]

The artificial nature of games and their theoretical separation from the 'real' world allowed the competition for prestige to be engaged in with relative safety and without threatening unacceptable levels of social conflict. It may be that England survived many of its political traumas because the key battles were fought not in Parliament or on the streets of London, but on the Heath at Newmarket and the card-tables of Bath.

Women especially used gaming to enhance their status. Disadvantaged by their sexual position, the pastime allowed them to enjoy the unfeminine thrill of competition, engage in monetary transactions, and compete on equal terms with men. In a poem of 1741 Mrs C—— declared how, under the influence of gambling,

Men oft-times sued in vain, with various arts,
To seduce me from my charming ace of hearts,
To no effect, I baffled all their skill,
I scorned their offers, and pursued my will.

Steele, after a visit to Harrison's table in Bath, reported that 'I am satisfied that the gamester ladies have surmounted the little vanities of showing their beauty, which they so far neglect, as to throw their features into violent distortions and wear away their lilies and roses in tedious watching and restless lucubrations. I should rather observe that their chief passion is an emulation of manhood'.[73]

7. PUBLICATIONS AND PUBLIC WORKS

Not all status had to be obtained in the white heat of competition. More sober channels existed in the majority of provincial towns

---

[72] C. Geertz, 'Deep Play: Notes on the Balinese Cock-Fight', in C. Geertz, *The Interpretation of Cultures* (London, 1975), 432–42; 'On the Game of Whisk', in *The Bath Miscellany for the Year 1740* (Bath, 1741), 8.

[73] 'Mrs C——'s Complaint for the Loss of the Ace of Hearts', in *Bath Miscellany*, 25; *The Guardian*, No. 174, 30 Sept. 1713, in *The Tatler and The Guardian* (Edinburgh, 1880), 257.

through which a person could make a mark on the world. Among the most important of these were publications and public works. Several printed maps and prospects were bordered by miniature drawings of the leading citizens' homes,[74] and town histories frequently contained descriptions of fashionable streets and residences. In his study of Leeds, Thoresby let it be known that 'John Atkinson esq, Justice of the Peace for the West Riding, and mayor of Leeds, 1711, is now building a delicate house, that for the exquisite workmanship of the stonework, especially the dome, and for the painted staircase . . . exceeds all in town', and the finished product is illustrated on Cossins's map of 1725 (see Fig. 1).[75] Newspapers were also used as a medium for obtaining public recognition. At the resorts they carried lists of the most distinguished visitors and in other towns the papers recorded the name of those attending prestigious local events like a race ball.[76]

One of the most effective devices for self-advertisement was the subscription system, which conferred on its users both the prestige of patronizing some culturally elevating project, and that of being ranked alongside more illustrious contributors. The list of subscribers that prefaced Wood's *Description of the Exchange of Bristol* permitted men such as Mr Joshua Ross, gilder and frame-maker of Bath, and Mr Joseph Smith, watchmaker of Bristol, to associate, at least on paper, with the Earl of Orrery and the Bishop of Bath and Wells. The subscribers to the building of the York assembly rooms enjoyed the pleasure of seeing their names collected together on a printed broadsheet with those of the cream of city and county society.[77] Contributions to public works and charities endowed particular prestige, since they conveyed the image of a selfless benefactor, interested in public rather than private improvement.[78] These gifts were rarely cloaked in anonymity. The chapel of King Charles the Martyr at Tunbridge Wells was erected in the late seventeenth century with the money raised from over 2,500 subscriber-visitors, whose names were recorded in two great framed lists. The

[74] See, for example, Gilmore, *Map of Bath*; Cossins, *Plan of Leeds*; J. Corbridge, *The West Prospect of the Town of Great Yarmouth in Norfolk*, pub. 1726, reproduced in Hyde, *Gilded Scenes*, 94-5.
[75] Thoresby, *Ducatus Leodiensis*, 76; Wood, *Bath*, 96, 245.
[76] McIntyre, 'Rise of a Resort Town', 208; Little, 'Gloucestershire Spas', 175, 186; Fairfax-Blakeborough, *Northern Turf History*, iii. 198-9.
[77] 'Proposals for . . . Assembly Rooms', YCA; and also Ross, *Tatler and Spectator*, 487-502.
[78] On the role of the subscription system in charities see Brewer, 'Commercialization and Politics', 225-8.

original building accounts included payments for 'digesting into an exact alphabet, all the contributors' names, engrossing them annually with those of former years in a book, with fair catalogues and scrolls, exposed for the satisfaction of the company'.[79] The county and town histories of the period also frequently chronicled acts of munificence. Wood's *Bath* contains a list of over 200 subscribers and 101 governors of the city's General Hospital (opened in 1742), a charity for which it had been the practice to produce 'annual printed lists of contributors'. Membership of the hospital's board of governors was an honour guaranteed by the payment of £20 (later raised to £40).[80]

Philanthropy therefore provided an altruistic façade behind which to pursue self-centred ambition, and though it may be thought a little uncharitable to argue, as Mandeville did, that 'pride and vanity have built more hospitals than all the virtues together', one cannot ignore the contribution of these baser aspirations to financing an escalating programme of public works.[81] Moreover, benefactions of this type had one particular advantage over most other forms of status acquisition, in that they provided a potentially infinite return on investment. When the *arriviste* London physician John Radcliffe died in 1714, he left a substantial portion of his huge fortune to Oxford University, prompting Mandeville to comment,

A rich miser, who is thoroughly selfish, and would receive the interest of his money even after his death, has nothing else to do than to defraud his relations, and leave his estate to some famous university: they are the best markets to buy immortality at with little merit. . . . There men are profoundly skilled in human nature, and know what it is their benefactors want. . . .

Oxford did not fail. The Radcliffe Quadrangle was added to University College by 1719, but the *pièce de résistance* came thirty-five years after his death, when the splendid library or Camera was completed, its massive rotunda and dome dominating a prestigious site in the university, its entrance surmounted by a statue of the saintly and astute doctor. Nor does the story end there, for subsequently the Radcliffe trustees erected an infirmary (1759–70) and an observatory (completed 1794) which still bear his name.[82]

---

[79] The two lists are at present hanging in the nave of the church, and the quotation is from the 1688–96 table; Burr, *Tunbridge Wells*, 52–3; Savidge, *Tunbridge Wells*, 6–7.

[80] Wood, *Bath*, 274–303, 439; and also Nash, *Worcestershire*, Supplement, 94–6.

[81] Mandeville, 'An Essay on Charity and Charity Schools', added in 1723 to the *Fable*, 269.

[82] Holmes, *Augustan England*, 221–2; Mandeville, *Fable*, 273; RCHM, *City of Oxford* (London, 1939), 114; BE *Oxfordshire*, 263–4, 271–2, 305.

8. THE CIVIC DOMAIN

The prestige that accrued from public architecture was often focused not so much on any individual, as on the town and city as a whole. Such buildings formed part of a growing body of investment in the civic image of the town, which was designed to raise its collective status. During the opening ceremony for the Exchange at Bristol in 1743 it was declared that

Public edifices have, in all times, been had in esteem, and considered as manifestations of the wisdom and grandeur of a state. . . . That the trade of this city may flourish and increase, and the prosperity and reputation of it be daily advanced, are the ardent wishes of the corporation, this noble pile, raised by their liberal hand, more eminently testifies than words can express.[83]

A town could also enhance its prestige in print, and urban authorities widely supported the preparation and publication of maps, prospects, and histories. When Drake produced his lavish study of York, the city fathers contributed £50 'towards the expenses of engraving copper plates' for the volume, including several of recently erected public buildings, and formally thanked the author for 'the infinite labour pains and expense he has been at to revive and illustrate the honour and grandeur of this ancient city'.[84]

The pursuit of the city's honour could, like charity, prove a convenient cloak behind which to advance more personal ambitions. Civic prestige was a reservoir of status from which some were able to draw more heavily than others. The principal beneficiaries were the urban patriciate. They were the men invariably responsible for initiating and developing schemes, and though they might be utilizing town capital, they took personal credit for these ventures. Moreover, several of the new public edifices were directly associated with accommodating the urban élite, and doing so in some style. The surge of town hall building and rebuilding displayed considerable architectural pretensions which spread beyond the external structure. The larger halls usually contained several rooms for business and entertainment, many of which were decorated in the most fashionable manner. The mayor's residence at York was lavishly appointed, with the semi-basement containing kitchens and offices; the ground floor, a dining-room,

[83] Wood, *Exchange of Bristol*, 33–4; Grady, 'Public Buildings in the West Riding', chap. 5.

[84] Clark, 'Visions of the Urban Community', 117; House Book, 19 Sept. 1735, 26 Nov. 1736, YCA.

Fig. 26.　The State or Great Room, Mansion House, York

robing-room, and butter pantry; the second floor, several bedrooms; and the *piano nobile*, the resplendent 'great' or state room, with panelled walls, corinthian pilasters, and a decorated coved ceiling (see Fig. 26).[85] Such buildings provided town leaders with a physical setting and life-style that imitated that of the landed élite, and increasingly separated them from the majority of their fellow citizens.

The prestige which accrued from investment in the collective image of the town was therefore focused primarily on its ruling circle. Though some of its members may have baulked at the expense and time involved in holding office, most would have understood that public virtues had private benefits. One particularly valuable social reward that flowed for the town's rising status was the enhanced opportunity it provided for the urban élite to associate with the traditional gentry. Every opening was exploited to foster contacts. Growing numbers of country gentlemen were invited to become freemen, councillors, and even mayors. At Preston the strict admission

[85] The building, furnishing, and subsequent maintenance and improvement of the mayor's residence can be traced in House Book, from 21 Oct. 1724 onwards, YCA; Drake, *Eboracum*, 330, and facing plate; W. Camidge, *The Mansion House at York* (York, 1902); *VCH York*, 543–4. For other examples of fine interior decoration of civic buildings see Oswald, *Old Towns Revisited*, 25; Hall, *Beverley*, 49–50.

rules for the town's freedom were relaxed to permit 'the mayor and council to bestow such freedoms for the greater reputation, state, and credit of this incorporation, upon some persons of honour, nobility, or other gentry', and the fullest advantage was taken of this provision.[86] The flourishing round of civic ceremony was frequently used to cultivate convivial links between patriciate and squirearchy. As part of the festivities at York in 1702 to celebrate recent military victories, it was agreed that 'a general jubilation be made to the gentry and clergy then present, to dine at Merchants' Hall', and the annual Sheriffs' Riding in the city was attended by 'a great concourse of country gentlemen, citizens, etc., on horseback, who are invited to do this honour to, and afterwards dine with', the sheriffs. During his stay at Bath in 1730 Viscount Percival 'dined with the mayor, at his feast given by him on being chosen', and on 5 November he 'went to the mayor's invitation to drink the King's health at the town hall . . . the anniversary of the discovery of the Gunpowder Plot'.[87] Many civic and company halls must have been deliberately built or remodelled to accommodate prestigious guests. It was said that in the mansion house (built *c*.1691) at Newcastle-upon-Tyne, 'the mayor gives entertainment . . . to very large companies of the gentlemen of Newcastle and its vicinity, and is furnished for that purpose, with a valuable and elegant service of plate'. The new hall constructed at Preston for the Guild of 1762 was intentionally designed to house the splendid feasts and balls mounted by the corporation for the local gentry, and the event was perceived as a time 'when many persons of honour and gentry are to be treated in an extraordinary manner, for the greater applause and glory to the borough of Preston'. Since a high degree of social segregation was maintained during the Guild and the majority of Prestonians debarred from the exclusive junketings with the gentry, then it was on the town's élite that the 'applause and glory' ultimately devolved.[88]

This chapter has explored the self-promoting side of the Georgian character. Vanity, pride, and ambition were among the leading human passions, and infused even the most refined activities and most

---

[86] Clark, *Country Towns*, 19–20; Clark, 'Civic Leaders', 322–6; Rosen, 'Winchester', 182–4; Council Minutes, 7 Sept. 1697, BCA; White Book, 5 Mar. 1682/3, 18 Dec. 1724, PCMSS.

[87] House Book, 2 Dec. 1702, YCA; Drake, *Eboracum*, 197; HMC, *Egmont MSS*, Diary i. 113–14.

[88] Brand, *Newcastle*, i. 56; *Guild Merchant of Preston*, 14–17; [Kuerden], *Preston*, 47–92; Parker, 'Preston Guild Merchant', 115–18.

commendable projects. What made social emulation such a feature of the age was the growth in personal wealth, the ascendancy of the cultural definition of gentility, and the greater opportunities the Urban Renaissance offered for the pursuit of status. If this analysis conveys a rather cynical view of the period, then it should be balanced against the more elevated aspects of the new urban culture, an investigation of which forms the subject of the next chapter.[89]

[89] Contemporaries were acutely aware of the tension between private and public interests, and of the need, in an increasingly diverse, wealthy, and capitalist society, to find a new philosophical basis for reconciling the concerns of self and society. See J. Barrell, *The Political Theory of Painting from Reynolds to Hazlitt* (New Haven, Conn., and London, 1986), 1-68.

10

Civility and Sociability

1. THE ENLIGHTENMENT AND THE TOWN

The Urban Renaissance was not built solely on self-interest and social emulation; it also had its nobler, uplifting aspects, seeking to foster man's finer qualities. In this respect it was part of a wider movement, an English enlightenment, whose underlying mission was to rescue the nation from barbarity and ignorance; in a word, to *civilize* it.[1] This was a cause that gripped the contemporary imagination, and in which culture was seen as the principal agent for promoting change. This point was made by Jonathan Richardson in 1715, when he argued that if understanding 'paintings and drawings were made part of the education of a gentleman . . . the whole nation would, by these means be removed some degrees higher into the rational state, and make a more considerable figure amongst the polite nations of the world'.[2] Such was the progress of the arts in England over the next half century, that in 1769 Benjamin Franklin could celebrate the first exhibition of the Royal Academy with a call to

> Behold a brighter train of years,
> A new Augustan age appears,
> The time, nor distant far, shall come,
> When England's tasteful youth no more,
> Shall wander to Italia's classic shore;
> No more to foreign climes shall roam,
> In search of models better found at home.

Five years later the inscription on a plate placed under the foundation stone of the new assembly rooms at Newcastle-upon-Tyne confidently proclaimed it 'an age when the polite arts, by general encouragement

---

[1] For the idea of the Enlightenment, and its European context, see N. Hampson, *The Enlightenment* (Harmondsworth, 1984); W. Doyle, *The Old European Order 1660-1800* (Oxford, 1978), 149-218. The concept is used here in a way related to, though rather different from its European application.
[2] J. Richardson, *The Works of Jonathan Richardson* (London, 1773), 271-2.

and emulation, have advanced to a state of perfection unknown in any former period'.[3]

Towns were both affected by and contributed to this national enlightenment. Histories of the time emphasized the recent progress of urban communities from crudity to civility. Wood described mid-seventeenth-century Bath as a vulgar and primitive society:

the streets and public ways . . . were become like so many dunghills, slaughterhouses, and pigsties . . . soil of all sorts, and even carrion, was cast and laid in the streets, and the pigs turned out by day to feed and root among it; butchers killed and dressed their cattle at their own doors. . . . The baths were like so many bear gardens, and modesty was entirely shut out of them; people of both sexes bathing by day and night naked; and dogs, cats, pigs, and even human creatures were hurled over the rails into the water, while people were bathing in it.

If we are to believe Burr, pre-Restoration Tunbridge Wells was scarcely more cultivated: 'The amusements of the gentry were few, confined, and selfish . . . delicacy, politeness, and elegant pleasures, were then just building forth from amidst the rubbish of gothic barbarism'.[4] A century later both spas had become epitomes of civilized behaviour, a transformation which Wood's and Burr's histories recorded and celebrated. The story was one repeated by others. Richard Warner, surveying the development of Bath from the vantage-point of 1801, noted how the diversions at the Tudor and Stuart spa 'suited the grossness and simplicity of the times. . . . But as national manners gradually refined, the idea of elegance was proportionally enlarged, and public amusements insensibly approximated to the taste and splendour which they at present exhibit: balls, plays, and cards usurping the place of those rude athletic sports, or gross sensual amusements, to which the hours of vacancy had before been devoted.'[5] The march of civilization was not confined to the fashionable resorts. In 1777 Matthew Boulton proudly reported from Birmingham, that 'in the last century' the recreations enjoyed by the town's inhabitants 'were bull-baitings, cock-fightings, boxing matches, and abominable drunkenness. . . . But the scene is now much changed: the people are more polite and civilized . . . and we have also made a considerable progress in some of the liberal arts'. Twenty years earlier John Dyer

[3] Franklin in Denvir, *Eighteenth Century*, 191; Brand, *Newcastle*, i. 121.
[4] Wood, *Bath*, 216–17; Burr, *Tunbridge Wells*, 21–2.
[5] R. Warner, *The History of Bath* (Bath, 1801), 349.

compared the rise of England's industrial towns to the building of the
great cities of antiquity:

> Thus all is here in motion, all is life:
> . . . .
> . . . scaffolds rise,
> And growing edifices; heaps of stone,
> Beneath the chisel, beauteous shapes assume
> Of frieze and column. Some, with even line,
> New streets are marking in the neighbouring fields,
> And sacred domes of worship. . . .
> . . . .
> . . . Such was the scene
> Of hurrying Carthage, when the Trojan chief
> First viewed her growing turrets. So appear
> Th'increasing walls of busy Manchester,
> Sheffield, and Birmingham, whose reddening fields
> Rise and enlarge their suburbs.[6]

The polite arts and pastimes were thought to play a critical role in
civilizing English townsmen. In 1734, at the opening night of York's
first permanent theatre, the audience was reminded that,

> When Athens flourished, and the Grecian state,
> Submissive, on its great decrees did wait,
> Over their manners then the stage did rule,
> Approved with wit, condemned by ridicule,
> Each virtuous mind, by just example formed;
> And showed how vice and folly should be scorned.

Similar claims were advanced during the inauguration of the early
Liverpool theatre in 1772. Describing the initial impact of visiting
performers on the town, it was said that

> The muses next a willing visit paid;
> They came to pleasure's and to virtue's aid;
> A graceful ease and polish to impart,
> Refine the taste and humanize the heart.[7]

This was a view shared by John Hippisley, who when promoting a
project for a new playhouse in Bath in the late 1740s, maintained that

---

[6] HMC, *Dartmouth MSS*, iii. 235; *The Fleece*, in D. Davison (ed.), *The Penguin
Book of Eighteenth-Century English Verse* (Harmondsworth, 1973), 91-2.
[7] The York epilogue is reproduced in Rosenfeld, *Strolling Players*, 119; the
Liverpool prologue, in Enfield, *Liverpool*, 64.

'Theatrical performances, when conducted with decency and regularity, have always been esteemed the most rational amusements, by the polite and thinking part of mankind.' In Birmingham, Boulton was so impressed by the theatre's elevating influence, that he gave his 'designers, painters, and modellers, tickets to the play, in order to improve them in those arts by which they are to live and gain reputation'.[8]

Just as theatre helped to refine behaviour, so also could architecture, which was felt to be an essential feature of civilization. In his *Origin of Building*, Wood observed that 'men . . . at first led a rude and brutish sort of life, wandered up and down in the fields, and fed upon herbs and the natural fruit of the trees, being as yet naked, without houses', and Neve contended that 'where there is no architecture in a nation, there can, by consequence, be no princely government . . . where such a power is wanting, people are so savage and barbarous, that they live more like brutes than rational men'.[9] The most noble of building models was thought to be that based on the ideal human form, thereby emphasizing the contrast with the primitive and animal world: Wood insisted that 'In the works of the Divine Architect of all things, we find nothing but perfect figures . . . to illustrate which, the figure of a man, created in the image of God, is the most notable example. . . . Man is a complete figure and the perfection of order.'[10] The human standard beloved of Renaissance architects was one that flourished in the building manuals of the eighteenth century. A favourite convention was to treat the classical orders in an anthropomorphic fashion. Ware suggested that 'as the doric has been always understood to represent a well-proportioned man, the ionic may be considered as the image of a well-proportioned female, not the girl, for the elegance and slenderness of the corinthian more naturally is brought in for that resemblance'.[11] The introduction of classical architecture into English towns would therefore have been seen as a humanizing and civilizing influence. This was particularly so because the style which only recently preceded it, known perjoratively as 'gothic', was stigmatized

[8] Wood, *Bath*, 444; HMC, *Dartmouth MSS*, iii. 235.

[9] Wood, *Origin of Building*, 12; Neve, *Dictionary*, p. viii.

[10] Wood, *Origin of Building*, 71.

[11] Ware, *Body of Architecture*, 176; R. Wittkower, *Architectural Principles in the Age of Humanism* (London, 1967), 14–16; Neale, *Bath: A Social History*, 190–2; A. Palladio, *The Four Books of Andrea Palladio's Architecture*, trans. I. Ware 1738, repr. (London, 1965), second book, 38; Neve, *Dictionary*, 71, 84–8, 210–11; Langley, *Chest-Book*, 29; Wood, *Origin of Building*, 185–97.

as barbaric and chaotic. Neve described its ornaments as 'wild and chimerical', and Ware found it 'A wild and irregular manner of building, that took [the] place of the regular antique method at the time when architecture, with the other arts, declined.'[12]

As a result of the impact of fashionable culture, many towns came to be seen as fountains of civilization, enjoying a widespread aesthetic approval before the ravages of the Industrial Revolution tarnished their reputation. When in 1741 William Hutton was first 'cast into those regions of civility' then occupied by Birmingham, he found the inhabitants 'were a species I had never seen: they possessed a vivacity I had never beheld: I had been among dreamers, but now I saw men awake. . . . Their appearance was strongly marked with the modes of civil life'. Moreover, the positive influence of the urban environment was not confined to those who resided in it. Since rural society widely used urban cultural facilities, towns were perceived as agents for spreading polite behaviour throughout the nation. Goldsmith claimed that Nash (and the two great resorts he ruled) 'first taught a familiar intercourse among strangers at Bath and Tunbridge, which still subsists among them. That ease and open access first acquired there, our gentry brought back to the metropolis, and thus the whole kingdom by degrees became more refined by lessons originally derived from him.'[13]

From his bastions at Bath and Tunbridge, Nash was engaged in a crusade to civilize the rural gentry and rescue them from the uncouthness of country living. His most effective weapon was that of negative propaganda, by which he sought to stigmatize rural dress and habits. To this end he composed several satirical entertainments, including a puppet-show,

in which Punch came in booted and spurred, in the character of a country squire. He was introduced as courting his mistress, and having obtained her consent to comply with his wishes, upon going to bed, he is desired to pull off his boots. My boots, replies Punch, why, madam, you may as well bid me pull off my legs. I never go without boots. . . . Thus he goes on, till his mistress, grown impatient, kicks him off the stage.

Goldsmith went on to add, 'from that time few ventured to appear at the assemblies in Bath in a riding-dress: and whenever any gentleman, through ignorance, or haste, appeared in the Rooms in boots,

---

[12] Neve, *Dictionary*, 154-5; Ware, *Body of Architecture*, 19.
[13] Hutton, *History of Birmingham*, 63; Goldsmith, 'Life of Nash', 288-9.

Nash would make up to him, and bowing in an arch manner, would tell him, that he had forgot his horse. Thus he was at last completely victorious.' Nash's success was evident in a rule operating in the spa in the 1760s, which reminded 'gentlemen frequenting the Rooms . . . that leather breeches are by no means suitable to the decorum of the place', doubtless because of their bucolic associations.[14]

The campaign to re-educate the rural gentry to more urban and civilized values by lampooning their behaviour and beliefs was one which attracted many fashionable writers. The character of the boorish country squire, invariably ill at ease in town society and always associated with hunting and animals, became a stock figure in literature. The thoughts of Fielding's fuddled and blasphemous Squire Weston were 'generally either in the field, the stable, or the dog kennel', and Pope's Zephalinda, transplanted from town, could anticipate only the attentions of a country booby, who

> . . . with his hounds comes hollowing from the stable,
> Makes love with nods, and knees beneath a table;
> Whose laughs are hearty, though his jests are coarse,
> And loves you best of all things—but his horse.

A verse of 1748 satirized 'the angry sportsman', who

> . . . hates the Bath, and its diversions too,
> Vexed that he is unable to pursue
> His own diversions of a nobler kind;
> Whether the hare, the fox, the stag, or hind:
> Crippled with gout and pains he must endure,
> He frets, like culprits, in the stocks secure.[15]

This vein of criticism was most effectively deployed in the highly influential pages of *The Tatler* and *The Spectator*. As propagators of urban civilization, these periodicals contained some savage portraits of the hunting gentry. Steele asked, 'how shall I celebrate Mrs Alse Copswood, the Yorkshire huntress, who is come to town lately, and moves as if she were on a nag, and going to take a five-bar gate?' and complained of those who 'with an estate that might make' them 'the blessing and ornament of the world round' them, have 'no other view and ambition, but to be an animal above dogs and horses, without the

[14] Goldsmith, 'Life of Nash', 306; Penrose, *Letters*, 136.
[15] H. Fielding, *The History of Tom Jones*, ed. R. P. C. Mutter (Harmondsworth, 1971), 163–4; 'Epistle to Miss Blount, on her Leaving the Town, after the Coronation', in *The Poems of Alexander Pope*, ed. J. Butt (London, 1965), 243; *Bath: A Poem*, 19.

relish of any one enjoyment, which is peculiar to the faculties of a humane nature'.[16] Addison's Sir Roger De Coverly (old-fashioned, slightly bumbling, stiff, paternalistic, superstitious, but basically good-hearted) was a gentler portrait of the provincial squire. But then it was probably all the more effective for that, since few country gentlemen would fail to recognize just a little of Sir Roger in themselves, and feel the need for personal reform.[17]

2. MIND, MORALITY, AND THE PASSIONS

The purpose behind the sort of urban propaganda to be found in *The Tatler* and *The Spectator* was to create a new type of gentleman who was to be characterized by his civilized nature. The changes required were not meant to be superficial ones; rather they were intended to reach the very core of a person's identity, providing a cultural template by which to live. Three areas of personality and behaviour attracted especial attention: the mind, morality, and the passions.

The rational and cultivated mind was considered the pre-eminent human faculty. Even in a manual art like architecture, it was essential that the brain ruled the body. Wood reminded his readers that 'the vast and great superiority of the labour of the mind, to that of the hands, in works of architecture, is very largely, and in the strongest terms, set forth by Plato', and Ware warned about the risks of trusting one's senses in matters of design, arguing 'that the change of proportions, in respect of the laws of optics, is always wrong. . . . Though sight be an effect of sense, the conception we form of it depends upon the mind'.[18] The latter's *Complete Body of Architecture* relentlessly promotes a cerebral approach to the subject by regularly referring to such faculties as 'the eye of reason', and the 'eye of judgement', and by exhortations to 'consult reason first', and base choice on 'discretion and judgement, not as hazard, or as fancy directs'.[19]

The capacity to exercise 'judgement' was not something which emerged of its own volition, but needed to be diligently cultivated through study and instruction. Steele considered 'the soul of man, as the ruin of a glorious pile of building. . . . Virtue and wisdom are

[16] *The Tatler*, No. 37, 2–5 July 1709, in Ross, *Tatler and Spectator*, 100–2.
[17] Ross, *Tatler and Spectator*, 216–50.
[18] Wood, *Origin of Building*, 67; Ware, *Body of Architecture*, 260–1.
[19] Ware, *Body of Architecture*, 136, 290, 374–5.

continually employed in clearing the ruins. . . . A happy education, conversation with the finest spirits, looking abroad into the works of nature, and observations upon mankind, are the great assistance to this necessary and glorious work.'[20] Addison suggested that 'the mind that lies fallow but a single day, sprouts up in follies that are only to be killed by a constant and assiduous culture', and another commentator remarked that 'taste . . . is acquired by toil and study, which is the reason so few are possessed of it'.[21] A central feature of the Urban Renaissance was the way in which it provided access to learning through its clubs, societies, libraries, books and bookshops, newspapers, journals, and other amenities. The original statutes of the Spalding Gentlemen's Society were specifically described as, 'Proposals for establishing a society of gentlemen for the supporting mutual benevolence, and their improvement in the liberal sciences and polite learning.'[22]

The pursuit of civility was not only a question of personal intellectual development and the pleasures that accrued from this. It was also seen as a morally improving experience. Shaftesbury asserted that 'the most natural beauty in the world is honesty and moral truth', Steele maintained that 'the general purpose of the whole' of his writing in *The Tatler* had 'been to recommend truth, innocence, honour, and virtue as the chief ornaments of life', and Johnson wrote of Addison that 'no greater felicity can genius attain than that of having purified intellectual pleasure, separated mirth from indecency, and wit from licentiousness'.[23] A concern for the moral context of behaviour can be discerned in the contemporary desire to refine sexual relations. In early seventeenth-century Bath, naked or semi-naked bathing appears to have been a common practice. Subsequently such conduct was frowned upon, though as late as 1737 the corporation still felt the need to direct 'that no male person above the age of ten years shall at any time hereafter go into any bath . . . without a pair of drawers and a waistcoat . . . and . . . no female person . . . without a

[20] *The Tatler*, No. 87, 27–9 Oct. 1709, in Ross, *Tatler and Spectator*, 123.

[21] *The Spectator*, No. 10, 12 Mar. 1710/11, in Ross, *Tatler and Spectator*, 210; *Weekly Register*, 6 Feb. 1731, in Denvir, *Eighteenth Century*, 63.

[22] Owen, *Spalding Gentlemen's Society*, p. x.

[23] 'An Essay on the Freedom of Wit and Humour' (1710), in A. A. Cooper, Earl of Shaftesbury, *Characteristics of Men, Manners, Opinions, Times*, 4th edn. (London, 1727), i. 142; *The Tatler*, No. 271, 30 Dec. 1710–2 Jan. 1710/11, in Ross, *Tatler and Spectator*, 189; S. Johnson, *Johnson: Prose and Poetry*, ed. M. Wilson (London, 1970), 876.

decent shift'. Sixteen years later an attempt was made 'to restrain men and women bathing together', by allocating them different days for using the facilities, though later this order was rescinded.[24]

In spite of its inanimate nature, architecture could also be perceived in moral terms. Ware frequently stressed the need for 'propriety' in matters of design, warned against 'impropriety and confusion by adding false decorations', and advocated caution in the use of 'the fanciful orders', based as they were on 'the free licentiousness of fancy'.[25] Some writers followed an influential Renaissance tradition that overtly linked architecture and religion. Neve informed his readers that 'the Divine Architect of this world hath been pleased to honour this excellent art [of architecture] so far, as to vouchsafe to give necessary precepts and rules concerning some buildings', and reminded them that 'our Blessed Redeemer . . . was pleased to exercise this art of architecture, and to be a mechanic'.[26] Wood's whole approach to building was infused with a strong religious purpose and symbolism, striving to reveal God to man through physical forms. A major difficulty was that the classical style appeared to be pagan in origin. To counter this Wood composed a treatise on *The Origin of Building: Or the Plagiarism of the Heathens Detected*, in which he developed the argument (already in currency) that classicism originated among the Jews, to whom it was transmitted by God, and was later 'plagiarized' by heathen antiquity. Wood concluded his 'debate . . . between sacred and profane history' with a call to render 'unto Caesar, the things which are Caesar's; and, unto God, the things which are God's', assured that his own works were firmly lodged in the latter camp.[27] Such an explicitly spiritual interpretation of building design may not have been shared by all, but in Ware's frequent references to 'grace', it is perhaps possible to detect a latent religious feeling that many may have experienced towards classical architecture.[28]

The moral seriousness of polite culture expressed itself especially in the field of charity. The act of providing for the poor and under-

---

[24] Wood, *Bath*, 217, 408-9; P. R. James, *The Baths of Bath in the Sixteenth and Early Seventeenth Centuries* (Bristol, 1938), 80-4; Neale, *Bath: A Social History*, 14, figure 1; Council Minutes, 26 Sept. 1737, 8 Jan. and 26 Apr. 1753, BCA.

[25] Ware, *Body of Architecture*, 236, 444, 448.

[26] Neve, *Dictionary*, pp. iii, v; Wittkower, *Architectural Principles*, 1-32.

[27] Wood, *Origin of Building*, 231-5; Neale, *Bath: A Social History*, 189-99; R. Wittkower, 'Frederico Zuccari and John Wood of Bath', *Jnl. of the Warburg and Courtauld Institutes*, v (1943), 220-2.

[28] See, for example, Ware, *Body of Architecture*, 197, 327, 438.

privileged was seen not only as commendable in itself, but as elevating
for the benefactors, and, in the words Enfield used to describe the
generosity of Liverpool's citizens, as a sign of 'humanity and public
spirit'.[29] To this end, fashionable culture was often associated with
charitable activities. Visitors to Bath were frequently assailed by
collections for worthy local causes, and were expected to give
generously. In 1755 it was reported from Stamford that 'three
charitable card assemblies are kept at this place every week', and in
mid-eighteenth-century York the theatre's winter season customarily
opened with a benefit performance for the city's new hospital.[30] Music
seems to have been a particular vehicle for philanthropy. At Bath in
the 1740s the profits from the concert breakfasts at the assembly
houses were 'presented to the General Hospital', at York in 1740 the
directors of the music assembly were allowed the use of the assembly
rooms 'for a benefit concert towards the relief of the poor . . . if they
think fit', and musical festivals, such as the Three Choirs or that
at Birmingham, often raised funds for humanitarian ventures.[31] In
eighteenth-century England charity and the liberal arts were intimately associated, precisely because both were seen to promote the
moral improvement of their devotees.

If the new model of gentility required one to cultivate mental and
ethical capacities, so also it demanded that one must learn to curb the
passions. Steele warned that 'it is to the very end of our days a struggle
between our reason and our temper, which shall have the empire over
us',[32] and it became a touchstone of civility to ensure that it was the
empire of reason rather than that of passion which prevailed. Excesses
of all types were to be eschewed, particularly violence. Duelling came
under considerable criticism,[33] and sports which involved cruelty to
animals were increasingly viewed with distaste,[34] though one suspects

[29] Enfield, *Liverpool*, 48.
[30] Wood, *Bath*, 418; Penrose, *Letters*, 59, 82-3, 130; *Gentleman's Magazine*, xxv
(1755), 164; Rosenfeld, *Strolling Players*, 138, 146.
[31] Wood, *Bath*, 439; Assembly Rooms Minute Book, 23 Dec. 1740, YCA; Smith,
Music in Birmingham, 23-7; Shaw, *Three Choirs Festival*, 3-5; Bisse, *Sermon*, 16-20;
Mackerness, *Social History of English Music*, 112-13; and also Suffolk RO, E2/20/1A,
fo. 4; Fawcett, *Music in Eighteenth-Century Norwich*, 13-17.
[32] *The Tatler*, No. 172, 13-16 May 1710, in Ross, *Tatler and Spectator*, 155.
[33] *The Tatler*, No. 25, 4-7 June 1709, and No. 31, 18-21 June 1709, in Ross, *Tatler
and Spectator*, 86-8, 93-7; D. T. Andrew, 'The Code of Honour and its Critics: The
Opposition to Duelling in England 1700-1850', *Social History*, v, No. 3 (1980), 410,
416-20.
[34] Thomas, *Man and the Natural World*, 143-4, 150-65, 173-81.

not so much because of any concern for the creatures themselves, but because their struggles excited man's savage instincts. The call for moderation also extended to architecture. In the design of the tuscan pedestal Ware stressed the importance of 'keeping a medium between the two extremes of plainness and decoration', and maintained that in the composite cornice, 'there is a medium between the excesses that have been made in the proportions and projectures' of the 'several parts'.[35] All this proved too much for Mandeville, who declared 'that boasted middle way, and the calm virtues recommended in the *Characteristics* [of Shaftesbury], are good for nothing but to breed drones, and might qualify a man for the stupid enjoyments of a monastic life, or at best a country Justice of the Peace'. But to those who understood its virtues, the *via media* was an invigorating and civilizing road to travel. Steele argued, that its devotees had little need of primitive pastimes to occupy them: 'with great respect to country sports . . . this gentleman [Isaac Bickerstaff] could pass his time agreeably, if there were not a hare or fox in his county. That calm and elegant satisfaction which the vulgar call melancholy, is the true and proper delight of men of knowledge and virtue.'[36]

3. SOCIABILITY

One of the most commendable activities a gentleman could engage in, and one in which moderation and an even temper were considerable assets, was simply that of meeting and mixing with his fellow human beings. Indeed, sociability was considered one of the foremost civilizing influences. William Hutton, in the confident tones of the English enlightenment, wrote that 'Man is evidently formed for society: the intercourse of one with another, like two blocks of marble in friction, reduces the rough prominences of behaviour, and gives a polish to the manners.'[37] For this reason eighteenth-century England developed a thirst for human contact. It was natural that the town should play a key role in servicing this demand, since it was the traditional point of exchange and meeting-place for society. Over and above this, the cultural facilities developed during the Urban

[35] Ware, *Body of Architecture*, 221, 234, and also 270–1.
[36] Mandeville, *Fable*, 337; *The Tatler*, No. 89, 1–3 Nov. 1709, in Ross, *Tatler and Spectator*, 128.
[37] Hutton, *History of Birmingham*, 259.

Renaissance were specifically designed, in their organization and ethos, to promote sociability.

In no case did this spirit of fraternity more reveal itself than in the formation of clubs and societies.[38] Though these were often devoted to some particular cultural activity, such as music or science, they were also treated as social institutions in which ties of friendship and good company could be cultivated. Maurice Johnson hoped to establish the Spalding Gentlemen's Society 'on the foot of a universal literary meeting for the sake of improvement in friendship and knowledge', and rules were framed to encourage social contact and amity. A president was appointed 'to moderate in all disputes', those regularly failing to attend meetings (without an adequate excuse) were to be fined, and alcoholic beverages were restricted to 'a tankard of ale holding one quart and no more'. Johnson also promoted links between the society and outside world, and many guests were invited to attend the normal meetings, suggesting the existence of a genuine community of learning in which the pleasure derived from knowledge lay as much in its exchange as in its discovery.[39]

The convivial ethos of the Spalding Gentlemen's Society was one shared by the many clubs and cultural organizations that sprang up in provincial towns. Claver Morris affectionately referred to the music club in early eighteenth-century Wells as 'our music-meeting', and to his fellow members as 'clubbers', and in 1729 Dr Bisse described the origins of the Three Choirs Festival as a 'fortuitous and friendly proposal between a few lovers of harmony, and brethren of the correspondent choirs, to commence an anniversary visit, to be kept in turn: which voluntary instance of friendship and fraternity was quickly strengthened by social compact'. Thomas Naish wrote that during the anniversary meeting of the Salisbury music society two years earlier, 'such a serene cheerfulness was seen in every face, and such endearments of friendship and affection mutually passed among all, as if the whole audience had but one heart and one mind'.[40]

The clubbing spirit was not confined to formal institutions. Viscount Percival found that among the visitors at Bath and Tunbridge Wells,

---

[38] Clark, *English Alehouse*, 234–5; Brewer, 'Commercialization and Politics', 217–23.

[39] Owen, *Spalding Gentlemen's Society*, especially pp. ix–x.

[40] Hobhouse, *Diary of a West Country Physician*, 99; Bisse, *Sermon*, 20; T. Naish, *A Sermon Preached at the Cathedral Church of Sarum, November the 30th, 1727* (London, 1727), pp. iii–iv.

'a few who are of the same turn of conversation . . . naturally select one another out and form a sort of society'. The circle Percival joined in Bath appears to have met regularly at a coffee-house, a class of establishments which in their own right constituted informal clubs, whose membership could drift freely in and out and yet be sure of a hospitable welcome. As one admirer asked, 'where can young gentle-men, or shopkeepers more innocently and advantageously spend an hour or two in the evening, than at a coffee-house? Where they shall be sure to meet company, and, by the custom of the house, not such as at other places, stingy and reserved to themselves, but free and communicative'.[41] Such openness must have been encouraged by the cultural message of sociability that coffee-drinking carried. An informal society of a rather different sort was that forged between newspapers and magazines, and their readership, since the regular purchase of these publications made one a member of a type of literary circle. Editors encouraged this impression by running competitions, answering readers' questions, and printing their contributions and letters. A number of journals, such as *The Tatler*, *The Spectator*, and Defoe's *Review*, organized a portion of their material around the club motif, *The Spectator* claiming to report the transactions of a 'society' of gentlemen.[42]

The promotion of social accord was something encouraged not only by the context in which cultural activities occurred, but also by their content. In 1731 the *Weekly Register* called taste 'the friend of society',[43] and many felt that the arts could exert a harmonizing influence both within and between individuals. When Thomas Naish delivered a sermon to the Society of Lovers of Music in Salisbury in 1700, he reminded his audience that 'now, as the true pleasure of life consists in the due and regular obedience of our passions, so music serves to bring them into harmony and order. . . . It abateth spleen and hatred'. These were sentiments echoed by the Newcastle-upon-Tyne composer Avison, when he argued in 1752 that 'every species of musical sound must tend to dispel the malevolent passions . . . and nourish those which are benevolent', and 'that it is the peculiar

[41] HMC, *Egmont MSS*, Diary i. 117; 'Coffee-Houses Vindicated. In Answer to the Late Published Character of a Coffee-House', repr. in *The Harleian Miscellany*, vi (1745), 435.
[42] Cranfield, *Development of Provincial Newspaper*, 102–3; Ross, *Tatler and Spectator*, 24–5, 144–7, 201–5. .
[43] *Weekly Register*, 6 Feb. 1731, in Denvir, *Eighteenth Century*, 63.

quality of music to raise the sociable and happy passions, and to
subdue the contrary ones'.[44] Such qualities were also to be discovered
in classical architecture. Robert Morris suggested that 'there are certain
proportions in building which affect the mind through the eye, as well
as music does through the ear', and Shaftesbury felt that 'true
proportions' make 'the beauty of architecture; as true measures that of
harmony and music'.[45] The essence of proportion and symmetry,
which were such crucial factors in the evolution of the façade, was the
creation of a compatible relationship between the individual parts of a
building and the whole. Architecture could therefore be perceived as a
symbol and model of social harmony, and this could account for the
emotive emphasis contemporaries placed on regularity and balance.
Wood argued that 'beauty and proportion in a fine figure are insepar-
able', Ware 'that proportion and regularity are real sources of beauty',
and a visitor to Bath in 1769 felt that 'the regular symmetry of the
whole [of the Circus] is the principal foundation of its beauty'.[46]

   In classical architecture the harmonies to be found within a building
should ideally also extend to its relationship with its neighbours.
Travellers frequently referred to this when they commended, in a word
charged with significance, the 'uniform' character of a town's houses.
This quality was a product of two aspects of urban classicism. First, in
its more purist form the new style discouraged excessive ornamentation, idiosyncrasy, and individualism. Thus it reflected a wider neo-
classical movement, which stressed archetypal forms and saw it as the
artist's duty to highlight those characteristics people shared in
common. Hume argued that 'the principles of taste be universal, and
nearly, if not entirely the same in all men', Shaftesbury that 'the good
poet and painter . . . hate minuteness, and are afraid of singularity',
and Reynolds asserted that in the painter's subject, 'there must be
something either in the action, or in the object, in which men are
universally concerned'.[47] When developed in an architectural context

   [44] T. Naish, *A Sermon Preached at the Cathedral Church of Sarum, Novemb. 22,
1700, before a Society of Lovers of Music* (London, 1701), 12-13; C. Avison, *An Essay
on Musical Expression* (London, 1752), 5, 8.

   [45] R. Morris, *Select Architecture: Being Regular Designs of Plans and Elevations Well
Suited to Both Town and Country,* 1757, repr. (New York, 1973), 4; Cooper,
Characteristics, i. 142.

   [46] J. Wood, *A Dissertation upon the Orders of Columns* (London, 1750), 12; Ware,
Body of Architecture, 295; HMC, *Verulam MSS,* 249.

   [47] 'Of the Standard of Taste', in D. Hume, *Essays Moral, Political, and Literary,* ed.
T. H. Green and T. H. Grose (London, 1875), i. 278; Cooper, *Characteristics,* i. 144;
J. Reynolds, *Discourses on Art,* ed. R. R. Wark (London, 1969), 55.

such sentiments inevitably tended to increase the similarity between buildings. Second, cohesiveness was achieved, as we have seen, by the growing fashion for subsuming individual dwellings within a larger physical unit. The impact of such ventures, and of uniformity in general, was to create a more 'gregarious' urban landscape, in which sociable architecture was the order of the day.

It is no accident that the town that played such a formative part in the evolution of multi-dwelling buildings should be Bath, for resorts enjoyed a very special role in fostering sociability. Their visitors were drawn from a much wider geographical area than most towns; this tended to erode localized practices and values and to accentuate cosmopolitan and universal standards. The two leading spas were portrayed as melting-pots of society. In 1749 Elizabeth Montagu described Tunbridge Wells as 'the parliament of the world, where every country and every rank has its representative: we have Jews of every tribe, and Christian people of all nations and conditions', and Lady Bristol found Bath in 1721, 'as full as possible, but such a mixture as was never got together at the building of Babel'. One poet wrote of Lindsey's assembly rooms at Bath,

> There Pagan, Turk, the Papist, and the Jew,
> And all mankind's epitome you view;

and another,

> Now from all parts the company resort,
> Sailing, like vessels, to this neutral port:
> Bath, Lisbon-like, for ever will admit
> Those of all nations for her benefit.[48]

The very presence of such a collection of people was in itself likely to dissolve social barriers. But there were also a number of rituals and facilities that positively encouraged gregarious behaviour. At the very outset, it was difficult for a visitor to slip into a resort unnoticed, and live anonymously. At Bath it was customary for strangers (particularly people of distinction) to be welcomed by ringing the Abbey bells, and at Bath and Tunbridge Wells by a salute outside their lodgings from a band of musicians. Through such practices the company 'have the pleasure', as Wood noted, 'of knowing, directly, the name of every

[48] E. Montagu, *The Letters of Mrs Elizabeth Montagu*, ed. M. Montagu, 1809–13, repr. (New York, 1974), iii. 90; Hervey, *Letter-Books*, ii. 202; Chandler, *Description of Bath*, 15; *Bath: A Poem*, 5.

family that comes to town: for upon the first sound of the bells, everybody sends out to enquire for whom they ring', a point confirmed by George Lucy when he wrote, 'I never hear the bells ring that I don't make enquiry'.[49] Information about those present was also spread through the detailed lists of new arrivals assembled in the local press, and at Scarborough by the custom of the various facilities maintaining subscription books that could be publicly scrutinized.[50]

A peal of bells and a musical serenade were more than simply a means of communicating the fact and identity of recent arrivals. They were also a ritual reminder to visitors, a sort of rite of passage, that they had entered a special community with its own codes and conventions, in which they were expected to live publicly rather than privately.[51] Indeed, spas may be seen as an elegant precursor of the modern holiday camp in which the visitors, or 'the company' as they were symbolically called, were projected into an orgy of socializing. Nothing enforced this more effectively than the existence of a rigorously organized daily routine of activities. At Bath this began in the early morning with a visit to the baths and the Pump Room before the ladies and gentlemen went their separate ways, the former to the toy shops and their lodgings, the latter to the coffee-houses. Later they met again for public breakfasts, concerts, lectures, and spiritual refreshment at the local chapels and churches. The hours between noon and dinner (served usually between two and three p.m.) were free time, and were often used for card-playing, walking, and longer outings. After dinner and evening prayers the company reassembled at the Pump Room, on the walks, and at the assembly rooms (for drinking tea), before 'the evenings . . . concluded', often in some splendour, 'with balls, plays, and mutual visits'.[52] Though other resorts, with the possible exception of Tunbridge Wells, could not

[49] Wood, *Bath*, 417; Warwickshire CRO, L6/1460; Burr, *Tunbridge Wells*, 114; Penrose, *Letters*, 26, 40, 176; *Step to the Bath*, 155; C. Anstey, *The New Bath Guide*, 1766, repr. (Bath, 1970), 12–14; Montagu, *Letters*, i. 74.

[50] McIntyre, 'Rise of a Resort Town', 208; *Bath Advertiser*, No. 1, 18 Oct. 1755; Warwickshire CRO, L6/1467; Warwickshire CRO, CR.1368, v, fo. 36; *Journey from London to Scarborough*, 33; *A List of the Nobility, Quality, and Gentry, at Scarborough, during the Spa Season in the Year 1733. Taken from the Subscription Books at the Spa, and the Long Room, the Bookseller's Shop, and the Coffee-House* (London, 1734).

[51] A. van Gennep, *The Rites of Passage* (London, 1977), 15–40.

[52] This account is based especially on Wood, *Bath*, 437–46. See also Students Diary, fos. 114–15; HMC, *Verulam MSS*, 249; Defoe, *Tour*, ii. 34–5; Goldsmith, 'Life of Nash', 391; Penrose, *Letters*, 70–5; Pigott Diary, i, articles 488–9; *Bath: A Poem*, 12–30; Barbeau, *Bath*, 53–8.

match the complexity and sophistication of this programme, the basic outline remained the same. It was said of Bristol Hot Wells in 1769, 'The method of spending time here is so much the same with that of other places that I shall not think it necessary to give a description of it.'[53] The existence of such an inexorable social round, and one so widely understood, forced the company into contact with each other, since it ensured that they were generally doing the same thing, at the same time, and in the same place. As was suggested in 1737, 'you cannot well be a free agent, where the whole turn is to do as other people do; it is a sort of fairy circle; if you do not run round in it, you cannot run at all, or are in everybody's way'.[54]

To enable the company to congregate simultaneously in the same place, large public arenas were built (such as pump rooms, assembly rooms, theatres, chapels, walks, gardens, squares, and circuses), and at Bath several of these were subsequently remodelled to accommodate the growing number of visitors.[55] One of the features of such spaces was their open plan, with a minimum of obstacles to interfere with the vision of those using them, and few nooks and crannies for the shy to hide in. New chapels at the spas, such as the Octagon in Bath, were so constructed as to give the congregation maximum exposure.[56] Even where, as was common in the larger assembly houses, there were a number of separate rooms, these were interconnected in a roughly circular fashion so as to encourage the free flow of the guests.[57] Within the assemblies, any attempt to create private space was frowned upon. In the 1760s a rule operated at Bath that 'no large screens can be brought to any card party in the Rooms on any account, as they . . . divide the company into secluded sets, which is against the fundamental institution of these places'.[58] Squares and circuses were, in effect, open-air rooms, and when, as in the case of the Circus at Bath,

[53] HMC, *Verulam MSS*, 250-1. For the daily routine at spas other than Bath, see Burr, *Tunbridge Wells*, 116-21; Macky, *Journey*, i. 89-91; Barton, *Tunbridge Wells*, 177; Lennard, 'Watering-Places', 55-6; V. Waite, 'The Bristol Hotwell', in P. McGrath (ed.), *Bristol in the Eighteenth Century* (Newton Abbot, 1972), 119; Powys, *Diaries*, 30-1, 49; Defoe, *Tour*, i. 160-1.

[54] *English Magazine* (Dec. 1737), quoted in Barbeau, *Bath*, 49-50.

[55] Ison, *Bath*, 49-50, 60-4; B. Mitchell, *An Illustrated Guide to the Pump Room, Bath* (Bath, 1981); Council Minutes, 27 Nov. and 21 Dec. 1705, 21 Jan. 1705/6, 1 July 1706, 26 Feb. 1750/1, 10 and 30 May 1751, 11 Feb. 1752, BCA.

[56] Ison, *Bath*, 72-3, and plates 23-4; A. Savidge, *The Story of the Church of King Charles the Martyr*, 2nd edn. (1978).

[57] Ison, *Bath*, 51; Drake, *Eboracum*, plan facing 338; and also Girouard, *English Country House*, 181-212.

[58] Penrose, *Letters*, 136.

the surrounding façade looked uncommonly like a bank of theatre boxes, then those who ventured into these spaces must have felt themselves exposed to the full glare of public examination (see Fig. 24).

Sociability was promoted not only by a conducive arrangement of time and space, but also by the actual activities visitors engaged in. A heavy round of visiting and entertaining was a public duty.[59] Large-scale commensality particularly helped to induce cordial behaviour. At Buxton in 1747 there was 'an ordinary which everybody eats at'; a visitor to Matlock in 1769 found 'the company . . . live, as in most other public places, in a very sociable manner, always meeting at meals in a common room'; and Harrogate in 1781 contained 'several detached inns, at each [of which] all the company breakfast, dine, and sup together'.[60] One of the most popular forms of communal dining was the 'public breakfast' and the 'public tea'. At Tunbridge Wells it was 'customary for the gentlemen to treat the ladies, and their male acquaintance, every one in their turn, and frequently to give a public breakfast to the whole company without exception'.[61] In 1762 George Lucy reported from Bath on a gargantuan breakfast given 'for about 700 people', but the party of seventeen joined by John Penrose four years later at the Spring Gardens must have been more typical. On this occasion there was no shortage of food and drink to stimulate the senses and inspire an atmosphere of conviviality:

When we entered the room, the tables were spread with singular neatness. Upon a cloth white as snow were ranged coffee-cups, tea dishes of different sizes, chocolate cups, teapots, and everything belonging to the equipage of the tea table, with French rolls, pots of butter, all in decent order, and interspersed with sweet-briar, which had a pretty effect both on the sight and smell. At the word of command were set on the table chocolate, coffee, tea, hot rolls buttered, buttered hot cakes.[62]

Socializing the visitors was a matter both of encouraging them to mix, and discouraging them from engaging in practices which inhib-

[59] Warwickshire CRO, L6/1451, 1453, 1460, 1474; letters of 1759 between Margaret Luttrell and Henry Luttrell, Somerset RO, DD/L; Penrose, *Letters*, 45, 75, 88, 90-2; HMC, *Egmont MSS*, Diary i. 291-2, 400-2; Hervey, *Letter-Books*, ii. 161, 170, 173, 178, 191, 280, 287, 295-6.

[60] M. Conyers, 'Account of a Tour from Arbury to Derbyshire and Nottinghamshire' (1747), fo. 8, Warwickshire CRO, CR.136/2668; HMC, *Verulam MSS*, 233; Pigott Diary, ii, article 840.

[61] Burr, *Tunbridge Wells*, 116; Pigott Diary, i, article 457; Wood, *Bath*, 438; Penrose, *Letters*, 106, 119, 122, 164, 198; Waite, 'Bristol Hotwell', 120; Smith, *Malvern*, 175.

[62] Warwickshire CRO, L6/1467; Penrose, *Letters*, 96.

ited this. A factor that potentially posed a serious barrier to free intercourse was the rigorous observation of formal status distinctions. As Burr noted of early Stuart Tunbridge Wells, 'the company, thus assembled, formed no general society. . . . The great brought with them all the haughtiness of nobility, and knew not how to let themselves down with grace.' The stiff, as opposed to subtle acknowledgement of title, became increasingly outmoded and was even derided in fashionable circles. In 1711 *The Spectator* reported that 'at present . . . an unconstrained carriage, and a certain openness of behaviour, are the height of good breeding. . . . A polite country squire shall make you as many bows in half an hour, as would serve a courtier for a week.'[63] During the eighteenth century the spas became famed for their relaxed (though not neutral) attitude to social rank. In the early 1730s it was reported from Scarborough that 'gentlemen appear in all places naked (i.e. without their swords) . . . from a polite declaration, that in places of public resort, all distinctions ought to be lost in a general complaisance'. A visitor to Matlock in 1757 noted how at dinner 'everyone sits down without any form, those who come first by the rule taking the uppermost seats at the long table', and in the 1760s it was said that 'in the great assembly rooms' at Tunbridge Wells, 'all ranks are mingled together without any distinction'.[64] Even Bath, which attracted the grandest in the land, eventually conformed to this pattern. In the early eighteenth century 'general society among people of rank and fortune was so far from being established . . . that the nobility would not associate with the gentry at any of the public entertainments of the place: but when proper walks were made for exercise, and a house built for assembling in, rank began to be laid aside'. Penrose confirmed this picture of informality, when he reported in 1766 the disgruntled reaction (unjustified as it transpired) of the company to a visit from William Pitt:

I was in hope to have seen him this morning at the Pump Room: but, it seems, he never comes thither, always sending for his water. Perhaps . . . being conversant with kings and princes, he chooses not to mix with the herd at Bath, who would not in their carriage distinguish between him and lesser men: for Bath, like "Caesar's arms, doth throw down all distinction". . . .[65]

[63] Burr, *Tunbridge Wells*, 21; *The Spectator*, No. 119, 17 July 1711, in Ross, *Tatler and Spectator*, 277.
[64] *Journey from London to Scarborough*, 44; Powys, *Diaries*, 31; Burr, *Tunbridge Wells*, 120-1; and also Waite, 'Bristol Hotwell', 121.
[65] Wood, *Bath*, 411; Penrose, *Letters*, 86.

A further threat to the cohesion of spa society came from disorderly or personally divisive behaviour. As centres devoted to the pursuit of pleasure, resorts always ran the risk that normal social conventions might be relaxed too far, encouraging unacceptable levels of high-spiritedness and rivalry. The assembly rooms and theatres at Bath and Tunbridge Wells experienced the occasional disturbance and even riot caused by some petty dispute, or a practical joke that backfired.[66] More dangerous, however, was the risk posed by uncontrolled gossiping and spitefulness, practices which were prevalent when issues like sexual relations, marriage, and status were at stake. To maintain a reasonable level of discipline among the company, a number of spas developed a body of informal rules, or 'honorary laws' as Wood called them, which, though they possessed no legal validity, carried the force of custom. Versions of these existed at Bath by the 1740s, where they were subsequently updated, and at Bristol Hot Wells and Buxton by the end of the century.[67] Most of the regulations were concerned with the conduct of the balls, seeking specifically to control the dress of guests and the duration of the events, and more generally, to curb excessive or impulsive behaviour. The early Bath laws were designed to suppress scandalmongering and overt manifestations of jealousy, and contained a number of specific exhortations to this effect. At Bath and Tunbridge Wells unwritten conventions governed the organization of the dancing in order to prevent an unseemly scramble for the most attractive partners. Burr wrote of the Kent spa, 'the ball is always opened with a minuet by two persons of the highest distinction: when this is concluded the lady returns to her seat, and the master of ceremonies brings the gentleman a new partner. The same order is observed by every succeeding couple, each gentleman being obliged to dance with two ladies, till the minuets are over.'[68]

The master of ceremonies, as Burr's description suggests, was an important supervisor of fashionable resort life. During the eighteenth century such an office existed at Bath, Bristol Hot Wells, Buxton, Cheltenham, Epsom, Scarborough, as well as Tunbridge Wells.[69] The

[66] Warwickshire CRO, L6/1470; Tyte, *Bath*, 28; Barton, *Tunbridge Wells*, 248.

[67] Wood, *Bath*, 248-50, 412-13; *New and Correct Plan of Bath* (1750); Penrose, *Letters*, 135-7; Tyte, *Bath*, 29-30; *The New History, Survey, and Description of the City and Suburbs of Bristol* (Bristol, 1794), 104-5; Heape, *Buxton*, 31-2, and plates opposite.

[68] Burr, *Tunbridge Wells*, 122; Wood, *Bath*, 443; Pigott Diary, i, article 477.

[69] Waite, 'Bristol Hotwell', 120-1; Heape, *Buxton*, 32; Hart, *Cheltenham*, 130-2; Little, 'Gloucestershire Spas', 188; Clark, 'Epsom Spa', 35-6; McIntyre, 'Health and Pleasure Resorts', 199.

most famous of these social leaders was Richard oɪ 'Beau' Nash, who
operated in both Bath and Tunbridge Wells, and was already something of a legend in his own time.[70] Contemporaries portrayed him as
a larger-than-life character, conceited, extrovert, extravagant ('he
usually travelled to Tunbridge, in a post-chariot and six greys, with
outriders, footmen, French horns, and every other appendage of
expensive parade'), sometimes buffoon-like, and there was more than
a hint of sarcasm when he was referred to as the 'king' of Bath and
'this Bathonian sovereign'.[71] Yet behind the epithet lay a germ of
truth. For Bath was a pseudo-kingdom, a parallel society sealed from
the outside world where conventions of rank were temporarily relaxed
to create an egalitarian commonwealth in which visitors could cultivate
and refresh their gregarious natures. In such a community, it was
natural that the court fool should be permitted to play the part of the
king, governing his potentially unruly subjects not with physical force
but with the scourge of satire.[72]

Though the claims for Nash's influence have frequently been exaggerated, there is little doubt that he made an important contribution
to regulating the behaviour of the company and fostering its unity.
Burr claimed that before Nash arrived at the country's two leading
spas, 'the company was generally disunited and unsocial', and a poem
of 1740 expressed the fear that when he temporarily left Bath,

> The fair assembly thus will be
> Into confusion hurled,
> Like second Babylonians we,
> Shall have a jargon world.

Twelve years later Lady Luxborough maintained that 'to promote
society, good manners, and a coalition of parties and ranks; to
suppress scandal and late hours, are his views: and he succeeds rather
better than his brother monarchs generally do', and after Nash's death
Dr King's epitaph praised how

[70] L. Melville, *Bath under Beau Nash* (London, 1907); Connely, *Beau Nash*;
J. Walters, *Splendour and Scandal: The Reign of Beau Nash* (London, 1968); 'Memoir
of Beau Nash', in *Bentley's Miscellany*, ii (1837), 414-25; 'The Monarch of Bath',
Blackwood's Magazine, xlviii (1840), 773-92; 'A Little King and his Little State',
Chambers Jnl., xxxii (1859), 250-4.

[71] Goldsmith, 'Life of Nash', 311; *Bath: A Poem*, 30; Wood, *Bath*, 184.

[72] V. W. Turner, *The Ritual Process: Structure and Anti-Structure* (Chicago, 1969),
chap. 3.

His chief care was employed,
In preventing obscenity or imprudence
From offending the modesty or the morals of the fair sex,
And in banishing from their assemblies
Tumult, clamour, and abuse.[73]

The promotion of sociability sits rather uneasily alongside that other great preoccupation of urban culture, the pursuit of status. Whereas one sought to unify society, the other encouraged fragmentation. The two motives cannot be easily harmonized; nor should they be. Then, as now, people were perfectly capable of behaving in a contradictory fashion. However, there were a number of ways in which it was possible to reconcile the striving for personal status with the desire for more intensive and amicable social relations. There was little point in ornamenting the body and refining the mind if there was no one to admire and praise the results. Society was therefore a pre-condition of status, and the ambitious cultivated company if only to acquire an audience. Similarly, even the most ruthless social climber had to realize that unrestrained individual competition might explode in counter-productive levels of verbal and physical violence, unless controlled by strong conventions of inter-personal behaviour. There were also more subtle reasons for the gregarious and egalitarian ethos of the new urban culture. If there was to be anything approaching a free exchange of status and wealth between the growing middling groups and the traditional landed élite, it would have to be done on relatively equal terms. Undue consideration of rank, especially of an inherited nature, would impede contact between the two parties and inhibit the efficient operation of the market. Sociability was therefore a means of facilitating a regime of free-trading.

Market dynamics can go only so far in explaining the contemporary commitment to congenial and convivial relations. Behind this also lay a deep apprehension about the well-being and cohesion of society. The cause of such fears was undoubtedly the bitter political and religious divisions that had plagued the nation's leaders ever since the Civil War. The tensions and prejudices bred during the Great Rebellion continued to infect the political process long after the Restoration. The Glorious Revolution, different as it was from its mid-

[73] Burr, *Tunbridge Wells*, 113; 'On Mr Nash's Going from the Bath', in *Bath Miscellany*, 22; quoted in M. Williams, *Lady Luxborough Goes to Bath* (Oxford, [1945]), 6; W. King, 'The Epitaph of Richard Nash, Esq', in Melville, *Bath under Beau Nash*, 297.

century predecessor, inevitably resuscitated the memories and anxieties of the 1640s and 1650s. The years after 1688 also saw the emergence of new conflicts, which merged with the old problems to create the intense party strife of the early eighteenth century.[74] When viewed in the light of these divisions and the emotions they generated, the mission to civilize and socialize the gentry may be seen as part of a subtle campaign to reunite a divided élite. The appeal to the polite gentleman to cultivate learning and morality, and to learn to curb his passions, was an attempt to produce a more balanced and thoughtful, less prejudiced and quick-tempered individual, who was more likely to understand his neighbours and peacefully coexist with them. The promotion of sociability went even further to stress the virtues of fellowship and good company, and practically encouraged this by providing controlled contexts in which people of different persuasions could mix together. The new urban culture can therefore be seen as a balm to soothe and heal long-standing wounds, which if left untreated could threaten the health of the body politic.

However, it would be wrong to assume that fashionable culture always had such salutary effects. Newspapers, journals, plays, operas, clubs, and coffee-houses were often associated with political causes. Seemingly innocuous recreations could be contaminated by the toxin of party.[75] The Tory celebrations at Chester, following their county victory in the 1710 general election, 'concluded with a ball for the ladies', and after a riot on the racecourse at Lichfield in 1747, Whigs and Tories mounted separate meetings for the next six years.[76] Even architecture reflected the opposing political and religious forces. The 'fifty new churches' project in London was part of a Tory/High Church campaign, initiated after their success in the 'Church in Danger' election of 1710 to restore the pride and prestige of the Anglican church, and the lavish and 'Romanish' baroque designs adopted were clearly meant to support this. Outside the metropolis, the strikingly different styles of St Philip's Birmingham (1709–15), curvaceous and Italian in inspiration (see Fig. 4), and St Ann's Manchester (1709–12), relatively simple and functional, almost certainly echoed the contrasting political attitudes of their promoters:

[74] G. S. Holmes, *British Politics in the Age of Anne* (London, 1967), especially chap. 5; Speck, 'Conflict in Society', 135–54.

[75] Holmes, *British Politics*, 21–4, 30–3; Williams, 'Henry Cross-Grove', 206–19; Loftis, *Politics of Drama*; Money, *Experience and Identity*, *passim*.

[76] *Post Boy*, No. 2415, 2–4 Nov. 1710; Kettle, 'Lichfield Races', 39–41. I owe the former reference to Geoffrey Holmes.

a body of gentry commissioners in Birmingham, and the Low Church Lady Bland in Manchester.[77]

Polite urban culture, therefore, was not sealed from the conflicts that raged around it and could be readily exploited as a vehicle for promoting partisan causes. But the tendency for this to occur probably began to diminish from the 1720s. Moreover, even before this date, fashionable town culture developed an apolitical, even anti-political complexion, that may have helped to stem the tide of party prejudice and warfare.[78] Several observers suggested that the combined influences of spa and coffee-house assisted in defusing political and religious tensions. John Toland, in his *Description of Epsom*, published in 1711, felt that 'I must do our coffee-houses the justice to affirm, that for social virtue they are equalled by few, and exceeded by none, though I wish they may be imitated by all. A Tory does not stare and leer when a Whig comes in, nor a Whig look sour and whisper at the sight of a Tory. These distinctions are laid by with the winter suit at London'. In a similar vein Burr observed that in mid-eighteenth-century Tunbridge Wells,

the coffee-house, and the bookseller's shop, are places where the social virtues reign triumphant over prejudice and prepossession. The easy freedom, and cheerful gaiety, arising from the nature of a public place, extends its influence over them, and every species of party spirit is entirely stripped of those malignant qualities which render it so destructive of the peace of mankind. Here divines and philosophers, Deists and Christians, Whigs and Tories, Scotch and English, debate without anger, dispute with politeness, and judge with candour. . . .[79]

Public assemblies and balls also seem to have had a predominantly apolitical character. Even at York, where separate party assemblies operated in the early eighteenth century, Macky noted that 'My Lord Carlisle hath been so good, as to endeavour to remove the names of distinction from the two assemblies, by carrying mixed company to both; and the officers of the army make no distinction, strangers go equally to both.' The regulations governing the foundation of the new rooms in the city in 1730 guarded against a resurgence of these earlier

[77] H. M. Colvin, 'Fifty New Churches', *Architectural Review* (Mar. 1950), 189–96; *BE Warwickshire*, 106–8; E. Saxon, *The Story of St Ann's Church, Manchester* (n.d.).

[78] For the role of the provincial town as a 'social welder of exceptional importance', see Holmes, 'Achievement of Stability', 20–2.

[79] [Toland], *Description of Epsom*, 15; Burr, *Tunbridge Wells*, 126–7.

divisions by severely limiting the size of any one individual's share-holding, thereby effectively preventing the establishment falling into the hands of a small party clique.[80]

Several clubs and societies seem to have deliberately cultivated an atmosphere of neutrality. In 1781 the Birmingham Subscription Library declared that 'this institution can never answer the purpose of any party, civil or religious, but, on the contrary, may be expected to promote a spirit of liberality and friendship', and ten years earlier the musical society at Swaffham reminded potential recruits, 'N.B. Swaffham concert is no party concert'. In 1733 the Spalding Gentlemen's Society expressed its aversion to partisan discussion at its meetings, when it noted of several issues of 'a new paper called the *Weekly Miscellany* . . . nothing was read out of them that was political, and as being newspapers that was guarded against with good caution according to our 3rd rule'.[81] The printed media, of course, frequently demonstrated a strong party bias, though it is unclear how common this was outside London. In 1750 the Stratford-upon-Avon printer James Keating felt he could succeed with quite the opposite tack, when in the first issue of his new publication he wrote that 'a good family paper, free from the prejudices of party, is most certainly wanted; and such this is intended to be'.[82] Even as politically committed a journalist as Addison, who was intimately associated with the Whig establishment, could criticize and satirize 'the rage of party'. In 1711, at the height of the conflict, he warned his *Spectator* reader that 'a furious party spirit, when it rages in its full violence, exerts itself in civil war and bloodshed . . . it fills a nation with spleen and rancour, and extinguishes all seeds of good nature, compassion, and humanity', and he advocated that 'we should not any longer regard our fellow subjects as Whigs or Tories, but should make the man of merit our friend, and the villain our enemy'. Though *The Tatler* and *The Spectator* reflected the Whig sentiments of their authors, it was the journals' vein of moderation that impressed later eighteenth-century commentators like Johnson, who argued that 'to

[80] Macky, *Journey*, ii. 211; 'Proposals for . . . Assembly Rooms', proposal No. 3, YCA.

[81] *Aris's Birmingham Gazette*, quoted in Kaufman, 'Community Library', 32; *Norwich Mercury*, 1 June 1771, quoted in Fawcett, *Music in Eighteenth-Century Norwich*, 38; Owen, *Spalding Gentlemen's Society*, 6; and also Brewer, 'Commercialization and Politics', 219.

[82] *Stratford, Shipston, and Alcester Jnl.*, i, No. 1, 5 Feb. 1749/50.

minds heated with political contest, they supplied cooler and more inoffensive reflections'.[83]

From the 1720s a period of comparative political and religious stability began to set in. Though the divisions of earlier years persisted for several decades, their bitterness and prominence began to moderate somewhat.[84] There were strong political reasons for this, but stability also owed much to a mounting reaction against the bigoted ideological conflict that had afflicted the nation for generations. The new urban culture, though at times coloured by the struggles that raged around it, helped nurture this moderate backlash. It also contributed to stability in practical ways by providing attractive contexts in which the traditional élite and the growing middling ranks could freely mix and acquire and exchange status and wealth, thereby neutralizing the potentially most dangerous of all divisions in post-Restoration Britain. During the early Georgian period a new sense of cultural community was emerging, one pioneered by the town, in which civility and sociability replaced the divisive aspects of politics and religion. In its wake developed a growing social cohesion, often as yet tenuous and fragile, within and between the upper and middling strata of English society. A new élite was being forged, at once more inclusive and exclusive than its predecessor.[85]

This chapter has suggested that the Urban Renaissance was fired not only by self-interest but also by idealism, for it was part of an English enlightenment that was determined to deliver the nation from barbarism into the ranks of the civilized world. At the personal level this involved reforming and refining the individual's mental, moral, and emotional capacities; in the collective sphere it required the assiduous cultivation of sociable behaviour. Public affability, though laudable in its own right, was also of critical value to the cohesion of the nation, for it helped to absorb and reconcile the tensions generated within a politically divided, competitive, and expanding élite. However, there

[83] *The Spectator*, No. 125, 24 July 1711; and also No. 50, 27 Apr. 1711; No. 57, 5 May 1711; No. 81, 2 June 1711; in Ross, *Tatler and Spectator*, 444–7, and also 252–4, 434–5, 440–7; Johnson, *Prose and Poetry*, 874.

[84] Plumb, *Growth of Political Stability*, 161–88; Cannon, *Whig Ascendancy*, *passim*; for the continuation of party alignments, see L. Colley, *In Defiance of Oligarchy: The Tory Party 1714–60* (Cambridge, 1982); J. C. D. Clark, *Revolution and Rebellion: State and Society in England in the Seventeenth and Eighteenth Centuries* (Cambridge, 1986), 141–55.

[85] It should be stressed that the definition of élite used here is far broader than that employed by Stone in his *Open Élite*.

were limits to sociability: the hand of friendship stretched only so far down the social ladder. It is these limits that will be explored in the following chapter.

11

Cultural Differentiation

Towards the end of his *Description of Bath*, Wood commends the egalitarian and sociable influence of the spa's leisure facilities: 'but when proper walks were made for exercise, and a house built for assembling in, rank began to be laid aside, and all degrees of people, from the private gentleman upwards, were soon united in society with one another'.[1] 'From the private gentleman upwards': this caveat (almost an afterthought, because such qualifications were scarcely necessary for contemporaries) reveals one of the paradoxes of the Urban Renaissance. Just as it brought the higher echelons of society into greater contact, so it opened a cultural gap between them and the populace as a whole. In practice these two developments complemented each other. If the boundaries of the élite were to be extended, as was essential if the swelling middling ranks were to be accommodated, it was of paramount importance that the newly established frontiers should be doubly fortified. An expanding and competitive élite was only tolerable if accompanied by more intensive segregation within society in general. One way this was achieved was by accentuating the cultural differences between those in the élite (as newly defined), and those outside it. The impact of this development was to be powerful and pervasive, but it should not be overemphasized. Commercialization, social emulation, the pluralist nature of society, and the need to retain a core of shared values engendered diverse and ambivalent attitudes which prevented a rigid polarization of beliefs. The following chapter will examine the process of cultural differentiation (both its scope and limits) by exploring the related development of separate polite and popular cultures, the use of charity to accentuate the social divide and reinforce social control, and the strategies employed to preserve the long-term exclusivity of fashionable leisure.

[1] Wood, *Bath*, 411.

1. POLITE AND POPULAR

For centuries there had been a distinct élite culture, lavish, courtly, and private in character. However, it seems that the wealthy minority who enjoyed its pleasures also participated in a more broadly based corpus of traditional (but not unchanging) beliefs, customs, recreations, and festivals. Because this was shared by gentry and populace alike, though often on an unequal basis, it contributed a good deal to social cohesion. From the Reformation onwards the strength and integrative influence of traditional culture was placed under a severe strain, as many among the upper and middling ranks began both to withdraw from it and to attack it.[2] The timing of this process is as yet unclear. Some historians have detected considerable cultural polarization during the Tudor and early Stuart period,[3] whereas others have stressed the continuing importance of common values and customs up until 1700, and even beyond.[4] It is argued here that whatever the prior situation, from the very end of the seventeenth century there was a marked acceleration in the rate at which the privileged and affluent withdrew from traditional beliefs and leisure activities, as these became associated not only with ungodliness (as was previously the case), but also, and more damningly, with social inferiority. The long-term consequence was that a widening cultural gap emerged between polite society and the majority of ordinary people, and with it the transformation of an inclusive traditional culture into an exclusive popular one. As early as 1725 Henry Bourne was able to write of the

---

[2] P. Burke, *Popular Culture in Early Modern Europe* (London, 1979), 23-9, 207-43, 270-81.

[3] Phythian-Adams, 'Ceremony and the Citizen', 79-80; Burke, *Popular Culture*, 277-8; K. Wrightson and D. Levine, *Poverty and Piety in an English Village: Terling 1525-1700* (New York, San Francisco, and London, 1979), chaps. 5-7; K. Wrightson, 'Alehouses, Order, and Reformation in Rural England, 1590-1660', in E. and S. Yeo (eds.), *Popular Culture and Class Conflict 1590-1914: Explorations in the History of Labour and Leisure* (Brighton, 1982), 1-27; Wrightson, *English Society*, 183-221; Clark, *English Alehouse*, 151-7.

[4] M. Ingram, 'Ridings, Rough Music, and the "Reform of Popular Culture" in Early Modern England', *Past and Present*, cv (1984), 79-113. Jonathan Barry's work on seventeenth- and eighteenth-century Bristol has stressed the extent to which the majority of citizens continued to share a broad range of cultural practices and attitudes (both old and new), and suggested that where divisions occurred political and religious factors were more important than social ones. See Barry, 'Cultural Life of Bristol', especially 11-14, 182, 339-44; J. Barry, 'Popular Culture in Seventeenth-Century Bristol', in B. Reay (ed.), *Popular Culture in Seventeenth-Century England* (London and Sydney, 1985), 59-90.

'vast number of ceremonies and opinions, which are held by the common people', that 'though some of them have been of national and others perhaps of universal observance, yet at present they would have little or no being, if not observed among the vulgar'.[5]

The Urban Renaissance played a critical part in this process of cultural differentiation. It transformed the whole scale and nature of élite pastimes, so that they could cope with the demands of a much larger clientele, and thereby free respectable society from the need to continue patronizing older customs and recreations. Moreover, by its very presence it encouraged, and by its propaganda it pressured those with status aspirations to abandon their contact with traditional culture. The Enlightenment, whose values urban centres disseminated, was in part a campaign to reveal to the gentry the error of plebeian ways. Civilizing and social distancing, therefore, went hand in hand. Polite and traditional (later popular) culture diverged over a range of mental fields. Five of these, closely associated with the influence of the town, are briefly explored here: space, literacy, language, leisure, and time.

The spatial perceptions embodied in traditional culture focused *inwards* on local custom and practices, whereas those of its polite counterpart looked *outwards* towards London and the continent. The towns of the Urban Renaissance were fashionable provincial society's window on the world outside. For example, leisure centres frequently imported theatrical and musical performers from the metropolis and Europe, and their musical clubs and festivals were often modelled on institutions pioneered in the capital. The names of the fabulous London pleasure grounds were appropriated to grace the gardens of several towns: in the 1760s Bath and Birmingham possessed a 'Vauxhall Gardens', Newcastle-upon-Tyne a 'New Ranelagh Gardens', and by the late eighteenth century Norwich had one of each.[6] The metropolis provided a blueprint for many other areas of

[5] H. Bourne, *Antiquitates Vulgares: Or, the Antiquities of the Common People* (Newcastle-upon-Tyne, 1725), p. ix; P. Borsay, ' "All the Town's a Stage": Urban Ritual and Ceremony 1660–1800', in Clark, *Provincial Towns*, 246–52; E. P. Thompson, 'Patrician Society, Plebeian Culture', *Jnl. of Social History*, vii, Part 4 (1974), 382–405; E. P. Thompson, 'Eighteenth-Century English Society: Class Struggle without Class?', *Social History*, iii, No. 2 (1978), 133–65; H. Payne, 'Elite versus Popular Mentality in the Eighteenth Century', in R. Runte (ed.), *Studies in Eighteenth-Century Culture*, viii (Wisconsin, 1979), 3–32.

[6] Above, chap. 5; Sydenham, *Bath Pleasure Gardens*, 6; Money, *Experience and Identity*, 80; Brand, *Newcastle*, ii. 538; Fawcett, *Music in Eighteenth-Century Norwich*, 29.

provincial urban life, so much so that in 1761 it was claimed that 'the several great cities, and we might add many poor country towns, seem to be universally inspired with the ambition of becoming the little Londons of the part of the kingdom wherein they are situated'.[7]

One vital way in which the provincial town provided access to cosmopolitan attitudes was through its production and distribution of print. Simply by purchasing a newspaper or borrowing a periodical or book from the local circulating library or club, a country dweller could be put into contact with national and international news and fashions. However, such contact depended upon the capacity to read, and to read well. This had not been a central feature of traditional culture, which though by no means isolated from the written language, laid greater emphasis on oral and visual forms of communication. Therefore, the use of the printed word represented a second characteristic that divided the polite and popular spheres. Socially this was reinforced by the concentration of literacy in the upper strata of society. Already by the later Tudor period it seems that almost all the male gentry and members of the leading professions were able to read. During the late sixteenth and seventeenth centuries this skill percolated down the social scale, though at an uneven pace, to embrace a substantial majority of the middling ranks. Literacy came far more slowly to the rest of the populace, among whom in 1700 only a minority of adult males (and even fewer women) would have directly enjoyed its benefits. Indirectly, of course, the uneducated could acquire access to the printed word through the services of intermediaries. Moreover, the reading ability of the ordinary man and woman should not be underrated. Skilled workers and townspeople were generally more literate than plebeian society as a whole, and there existed a buoyant trade in cheap publications to supply the popular market.[8] However, the social divide between the two cultures revolved not only around the basic ability to read, but also the quality

[7] *Annual Register* (1761), quoted in Falkus, 'Lighting in the Dark Ages', 259; McKendrick, 'Commercialization of Fashion', 50-1.

[8] D. Cressy, 'Levels of Illiteracy in England 1530-1730', *Historical Jnl.*, xx (1977), 1-23; D. Cressy, *Literacy and the Social Order: Reading and Writing in Tudor and Stuart England* (Cambridge, 1980), especially chaps. 6 and 7; Wrightson and Levine, *Poverty and Piety*, 142-53; Wrightson, *English Society*, 184-99; M. Spufford, *Contrasting Communities: English Villagers in the Sixteenth and Seventeenth Centuries* (Cambridge, 1979), 192-205; M. Spufford, *Small Books and Pleasant Histories: Popular Fiction and its Readership in Seventeenth-Century England* (London, 1981); Barry, 'Popular Culture', 61-70; R. A. Houston, 'The Development of Literacy: Northern England 1640-1750', *EcHR*, 2nd ser., xxxv, No. 2 (1982), 199-216; R. A.

of this skill, and the uses to which it was put. The majority of literate common people would not have been educated to a level where they could easily cope with linguistically and intellectually demanding texts, nor would they have had the purchasing power to afford such literature. Instead they would seek out more popular and less expensive genres. Literacy was thus an ambivalent cultural force that divided as much as it united those who possessed it.[9]

The Urban Renaissance widened the gap that existed between the literate and illiterate, the skilled and the simple reader, by enormously increasing the range and sophistication of printed material. The well-educated person acquired access to a much wider field of knowledge than ever before, and this necessarily highlighted the apparent ignorance of those unable to tap this vein of learning. The growth in publications and the socially selective entrée to these also led to diverging attitudes in a third area, the use of language. Traditional culture, with its oral and local character, encouraged a rich diversity of dialects, vocabulary, and syntax. However, the printed word moved in quite the opposite direction. Its effective use depended upon the existence of a relatively standardized language; at the same time its dissemination promoted the development of linguistic uniformity. As Johnson argued in the preface to his *Dictionary of the English Language* (1755), 'the various dialects of the same country . . . will always be observed to grow fewer, and less different, as books are multiplied', and he planned his dictionary to be a means 'by which the pronunciation of our language may be fixed, and its attainment facilitated'. Since only the literate were directly subject to such influences, there emerged a widening gulf between the polite, who communicated through standardized 'received' English, and the vulgar, who continued to articulate their multiplicity of regional accents and words.[10]

Houston, *Scottish Literacy and the Scottish Identity: Illiteracy and Society in Scotland and Northern England 1600-1800* (Cambridge, 1985), 20-83, 193-210.

[9] R. Chartier, 'Culture as Appropriation: Popular Cultural Uses in Early Modern France', in S. L. Kaplan (ed.), *Understanding Popular Culture: Europe from the Middle Ages to the Nineteenth Century* (Berlin, New York, and Amsterdam, 1984), 229-53; B. Capp, 'Popular Literature', in Reay, *Popular Culture*, 231-2; Spufford, *Small Books and Pleasant Histories*, 46-8; Houston, *Scottish Literacy*, 199, 228-9, 243; K. Thomas, 'The Meaning of Literacy in Early Modern England', in G. Baumann (ed.), *The Written Word: Literacy in Transition* (Oxford, 1986), 99-101, 116-18, 121; Barry, 'Cultural Life of Bristol', 85-91.

[10] Johnson, *Prose and Poetry*, 138, 302. For the Glamorgan gentry's withdrawal from the Welsh language see Jenkins, *Ruling Class*, 205-6, 209-10, 213-16.

Leisure was a fourth area where the two cultures diverged. Emphasis on the contemplative pleasures derived from literacy and learning inevitably drew fashionable society away from the rough and tumble of traditional recreations, whose appeal persisted among the majority of the population. The educated were further alienated by a mounting intellectual scepticism towards the magical beliefs that often infused and supported the older customs and festivals.[11] The pastimes of the polite therefore emerged as cerebral and enlightened, while those of the common people appeared to be physical, sensual, superstitious, and ignorant.[12] The withdrawal of the élite from traditional leisure also led to a divergence of attitudes in a fifth field, that of time. The religious and festival calendar came to play a declining role in the lives of the fashionable, as they adopted a new timetable based on polite recreations, which cut right across that of the customary year. Whereas the historic calendar was divided at December (Christmas) and late June (Midsummer) into ritualistic and secular halves, the new one was separated at roughly October and April, into winter and summer seasons. On the other hand, ordinary people continued to respect the traditional annual cycle, and to celebrate its climactic points, such as Shrove Tuesday, Easter Day, May Day, and Midsummer's Eve. Moreover, whereas popular festivals (particularly fairs and wakes) were deliberately timed to mesh with the agricultural calendar, this appears to have had little impact on the organization of polite leisure.[13]

In several respects the development of urban architecture encapsulated the process of cultural differentiation. The wealthy and prosperous eagerly adopted the new vogues in building, but the majority of people continued to occupy houses largely constructed in the traditional vernacular manner. Whereas a defining feature of the vernacular style was its local character, classicism was an overtly outward-looking and international style.[14] As in the field of entertainments,

[11] K. Thomas, *Religion and the Decline of Magic: Studies in Popular Beliefs in Sixteenth and Seventeenth-Century England* (Harmondsworth, 1973), 767–800; *The Spectator*, No. 110, 6 July 1711, and No. 117, 14 July 1711, both in Ross, *Tatler and Spectator*, 225–8, 236–8; Wood, *Bath*, 452–6; Penrose, *Letters*, 106–8.

[12] J. Harris, *Hermes: Or a Philosophical Inquiry Concerning Language and Universal Grammar*, 1751, repr. (Menston, 1968), 350; *The Tatler*, No. 89, 1–3 Nov. 1709, in Ross, *Tatler and Spectator*, 128.

[13] Above, chap. 5; C. Phythian-Adams, *Local History and Folklore: A New Framework* (London, 1975), 21–5; Phythian-Adams, 'Ceremony and the Citizen', 70–9; Malcolmson, *Popular Recreations*, 18, 24–5.

[14] Brunskill, *Handbook of Vernacular Architecture*, 25–6; Mercer, *Vernacular Houses*, 1–2.

London was the entrepôt for continental ideas, and provincial urban buildings were frequently praised for their similarity to those in the metropolis. One writer found Liverpool 'mostly new built houses of brick and stone after the London fashion . . . its London in miniature as much as ever I saw anything', another considered the elegant houses of Temple Row Birmingham (constructed from 1710 onwards) to be 'as lofty, elegant, and uniform as those of Bedford Row', while Queen Square Bristol (1700–27) was described as 'somewhat like Lincoln's Inn Fields', and the port's new Exchange (1741–3) as 'in miniature the Change at London'.[15] Direct international allusions could be seen, for example, in the Circus at Bath, clearly based on the Coliseum at Rome (see Fig. 24), or in the new assembly rooms at York, whose centre-piece was a ballroom modelled on Palladio's interpretation of the Egyptian hall described by Vitruvius (see Fig. 13).[16]

Unlike the vernacular tradition, classicism had a strong literary basis. Building treatises had been powerful agents in the development and dissemination of Italian Renaissance architecture. During the eighteenth century several of these texts were translated and reprinted in England, in addition to which a growing body of theoretical works and manuals flowed from the presses. Architecture, therefore, became an increasingly bookish subject, and for anyone who practised or studied it, and wished to keep abreast of the latest fashions, literacy was a valuable, even essential skill. The publication of pattern-books also had the effect of standardizing the language of polite architecture, not only because classicism was itself a theoretically universal style, but also because printed material passed freely across regional boundaries. Some manuals self-consciously presented themselves as building lexicons. Neve's contribution to the genre was called *The City and Country Purchaser and Builder's Dictionary*, and the first chapter of Ware's *Complete Body of Architecture* was titled, 'An Explanation of the Terms of Art, Which Are Used in Writing or Speaking of Buildings', and was arranged in the form of a dictionary.[17]

The stress in classicism was on an international, literate, and standardized style of architecture, which divorced it physically and

[15] Fiennes, *Journeys*, 183–4; Toldervy, *England and Wales Described*, 349; Students Diary, fo. 121; HMC, *Verulam MSS*, 250.

[16] HMC, *Verulam MSS*, 249; Summerson, 'English Town-Planning Tradition', 98–101; R. Wittkower, *The Earl of Burlington and William Kent*, York Georgian Soc., Occasional Paper No. 5 (1948), 20–3.

[17] Above, chap. 2; Ware, *Body of Architecture*, 1.

mentally from the vernacular tradition. Since popular society lacked the means to dabble in the new fashions, and often the literate skills to understand them, then the rise of classicism further widened the cultural gap. Artisans in the building trades inevitably had close contact with high architecture, but the appreciation of the subject was essentially a polite concern. Pattern-book authors stressed that their publications were aimed at gentlemen as well as craftsmen. Ware intended his *Complete Body of Architecture*, 'to acquaint the gentleman with what . . . he should design in his edifice; and to instruct the practical builder in not only what he ought to do, but how he should execute it, to his own credit, and the advantage of the owner', and promised to 'omit the common and vulgar terms understood by every labouring person'.[18] Ware's volume is intensely élitist in nature, suggesting the gulf between the aesthetic faculties of the educated and the ignorant. He warns against 'idle ornaments' that 'charm the vulgar, but disgust the judicious', exhorts the architect to 'leave vulgar shifts to common judges', and disapproves of the man who will 'justify the construction from the opinion of the common eye'.[19]

Though the emergence of fashionable urban culture encouraged the development of diverging polite and popular *mentalités*, this did not always lead to a rigid social divide between the groups involved. The glittering pleasures of the beau monde inevitably attracted the attention of plebeian interlopers. For this reason it was necessary to build into the new urban leisure a good measure of positive segregation. Most élite pastimes were protected by some form of entry barrier, the most effective of which was cost. In 1759 one correspondent reported from Bath that 'anybody may go for 19*d.*' to the Spring Gardens. However, this would have involved about a full day's wages for a provincial craftsman, rather more for a labourer. Even if this was possible, such men could scarcely have afforded the guinea needed to gain admission to the great race assemblies at York, or even the five shillings required on these occasions 'for the liberty of . . . going up to the gallery to look upon the company'.[20] But entrance fees represent only a fraction of the true cost of polite leisure. To cut a respectable

[18] Ware, *Body of Architecture*, Preface, and p. 2; Neve, *Dictionary*, advertisement; Langley, *Chest-Book*, title page.

[19] Ware, *Body of Architecture*, 137, 154, 683.

[20] Margaret Luttrell to Henry Luttrell, [?] 1759, Somerset RO, DD/L; E. W. Gilboy, 'Wages in Eighteenth-Century England', *Jnl. of Economic and Business History*, ii, No. 4 (1930), 603-29; Assembly Rooms Minute Book, 8 Aug. 1732, YCA; and also Barry,

figure at the pleasure gardens and assemblies large sums had to be invested in physical and mental accoutrements. A lengthy stay at one of the resorts necessitated substantial expenditure on transport, accommodation, servants, food, and a whole range of charities and recreational facilities.[21] Cost would therefore deter the majority of people from participating in fashionable pastimes, even if they had the inclination to do so. As an additional safeguard, subscription libraries, book clubs, and learned societies frequently subjected prospective members to vetting or balloting procedures.[22]

Even where effective cost barriers existed, there was always the risk that the lower orders might attempt to gain unauthorized access, either to ogle, or to pursue more nefarious activities. In 1732 the directors of the York assembly rooms instructed that a shed abutting the establishment be demolished, because it was 'a great nuisance by reason of people's getting upon it, and looking in and lifting up the sashes'. Despite such preventative action the threat from voyeurs and intruders continued, and in 1736 it was further 'ordered that four iron pins be made for the windows in the weekly assembly room to hinder people on the outside from lifting up the sashes'.[23] Many respectable public entertainments employed commissionaires who could double as bouncers to exclude unsuitable or unruly elements. Preston Guild customarily appointed two 'groom-porters . . . to keep off [the] crowd and let in gentry and strangers into the hall or butteries'; the Blake Street rooms in York appear to have been protected by a doorman who in 1734 was 'vindicated for resisting Mr Stones in forceably entering the assembly rooms in the last race week without a ticket'; and at Bath the late seventeenth-century assemblies in the town hall were guarded by 'a couple of brawny beadles to keep out the mobility, looking as fierce as the uncouth figures at Guildhall'.[24]

Access to open-air facilities, such as public walks, was less easy to control. Gates existed on the New Walk at York (where they were

'Cultural Life of Bristol', 200–4, which argues that cost was more effective as a social barrier in the fields of music and drama than in those of literature and the pictorial arts.

[21] Castle Accounts, 1695, Warwickshire CRO, Warwick Castle MSS, show that for a six-week stay in Bath Lord Brooke's expenses, including travel, came to £228.12*s*.10*d*. See also Pigott Diary, i, article 457; Burr, *Tunbridge Wells*, 114–15; Defoe, *Tour*, i. 127; 'Letter from Tunbridge'; Neale, *Bath: A Social History*, 38–9.

[22] Kaufman, 'Community Library', 33; Kaufman, 'English Book Clubs', 24; Owen, *Spalding Gentlemen's Society*, 4–6.

[23] Assembly Rooms Minute Book, 23 Aug. 1732, 29 Nov. 1736, YCA.

[24] [Kuerden], *Preston*, 67–8; Assembly Rooms Minute Book, 26 Oct. 1734, YCA; *Step to the Bath*, 165.

closed every evening), and on Avenham Walk Preston, though it is unclear whether these were permanently attended, or if they were used to exclude people. Another solution was to build separate parades for rich and poor, as in the case of the Gravel Walks at Bath (before their redevelopment) and the Pantiles at Tunbridge Wells, both of which were constructed on two levels, with the lower promenade reserved for the 'common sort of people' (see Fig. 19).[25] A different type of policy was adopted to protect the New Walk at York. Its riverside location had traditionally been used by the city's washerwomen for drying clothes, and by the local youth for swimming. When the walks were upgraded in the 1740s, it was decided to terminate these plebeian intrusions by employing 'proper persons . . . to devise means . . . for preventing peoples hanging clothes upon the hedge in St George's Close Walk', and by placing 'advertisements' in the local paper 'against persons exposing themselves naked in the water, or out of the water, within the view of the New Walk'.[26]

One section of the lower ranks who necessarily had contact with fashionable society and their pastimes was servants. They were to prove a persistent headache for the directors of the York assembly rooms. The original plan for the building included 'two vaults or rooms to be dug for the footmen', but it appears that this subterranean accommodation proved ineffective at separating servants from their masters, perhaps because it was unattractive. The directors attempted to solve the problem by adding a ground-floor 'passage as a room for the servants in waiting, which is very much wanting to preserve the front rooms of the assembly free from them, who notwithstanding all our endeavours crowd in with their flambeaus and torches, and spoil the stucco work and chimney-pieces'.[27] Despite the new facilities the footmen continued to be a nuisance. In 1750 complaints were made 'of the company having been crowded and annoyed by servants pressing into the assembly rooms', which led the directors to order 'that the steward and his assistants do cause them to be turned out in case any of them presume to force in'.[28]

Similar problems to those at York, though of a more acute character, existed at Bath. The spa's chairmen, who provided the principal

[25] House Book, 7 Dec. 1732, YCA; Council Minutes, 6 Apr. 1736, PCMSS; Wood, *Bath*, 343; Barton, *Tunbridge Wells*, 117.

[26] Drake, *Eboracum*, 249; House Book, 28 Apr. and 14 July 1742, YCA.

[27] Assembly Rooms Minute Book, 4 May 1730, 4 Feb. 1730/1, 2 Mar. 1735/6, YCA.

[28] Ibid. 16 Jan. 1748/9, 4 Aug. 1750, 14 May 1752, 26 July 1755.

means of transport within the city, were a notoriously unruly bunch. Wood reported how it was 'usual with those turbulent people to provoke gentlemen to draw their swords upon them: and then, by defending themselves with their chair poles, the danger of murder frighted the ladies to such a degree, that the public assemblies for diversion seldom ended without the utmost confusion'. To control this fractious interface between polite and popular society, the authorities introduced a system of strict licensing and standardized fares, arranged a weekly meeting of commissioners 'to hear and determine complaints relating to the chairmen', and from 1754 ordered the town 'beadles [to] attend every night at the public rooms, eight to eleven, by turns, for the better regulation of the chairmen'.[29]

The exclusion of the lower ranks from fashionable recreations was part of a broader process of spatial segregation encouraged by the Urban Renaissance. Towns had long been socially zoned. In early modern Exeter, Newcastle-upon-Tyne, Warwick, Worcester, and York, the more prosperous and prestigious parishes and wards formed a rough core, from which the poorer districts radiated outwards.[30] The selective adoption of classical architecture accentuated this pattern by sharpening the visual contrast between the wealthier and the more impoverished areas. But its impact went deeper. The high-status districts had always contained a significant proportion of poorer households, and as the centres of commercial activity they also attracted a broad spectrum of society during the working day. However, many of the new classical streets and squares were planned primarily as select residential developments, from which the poor, along with unpleasant trades and manufactures, were to be excluded. Leases for Queen Square in Bristol required that 'no tenement be let out to any sort of tenants, particularly no smith's shop, brew-house, nor to any tallowchandler or any other tradesman who by noise, danger of fire, or ill smells shall disturb or annoy any of the inhabitants who shall build

[handwritten margin note: ORDER]

---

[29] Wood, *Bath*, 379–81, 411–12; *The Bath and Bristol Guide: Or, the Tradesman's and Traveller's Pocket-Companion*, 3rd edn. [1755], repr. (Bath, 1969), 27–39; Council Minutes, 3 Sept. 1754, BCA.

[30] P. Slack, 'Social Problems and Social Policies', in Phythian-Adams *et al.*, *Traditional Community under Stress*, 87; Hoskins, *Exeter*, 116; R. Howell, *Newcastle-upon-Tyne and the Puritan Revolution* (Oxford, 1967), 11–12; J. Langton, 'Residential Patterns in Pre-Industrial Cities: Some Case Studies from Seventeenth-Century Britain', *Trans. of the Institute of British Geographers*, lxv (1975), 7–11; Borsay, 'Landscape and Leisure', 132–4; Dyer, *Worcester in the Sixteenth Century*, 178; *VCH York*, 165; and also Clark and Slack, *Towns in Transition*, 114, 122; Patten, *English Towns*, 36–9, 194–6.

near it', and at the Square in Birmingham it was stipulated 'that no building for a butcher, or a baker, or a smith should be erected, except the shop fronting Bull Street . . . which lately was a smith's shop'. Lease control was used to ensure 'that the utmost good order may be preserved in Queen Square' Bath, and that 'it may be looked upon as a perfect sample of a well regulated place: upon the certainty of which, most of the houses are now purchased and inhabited by people of distinction and fortune'.[31] The aim of such exclusive ventures was both to encourage a sense of common identity among those dwelling there, and to segregate the occupants more effectively from the mass of people. As Wood argued, 'the intention of a square in a city is for people to assemble together: and the spot whereon they meet, ought to be separated from the ground common to men and beasts, and even to mankind in general, if decency and good order are necessary to be observed in such places of assembly'.[32]

The spatially divisive impact of the fashionable new building projects was reinforced by the beginnings of a trend among the more affluent citizens to leave the previously prestigious central districts for pleasanter dwellings in the suburbs.[33] As early as the 1730s Bourne could describe how the houses of the Close at Newcastle-upon-Tyne, 'formerly the part of the town where the principal inhabitants lived', have 'of late years . . . been forsaken and their wealthier inhabitants have chosen the higher parts of the town'. One area he undoubtedly had in mind was the suburban street to the north of the city (beyond Pilgrim Street Gate), which he found 'very well built . . . having in it some very pretty houses. . . . This street is the most pleasant of any within or without the town'.[34] In post-Restoration Leeds the gentlemen merchants vacated the main commercial street Briggate, for a district towards the south-eastern edge of the town. By the mid-eighteenth century this area itself was beginning to descend in tone (in 1816 it was called a place of 'dirt, smoke, and raff yards') as Leeds expanded and its leaders pushed further into the town's rural belt.[35] During the eighteenth century the village of Clifton emerged as an

[31] Lease quoted in Ison, *Bristol*, 142; lease quoted in Hill and Dent, *Old Square*, 17; Wood, *Bath*, 347.

[32] Wood, *Bath*, 345.

[33] Clark, *Provincial Towns*, 43-4.

[34] Bourne, *Newcastle*, 126, 151; Ellis, 'Social Relations in Newcastle', 198-9; Howell, *Newcastle*, 4, 350-2.

[35] Wilson, *Gentlemen Merchants*, 195-8; Thoresby, *Ducatus Leodiensis*, 76, and notes; Cossins, *Plan of Leeds*.

important suburb of Bristol, providing an arcadian retreat from the
environmental and social pressures of the city. In 1777 a visitor could
report

what a different world you find yourself in after crossing this large town and
got on Clifton hill: hence I thought myself in a parallel situation with Aeneas,
who after passing the abode of the unhappy, found himself in the Elysian
fields. The village of Clifton is by everybody known for the salubrity of the air,
its beautiful and extensive prospects, and the cleanness, neatness, and beauty
of its buildings. . . .[36]

2. CHARITY, LEISURE, AND SOCIAL CONTROL

For society's leaders one of the costs of their pursuit of greater
exclusiveness was the loss of those common residential and cultural
contexts in which deferential attitudes could be personally fostered. By
way of compensation, new and more overt forms of social control were
required. One area where this can be clearly discerned is that of
charity, whose development during the period was intimately associated
with that of fashionable recreations. Such close links reflected not only
the manner in which philanthropy serviced the internal needs of polite
leisure, but also its external aims. Charity was undergoing an
important shift away from personal to institutional forms of giving, as
exemplified in the rise of the blue-coat schools and subscription
hospitals. This allowed assistance to be dispensed through an inter-
mediary organization, thereby reducing the contact between rich and
poor and strengthening the barrier between the two groups. On the
other hand, institutionalization also helped neutralize the potentially
erosive influence of cultural differentiation on attitudes to authority
by accentuating philanthropy's role as an agent of education and
discipline among the poor.

The giving and receiving of alms became increasingly a symbolic
and exemplary exercise, as much an act of control as of relief. The
inmates of the new charitable establishments were normally subject to
the strictest of regimes. At the General Hospital in Bath (opened in
1742) the mixing of the sexes, smoking, bad language, and games
were forbidden inside the building, a porter was placed on the door to

[36] Pigott Diary, i, article 495; *New History of Bristol*, 107; Little, *City and County of
Bristol*, 230-7.

prevent the patients leaving without permission, and when they were allowed outside, they were not to 'loiter about the city, or to go to an alehouse, on pain of expulsion'. Similar rules operated at the Liverpool Infirmary (opened in 1749).[37] In addition to greater regulation, there was a growing tendency to physically distinguish those in receipt of assistance,[38] and to publicly display them in regimented formation. St Peter's church in early eighteenth-century Leeds possessed a special pew 'under the north wall . . . for the master and mistress of the charity school, with 40 poor boys and girls decently clad in blue', and at a service in Bath in 1742, John Penrose found the charity children 'all ranged along the Abbey . . . the boys on one side, the girls on the other, forming a lane for the congregation to pass through. They were all new clothed, in blue, with white stockings. . . . They made a decent appearance, and I was much affected with the sight.' To benefactors such spectacles were a comforting demonstration of deference and order among the poor, and a reminder of their power over such people. As Mandeville noted, 'it is diverting to the eye to see children well matched, either boys or girls, march two and two in good order; and to have them all whole and tight in the same clothes and trimming must add to the comeliness of the sight. . . . In all this there is a shadow of property'.[39] For the beneficiaries, institutional philanthropy was a form of discipline, and one intended to catch many during the impressionable years of youth. Its overtly public and ritual nature also served as a lesson to all the populace, whether objects of relief or not, of how they were expected to behave themselves.

At Bath the relationship between charity, leisure, and social control was a particularly complex affair. One of the attractions of the spa for the fashionable visitor was its apparent freedom from the huge indigenous working population that thronged London, and whose presence was inescapable, even in the West End.[40] In reality, however, the image of Bath as a safe and select retreat was one that was difficult to sustain. Servants, chairmen, craftsmen, and labourers were essential to attend to the needs of rich visitors and residents. Moreover, the very

[37] Wood, *Bath*, 297-9; G. McLoughlin, *A Short History of the First Liverpool Infirmary 1749-1824* (London and Chichester, 1978), 83-4.

[38] Taylor, *Problem of Poverty*, 29, 104; Wood, *Bath*, 297.

[39] Thoresby, *Ducatus Leodiensis*, 40; Penrose, *Letters*, 82; Mandeville, *Fable*, 288-9; and also Jones, *Charity School Movement*, 71-109.

[40] Corfield, *English Towns*, 78-9; M. Reed, *The Georgian Triumph 1700-1830* (London, 1983), 113-17.

concentration of wealthy people in the spa made it attractive to those seeking employment or alms, and also to semi-illicit and criminal elements. The lower ranks, many of them migrants and living in considerable poverty, therefore composed a substantial stratum in Bath society. It is not surprising that they were perceived by their superiors as an ever-present threat to public order. In 1730, after a city tradesman received an anonymous blackmail letter threatening him with arson and murder unless a sum of money was forthcoming, fifteen constables were dispatched 'to search and take up all vagrants and persons who will give no account of themselves, and accordingly forty were seized . . . all night-walkers [were] examined . . . and all the hedge alehouses within a mile searched for suspicious persons'. Thirty-six years later George Lucy complained that 'we are in a sad way here . . . Thursday last a gent riding out in a chaise' was 'attacked and robbed. . . . If the magistrates don't take a little more care it will be well soon if we don't lose our lives as well as our money'. Even where there was no direct danger to property or life, the presence of so many undesirable elements was seen as an unpleasant and aggravating nuisance, leading one poet to lament in 1737 that

> Beggars in shoals (whose joint permission-fee
> May serve for life, to buy the May'ress tea)
> With counterfeited mis'ry's grating din,
> Stun us alike without doors or within:
> Dogs, howling chairmen; and the jarring yells
> Of lackeys louder yet than th' Abbey bells:
> And last of colliers a rude sable breed
> (Whose brawls and filthy garb all terms exceed)
> Deafens the sense, the pass obstructs, and makes
> Of the whole town a second Elean Jakes.[41]

The presence of disorderly elements—and the existence of reports that stressed this—was cause for serious concern in a resort whose livelihood depended upon an image of exclusiveness and security. To some extent the threat could be countered by reassuring publicity. The Bucks noted that 'the magistrates take great care in preserving good order', John Wood's 1736 *Plan* advised that 'great care is taken' by the corporation 'to preserve . . . peace and good order', and his

---

[41] Neale, *Bath: A Social History*, chaps. 3 and 9; McIntyre, 'Rise of a Resort Town', 222; HMC, *Egmont MSS*, Diary i. 117; Warwickshire CRO, L6/1466; *The Diseases of Bath: A Satire* (London, 1737), 15.

Description of Bath includes ten chapters lavishly detailing 'the statute, patent, and other laws relating to the city'.[42] But more than propaganda was required to keep the plebeian peril at bay. Direct action was taken, as we have seen, to curb the unruly chairmen. However, the most serious menace came from the considerable pool of subsistence migrants.[43] In dealing with such people, an inhibiting factor for the authorities was that the infirm poor had over many generations established a customary right of access to the town's curative waters, and one that was to a limited degree embodied in legislation.[44] As Bath emerged as a major fashionable resort such rights became increasingly anachronistic and troublesome to the city fathers.

The first step towards solving the problem of the non-indigenous poor was taken in 1714, when the statute protecting their access to the baths came up for renewal and was permitted to lapse. This allowed the city's magistrates to turn the full force of the vagrancy and settlement laws on their unwanted visitors. But, on its own, this policy was unsatisfactory, since it tarnished the authorities' caring and paternalistic image. To justify the attack on the customary rights of the impoverished, a parallel scheme was needed that permitted a measure of popular access to the spa's facilities, but on a highly regulated basis. A number of smallish charitable establishments already existed in the town, but something of a more substantial nature was required. The answer was the General Hospital project, which significantly first emerged in 1716, shortly after the lapse of the protective legislation. The scheme was heavily patronized by fashionable society, but it took several decades to reach fruition, and the hospital was not opened until 1742. By the latter part of 1750 it could accommodate 110 patients, who had to be vetted and proposed by a doctor, and guaranteed by their home parish.[45]

The underlying purpose of the project, that of providing a moral lever with which to tackle the wider problem of vagrancy in the city, seems to have been widely understood. As Wood wrote,

[42] Buck, *Antiquities*, iii, Bath; Wood, *Plan of Bath*; Wood, *Bath*, 353–415.

[43] Wood, *Bath*, 279, for comments on vagrants.

[44] Ibid. 198–200, 206; James, *Baths of Bath*, 32–4, 78, 101–3; Lennard, 'Watering-Places', 4–5, 39; Cunliffe, *City of Bath*, 99–101, 105.

[45] Wood, *Bath*, 206–7, 275, 280, 303–6; James, *Baths of Bath*, 18, 68–70, 104–9; *Bath and Bristol Guide*, 17–19; G. D. Kersley, *The Three Rs: Rheumatism Rehabilitation Research as Viewed from Bath* (Bath, n.d.), 27–30.

the end and design of this charity was to provide for real objects, whose cases require the Bath waters, but cannot have them without such assistance, and to clear the city of all sorts of beggars. For these ends the magistrates of Bath were, in the strongest terms, called on by the contributors to expel and punish vagrants and impostors, while the trustees of the charity were directed to relieve no person who should . . . come to the town without their express order, to take off every pretence which idle people make for coming to Bath, and teazing people of fashion for relief.

This aim was confirmed by the fact that the statute which formally provided for the establishment of the hospital also made provision 'to rid the town of loose and disorderly people in the day time', and was accompanied by an act empowering the authorities to clear 'the town of vagabonds during the recess of the night'. In 1749 the regulations were further tightened, when the corporation agreed to fine unlicensed carriers in the city and confiscate their equipment, because 'the employment of poor strangers in carrying meat and other provisions for hire, hath encouraged many such to resort to the said city and liberties, and has burdened the inhabitants thereof with a great increase of poor'.[46]

3. PRESERVING EXCLUSIVITY

It has been the argument of this chapter that the development of fashionable urban architecture and leisure opened a widening cultural gap between polite and popular society. This was necessary to protect the exclusive nature of a more inclusive élite. However, it would be dangerous to exaggerate the degree to which cultural differentiation was effective in separating the two social groups. First, a significant number of the traditional gentry continued to patronize popular recreations, and among the urban bourgeoisie there were puritan elements who felt little sympathy with either of the two major cultures. Second, though in theory the line between those inside and outside the élite was intended to be a clear one, in practice it was inevitably blurred. The increasing imprecision in the definition of a gentleman, allied to the expansion of the middling ranks, meant that the circle of polite society must have developed a wide penumbra. Defoe hinted at the existence of groups occupying a marginal zone in his *Complete*

---

[46] Wood, *Bath*, 282, 387–8; Council Minutes, 8 Dec. 1749, BCA; and also McIntyre, 'Rise of a Resort Town', 238.

English Tradesman, when he wrote of 'young shopkeepers' who 'keep horses, ride a hunting' and 'learn dog language', of 'young beginners' who 'ape the gaieties of the court', and claimed 'that not a family, no, hardly of the meanest tradesman, but trust their friends with wine, or punch, or fine ale; and have their parlours set off with the tea table, and chocolate-pot, and the silver coffee-pot, and oftentimes an ostentation of plate into the bargain'.[47]

A third factor which undermined the segregative impact of polite culture was that parts of it had a considerable appeal among sections of the populace. Foremost were servants and some apprentices, who because of their close contact with their masters came to acquire the cultural standards of the fashionable world. Steele complained that servants 'are but in a lower degree what their masters themselves are; and usually affect an imitation of their manners', and Mandeville argued that it was 'undeniable that servants in general are daily encroaching upon masters and mistresses, and endeavouring to be more upon the level with them'.[48] Those working in the luxury trades may also have shared similar attitudes. But for the majority of the common people polite culture as a whole had a more limited appeal, and they selected from it those specific constituents that had some association with traditional pastimes and to which there was relatively easy access. A final factor which potentially narrowed the social divide was commercialization, since it tended to increase the supply and lower the price of high culture.

Fears about plebeian encroachment on polite pastimes, and a consequent lowering of standards, stimulated a chorus of complaints. The attack on the circulating library and Grub Street, with their propensity to expand the availability of publications, reflected deep-seated anxieties about the impact of commercialization on literature.[49] Pope's *Dunciad*, like Eliot's *Waste Land* two centuries later, was a bitter polemic against the threat posed by the mass market to the aesthetic standards and social exclusivity of high culture. Similar concerns about the effect of popularization on the arts were visible in the world of architecture and drama. In 1754 John Boyle, Earl of Cork and Orrery, after a satirical description of a citizen's country retreat, remarked that 'if the taste for building increases with our opulence,

[47] Defoe, *Tradesman*, 66, 71, 76.
[48] *The Spectator*, No. 88, 11 June 1711, in Ross, *Tatler and Spectator*, 294; Mandeville, *Fable*, 311; McKendrick, 'Commercialization of Fashion', 57-60.
[49] Kaufman, 'Community Library', 22-4.

for the next century we shall be able to boast of finer country seats belonging to our shopkeepers, artificers, and other plebeians, than the most pompous descriptions of Italy or Greece have ever recorded'. When in 1747 John Hippisley presented his proposals for a new theatre in Bath, one of the reasons he gave for the project was that 'the present playhouse, or rather play-room, is so small and incommodious . . . And nothing can be more disagreeable, than for persons of the first quality, and those of the lowest rank, to be seated on the same bench together'.[50]

The area of fashionable pastimes most vulnerable to popular intrusion was sport. Cricket matches often drew a considerable body of plebeian spectators, especially in the vicinity of London (where crowds could be numbered in thousands), and occasionally contests, heightened by heavy betting, degenerated into riots.[51] In 1743 the *British Champion* complained that cricket 'draws numbers of people from their employments, to the ruin of their families. It brings together crowds of apprentices and servants, whose time is not their own. It propagates a spirit of idleness. . . . It is a most notorious breach of the laws, as it gives the most open encouragement to gaming'. The *Champion* went on to ask 'can there be anything more absurd, than making . . . matches for the sake of profit, which is to be shared amongst people so remote in their quality and circumstances?'.[52] Even more attractive to popular society was horse-racing, with its large open courses (usually well endowed with drinking booths), and its rich opportunities for petty gambling. Already by the 1660s hordes of Londoners were flocking to Epsom on race days. With the explosion of meetings in the early eighteenth century, the sport became accessible to thousands of ordinary people. On the periphery of London existed a battery of petty venues (such as Belsize, Finchley, Hampstead, Highgate, Kentish Town, and Tothill Fields), 'frequented', it was said in 1738, 'chiefly by apprentices, servants, and the lowest sort of tradesmen'.[53] The common race-goer was also attracted to the great county meetings, where he mingled with his superiors in an unbecoming social *mélange*. As Drake complained in 1736, when writing of the

[50] *Connoisseur*, No. 33, 12 Sept. 1754, in Denvir, *Eighteenth Century*, 84; Wood, *Bath*, 444.
[51] Buckley, *18th Century Cricket*, 6, 18-19, 42; Altham and Swanton, *History of Cricket*, 31, 39; Brookes, *English Cricket*, 49.
[52] Reprinted in the *Gentleman's Magazine*, xiii (1743), 486.
[53] Hunn, *Epsom Racecourse*, 30; below, Appendix 7; *Craftsman*, 26 Aug. 1738, quoted in Malcolmson, *Popular Recreations*, 51.

York meeting, 'the attraction of this, at the best but barbarous diversion, not only draws in the country people in vast crowds, but the gentry, nay even the clergy and prime nobility are mixed amongst them. Stars, ribbons, and garters here lose their lustre strangely, when the noble peer is dressed like his groom.'[54]

Anxieties about the vulgarization of polite culture were therefore widespread and persistent, if generally exaggerated, reflecting the crucial role that art and leisure played in separating the social ranks. Between about 1735 and 1750 the chorus of criticism reached a special pitch of intensity, suggesting that contemporaries viewed the years as ones of crisis. This was almost certainly more than a paranoid illusion. By the 1730s the first phase of the commercialization of fashionable leisure was reaching its peak, substantially expanding the level of supply, and exerting a depressive influence on prices. It also appears that by this period many working people were enjoying the combination of a decline in food prices and a rise in money wages, enhancing their purchasing power, or if they preferred, allowing them greater time for leisure.[55] Together these factors permitted a popular invasion of specific areas of élite culture, which it was felt required positive action to halt if it was not to spiral out of control.

One way of reinforcing exclusivity was to raise the entrance fee to entertainments. In 1744 the proprietor of the Artillery cricket ground in London decided to treble his admission charges, after the previous match had been attended by 'great disorder', resolving 'for the future . . . each person pay for going into the ground sixpence, and there will be for the better conveniency of all gentlemen that favour me with their company, a ring of benches that will hold at least 800 persons'.[56] However, by this date private initiatives had been overtaken by public legislation. Between 1737 and 1740 acts were introduced which sought to restrict severely the provision of theatre (1737), gaming (1739), and horse-racing (1740). The terms of the legislation were Draconian. All theatre companies were required to obtain either letters patent from the King or a licence from the Lord Chamberlain, who was to vet all new plays and alterations to old ones. Performances were apparently to be limited to Westminster or the location of the King's residence. A wide variety of card and dice games were forbidden, and when new ones inevitably emerged to replace them, these were added to the list

[54] Drake, *Eboracum*, 241.
[55] Coleman, *Economy of England*, 102-3.
[56] *Daily Advertiser*, 30 June 1744, quoted in Buckley, *18th Century Cricket*, 18-19.

of proscribed pastimes. With a few exceptions, horse-races worth less than £50 (a hefty sum by the standards of the early Georgian turf) were declared illegal.[57] The impact of this formidable body of recreational law is difficult to gauge without further research, but it has been shown that in the case of racing its effects were considerable, pruning back the luxuriant growth of the early eighteenth century. Though the Theatre Act did not destroy provincial drama, it seems likely that it temporarily curtailed its growth, and forced managers to adopt a much lower profile. Similarly, the gambling legislation was far from ineffective, and there is evidence from York and Bath of the city authorities arresting and prosecuting illegal gamesters.[58]

The attack on fashionable recreations appears to have been a highly selective one, deliberately targeted to destroy areas of popular encroachment. It was the larger prestigious courses that survived the ravages of the Racing Act, and the terms of the theatre and gaming laws depended entirely upon local implementation, allowing magistrates to turn a blind eye to those gambling facilities and theatre companies that serviced fashionable society. At Bath gaming seems to have continued uninterrupted in the assembly rooms, and the basement of Hawley's (later Simpson's) Rooms acted as the main theatre in the spa, until drama resurfaced in about 1750 to occupy purpose-built establishments.[59] Though the leisure laws were instituted for a variety of motives (the Theatre Act was also a crude attempt to silence an increasingly vociferous political stage in the metropolis),[60] the need to reduce popular participation was undoubtedly a principal concern. This was implied during the passage of the Theatre Act, when it was 'remarked that the excess of theatrical entertainments fills both town and country with idleness and debauchery', and more directly articulated in the preamble to the Racing Act, whose restrictions were justified on the grounds of 'the great number of races for small plates, prizes, or sums of money, [which] have contributed very much to the encouragement of idleness, to the impoverishment of many of the meaner sort'.[61] In the short term this legislation may have been

---

[57] 10 Geo. II, c. 28; 12 Geo. II, c. 28; 13 Geo.II, c. 19; Wood, *Bath*, 388-91.

[58] Above, chap. 7; Rosenfeld, *Strolling Players*, 7-9; House Book, 29 Jan. 1749/50, 18 Dec. 1751, YCA; Tyte, *Bath*, 55.

[59] McIntyre, 'Rise of a Resort Town', 238; Rosenfeld, *Strolling Players*, 178-86.

[60] Loftis, *Politics of Drama*, chap. 6; Hartnoll, 'Theatre and the Licensing Act', 165-86.

[61] *Sherborne Mercury*, No. 16, 7 June 1737, quoted in Wiles, *Freshest Advices*, 228; 13 Geo. II, c. 19.

successful in stemming the tide of popularization, but in the longer run further readjustments were necessary. With the number of smaller race-meetings permanently reduced, plebeian lovers of the turf turned their attention to the great gentry meetings. The élite responded by constructing a string of elegant grandstands, such as those at Doncaster (1751), York (1754), Manchester (*c*.1760), Newmarket (1760s), Stamford (1766), and Beverley (1767), as a means of protecting their social territory.[62]

The legislation of the late 1730s represented a heavy-handed approach appropriate only to a crisis. A less dramatic solution, aimed at those on the margins of high society rather than the populace as a whole, was to redefine aesthetic standards so as to push out of the charmed circle all those who could not afford to regularly replace their cultural capital. The natural movements in fashion ensured that subtle adjustments in taste were continuously occurring, but occasionally more substantial modifications were required. Under the early Georgians classical architecture faced the threat of becoming socially debased after several decades in which the new style had permeated deep into the middling ranks. The logical way forward was to develop a more complicated and lavish version of classicism, that demanded greater expense and enhanced the opportunities for personal display. However, the road of ever-increasing degrees of ostentation was not one that stretched into infinity, and by the late 1710s the end was in sight. To elaborate on the reigning baroque style would have risked entering the realms of the aesthetically ridiculous. Moreover, as a style its social effects were increasingly counter-productive. By highlighting the ornamental and theatrical aspects of architecture, it suggested that the prestigious qualities of a building were essentially superficial ones. Therefore, considerable status could be acquired simply by refacing a house. Baroque's individualistic nature also made it difficult to establish the social value of architecture, since criticisms derived from objective external standards could be deflected by stressing the originality of a design.

To escape from this cultural cul-de-sac a major reversal of style was necessary. Palladianism was the answer. Emerging in the mid-1710s, and developed under the leadership of the suitably austere and aristocratic Earl of Burlington, the movement came to exert a powerful grip

[62] Rice, *British Turf*, ii. 28; Fairfax-Blakeborough, *Northern Turf History*, iii. 38–9, 62–3; Hodgkinson and Pogson, *Early Manchester Theatre*, 22–3; *VCH Cambridgeshire*, v. 281; RCHM, *Stamford*, pp. xliii–xliv; Gill, *Racecourses*, 33.

on English architecture until the middle of the century. The leitmotiv
of the new style was simplicity, the very obverse of the baroque stress
on elaboration. Ware claimed that 'there is a nobleness in simplicity
which is always broke in upon by ornament . . . the simple and the
natural is the proper path to beauty', and Robert Morris declared that
'a building, well proportioned, without dress, will ever please, as a
plain coat may fit as graceful, and easy, on a well-proportioned
man. . . . But if you will be lavish in ornament, your structure will
look rather like a fop, with a superfluity of gaudy tinsel, than real
decoration'.[63] Ostentation had become a sign of the uncultivated, and
all those who continued to build or live in baroque houses risked being
branded as old-fashioned, ignorant, even vulgar. Palladianism was
also thought to be founded upon absolute and objective rules: as Ware
proclaimed, 'whatever the false taste of any particular time may adopt,
the builder . . . must never suppose that caprice, or fashion, can
change the nature of right and wrong. He must remember that there is
such a thing as truth'.[64] Consequently, though it was recognized that
'genius' played an important role in design, there was to be no licence
for the sort of heroic individualism that threatened the establishment
of firm architectural standards, and by implication, encouraged
cultural and social anarchy.

By emphasizing the simple rather than the ornate in classical
architecture, Palladianism ran the risk of making polite culture more
rather than less accessible. On the face of it, a plainer house was
cheaper and easier to construct than an elaborate one. However,
two factors militated against this. First, the enormous weight that
Palladians placed on 'true proportions', 'harmony', and 'regularity',
suggested that a building had to be treated *as a whole*; change one
part, add to another, and the complete structure might have to be
rebuilt. In such circumstances, cheap ruses to keep up with the
prevailing fashions, such as refronting, the construction of extra
rooms, or the addition of superficial decoration, were inadequate.
Only a new house, or at the very least substantial alterations, would be
acceptable, and this was necessarily an expensive procedure. Second,
although Palladianism was simple it was not straightforward. The
movement's architectural treatises are profusely laced with terms such
as 'beauty', 'grace', 'elegance', 'taste', 'nobility', and 'dignity': a

63 Ware, *Body of Architecture*, 136–7; Morris, *Select Architecture*, Preface.
64 Ware, *Body of Architecture*, 295.

random eleven pages of Ware's *Complete Body of Architecture* contains twenty-seven references to beauty, five to elegance, four to taste, three to nobility, and one each to dignity and grace.[65] These keywords represented central concepts in the Palladian aesthetic, yet they are virtually undefinable. Contemporary efforts to do so tend to be less than illuminating. Wood called 'beauty . . . that sort of object which gives delight to the mind', and in 1731 a contributor to the *Weekly Register* described taste, as 'a peculiar relish for an agreeable object, by judiciously distinguishing its beauties'.[66] Such vague concepts were an ideal screen behind which to build an élitist culture. They were so elevated that only men of the most refined intellect and sensibility could understand them, and so nebulous that those outside the circle of initiates could do little to challenge such men's judgement. Palladianism thus helped to wrestle away cultural control from the mass market at a time when standards were at risk of becoming socially debased, and placed authority back into the hands of a narrow group of *cognoscenti* and patrons who could afford to employ their services. Later the secrets of the new architecture were themselves to be widely disseminated through the publication of detailed manuals, necessitating further alterations and revolutions in style. The existence of a buoyant and commercialized consumer market made the preservation of the exclusive character of polite culture a labour of Sisyphus.

This section of the book has revealed that the Urban Renaissance was a complex and ambivalent phenomenon. On the one hand, it was a socially exclusive movement, but on the other hand, much of the wealth and entrepreneurial skill behind it came from the expanding middling groups, who were pressing for admission to the ranks of the gentility. On the one hand, it serviced the needs of self-interest and social emulation, on the other, those of cultural idealism, civility, and sociability. And, on the one hand it sought to harmonize the bitter rift among the traditional rulers, and the potential division between the new and old gentry; while, on the other, as this chapter has argued, it attempted to drive a cultural wedge between the new, expanded élite and the rest of society, and strove continuously to sustain the fissure between the polite and popular spheres. Such arguments about the impact of the Urban Renaissance raise fundamental questions about

[65] Ibid. 127-37.
[66] Wood, *Origin of Building*, 73; *Weekly Register*, 6 Feb. 1731, in Denvir, *Eighteenth Century*, 63.

the nature of English society in the period. The point has now been reached where it would be useful to summarize the various themes developed in this book, and to assess their wider implications.

V
CONCLUSION

12

Town and Nation

This book has attempted to treat its subject as an integrated and evolving process, not an autonomous or static cultural movement. The emphasis has been on change, on the interaction between economic, social, political, and aesthetic factors, and on synthesis. Such an approach has led urban culture to be investigated not only (or even primarily) in its own right, but also as a window through which to view the workings of society *in toto*. Therefore, this conclusion will draw out both the narrower and wider implications of the thesis of an urban renaissance. Initially attention focuses on the impact on the town itself, but later the perspective broadens to take in the nation as a whole.

1. THE TOWN

For provincial towns the most striking effect of the Urban Renaissance was the rehabilitation of their cultural prestige. What the Reformation, warfare, and economic crises had so badly damaged, the flowering of fashionable culture restored. If Georgian York could not quite match the glories of its medieval past, the Bath of Nash, Allen, and the Woods excelled any of its earlier incarnations. By 1770 provincial towns were again at the forefront of English cultural life. Not all urban centres shared equally in the revival. The mass of smaller market towns and ports were much less affected than the regional centres and provincial capitals. But it was the larger towns that were the flagships of the urban system, the representatives by which its achievements would be judged.

Cultural prestige was no mere ornament. It possessed a real financial value which contributed significantly to the economic resurgence enjoyed by many towns. The demand for new building and rebuilding in the classical style stimulated the urban construction industry. In York the building and furnishing trades' share of the admissions to

the city's freedom grew from 7.7 per cent between 1600 and 1609, to
9.2 per cent between 1650 and 1659, and 16.2 per cent by the last
decade of the century; and in Northampton the average number of boys
apprenticed per decade to the building trades rose from one between
1562 and 1642, to nine between 1654 and 1715, and twenty-eight
between 1716 and 1776.[1] Though the initial rise at Northampton may
be explained by the fire of 1675, the later figure reflects the
continuing importance of the building sector. Leisure services would
not normally have occupied as large a niche in the urban economy as
the construction industry, but in the resorts and county centres they
generated substantial extra income and employment. However, of
deeper economic significance than the direct contribution of cultural
provision were its indirect effects. More fashionable and comfortable
housing, better civic facilities, and the existence of an appealing new
range of recreational services were critical in attracting the wealthy to
visit towns and reside in them. The presence of such people stimulated
the urban economy as a whole, particularly raising the level of demand
for superior lodging and feeding facilities, domestic and professional
services, and luxury crafts and trades. In a number of shire towns and
provincial capitals, which had undergone an economic crisis during
the early modern period as their staple industries declined, catering to
the gentry became their high road to recovery.

An influx of gentry and their families inevitably affected the urban
social structure. The impact might only be of a temporary and superficial nature, as when York hosted the great and gallant during its
annual race week. On the other hand, the gentry who resided for the
season at a shire town or resort would have had a more sustained
effect. As long as they or people of a similar background returned
regularly, they would have altered the long-term social profile of these
centres. The gentrification of the town was not only due to the presence
of an increasingly mobile rural élite. Because urban life became so
attractive, men and women of independent means were choosing to
settle permanently in fashionable centres. To these so-called pseudo-
gentry can be added the growing ranks of the professions and
merchants, who no longer found it necessary to flee the town to pursue
status and civilized living. The rise in the cultural prestige of the larger
urban centres, as well as directly expanding their upper strata, must
also have indirectly enlarged the domestic service sector of their

[1] *VCH York*, 167; Everitt, *Ways and Means*, 36-7.

working population, as is suggested by the relatively high ratios of women to men generally found in these communities.[2]

To what extent did the Urban Renaissance make provincial towns more *urban*? This is an important question, but a difficult one to answer, since many of the features of the cultural revival can also be discovered in the countryside. Classical architecture was universally used in the new or rebuilt country houses of aristocrats, gentlemen, and prosperous farmers, and music-making, drama, reading, dancing, walking, bowling, cricket, hunting, horse-riding, and horse-racing were all aspects of fashionable rural life. However, there were differences between town and country in the particular *forms* these elements took, and in the *contexts* in which they occurred. These variations helped to accentuate urban identity. Many public buildings, such as civic halls, market halls and crosses, exchanges, and custom-houses, were quite specific to the town. By indicating the existence of a civic body or commercial function, and proclaiming this in an elaborate physical form, they both identified and celebrated precisely those features which distinguished the urban from the rural environment. The grand mayoral house at York (1725–30), with the city arms framed in the pediment (see Fig. 11), or the splendid merchants' exchange at Bristol (1741–3) (see Fig. 12), adorned with the arms of the city (south front) and the merchants' company (courtyard), declared their respective settlements to be corporate or trading communities, and thus quite different from the surrounding villages.[3] The sheer quantity and quality of public buildings, and this would include types such as churches and almshouses which could also be found in the countryside, further distinguished towns from their rural neighbours.

If the heavy investment in public edifices reinforced urban consciousness, so also did that in domestic architecture. Again it was a matter of different forms. Pressure of space generally made compactness an important criterion in the design of the classical town house, unlike that of rural residences, leaving relatively little scope for the treatment of the area surrounding a dwelling, and throwing the emphasis on the façade and particularly the door-case. The proximity of other properties also encouraged builders to adopt a broadly common approach to design, and to exercise a certain restraint in decorative treatments, so as to avoid any serious clashes of style. A

---

[2] D. Souden, 'Migrants and the Population Structure of Later Seventeenth-Century Provincial Cities and Market Towns', in Clark, *Provincial Towns*, 149–61.
[3] *VCH York*, 543–4; Wood, *Exchange of Bristol*, 25.

number of developers took matters even further, seeking to stress the
common identity of town buildings by combining individual residences into larger blocks, such as formal terraces, crescents, circuses,
squares, and planned units. With the exception of estate villages, such
building forms were a unique and (to a large extent) novel urban
feature that highlighted the visual differences between town and
country.

It is possible that the shared physical environment of multi-dwelling
units, such as crescents and squares, encouraged their occupants to live
more public and sociable lives. Certainly these qualities distinguished
town recreations from their rural counterparts. Urban plays, concerts,
and assemblies were normally freely open to all respectable people and
were deliberately designed to promote social contact. Access was not
restricted, as during a country-house ball or musical evening, to family
and friends. Similarly, whereas walking and riding in the countryside
were essentially private pleasures to be shared at most with a few close
associates, the promenades of York and Tunbridge Wells and the
riding rings at Epsom and Bath were public arenas. The general trend
towards a more gregarious pattern of leisure also enhanced the specifically urban content of several sports, such as racing and hunting,
which increasingly needed the sort of service infrastructure which only
a town could offer to justify their role as sociable and not merely
physical recreations.

Due to its public character, urban leisure attracted people of a wider
social and geographical background than did rural pastimes. This
made it more cosmopolitan, and more of a channel for communicating novel or differing attitudes and opinions. The Pump Room,
walks, and assembly houses at Bath must have been extraordinarily
rich and bustling markets for the exchange of news, gossip, knowledge, and fashions among the nation's élite. Communication and
innovation were also associated with the town because of its close links
with the literary and intellectual arts. Urban printers, publishers,
bookshops, libraries, clubs, lectures, inns, and coffee-houses were all
powerful media for the transmission of new ideas and vogues. And
because these were usually imported, especially from the metropolis,
urban culture was inclined to be more outward-looking than that in
the countryside.

Not all aspects of the cultural renaissance strengthened the urban
character of towns, however. The development of public walks and
gardens, and the townsman's private passion for horticulture and its

related societies, could be seen as a reaction against the de-naturalizing impact of urbanization. Most walks were lined with trees or hedges, and many were located on the town's periphery, almost seducing their promenaders out of the city and into the country. Even today, the New Walk at York, having enticed its strollers along the tree-lined banks of the Ouse, gently decants them into a lush meadow (see Fig. 16). Several spas near London, particularly Epsom and Tunbridge Wells, seem to have deliberately cultivated a rural profile to attract their metropolitan patrons. However, this did not represent a threat to urban identity, for the nature re-created in town gardens and viewed from the carefully tended corridors of the promenade was not that to be found in the countryside. It was a sanitized and idealized rusticity without muck and smells, one created for pleasure rather than production, a pastoral myth born out of the bustle and pressures of the city. In essence it was a townsman's view of the countryside, and as such was as much a part of urban culture as the coffee-house or assembly room.

2. THE NATION

It might be imagined that the Urban Renaissance, with its emphasis on the special cultural identity of the town, intensified the divide between the urban and rural spheres. The contrasts between the two types of environment, and the contribution of leisure to accentuating these, are certainly evident in the literature of the period.[4] However, it would be dangerous to assume that such accounts reflected a general or deepening alienation between town and country. In reality, the two worlds were inextricably bound together, particularly at the provincial level. The various roles played by the town—centre for the exchange of agricultural and industrial raw materials and products, provider of administrative, political, and recreational services—meant that urban and rural communities complemented rather than contradicted each other. Indeed, the notion of a town fundamentally dissociated from the country made little sense until the nineteenth century, when centralized industrial production allowed the city a self-sustaining economic identity. This mutuality of interests was also reflected at the

---

[4] Thomas, *Man and the Natural World*, 243–54; H. Love (ed.), *The Penguin Book of Restoration Verse* (Harmondsworth, 1968), 245–85; Davison, *Eighteenth-Century English Verse*, 91–110.

level of the individual. The vast majority of country dwellers must have made regular use of urban markets and services. A significant proportion of ordinary working people would have spent a part of their lives in urban employment, and the country gentry made frequent and lengthy visits to the resorts and county centres, and were probably more urbanized than the permanent inhabitants of the smaller towns. Therefore, the urban and the rural in early modern England were different but interrelated parts of the same organism: and if the full impact of the Urban Renaissance is to be understood, we must look beyond the confines of the town to the nation as a whole.

In the years after the Restoration the English economy entered a new phase of growth and prosperity. The cultural renaissance contributed to this at several levels. First, there was the direct input through the urban building and recreational industries, and more broadly through the town's luxury craft, trade, and service sectors. Second, because the cultural economy was often highly innovative and business-oriented, it helped to educate those involved in it, or those who used its products and services, to an acceptance of change, modernity, and commercialization.[5] It is not too far-fetched to suggest that when the rural aristocracy and gentry engaged in the highly competitive world of horse-racing as owners, breeders, or gamblers, they were being subtly persuaded to more capitalistic beliefs. Moreover, the very association of the commercial ethic with high art and the élite helped to legitimize it, and therefore contributed to the general acceptance of values that were conducive to economic development.

Third, much of the economic growth of the eighteenth century and the Industrial Revolution was founded on the demand for luxury and semi-luxury goods, such as light and highly patterned cloths, ribbons, fancy figurines and tableware, 'toys', buckles, and buttons. If a market was to be created for these types of products, they required appropriate contexts in which they could be displayed. For the consumer, the classical town house provided a suitably elegant show-case for domestic extravagance, while theatres, assembly rooms, town halls, and walks provided for the public display of personal finery. For producer and shopkeeper, such urban arenas accommodated a perpetual real-life fashion show, stimulating new consumer aspirations and demands.

Luxury products and services were intimately associated with the pursuit of status, since they were one of the principal means by which

[5] Plumb, 'Acceptance of Modernity', 316–34.

the élite acquired and consolidated its position in society. Thus the rapid expansion of the luxury economy promoted by the Urban Renaissance allowed more and more people access to gentility. The major beneficiaries were the wealthier middling groups (such as merchants, doctors, lawyers, and military officers), the gentry's younger sons (many of whom entered trade and the professions), and the pseudo-gentry. The result was a reshaping of the nation's social structure, as a broader and more diverse élite began to emerge. In this process the town was the crucible of change, providing the cultural artefacts and channels through which status could be acquired and the new and traditional social elements fused together.

The pursuit of personal prestige inevitably meant that fashionable town life, for all its apparent ease and elegance, was often riddled with ambition and jealousy. None the less, polite culture also possessed a genuinely elevated and altruistic side, the principal aim of which was the creation of a more civilized humanity. Some saw this mission as part of a specifically urban enlightenment, aimed at dispelling a pervasive rural brutishness and ignorance. Though this represented a particular view of the civilizing process, towns undoubtedly played an important part in disseminating more cosmopolitan, literate, educated, and refined attitudes among the more affluent country dwellers, and in eroding their attachment to vernacular traditions and pastimes.

Fashionable urban culture also appears to have possessed a political dimension. Though this is not a subject examined in any detail in this study, it is one that demands consideration, albeit of a speculative nature. Long-term political stability depends to a large extent on society meeting the aspirations of the individuals and groups within it. From the late seventeenth century the personal wealth produced by national economic prosperity, allied to a series of large-scale wars, was creating a considerable growth in the middling ranks, which brought with it a rise in their social and political expectations. A failure to reasonably satisfy these might have engendered frustration and potentially serious conflict. On the other hand, were the aspirations of the *nouveau riche* accommodated too easily, and without respect for the traditional élite, then there might have been a dangerous conservative backlash: some of the Tory propaganda of Anne's reign was inspired by this.[6] The Urban Renaissance provided the cultural mechanisms through which the social expectations of the new and old gentry could

---

[6] G. S. Holmes and W. A. Speck (eds.), *The Divided Society: Party Conflict in England 1694-1716* (London, 1967), 131-8; Holmes, *British Politics*, 148-82.

be expressed, negotiated, and to the extent necessary to retain stability, realized. This may have led to a good deal of inter-personal friction, but there were enough winners on both sides to prevent it degenerating into a conflict of social groups. The recreational forums in which exchanges of status were transacted may also have been employed as channels of political influence, though verifying this would require further investigation.

One of the reasons the new urban recreational facilities were so effective in ensuring the safe pursuit of status was the stress they laid on polite behaviour and sociability. This encouraged free competition unimpaired by barriers of rank or birth, while simultaneously suppressing the potentially explosive personal conflict that was generated during such rivalry. If civility and sociability were the flux that helped weld together the new and old gentry, they may also have contributed to bridging the divisions that had internally divided the latter group since the Civil War. The new culture's antipathy to ideological and religious bigotry, its emphasis on aesthetic rather than overtly political values, and its celebration of polite and gregarious behaviour provided a healing current to help mend the self-inflicted injuries of the traditional élite. The lowering of the party-political temperature from the 1720s may owe something to this influence.

But the encouragement of social intercourse had its limits. Access to fashionable urban life was intended to be restricted to those whose wealth or existing status gave them a legitimate claim to gentility, thus driving a cultural wedge between the upper and middling ranks on the one hand, and the populace on the other. It was a division accentuated by the nature of polite leisure, whose character and organization in so many ways contradicted that of traditional customs and recreations. As a consequence, the élite increasingly withdrew from participating in or patronizing the latter activities, and even sought to attack them. The common people now became the principal supporters and defenders of the older pastimes, which were thus transformed into a genuinely *popular* culture. The emergence of a true class society had to wait until the late eighteenth or early nineteenth century and further industrial and urban growth, but increasing cultural differentiation was already sowing the seeds of social polarization a century earlier.

The cracks appearing in the social fabric were not yet chasms. One reason for this was that although in theory fashionable urban culture should only be open to legitimate consumers, in practice it was difficult to enforce this. Petty traders decorated their houses with classical ornament, domestic servants read their masters' and mistresses' books, and apprentices and working people flocked to the proliferating race-courses. A further reason was that a number of the older gentry were loath to abandon cherished pastimes simply because these were now thought to be old-fashioned, uncivilized, and inferior. Such men often perceived traditional recreations and customs as part of a pater-nalistic organic society, to whose existence they hung on tenaciously. The social distinction between polite and popular leisure was therefore not a rigid one, and many individuals and groups operated outside their appropriate cultural spheres. However, there were strong pres-sures on the squirearchy to conform to the new segregative norms: and where the select character of fashionable pastimes was seriously threatened by popularization, then positive action was taken (such as through legislation or the redefinition of aesthetic standards) to preserve exclusivity. Though the Urban Renaissance promoted greater cohesion among the upper echelons of the nation, within society as a whole it was undoubtedly a divisive force.

This book opened with a description of a disaster, that of the fire of Warwick in 1694. It ends with a visual account which demonstrates how successfully the town responded to this calamity, creating a landscape at once grander and more refined than that before. In the mid-eighteenth century the Venetian scenic artist Canaletto was working in England. One of the men who called on his services was Lord Brooke (later Earl of Warwick). As well as painting several glowing canvases of the castle, Canaletto was apparently also commis-sioned to produce a drawing (1754–5) of the post-fire town, which had been rebuilt under the close direction of Brooke's grandfather (see Fig. 27). The view is of the very heart of the new Warwick, looking along the axis from the castle, through the crossing of Church, Castle, High, and Jury Streets, towards the church itself. In the foreground stands the fine baroque town hall of the late 1720s; the middleground is filled with fashionably dressed family groups strolling along the promenade formed by the widened crossing area and Church Street; and the background is occupied by the grandiosely rebuilt St Mary's and its new square, justifying Canaletto's title for the work, *Ingresso nella Piazza de Varik* (entrance to the square at Warwick). It is entirely fitting that this delightful sketch should have been executed by an artist from Italy, the cradle of the European Renaissance, for the influence of that great movement is everywhere evident in the scene

Fig. 27. 'Ingresso nella Piazza de Varik' (Entrance to the Square at Warwick), drawn by A. Canaletto, 1754–5

depicted. English provincial towns may have joined the mainstream of continental culture late in the day, but by the mid-eighteenth century, as a result of their own local renaissance, they were indubitably part of it.

APPENDICES

The following appendices should not be considered definitive or comprehensive, but should be treated as working handlists, which will need to be added to and modified as a consequence of further research. Asterisked items are those where I have evidence that a physical structure, facility, or event still survives (though squares are omitted, since many which retain the original name have subsequently been heavily altered).

APPENDIX 1

Provincial Urban Squares 1680–1770

BATH. (i) *Queen Square*. John Wood obtained the lease of the property to be used for the first part of the square Nov. 1728. Further leases acquired 1730–4. Began to prepare the ground for the foundations of the first houses Dec. 1728. Laid the first building stone Jan. 1729. Completed 1736.[1]

(ii) *Kingsmead Square*. Began to prepare the ground for building c.1727.

(iii) *Beaufort Square*. Began to prepare the ground for building c.1727.[2]

BIRMINGHAM. *The Square*. John Pemberton purchased Priory Close, on which the square was to be built, 1697. Several houses completed by 1713.[3]

BRISTOL. (i) *Queen Square*. First lease granted Oct. 1699. Construction appears to be underway by Feb. 1700, and most of the ground bordering the square was built upon by 1718. Last leases granted 1725, and seems completed by 1727.[4]

(ii) *St James's Square*. Ground prepared for building c.1707. Completed by 1716.[5]

(iii) *Orchard Street* (part of which was originally named Orchard Square). Proposals first put to corporation 1715. First lease granted 1718.[6]

(iv) *Dowry Square*. Ground prepared for building soon after 1720. Houses still being added 1746.[7]

(v) *King Square*. Ground prepared for building 1737. First houses erected c.1740. Considerable building activity c.1760. Still unfinished 1772.[8]

(vi) *Brunswick Square*. Building of first house begun 1766. Square still incomplete 1784.[9]

LIVERPOOL. *Derby Square*. Built on the site of the castle (demolished early 18th cent.) which was leased to the town in 1704. Corporation gave committee 'power to finish the new buildings and alterations in and about the castle now called Derby Square', 1709. Council orders that 'the houses over the piazzas in Derby Square be lotted and leased out to the highest bidder', 1725.[10]

---

[1] Wood, *Bath*, 243, 246.
[2] Ibid. 242.
[3] Hill and Dent, *Old Square*, 10, 16–17.
[4] Ison, *Bristol*, 141–4; Bristol Common Council Proceedings, 28 Feb. 1699/1700, Bristol AO.
[5] Ison, *Bristol*, 150.
[6] Ibid. 152–4.   [7] Ibid. 158–9.   [8] Ibid. 174–5.   [9] Ibid. 204–9.
[10] Picton, *Liverpool Municipal Archives*, 34–5, 60–1; Chandler, *Liverpool*, 55, 108.

MANCHESTER. (i) *St Ann's Square*. Act of Parliament passed for building St Ann's church 1708. The building of the square followed shortly after this. Laid out and planted with trees by 1720.[11]

(ii) *St James's Square*. Laid out *c*.1739.[12]

WARWICK. *The Square*. Built as part of the reconstruction of the town after the fire of 1694. Rebuilding commission ordered 'a large and spacious place, square, or street, to be opened over against the west front of' St Mary's, July 1695. Appears to be largely completed by Sept. 1704, when 'all the proprietors of houses in the new square' were ordered to make payments towards pitching the area.[13]

WHITEHAVEN. *St Nicholas's churchyard and burial ground*. Part of the late seventeenth-century development of the new town. Though not called a square, the intention was to treat it as such, with the corner houses of all the incoming streets (with the exception of Lowther Street) facing on to the area rather than on to the side streets. Church built 1687-93.[14]

---

[11] Aikin, *Manchester*, 186; Saxon, *Story of St Ann's Church*, 3; Defoe, *Tour*, ii. 262.
[12] Chalklin, *Provincial Towns*, 62.
[13] Memorials, 30 July 1695, 30 Mar. and 21 Sept. 1704.
[14] Draft typescript of chap. 2 of the RCHM forthcoming volume on Whitehaven.

APPENDIX 2

Provincial Town Halls and Mayoral Residences 1655–1770

ABINGDON. (i) County or Town Hall.* Built 1678–*c*.82. Open-arcaded ground floor with large sessions hall above; hipped roof, balustrade, and cupola. Cost *c*.£2,800. Used for assizes and public functions, therefore as much a county as a town hall.

(ii) Guildhall or Borough Buildings.* Contains the council-chamber built 1731–4, and the Bear Room or small council-chamber built 1759.[1]

BATH. Guildhall. Built 1625. Open-arcaded ground floor with accommodation above. Sash-windows added and interior wainscoted, 1710 and 1718. Extended 1724–6. Demolished and rebuilt* on a new site in High Street, outside the area of the street, *c*.1777.[2]

BEDFORD. Market house and town hall. Built *c*.1683, but never completed. Converted into a workshop. Arcaded ground floor; above, 'rooms which were designed for the session and public business of the town'.[3]

BEVERLEY. Guildhall.* Refaced and remodelled *c*.1760. Fine court-room and jury room. Present facade of 1832.[4]

BLANDFORD FORUM. Town Hall.* Built 1734, after earlier one destroyed in the fire of 1731. Ground floor has open loggia on street side; court-room and council-chamber above.[5]

BRACKLEY. Town Hall.* Built 1706. Arched ground floor windows, originally forming an open arcade; hipped roof and cupola.[6]

BRISTOL. Council House. Either newly built or substantially rebuilt 1701–4. Two lofty storeys of five bays, with rooms on each floor. Cost £1,147.[7]

CARLISLE. Town Hall.* Built 1717. Open ground floor. Later much altered.[8]

CHICHESTER. Council House.* Built 1731–3. Open-arcaded ground floor; council-chamber above; assembly rooms added to rear 1781–3.[9]

[1] Oswald, *Old Towns Revisited*, 18–25; Gilyard-Beer, *County Hall, Abingdon*.

[2] Wood, *Bath*, 213–14; Council Minutes, 26 June 1710, 16 May 1718, 1 Dec. 1724, 10 May 1725, 26 June 1726, BCA; McIntyre, 'Rise of a Resort Town', 231.

[3] Fiennes, *Journeys*, 340.

[4] *BE Yorkshire: York and the East Riding*, 184–5; Hall, *Beverley*, 49–50.

[5] RCHM, *Dorset*, iii, Part 1, 22–3.

[6] *BE Northamptonshire*, 117.

[7] Bristol Common Council Proceedings, 23 Oct. 1699, Bristol AO; Ison, *Bristol*, 90–1.

[8] Morrice, *Stuart and Baroque*, 149.

[9] *BE Sussex*, 172.

DEVIZES. Old Town Hall or the Cheese Hall.* Built 1750-2. Arched ground floor windows, originally forming an open arcade. Built to replace the old guildhall, and referred to originally as a 'public hall', it is unclear whether it was used for council meetings. In 1806-8 a new town hall* was built nearby. [10]

DONCASTER. Mansion House.* Built 1745-8. Entrance hall and grand staircase on ground floor; splendid ballroom on first floor. Cost £8,170. [11]

EYNSHAM. Town Hall.* Built late 17th cent. Originally open-arcaded ground floor (now blocked up), with room above. [12]

FARINGDON. Town Hall.* Built late 17th cent. Arcaded ground floor. [13]

HEREFORD. Guildhall. Built soon after 1759. [14]

HIGH WYCOMBE. Guildhall.* Built 1757. Open-arcaded ground floor with two rooms above; cupola. [15]

LEEDS. The Town or Moot Hall. Partly rebuilt and extended 1710-11. Open-arcaded ground floor with accommodation above; cupola. Cost £210. [16]

LICHFIELD. Guildhall.* Rebuilt c.1707. Cost £83. [17]

LIVERPOOL. (i) Exchange and Town Hall. Built 1673-5. Open-arcaded ground floor used by merchants; 'a very handsome town hall' above; tower and cupola. [18]

(ii) The Exchange. Built 1749-54. 'Spacious covered piazza' on ground floor; separate town hall, council-room, and assembly room above; dome and cupola. [19]

MORPETH. Town Hall. Built 1714. Reconstructed to original design after fire of c.1875. [20]

NEWCASTLE-UPON-TYNE. (i) Exchange and Town Court. Built 1655-8. Arcaded ground floor, containing a weigh-house and a house for the collection of the town revenues; a separate court-room, town chamber, and withdrawing-room above. Cost over £10,000. [21]

---

[10] *BE Wiltshire*, 209, 212-13; Cunnington, *Devizes*, 220-2; R. Sandell, *Devizes Town Trail* (Devizes, n.d.).

[11] *BE Yorkshire: The West Riding* (Harmondsworth, 1979), 183-4; Grady, 'Public Buildings in the West Riding', Gazetteer.

[12] *BE Oxfordshire*, 601.

[13] *BE Berkshire* (Harmondsworth, 1975), 141.

[14] Lobel, *Atlas*, i, Hereford, 11.

[15] *BE Buckinghamshire*, 163-4.

[16] D. Linstrum, *Historic Architecture of Leeds* (Leeds, 1969), 20; Grady, 'Public Buildings in the West Riding', Gazetteer; Cossins, *Plan of Leeds*.

[17] P. Laithwaite, *The History of the Lichfield Conduit Land Trust* (Lichfield, 1947), 57-8; *BE Staffordshire*, 194.

[18] Fiennes, *Journeys*, 184; Tupling, 'Lancashire Markets', 4-6; Chandler, *Liverpool*, 195.

[19] Enfield, *Liverpool*, 58-9; Chandler, *Liverpool*, 202.

[20] Morrice, *Stuart and Baroque*, 173.

[21] Bourne, *Newcastle*, 125; Brand, *Newcastle*, i. 29-30; Fiennes, *Journeys*, 210.

(ii) Mansion House or mayoral residence. Built *c*.1691. Cost £6,000. [22]

PETERBOROUGH. Guildhall.* Built 1671. Open-arcaded ground floor; accommodation above. [23]

PORTSMOUTH. Guildhall. Rebuilt 1738. Open-arcaded ground floor; hall, record room, etc. above; cupola and dome. [24]

PRESTON. Town Hall. Repairs and improvements 1705 and 1716. Addition of a cupola 1718-19. Substantially rebuilt 1727-8. Guildhall built at cost of *c*. £1,650, adjoining to the town hall, 1760-2. Repair of the jury room 1763. [25]

ROCHESTER. Guildhall.* Built 1687. Open-arcaded ground floor; hall above. [26]

ROTHERHAM. Town Hall and Grammar School. Built 1739-43. School on ground floor; hall above. Cost £550. [27]

RYE. Town Hall.* Designed 1743. Open-arcaded ground floor; council-chamber above; parapet and cupola. [28]

SALISBURY. Council House. Fairly extensive repairs 1734 and 1757. Burnt down 1780. [29]

SHEFFIELD. Town Hall. Built 1700-1. Ground floor used for shops and prison cells; room above used for quarter sessions, manor court, and meetings of the town trustees. Cost £220. [30]

TAMWORTH. Town Hall.* Built 1701. Open-arcaded ground floor; accommodation above; cupola. [31]

WARWICK. Court House.* Built *c*.1724-30. Kitchen in basement; mayor's parlour on ground floor; assembly room on first floor. Cost £2,254. [32]

WIGAN. Town Hall. Built 1720-3. Cost well over £2,000. Demolished 1882. [33]

WINCHESTER. Guildhall.* Built 1713. Arcaded ground floor, originally open. Now Lloyds Bank. [34]

---

[22] Bourne, *Newcastle*, 127; Brand, *Newcastle*, i. 56.

[23] BE *Bedfordshire and the County of Huntingdon and Peterborough* (Harmondsworth, 1968), 326.

[24] N. W. Surry and J. H. Thomas (eds.), *Portsmouth Record Series: Book of Original Entries* (Portsmouth, 1976), p. xviii.

[25] Council Minutes, 3 Dec. 1705, 4 July 1709, 27 July and 13 Aug. 1716, 26 June and 31 July 1718, 31 Mar. and 9 July 1719, 6 Feb. 1726/7, 10 May and 20 Sept. 1728, 28 Sept. 1759, 22 Feb. and 20 June 1760, 11 May 1761, 13 Apr. 1762, 22 Apr. and 1 June 1763, PCMSS; White Book, 4 Aug. 1727, 2 May, 20 June. and 9 Aug. 1760, 23 Apr. 1761, PCMSS; Hewitson, *History of Preston*, 356-7.

[26] BE *West Kent and the Weald* (Harmondsworth, 1969), 472.

[27] Grady, 'Public Buildings in the West Riding', Gazetteer.

[28] BE *Sussex*, 597.

[29] *VCH Wiltshire*, vi. 87, 109.

[30] Grady, 'Public Buildings in the West Riding', Gazetteer.

[31] BE *Staffordshire*, 278.

[32] Kemp, *History of Warwick*, 173-7; Styles, 'Corporation of Warwick', 72.

[33] Tupling, 'Lancashire Markets', 7 n. 1.

[34] BE *Hampshire*, 715.

WINDSOR. Town Hall or Guildhall.* Built 1689-90. Arcaded ground floor; accommodation above. Cost £2,000.[35]

WORCESTER. Guildhall.* Built 1721-3. Nine bays in centre, with three-bay wings (two bays deep); ground floor containing long entrance hall; grand assembly room above; lantern.[36]

YARM. Town Hall.* Built 1710. Arcaded ground floor, originally open; accommodation above; hipped roof and lantern.[37]

YORK. Mansion House or mayoral residence.* Largely built 1725-30. First used for public entertainment Oct. 1727; first occupied by mayor 1730; state-room not finished until Feb. 1731. Kitchens and offices in semi-basement; dining-room, robing-room, and butler's pantry on ground floor; state or banqueting room on first floor; bedrooms on second floor.[38]

Explanatory Note: It is not always easy to distinguish between a town hall and (a) a county hall, or (b) a market hall. Most town halls of this period would in fact have accommodated a market or other commercial activities on the ground floor. The buildings listed here are ones that appear to have possessed some type of civic function.

[35] *BE Berkshire*, 301.
[36] Green, *History and Antiquities of Worcester*, ii. 6-11; *BE Worcestershire*, 323.
[37] *BE Yorkshire: The North Riding*, 407.
[38] House Book, 9 Oct. 1727, 2 July and 5 Dec. 1729, 1 Feb. 1730/1, YCA; *VCH York*, 543-4.

APPENDIX 3

Provincial Urban Theatres 1700–1770

BATH. (i) Junction of Borough Walls and Vicarage Lane. Built 1705. Cost £1,300.

(ii) Kingsmead Street. Operating by 1750.

(iii) Orchard Street. Opened 1750. Cost of original scheme, launched in 1747, c. £1,000 (Wood), 70 × £20 shares = £1,400 (Tyte). This may have been altered later.[1]

BEVERLEY. Nos. 90–92 Walkergate. Built c.1754.[2]

BIRMINGHAM. (i) Moor Street. Built c.1740.

(ii) King Street. Built 1752.

(iii) Smallbrook Street. Operating by 1759.[3]

BRISTOL. (i) Newly erected playhouse 1706.

(ii) St Augustine's Back. In regular use by 1726. Closed down 1731. Converted into an assembly room shortly before 1742.

(iii) Jacob's Well, Clifton. Built 1729. Adjoined an alehouse or tavern. Cost 18 × £300 shares = £5,400 (but this figure seems rather high). It has been suggested (Barry) that this was a temporary building, and that Jacob's Well only opened as Bristol's chief theatre in 1737.

(iv) King Street. Built 1764–6. Cost 48 × £50 shares + an extra £1,400 subscribed by various patrons + an advance of £1,000 = £4,800.[4]

COLCHESTER. Behind the Moot Hall. Built 1764. Accommodated 200.[5]

HARROGATE. High Harrogate. Operating by 1769.[6]

HULL. Lowgate. Operating by 1743.[7]

IPSWICH. (i) St Nicholas Street. Operating by 1733.

(ii) Tankard Street. Built c.1736. Appears to have been rebuilt 1754.[8]

LICHFIELD. Playhouse existed from c.1736.[9]

LIVERPOOL. (i) Old Ropery. Earliest regular theatre in Liverpool.

(ii) Drury Lane. Renovated and reopened 1759.

---

[1] Wood, *Bath*, 223, 444–6; Rosenfeld, *Strolling Players*, 182–3; Tyte, *Bath*, 104–5.

[2] Hall, *Beverley*, 3.

[3] Hutton, *Birmingham*, 125, 127; Smith, *Music in Birmingham*, 16–18.

[4] Barker, *Bristol at Play*, 4–12; Ison, *Bristol*, 123–7; Watts, *Theatrical Bristol*, 41–2, 63–72; Barry, 'Cultural Life of Bristol', 187–9.

[5] Brown, 'Colchester in the Eighteenth Century', 163; Morant, *Essex*, i. 114.

[6] Jennings, *Harrogate and Knaresborough*, 236, and plate 15.

[7] Rosenfeld, *Strolling Players*, 132.

[8] Ibid. 66, 85, 98–9.

[9] H. Thorpe, *Lichfield: A Study of its Growth and Function* (1950–1), 56 n. 190.

(iii) Theatre Royal, Williamson Square. Opened 1772. Cost 30 × £200 shares = £6,000.[10]

MANCHESTER. King Street or Marsden Street. Operating by 1753, and probably built around this date.[11]

NEWCASTLE-UPON-TYNE. Walls of St Bartholomew's Hospital, near the Nun's Gate. Built *c*.1748.[12]

NORTHAMPTON. Theatre in the town by the end of George II's reign.[13]

NOTTINGHAM. Theatre built 1760.[14]

NORWICH. (i) The White Swan, near the west end of St Peter Mancroft. The chief theatre in the city, and the regular playhouse of the Norwich company until 1758. Operating at least by 1723. Altered and improved 1739, 1742, and 1747.

(ii) The Angel, in the Market-Place. Operating by 1692. Gallery collapsed in 1699 and was reconstructed in 1722. Plays were also performed at the Red Lion and the King's Arms, though it is unclear if separate and permanent playhouses existed at these inns.

(iii) Near Chapel Field and adjacent to the assembly rooms. Built 1757-8.[15]

PLYMOUTH. Theatre built sometime between 1736 and 1760.[16]

PORTSMOUTH. High Street. Operating by 1750. New theatre, possibly on different site in High Street, opened 1761.[17]

PRESTON. Fishergate. Called the 'Old Theatre' in 1762, and in use in that year for 'pantomime entertainments, humorous farces', etc.[18]

SAXMUNDHAM. New theatre built 1745.[19]

SCARBOROUGH. New theatre built 1767. In use 1768.[20]

SHEFFIELD. Norfolk Street. Theatre and assembly rooms. Completed 1762. Theatre accommodated 800. Cost of theatre and assembly rooms over £3,000. Raised by £100 shares.[21]

SOUTHAMPTON. New theatre built 1765-6.[22]

STAMFORD. New theatre, probably built 1768.[23]

---

[10] Chandler, *Liverpool*, 442; Enfield, *Liverpool*, 62.

[11] Hodgkinson and Pogson, *Early Manchester Theatre*, 3-24.

[12] Rosenfeld, *Strolling Players*, 164.

[13] Everitt, 'Urban Inn', 119.

[14] Hodgkinson and Pogson, *Early Manchester Theatre*, 50.

[15] Rosenfeld, *Strolling Players*, 42, 53, 64-6, 90-1; Burley, *Players of East Anglia*, 1-7.

[16] Chalklin, 'Building for Cultural Purposes', 53.

[17] Sargeant, *Portsmouth Theatres*, 3-6.

[18] *Guild Merchant of Preston*, 16-17.

[19] Rosenfeld, *Strolling Players*, 66.

[20] Chalklin, 'Building for Cultural Purposes', 54; HMC, *Verulam MSS*, 237.

[21] Grady, 'Public Buildings in the West Riding', Gazetteer.

[22] Hare, *Georgian Theatre*, 65; Chalklin, 'Building for Cultural Purposes', 54.

[23] Hodgkinson and Pogson, *Early Manchester Theatre*, 47-8.

STOCKPORT. Theatre operating in 1763.[24]

WHITEHAVEN. Roper Street. Opened 1769.[25]

YORK. (i) Lord Irwin's Yard, near the Minster. Opened 1734. Built from an adapted tennis court.

(ii) Mint Yard. Opened 1744. Built over the vaulted cloisters of the united hospitals of St Leonard and St Peter. New theatre built on site of old one, opened 1765. Accommodated *c*.550.[26]

Explanatory Note: This is a list of what appear to be permanent theatres, specially constructed or converted for the purpose of performing drama, and constituting separate buildings. However, it is by no means definite that all the cases listed fall into this category, since the sources consulted are often too brief or unclear to provide positive evidence on the relevant points. A particular problem is distinguishing between what may be a permanent building and what may have been simply a temporary booth erected for a short run of performances.

---

[24] Ibid. 37.

[25] Beckett, *Coal and Tobacco*, 188.

[26] Rosenfeld, *Strolling Players*, 116–21, 134; Fitzsimmons, 'Theatre Royal York', 169–72.

APPENDIX 4

Provincial Urban Music 1660–1770

Note: A = Concerts; B = Clubs and Societies; C = Festivals

BANBURY. A. First of twelve monthly subscription concerts and balls advertised June 1766. Apparently held at the Three Tuns Inn.[1]

BATH. A. Band of musicians playing at or near the baths from at least 1668. Concerts held from at least the early 18th cent., some in the assembly rooms. 'Private concerts' and 'concert breakfasts' in the assembly rooms, 1740s.

    B. George Lucy refers to 'our musical academy', 1765.[2]

BECCLES. A. Advertised that concert days will be Mondays, Wednesdays, and Fridays, 1758.[3]

BIRMINGHAM. A. Vocal and instrumental concerts, operas and oratorios, held in theatres, pleasure gardens, churches, assembly rooms, and inns, from at least 1740s.

    B. Several music clubs, 1720–60. Musical and Amicable Society founded 1762 (met at an inn), and the Oratorio Choral Society 1766.

    C. Birmingham Musical Festival founded 1768. Lasted three days. Used to raise money for building the General Hospital. Next festival 1778.[4]

BRISTOL. A. Concert advertised in 1714. Concerts became increasingly common after 1720s. Winter subscription concerts operating by at least the late 1740s.

    B. 'The gentlemen of the Musical Society' referred to in 1727.

    C. Regular benefit concerts held for the city musicians on St Cecilia's day. One- or two-day musical festivals held for charity 1757–60.[5]

BURY ST EDMUNDS. A. Proposals advertised to start weekly or monthly subscription concerts, 1721. Not known if effected, but a subscription series was started in 1734.[6]

---

[1] Gibson, 'Three Tuns', 5.

[2] Pepys, *Diary*, ix. 233–4; Tilmouth, 'Provincial Concert Life', 7–8; Hobhouse, *Diary of a West Country Physician*, 88, 99–100; *Bath Advertiser*, No. 1, 18 Oct. 1755; Wood, *Bath*, 438–9; Warwickshire CRO, L6/1473.

[3] Sadie, 'Concert Life', 22.

[4] Smith, *Music in Birmingham*, 10–27.

[5] Barry, 'Cultural Life of Bristol', 186.

[6] Sadie, 'Concert Life', 21.

COVENTRY. A. Concerts of vocal and instrumental music at the bowling-green and Spires's Spring Garden in 1740s.

B. Musical society operating 1755.[7]

DEDHAM. A. Subscription concerts by 1739.

B. Musical society in existence by 1739.[8]

DURHAM. A. Subscription concerts operating in mid-18th cent.[9]

EPSOM. A. Daily music from 'a consort of music' during the season, 1710.[10]

FAKENHAM. A. Subscription concerts operating 1750s.[11]

GLOUCESTER. C. Three Choirs Festival. Meeting at Gloucester from at least 1718.[12]

HEREFORD. C. Three Choirs Festival. Meeting at Hereford from at least 1720.[13]

IPSWICH. A. Fortnightly concerts throughout the year from 1730s.

B. Musical society in existence by 1730s.[14]

KING'S LYNN. A. Subscription concerts started 1750s.[15]

LEEDS. A. William Herschel appointed director of the public concerts at Leeds 1762.

B. Reference to 'the music-meeting', 1741.[16]

LICHFIELD. C. Annual St Cecilia's day concert from at least 1742.[17]

MANCHESTER. A. Regular concerts operating 1744.[18]

NEWCASTLE-UPON-TYNE. A. Subscription concerts operating from 1735. Held in the assembly rooms, with tickets one guinea for the season, 1736. Informal concerts held in a room at St Nicholas's vicarage, from *c*.1761.

B. Marcello Society founded 1750s.

C. The Sons of the Clergy charitable society established 1710. 'Anniversary meeting' held in 'our great church', with choral contributions, 1722.[19]

NORWICH. A. City bye-law required the waits to hold a monthly meeting for the 'diversion of the lovers of music', 1714. Uncertain if these meetings materialized, but other concerts were occurring in the city from the late 1710s.

B. First real concert society founded 1724, holding weekly concerts, probably only during the winter season.

[7] *VCH Warwickshire*, viii. 224.

[8] Sadie, 'Concert Life', 23.

[9] *New Grove*, i. 749.

[10] Tilmouth, 'Provincial Concert Life', 4.

[11] Fawcett, *Music in Eighteenth-Century Norwich*, 36.

[12] Shaw, *Three Choirs Festival*, 1–5.

[13] Ibid. 1–3.

[14] Sadie, 'Concert Life', 21.

[15] Fawcett, *Music in Eighteenth-Century Norwich*, 36.

[16] Turner, *Science and Music*, 24; Looney, 'Advertising and Society', 170.

[17] Money, *Experience and Identity*, 82; Hopkins, *Johnson's Lichfield*, 51.

[18] Young, *History of British Music*, 313.

[19] *New Grove*, i. 749; Young, *History of British Music*, 312–13; Ellis, 'Social Relations in Newcastle', 200.

C. St Cecilia's Day feast, 1714. Norwich Festival from 1770.[20]

OXFORD. A. Many concerts in post-Restoration period. The Sheldonian Theatre, after Smith's organ was installed in 1671, was increasingly used for larger public concerts. From the mid-18th cent. the Holywell Music Room* (built *c.*1742–8) housed a series of weekly subscription concerts.

B. At least three distinct musical societies operating in the 1730s.

C. St Cecilia's day celebration, 1696.[21]

SALISBURY. A. Regular subscription concerts by at least 1740s.

B. The Society of Lovers of Music in existence by 1700.

C. St Cecilia's day celebrations recorded 1700, 1726, and 1727. These appear to have developed into a festival proper, which from 1748 was extended to two days, and from 1768 to three.[22]

SAXMUNDHAM. A. Monthly concerts by 1760.[23]

SHREWSBURY. B. Musical society performances of vocal and instrumental music in Shrewsbury and Hereford, 1720.[24]

SPALDING. A. Regular weekly concerts at the Spalding Gentlemen's Society 'museum' from 1727.

B. The 'music meeting' or 'musical gentlemen' in existence by 1726.[25]

SWAFFHAM. A. Monthly subscription concerts established by 1745.

B. The subscription concerts were probably organized by the Philharmonic Society of Swaffham.[26]

TUNBRIDGE WELLS. A. Band of musicians maintained by at least the late 1690s to play while the waters were being drunk (morning), to accompany the promenaders on the walks and the dancing (afternoon). Weekly formal concerts started by 1703.[27]

WELLS (Som.) A. Regular concerts by the town's music club, at least some of which were open to non-members, operating by early 1700s.

B. A music club existed by at least 1704, called variously by one of its members, 'the music meeting', 'the lovers of music', 'our music', and the 'clubbers'.

C. Annual St Cecilia's day concert by at least 1709.[28]

WINCHESTER. A. Weekly concerts operating in 1760s. Subscription concert 1769.

C. St Cecilia's day concert, 1703. Annual festival founded 1760. Until

---

[20] Fawcett, *Music in Eighteenth-Century Norwich*, 3–4; Tilmouth, 'Provincial Concert Life', 11; *New Grove*, vi. 175.

[21] Tilmouth, 'Provincial Concert Life', 9; Mee, *Oldest Music Room*, 7–8, 14–17; Sadie, 'Concert Life', 20.

[22] *New Grove*, xvi. 421; Naish, *Diary*, 4, 42; *VCH Wiltshire*, vi. 142; Young, *History of British Music*, 313–14.

[23] Sadie, 'Concert Life', 22.

[24] Tilmouth, 'Provincial Concert Life', 14.

[25] Owen, *Spalding Gentlemen's Society*, pp. xii–xiii.

[26] Sadie, 'Concert Life', 22.

[27] Tilmouth, 'Provincial Concert Life', 7; Fiennes, *Journeys*, 135.

[28] Hobhouse, *Diary of a West Country Physician*, 39–43, and *passim*.

1766 this was spread over two evenings, but from the following year it was extended to three days.[29]

WORCESTER. B. Musical society by 1720.

   C. Three Choirs Festival. Meeting at Worcester from at least 1719.[30]

WYMONDHAM. A. Experimented with a quarterly series of subscription concerts 1753. Supported a subscription concert, though not necessarily continuously, until at least 1776.[31]

YARMOUTH. A. Concerts held in the early 18th cent.

   B. Wednesday music club started 1736. Another musical society also operated in the 1730s.[32]

YORK. A. Weekly subscription concerts held every Friday (by 1754 these appear to have moved to Wednesday) during the winter season in the assembly rooms, from at least the early 1730s. These were mounted by 'the music assembly'. In 1741 the concerts probably ran from mid-Oct. to early Mar. In 1761 there were twenty concerts from mid-Oct. to Mar., for which a season ticket cost half a guinea, and individual tickets 2s.6d. Morning concerts were also mounted in the assembly rooms during August race week from at least 1733.[33]

   B. York Musical Society apparently founded in 1676. Certainly in existence by 1767. Another music club may have been the 'concert held by a number of gentlemen', meeting weekly at the George Inn, 1741. The 'music assembly' or 'Friday consort' was founded by at least 1730.[34]

[29] *New Grove*, xx. 446; Sadie, 'Concert Life', 18.

[30] Shaw, *Three Choirs Festival*, 1-5; Tilmouth, 'Provincial Concert Life', 14.

[31] Fawcett, *Music in Eighteenth-Century Norwich*, 37.

[32] Tilmouth, 'Provincial Concert Life', 11; Fawcett, *Music in Eighteenth-Century Norwich*, 33-5.

[33] House Book, 24 Mar. 1732/3, 27 July 1733, 28 July 1752, 31 Dec. 1754, YCA; Drake, *Eboracum*, 240; Looney, 'Advertising and Society', 167-9.

[34] *New Grove*, xx. 575; Looney, 'Advertising and Society', 174-5; 'Proposals for . . . Assembly Rooms', YCA.

APPENDIX 5

Provincial Urban Assemblies, Assembly Rooms, and Balls 1660–1770

Place	*Date*	*Type*	*Building or Location*
ASTROP	*c*.1694		On the walks there is 'a room for the music and a room for the company'.[1]
	1740		On the walks a dancing room, and in the town an assembly room.[2]
BANBURY	June 1766	First of twelve monthly subscription concerts and balls advertised.	Meetings apparently held at the Three Tuns Inn.[3]
BARNSLEY	Early/ mid-18th cent.		The Free School (completed 1738) contained an assembly room.[4]
BATH	1670s	Dancing.	On the bowling-green.[5]
	1696, 1698	Balls.	In the town hall.[6]
	1708		Harrison's assembly rooms built on the Terrace Walk.
	1730		Lindsey's assembly rooms opened on the Terrace Walk.

[1] Fiennes, *Journeys*, 31–2.
[2] Lennard, 'Watering-Places, 39.
[3] Gibson, 'Three Tuns', 5.
[4] Grady, 'Public Buildings in the West Riding', 35, and Gazetteer.
[5] Barbeau, *Bath*, 19 n. 5.
[6] HMC, *Hastings MSS*, ii. 279; Fiennes, *Journeys*, 236.

Place	Date	Type	Building or Location
	1769-71		The Upper Rooms* built off Bennett Street. Cost c.£20,000.[7]
BECCLES	1733	Assembly each night of the races.	In the town hall.[8]
BEVERLEY	Early 18th cent.	Assemblies.[9]	
	1745		Assize judges to be invited to a collation at the assembly room or other public place.[10]
	1761-3		New assembly room built.[11]
BIRMINGHAM	1703		The Old Cross built, containing a first-floor assembly room.[12]
	c.1750		Appear to be three assembly rooms operating: (i) 'Mr Sawyer's Great Room', No. 11 The Square, formerly a school; (ii) No. 85 Bull Street; (iii) 'Mrs Fulwood's Assembly House', Colmore Row.[13]
BRISTOL: CITY	Early 18th cent.	Civic ball held in 1714. Winter assemblies were operating by at least the 1730s.	Assembly room in the Pithay.

[7] Wood, *Bath*, 225, 245, 319-20; Ison, *Bath*, 49-54.

[8] *Suffolk Mercury*, xxiv, No. 71, 7 May 1733.

[9] Macky, *Journey*, ii. 216.

[10] Macmahon, *Beverley Corporation Minute-Books*, 27.

[11] Hall, *Beverley*, 3.   [12] Gill, *Birmingham*, 68.

[13] Hutton, *History of Birmingham*, 131; Hill and Dent, *Old Square*, 84-5; Smith, *Music in Birmingham*, 15.

Place	Date	Type	Building or Location
	Shortly before 1742		Playhouse in St Augustine's Back converted into an assembly room.
	1754-5		Prince Street assembly rooms built. Opened 1756. Cost 120 × £30 shares = £3,600.[14]
BRISTOL: HOT WELLS	1722		Visitor 'saw the great new-built room for dancing'.[15]
	1725		The 'long room' described as a 'noble large one, having seven arched windows in front, is built with brick, and handsomely wainscotted and painted'.[16]
	mid-18th cent.	Balls twice a week from 1757.	A second long room opened 1768.[17]
BUCKINGHAM	c.1670		Assembly room built in Castle Street.[18]
BUNGAY	1736		Assembly room erected.
	1737	Race assemblies.[19]	
BURY ST EDMUNDS	Early 18th cent.	Regular assemblies during the fortnight of Bury Fair.[20]	
	1723, 1725	Race assemblies at Mr Eastland's.[21]	

[14] Ison, *Bristol*, 108-14, 123; Barry, 'Cultural Life of Bristol', 186, 324.

[15] Hobhouse, *Diary of a West Country Physician*, 93.

[16] Students Diary, fo. 128.

[17] Barry, 'Cultural Life of Bristol,' 168; Powys, *Diaries*, 49; Little, 'Gloucestershire Spas', 174-6.

[18] Clark and Slack, *Crisis and Order*, 15.

[19] *Suffolk Mercury*, xxiv, No. 280, 18 July 1737.

[20] Macky, *Journey*, i. 6; Hervey, *Letter-Books*, ii. 92.

[21] *Suffolk Mercury*, x, No. 9, 19 Aug. 1723; xvi, No. 4, 24 May 1725.

Place	Date	Type	Building or Location
	1760s, 1770s	Private and public balls; subscription assemblies; and assemblies during the Fair, and the assizes. [22]	
CANTERBURY	1750		Assembly room built. [23]
CHELTENHAM	*c*.1740		Small ballroom built near the wells, with billiard-room above.
	1750s	Balls twice a week.	Apparently the Upper Rooms were built about this time. [24]
CHESTER	Early 18th cent.	Regular assemblies. [25]	
	1710	Ball as part of the Tory victory celebrations after the 1710 election.	In the town hall. [26]
	1711	Assize balls. [27]	
CHESTERFIELD	1757	Race assemblies.	In the assembly room. [28]
CIRENCESTER	Early Georgian		Assembly room* in the Fleece Inn. [29]
COLCHESTER	1730s	Quarterly assemblies.	In the King's Head Inn.
	1750s	Monthly assemblies, with some additional balls.	In the King's Head Inn. [30]

---

[22] Suffolk RO, E2/25/1, fos. 60A, 63, 67, 71, 93, 134A, 153, 212; Suffolk RO, E2/25/2, fos. 116, 124, 131.

[23] Chalklin, 'Building for Cultural Purposes', 55.

[24] Hart, *Cheltenham*, 125, 127, 134–5.

[25] Macky, *Journey*, ii. 42, 214.

[26] *Post-Boy*, No. 2415, 2–4 Nov. 1710. I owe this reference to Geoffrey Holmes.

[27] Warwickshire CRO, CR.1368, i. fo. 75.

[28] Powys, *Diaries*, 24–5.

[29] Keverne, *Old Inns*, 108.

[30] Brown, 'Colchester in the Eighteenth Century', 163.

Place	Date	Type	Building or Location
CONGLETON	1752	Hunt ball.	In the Black Lion Inn.[31]
COVENTRY	Mid-18th cent.	Assemblies.	In the Draper's Hall and and St Mary's Hall.[32]
DERBY	Early 18th cent.	Assemblies.[33]	
	1763-4		Assembly rooms* built.[34]
DONCASTER	Mid-18th cent.	Race ball (1751).	The Mansion House, built 1745-8, contains a large ballroom, used for the race balls.[35]
EPSOM	c.1707		Ballroom built at the New Wells.
	Early 18th cent.		Ballroom built at the Old Wells.[36]
EYE (Suffolk)	Mid-18th cent.		Assembly room* added to the White Lion Inn.
GLOUCESTER	1769	Ball on last evening of the Three Choirs Festival.[38]	
HARLESTON (Norfolk)	Early 18th cent.		Assembly room* in the Swan Inn. The room was in existence and being used for balls by 1732.[39]

[31] Crossley, *Cheshire*, 75-6.
[32] *VCH Warwickshire*, viii. 224.
[33] Macky, *Journey*, ii. 176.
[34] *BE Derbyshire*, 118.
[35] Fairfax-Blakeborough, *Northern Turf History*, iii. 198-9; *BE Yorkshire: The West Riding*, 183-4.
[36] Fiennes, *Journeys*, 337-8, 349-50; Clark, 'Epsom Spa', 18-22.
[37] Keverne, *Old Inns*, 52.
[38] Shaw, *Three Choirs Festival*, 14.
[39] Keverne, *Old Inns*, 50; HMC, *Portland MSS*, vi. 151-2.

Place	Date	Type	Building or Location
HEREFORD	1756, 1765, 1771	Ball on each night of the meeting of the Three Choirs Festival.	In the College Hall (1756).[40]
HITCHIN	1770		Assembly room* added to the Sun Inn.[41]
HULL	First half 18th cent.	Assemblies.	In the grammar school.
	Mid-18th cent.		Assembly room built in Dogger Lane.[42]
KING'S LYNN	1766		Assembly room* built to the rear of the Guildhall.[43]
LEEDS	Before 1726		Assembly room built in in Kirkgate.[44]
LEICESTER	1741	Race ball.	
	c.1750		Building erected in Haymarket, with a first floor room used for assemblies.[45]
	1760	County hunt ball.[46]	
LEWES	1738	Weekly assemblies.	Held 'in a handsome house and a large room'.[47]
	1757	Race ball.[48]	

[40] *Gloucester Jnl.*, xxxv, No. 1789, 7 Sept. 1756; Shaw, *Three Choirs Festival*, 14.
[41] *BE Hertfordshire* (London, 1953), 136.
[42] *VCH Yorkshire: East Riding*, i. 209.
[43] *BE North-West and South Norfolk* (Harmondsworth, 1962), 230.
[44] Grady, 'Public Buildings in the West Riding', Gazetteer.
[45] Simmons, *Leicester*, 85, 119, 121.
[46] Suffolk RO, E2/20/1A, fo. 10.
[47] HMC, *Portland MSS*, vi. 68.
[48] Turner, *Diary*, 108.

Place	Date	Type	Building or Location
LICHFIELD	1733, 1748, 1769	Race balls.[49]	
	Mid-18th cent.	Winter subscription assemblies; hunt balls.[50]	
LINCOLN	Early 18th cent.	(i) Principal county assemblies.	In the Angel Inn.
		(ii) Fortnightly city assemblies.	Agreed (1731) that the Guildhall could be used for these.
	1744		Assembly room built.[51]
LIVERPOOL	1726	An assembly.[52]	
	1738		Assembly room let by the corporation.[53]
	1754	The Exchange opened with a grand ball, followed by a week of concerts and balls.	The Exchange contained an assembly room on the first floor.[54]
MAIDSTONE	Early 18th cent.	Assemblies introduced but then declined.[55]	
MANCHESTER	Early 18th cent.	Weekly subscription assemblies.	Construction of a building in King Street, with a first floor room used for assemblies.[56]

[49] HMC, *Hastings MSS*, iii. 18; Kettle, 'Lichfield Races', 41; Hopkins, *Johnson's Lichfield*, 56.

[50] Hopkins, *Johnson's Lichfield*, 54–5.

[51] Hill, *Stuart Lincoln*, 202; Hill, *Georgian Lincoln*, 15, 58.

[52] Blundell, *Diurnal*, iii. 19.

[53] Picton, *Liverpool Municipal Archives*, 134.

[54] Baines, *County Palatine of Lancaster*, i. 164; Enfield, *Liverpool*, 59; HMC, *Verulam MSS*, 270.

[55] Defoe, *Tour*, i. 115.

[56] Aikin, *Manchester*, 187.

Place	Date	Type	Building or Location
	1729		The Exchange built in the Market-Place, with an upper room used for balls.
	Mid-18th cent.	Balls.	Held in (i) the theatre built *c.*1753; (ii) the cockpit and assembly room, in use by 1754.[57]
MARGATE	1769	During the season the assemblies attracted 930 subscribers at 5*s.* each.	Assembly room opened.[58]
MATLOCK	1757	Evening balls for the visitors.	Held in the Long Room, built in 1734.[59]
NEWCASTLE-UPON-TYNE	Early 18th cent.		Bowling-green house used for assemblies.[60]
	1736		Assembly room used for concerts.[61]
	1766	Assize ball.[62]	
	1776		New assembly rooms opened. Cost *c.* £6,700. The old room became a coffee-house.[63]
NORTHAMPTON	Mid-18th cent.	Race balls; weekly subscription assemblies during the winter season.	Assemblies held in the leading local inns.[64]

[57] Hodgkinson and Pogson, *Early Manchester Theatre*, 6, 11–14, 22, 35.
[58] Whyman, 'Margate before the Railway', 142.
[59] Powys, *Diaries*, 30–1.
[60] Macky, *Journey*, ii. 217.
[61] Young, *History of British Music*, 312.
[62] Warwickshire CRO, CR.1368, v, fo. 36.
[63] Brand, *Newcastle*, i. 121–2.
[64] Everitt, 'Urban Inn', 116–17.

Place	Date	Type	Building or Location
NORWICH	1688, 1727	Dances and balls during sessions week.	Held in Chapel Field House.[65]
	1717	Dancing and card assemblies inaugurated.	In Chapel Field House.[66]
	1754		New assembly rooms* built near to Chapel Field, on the present day Theatre Street.[67]
NOTTINGHAM	Mid-18th cent.	Regular assemblies.[68]	
PRESTON	1682	'Balls and revellings' during the meeting of the Guild.[69]	
	1728		Corporation agreed that the 'ladies have the use of the town hall for the assembly till further order'.
	1747	Public ball to mark Lord Strange 'having lately brought his lady to town'.[70]	
	1762	During the month of the Guild there were five assemblies each week.	Held in the state-room of the Guildhall (opened 1762), and the adjoining town hall.[71]

[65] R. W. Ketton-Cremer, 'Assize Week in Norwich in 1688', *Norfolk Archaeology*, xxiv (1932), 15; Cranfield, *Development of Provincial Newspaper*, 217.
[66] Fawcett, *Music in Eighteenth-Century Norwich*, 3.
[67] *BE North-East Norfolk and Norwich*, 261.
[68] Chalklin, 'Building for Cultural Purposes', 54.
[69] [Kuerden], *Preston*, 80-1.
[70] Council Minutes, 20 Sept. 1728, 8 Aug. 1747, PCMSS.
[71] *Guild Merchant of Preston*, 16-17.

Place	Date	Type	Building or Location
ROTHERHAM	1739–43		Town hall and grammar school built (as one structure), in which the town hall was also used for assemblies.[72]
ST NEOTS	Mid-18th cent.		Assembly room* of this period on the upper floor of the George Inn.[73]
SALISBURY	Early 18th cent.	Weekly assemblies.[74]	
	Mid-18th cent.	Assize balls (1763).	St Cecilia's day concert in the assembly room in New Street (1740). This establishment was replaced by a new room in High Street in 1750. The assembly room was used in 1765 to accommodate plays.[75]
SCARBOROUGH	1733	Balls every evening during the season.	Held in the Long Room, built by at least 1725.[76]
SHEFFIELD	1733	Assemblies.	In the dormitory of the boys' charity school.[77]
	1762		Assembly room and theatre in Norfolk Street completed. Cost over £3,000.[78]

[72] Grady, 'Public Buildings in the West Riding', Gazetteer.
[73] Tebbutt, *St Neots*, 125–6, 244–5.
[74] Macky, *Journey*, ii. 41–2.
[75] Unidentified correspondent to Dolly Long, 29 July 1763, Wiltshire RO, 947; *New Grove*, xvi. 421; Hare, *Georgian Theatre*, 62.
[76] *Journey from London to Scarborough*, 38; Students Diary, fo. 40.
[77] Walton, *Sheffield*, 104.
[78] Grady, 'Public Buildings in the West Riding', Gazetteer.

Place	*Date*	*Type*	*Building or Location*
SHREWSBURY	Early 18th cent.	Weekly assemblies.[79]	
	c.1775–80		Ballroom* added to the Lion Inn.[80]
SOUTHAMPTON	1767		The old assembly room in High Street replaced by a new one near the West Quay.[81]
STAMFORD	Early 18th cent.	Monthly assemblies.	Held in a house in Barn Hill used for assemblies since before 1720. New assembly room* built c.1727 in St George's Square. Additions made in the 1790s.[82]
	1755	Monthly dancing assemblies; charitable card assemblies three times a week.	In a 'very large neat assembly room'.[83]
STRATFORD-UPON-AVON	1755	'Stratford assembly'.[84]	
SWAFFHAM	1737	Race assemblies.[85]	
TOPSHAM	1720s		Salutation Inn* built containing an assembly room.[86]

[79] Macky, *Journey*, ii. 140-1.
[80] *BE Shropshire*, 284.
[81] A. T. Patterson, *A History of Southampton 1700-1914*, vol. 1, Southampton Record Ser., xi (1966), 41.
[82] RCHM, *Stamford*, 49-50.
[83] *Gentleman's Magazine*, xxv (1755), 163.
[84] Warwickshire CRO, L6/1375.
[85] *Suffolk Mercury*, xxiv, No. 274, 6 June 1737.
[86] Hoskins, *Devon*, 498; *BE South Devon*, 288.

Place	Date	Type	Building or Location
TUNBRIDGE WELLS	Mid-17th cent.		Assembly room at Rusthall *c*.1655–64. This was moved to Mount Ephraim *c*.1665–70.[87]
	Late 17th cent.		Dancing on the bowling-greens or in the rooms attached to them.[88]
	1739		The public room on the Upper Walk enlarged as an assembly room.[89]
	1760s	Public balls twice a week; private balls also mounted.	Two sets of assembly rooms.[90]
WAKEFIELD	1727		Two-storey assembly room completed, adjoining the White Hart Inn.[91]
	1770s	Regular assemblies; private balls.[92]	
WARWICK	Early 18th cent.		In 1726/7 the room over the market hall (built 1670) hired for use during the assizes and horse-races, probably for balls. The Court House,* built *c*.1724–30, contains a first floor assembly room.[93]
	1755, 1769	Race balls.[94]	

[87] Burr, *Tunbridge Wells*, 38, 44–5.
[88] Lennard, 'Watering-Places', 54; Fiennes, *Journeys*, 135.
[89] Savidge, *Tunbridge Wells*, 63.
[90] Burr, *Tunbridge Wells*, 120–3; Barton, *Tunbridge Wells*, 342.
[91] Grady, 'Public Buildings in the West Riding', Gazetteer.
[92] Suffolk RO, E2/25/1, fos. 162A, 176, 183A, 246; Suffolk RO, E2/25/2, fo. 1.
[93] Kemp, *History of Warwick*, 173–7, 190.
[94] Newdigate Diaries, 27 Aug. 1755; printed Bill for Warwick Races (1769), Shakespeare Birthplace Trust, PR.64.

Place	*Date*	*Type*	*Building or Location*
WEYMOUTH	1769		Ad refers to a 'large elegant assembly room, new built', probably Delamotte's Public Rooms, an addition to an older coffee-house and tavern.[95]
WHITEHAVEN	1736		Plot taken in Howgill Street to build an assembly room.[96]
WINCHESTER	Early 18th cent.	Weekly assemblies.[97]	
WOBURN	Early Georgian	Regular winter assemblies.	Held in the early Georgian Bedford Arms Inn, which contains an assembly room.*[98]
WORCESTER	Early 18th cent.	Assemblies.[99]	
	1721-3		Guildhall* built, with first floor assembly room.[100]
	Mid-18th cent.	Balls during the Three Choirs Festival (1752, 1755, 1758, 1767, and 1770), and the races (1757).	Guildhall used for at least some of these.[101]

[95] McIntyre, 'Health and Pleasure Resorts', 310, 314.
[96] Beckett, *Coal and Tobacco*, 188.
[97] Macky, *Journey*, ii. 41-2; Defoe, *Tour*, i. 186.
[98] Keverne, *Old Inns*, 136.
[99] Macky, *Journey*, ii. 42.
[100] *BE Worcestershire*, 323.
[101] Shaw, *Three Choirs Festival*, 13-14; Gill, *Racecourses*, 230.

Place	Date	Type	Building or Location
YORK	Mid-17th cent.		Suggested that assemblies occurred in a theatre (1630s) and at the Old Boar Inn (from 1653).[102]
	Early 18th cent.	Weekly assemblies operating by at least 1710.	Held in (i) The King's Manor; (ii) Private house in Minster Yard.[103]
	1732	Race balls.	At the 'assembly house in Ogleforth'.[104]
	1732	The weekly Monday assemblies and assize and race balls were all held in the new rooms.	Blake Street assembly rooms* opened. Cost over £5,000.[105]

[102] Wittkower, *York Assembly Rooms*, 2; Defoe, *Tour*, ii. 230.

[103] McInnes, *English Town*, 21; Drake, *Eboracum*, 240; *VCH York*, 245; Macky, *Journey*, ii. 211.

[104] Fairfax-Blakeborough, *Northern Turf History*, iii. 51.

[105] Assembly Rooms Minute Book, *passim*, YCA.

APPENDIX 6

Provincial Urban Walks and Gardens 1630–1770

ASTROP. Hedge-lined gravel walk, observed c.1694. Two separate walks (the longer one was gravelled, hedged, and lined with benches) at right angles to each other; in between the two was a large garden house; all described 1740.[1]

BATH. (i) King's Mead walks, observed in or before 1687.[2]

(ii) Abbey Garden, Abbey Green, and Old Bowling-Green. All three shown in a map of 1694, and the walks in the Old Bowling-Green improved by the corporation 1693-4.[3]

(iii) The Gravel Walks or Orange Grove. Shown in a map of 1694. A paved walk, lined with shops, was added to their south side from the early 1700s, to form an upper promenade. This and the lower walk were merged together and the whole area relandscaped in the early 1730s.[4]

(iv) Harrison's gardens, attached to his assembly rooms (built in 1708). Close to the line of the city walls.[5]

(v) The Terrace Walk.* Developed from late 1728. Site of the two assembly rooms. Close to the line of the city walls.[6]

(vi) North and South Parades.* Built 1740-8.[7]

(vii) The Spring Gardens, later Vauxhall Gardens, in Bathwick Meadows. In existence by 1742.[8]

(viii) Informal walk along the bank of the Avon, west to Twerton. Partly landscaped by Wood, and described by him in the 1740s.[9]

BIRMINGHAM. (i) St Philip's churchyard. Tree-lined walk surrounding the area, described 1762.

(ii) Apollo Gardens, Aston. Closed down 1751.

---

[1] Fiennes, *Journeys*, 31-2; Lennard, 'Watering-Places', 39.

[2] Fiennes, *Journeys*, 20-1, 23.

[3] Gilmore, *Map of Bath*; Council Minutes, 11 Dec. 1693, BCA; Chamberlain's Accounts, 1693/4, BCA.

[4] Gilmore, *Map of Bath*; Wood, *Bath*, 224, 342-3; Macky, *Journey*, ii. 128; Council Minutes, 28 Dec. 1730, 20 Nov. 1732, and *passim*, BCA.

[5] Wood, *Bath*, 225.

[6] Ibid. 243-6.

[7] Ibid. 349-51; Ison, *Bath*, 145.

[8] Sydenham, *Bath Pleasure Gardens*, 2.

[9] Wood, *Bath*, 439.

(iii) Duddeston Hall, later Vauxhall Gardens. Operating mid-18th cent.[10]

BRISTOL. (i) The Marsh. Engraved prospect of the city shows a tree-lined walk along the bank of the River Avon, with a bowling-green attached, 1673. Fiennes observed the walks in 1698. Later the site of Queen Square, built *c*.1700-27, which itself contained a railed central area planted with trees.[11]

(ii) College Green. Described as 'handsomely planted with trees railed in', 1725.[12]

(iii) A Vauxhall Gardens operated 1751-7 (near the Hotwells) and 1776-7 (Redcliffe).[13]

CHELTENHAM. Upper and Lower Walks laid out 1739-40.[14]

CHESTER. Engraved prospect shows a walk around the city walls, 1728.[15]

CHICHESTER. (i) North Walls walk and rampart 'levelled, repaired, and beautified', 1724. An original row of trees may date from *c*.1689.

(ii) East Walls. Row of trees planted *c*.1720s.

(iii) Walk by the wall of the Priory, paved, and fenced with rails and posts, *c*.1730.[16]

COLCHESTER. St Mary's churchyard. Gravel walks, lined with lime trees, laid out 1714. The church itself was rebuilt 1713-14.[17]

COVENTRY. (i) Fiennes observed that 'there are several good walks about the town, a large park above the town which most people walk in', 1697.[18]

(ii) Spires's Spring Garden. Operating 1740s.[19]

DORCHESTER. Walk* of sycamores surrounding the town, observed 1760. Map of *c*.1774 shows four walks following the line of the town walls: North Walk, New Walk, Old Walks, and Chestnut Walk.[20]

DURHAM. (i) Public gardens and walks in the ruinated house of Sir Charles Musgrave, observed 1698.[21]

(ii) Engraved prospect shows 'The Prebend's Walk', *c*.1745.[22]

---

[10] Toldervy, *England and Wales Described*, 349; Smith, *Music in Birmingham*, 10-11.

[11] J. Millerd, *The City of Bristol*, reproduced in Hyde, *Gilded Scenes*, 58-9; Fiennes, *Journeys*, 238; Students Diary, fo. 121.

[12] Students Diary, fo. 120.

[13] Barry, 'Cultural Life of Bristol', 168-9; Barker, *Bristol at Play*, 13.

[14] Hart, *Cheltenham*, 126.

[15] Buck, *Antiquities*, iii.

[16] Spershott, *Memoirs*, 17-18.

[17] Morant, *Essex*, i. 108.

[18] Fiennes, *Journeys*, 114.

[19] *VCH Warwickshire*, viii. 224.

[20] Powys, *Diaries*, 64; J. Hutchins, *The History and Antiquities of the County of Dorset* (London, 1774), i. 371.

[21] Fiennes, *Journeys*, 215-16.

[22] Buck, *Antiquities*, iii.

EPSOM. (i) Old Wells. Tree-lined walk, observed c.1701-3.[23]

  (ii) New Wells, opened 1707. Grove and bowling-green attached.[24]

  (iii) High Street, south side. Paved terrace shaded by trees, described 1711.

  (iv) High Street, north side. The 'New Parade', constructed c.1710s.[25]

EXETER. (i) Northernhay Walk.* Laid out before the Civil War. During the hostilities converted into an outwork, and the trees felled. Levelled and replanted 1664. Fiennes observed 'a long walk, as well as broad, enclosed with rows of lofty trees . . . along by the ditch and bank on which the town wall stands', 1698.

  (ii) Fiennes observed 'another long walk within shady trees on the other side of the town, which leads to the grounds where the drying frames are set up', 1698.[26]

  (iii) The Haven Walk. Shown on a map following the line of the River Exe, 1765.[27]

HEREFORD. (i) Engraved prospect shows tree-lined walk in front of the city walls, 1732.

  (ii) Castle Green. Promenade* made in 1746.[28]

LEEDS. The 'Spring Garden' with a 'house of entertainment'. Situated on the west of the town, close to the River Aire, described 1715.[29]

LIVERPOOL. Corporation orders two public walks to be made, one at the north end and the other at the south end of the town, and agrees that land be purchased for this purpose. The Ladies' Walk, tree-lined and in a corner of the town next to the sea, observed 1750.[30]

MAIDSTONE. Engraved prospect shows 'The Meadow', an area ringed by trees, and containing a tree-lined walk along the bank of the River Medway, 1738.[31]

NEWCASTLE-UPON-TYNE. (i) The Forth or Firth. Situated to the west of the town outside the walls. Leased out as a bowling-green 1657. The corporation made several orders in the early 1680s to landscape and develop the area. Fiennes observed the results in 1698, describing the tree-lined gravel walks around the bowling-green; an entertaining house with a paved and covered walk in front of it; and an attached 'pretty garden . . . a sort of Spring Garden' with a greenhouse. Many of these features are shown in Bourne's

---

[23] Fiennes, *Journeys*, 338.

[24] Clark, 'Epsom Spa', 10, 18; Fiennes, *Journeys*, 349-50.

[25] Clark, 'Epsom Spa', 27.

[26] Lysons, *Magna Britannia*, vi. 185, 191; Fiennes, *Journeys*, 249. I owe the first of these references to Joyce Miles.

[27] Donn, 'Plan of Exeter'.

[28] Buck, *Antiquities*, iii; *BE Herefordshire* (Harmondsworth, 1977), 189.

[29] Thoresby, *Ducatus Leodiensis*, 92.

[30] Picton, *Liverpool Municipal Archives*, 137; Pococke, *Travels*, i. 5.

[31] Buck, *Antiquities*, iii.

map of the town of *c*.1730, which also indicates a tree-lined walk linking the town walls and the Forth.

(ii) Fiennes observed 'one broad walk by the side of the town . . . made with coal ashes', 1698.

(iii) Fiennes observed 'a walk all round the walls of the town', 1698. Bourne indicated a walk along the town walls near Pilgrim Street, *c*.1730.

(iv) New Ranelagh Gardens. Opened 1760.[32]

NORTHAMPTON. Cow Meadow. Developed as a pleasure garden and walks by the corporation, from at least 1703.[33]

NORWICH. (i) Chapel Field, in the west of the city, close to the walls. Walk mentioned 1688. Described as the 'Mall of Norwich', 1754.

(ii) The Gentlemen's Walk, in the Market-Place. Used in 18th cent.[34]

(iii) Moore's Spring Gardens, later known as Vauxhall Gardens. On a riverside site, operating by 1750.[35]

NOTTINGHAM. Engraved prospect shows 'the foot walk through the beautiful meadows', *c*.1743.[36]

PRESTON. Avenham Garden used by polite society in the late 1680s. The walk* was planted with trees and gravelled in the late 1690s, and a substantial improvement scheme was launched in 1737.[37]

SHAFTESBURY. (i) Park Walk.* Laid out 1753, observed 1760, described 1764.

(ii) Castle Hill walk, observed 1760.[38]

SHREWSBURY. (i) Abbey Gardens. Grass and gravel walks, gardens, and a greenhouse, observed 1698.[39]

(ii) The Quarry. Corporation orders landscaping 1719. Extension added across the river in Kingsland 1728. Engraved prospect shows the Quarry area, with tree-lined walks (some along the bank of the River Severn), a summer-house, and a bowling-green, 1739.

(iii) Walk established along the circuit of the walls, early 18th cent.[40]

TUNBRIDGE WELLS. (i) Walk by the wells, now called the Pantiles.* Green bank raised and levelled, and a double row of trees planted in 1638 to form the Upper Walk. Shops and other buildings added *c*.1676. Redeveloped after a

[32] Brand, *Newcastle*, i. 416-19; ii. 538; Fiennes, *Journeys*, 211; Bourne, *Newcastle*, 81, and plan.

[33] *VCH Northamptonshire*, iii. 23.

[34] Ketton-Cremer, 'Assize Week in Norwich', 16-17; Corfield, 'A Provincial Capital', 293.

[35] Fawcett, *Music in Eighteenth-Century Norwich*, 29.

[36] Buck, *Antiquities*, iii.

[37] Bellingham, *Diary*, 4-6; Hewitson, *History of Preston*, 320; Small Order Book, 23 May and 7 Nov. 1698, PCMSS; Council Minutes, 28 Jan. and 18 Feb. 1736/7, PCMSS.

[38] *BE Dorset*, 366; Powys, *Diaries*, 79; *England Illustrated*, i. 196.

[39] Fiennes, *Journeys*, 227.

[40] *Prospect of Shrewsbury*, reproduced in Hyde, *Gilded Scenes*, 78-9; information from Angus McInnes.

fire in 1687. Future Queen Anne gave money for paving 1698. Lower Walks improved 1728.

  (ii) Queen's Grove. Planted *c*.1702 to celebrate accession of Anne.

  (iii) Cold Bath, Rusthall. Built 1708 with attached ornamental gardens.

  (iv) Mount Sion. Grove planted 1703.

  (v) Southborough. Grove established by early 18th cent.[41]

WELLS (Som.). The 'water-walk and meadows',* observed 1709.[42]

WINCHESTER. The Arbour. Open space outside the walls, used for walking and shooting in the late 17th cent.[43]

WORCESTER. (i) Sansom or Sansome Fields Walk, described 1764.

  (ii) Dr Wall's Walk, described 1764.[44]

YARMOUTH. Tree-lined walk leading to St Nicholas's Church, observed 1732.[45]

YORK. (i) Lord Mayor's Walk. North of the Minster, adjacent to the city walls. Mayor given permission to plant trees on the walk 1719.[46]

  (ii) The New or Long Walk.* Tree-lined walk that runs south from the city walls for about a mile along the bank of the River Ouse. Probably first landscaped 1731-2. Substantially improved 1739-40.[47]

[41] Burr, *Tunbridge Wells*, 32, 50-1, 55-60; Barton, *Tunbridge Wells*, 117, 196.

[42] Hobhouse, *Diary of a West Country Physician*, 54.

[43] Rosen, 'Winchester', 180.

[44] V. Green, *A Survey of the City of Worcester* (Worcester, 1764), plan opposite 237. I owe this reference to Bruce Clarke.

[45] HMC, *Portland MSS*, vi. 154.

[46] Drake, *Eboracum*, 254; House Book, 31 Dec. 1719, YCA.

[47] House Book, 9 Mar. 1731/2, 16 Oct. and 29 Nov. 1739, 28 Feb. 1739/40, 12 Sept. 1740, YCA.

APPENDIX 7

Horse-Race Meetings 1500–1770

Abbreviations

B   Blundell, *Diurnal*
FB   Fairfax-Blakeborough, *Northern Turf History*
G   Gill, *Racecourses*
L   Longrigg, *Horse-Racing*
RC   *Racing Calendar*
Sh   *VCH Shropshire*, ii
SM   *Suffolk Mercury*

Explanatory Note: It must be stressed that this appendix is in no respect a comprehensive one. It is merely the result of combing through a variety of sources, and collecting a number of stray references. It should not be considered as anything more than a preliminary handlist. The *Racing Calendar* entries are drawn from a sample of seventeen years between 1730 and 1770: they are 1730, 1735–40, 1745–6, 1749, 1755–60, and 1770. This sample was chosen in the context of the sources available, and the need both to investigate certain key years and to provide a reasonable coverage of the period 1730–60. The counties referred to in column one are those which were operating prior to local government reorganization in 1974. The figures in column two are the number of years a meeting occurs in the seventeen-year sample described above. The frequency with which a meeting occurs may give some indication of its importance. The dates in column three are the earliest references I have discovered for these meetings. They cannot be taken to indicate the date at which a meeting was founded. More detailed and systematic research than was possible in this study, particularly on newspapers, would undoubtedly push back the majority of these dates. The asterisked meetings are ones which were still operating in 1975, as listed in Gill, *Racecourses*.

Place	Meetings Recorded In Calendar Sample (Max. No. = 17)	Earliest Reference	Source
BEDFORDSHIRE			
Bedford	13	1730	RC
Dunstable	3	1755	RC
Leighton Buzzard	1	1730	RC
Woburn	1	1736	RC
BERKSHIRE			
Abingdon	2	1730	RC
Ascot*	14	1711	L, 55
East Ilsley	3	1730	RC
Faringdon	2	1739	RC
Lambourn	8	1735	RC
Maidenhead	9	1730	RC
Newbury*	2	1738	RC
Reading	16	1730	RC
Wantage	1	1770	RC
Windsor*	3	1682	G, 222
BUCKINGHAMSHIRE			
Amersham	1	1730	RC
Aylesbury	8	Late 17th cent.	L, 49
Marlow	3	1725	SM, 11 Oct. 1725.
Newport Pagnell	8	1730	RC
Olney	3	1735	RC
West Wycombe	1	1736	RC
CAMBRIDGESHIRE			
Bottisham	1	1735	RC
Wisbech	9	1737	RC
CHESHIRE			
Chester*	17	1511	L, 29
Crabtree Green	2	1730	RC
Farndon	17	17th cent.	Crossley, *Cheshire*, 75.
Knutsford	13	1729	Crossley, *Cheshire*, 75.
Latchford	1	1755	RC

Place	Meetings Recorded In Calendar Sample (Max. No. = 17)	Earliest Reference	Source
Leasowe	—	16th cent.	Crossley, *Cheshire*, 75.
Little Budworth	3	Early 17th cent.	Crossley, *Cheshire*, 75.
Nantwich	3	1739	RC
Northwich	6	1755	RC
Stockport	1	1739	RC
Tarporley	—	1622	L, 41
Threapwood	1	1730	RC
Wallasey	2	*c*.1605	FB, ii
CORNWALL			
Bodmin	4	1757	RC
Launceston	7	1739	RC
CUMBERLAND			
Brampton	4	1736	RC
Burgh Barony	—	*c*.1684	FB, ii
Carlisle*	15	Late 16th cent.	G, 43
Cockermouth	1	1730	RC
Drigg	—	*c*.1670	FB, ii
Egremont	3	1730	RC
Langwathby	—	16th cent.	Bouch and Jones, *Short Economic and Social History of the Lake Counties 1500–1830*, 342.
Penrith	7	1730	RC
Workington	1	1687	FB, ii
DERBYSHIRE			
Bakewell	2	1730	RC
Chesterfield	17	1730	RC
Derby	8	1737	RC
Shirley	1	1745	RC
Tideswell	1	1737	RC

Place	Meetings Recorded In Calendar Sample (Max. No. = 17)	Earliest Reference	Source
DEVON			
Barnstaple	4	1736	RC
Colyton	1	1755	RC
Exeter*	1	Early 17th cent.	G, 63
DORSET			
Blandford Forum	12	1600	Weinstock, 'Blandford', 122.
Shaftesbury	1	1735	RC
DURHAM			
Barnard Castle	1	1718	FB, ii
Bishop Auckland	5	1662	FB, ii
Chester-le-Street	2	1735	RC
Darlington	4	1732	FB, ii
Durham	16	1613	FB, ii
Gainford	1	1734	FB, ii
Heighington	1	1730	RC
Sedgefield*	6	17th cent.	G, 192
Staindrop	1	1756	RC
Stockton-on-Tees*	13	1724	G, 199
Sunderland	6	Late 17th cent.	FB, ii
Winlanton	5	1735	RC
Wolsingham	1	1730	RC
ESSEX			
Brentwood	12	1736	RC
Chelmsford	3	1759	RC
Colchester	2	1755	RC
Epping	2	1738	RC
High Ongar	1	1735	RC
Holness	1	1738	RC
Maldon	4	1737	RC
Romford	4	1755	RC

Place	Meetings Recorded In Calendar Sample (Max. No. = 17)	Earliest Reference	Source
GLOUCESTERSHIRE			
Bisley	2	1736	RC
Chipping Campden	1	1730	RC
Chipping Sodbury	1	1739	RC
Cirencester	4	1755	RC
Gloucester	7	1735	RC
Tetbury	11	1730	RC
Tewkesbury	4	1721	*VCH Gloucestershire*, viii. 123.
HAMPSHIRE			
Andover	3	1757	RC
Basingstoke	11	1730	RC
Broadhalfpenny	1	1730	RC
Odiham	4	1758	RC
Ringwood	4	1735	RC
Stockbridge	15	1735	RC
Whitchurch	1	1755	RC
Winchester	17	1591	Thirsk, *Horses in Early Modern England*, 22.
HEREFORD			
Hereford*	8	1730	RC
Leominster	1	1756	RC
HERTFORDSHIRE			
Barnet	11	1620	L, 41
Berkhamsted	1	1730	RC
Odsey	9	1730	RC
Tring	1	1730	RC
HUNTINGDON			
Huntingdon*	17	1730	RC
St Ives	2	1730	RC
Sapley	—	1602	L, 30
Sawtry	1	1730	RC
Stilton	5	1735	RC

Place	Meetings Recorded In Calendar Sample (Max. No. = 17)	Earliest Reference	Source
KENT			
Barham	16	1735	RC
Bexleyheath	1	1739	RC
Bromley	3	1730	RC
Canterbury	17	1730	RC
Lynsted Park	1	1735	RC
Maidstone	5	1735	RC
New Romney	1	1739	RC
Tunbridge Wells	1	1738	RC
LANCASHIRE			
Aughton Moss	—	1705	B, i. 94
Childwall	2	1705	B, i. 93
Clitheroe	2	1617	FB, ii
Crosby	1	Early 17th cent.	B, ii. 237
Great Crosby	—	1704	B, i. 23
Knowsley Park	—	1726	B, iii. 193
Lancaster	5	1698	FB, ii
Leaton Heyes	—	1704	B, i. 60
Liverpool*	1	Early 17th cent.	B, ii. 237
Manchester	10	1730	RC
Newton-le-Willows	2	1730	RC
Ormskirk	6	1685	FB, ii
Prescot	1	1727	B, iii. 218
Preston	10	1669	R. Greinsworth to R. Kenyon, 19 Aug. 1669, Lancashire RO, DDKe (Kenyon MSS), 9/40.
Rochdale	1	1730	RC
LEICESTERSHIRE			
Burton-on-the-Wolds	1	1756	RC
Earl Shilton	5	1730	RC

Place	Meetings Recorded In Calendar Sample (Max. No. = 17)	Earliest Reference	Source
Hinckley	1	1738	RC
Leicester*	16	1603	G, 123
Loughborough	6	1735	RC
Lutterworth	2	1735	RC
Market Bosworth	1	1736	RC
Market Harborough	2	1735	RC
Melton Mowbray	6	1718	*Evening Post*, 9–12 Aug. 1718.
LINCOLNSHIRE			
Alford	5	1730	RC
Boston	2	1730	RC
Caistor	2	1736	RC
Fleet	1	1739	RC
Gainsborough	1	1730	RC
Grantham	16	1730	RC
Grimsby	1	1730	RC
Holbeach	1	1738	RC
Horncastle	2	1737	RC
Leadenham	1	1738	RC
Lincoln	17	1617	L, 40
Long Sutton	1	1730	RC
Louth	3	1755	RC
Sleaford	1	1736	RC
Spalding	4	1730	RC
Stamford	14	*c*.1619	RCHM, *Stamford*, p. xliii.
MIDDLESEX			
Belsize	2	1730	RC
Enfield	1	1755	RC
Finchley	3	1736	RC
Hampstead	7	1730	RC
Hampton Court	—	Late 17th cent.	L, 49

Place	Meetings Recorded In Calendar Sample (Max. No. = 17)	Earliest Reference	Source
Highgate	2	1737	RC
Hounslow	10	1725	SM, 27 Sept. 1725.
Hyde Park	—	1635	L, 41
Kentish Town	4	1733	SM, 9 July 1733.
Sunbury	1	1730	RC
Tothill Fields	4	1736	RC
MONMOUTHSHIRE			
Monmouth	7	1730	RC
NORFOLK			
Fakenham*	1	1758	RC
Holt	5	1727	SM, 15 May 1727.
North Walsham	2	1730	RC
Norwich	3	1710	Corfield, 'A Provincial Capital', 292.
Swaffham	13	1695	G, 231
Thetford	1	1726	SM, 25 Apr. 1726
Yarmouth*	—	1715	G, 231
Winterton-on-Sea	1	1730	RC
NORTHAMPTONSHIRE			
Daventry	4	1730	RC
Brackley	—	1612	L, 40
Harlestone	3	1632	Rice, *British Turf*, ii. 86.
Kettering	3	1735	RC
Northampton	15	1730	RC
Oundle	4	1736	RC
Peterborough	15	1730	RC
Rothwell	1	1730	RC
Thrapston	2	1736	RC
Wellingborough	1	1736	RC
Whittlebury	1	1770	RC

Place	Meetings Recorded In Calendar Sample (Max. No. = 17)	Earliest Reference	Source
NORTHUMBERLAND			
Alnwick	6	1654	FB, ii
Bellingham	—	1709	FB, ii
Berwick-upon-Tweed	5	1639	FB, ii
Blencarn	—	c.1630	FB, ii
Bywell	1	1737	RC
Hexham*	7	1721	G, 106
Milfield	6	1723	FB, ii
Morpeth	15	1720	FB, ii
Newcastle-upon-Tyne*	16	1621	G, 143
Stamfordham	1	1740	RC
Stanerton	3	1737	RC
NOTTINGHAMSHIRE			
Mansfield	5	1735	RC
Newark-on-Trent	6	1755	RC
Nottingham*	17	1689	G, 163–4
OXFORDSHIRE			
Banbury	4	1735	RC
Bicester	—	1718	*Evening Post*, 5–7 Aug. 1718.
Burford	11	1681	L, 47
Chipping Norton	15	1735	RC
Henley-on-Thames	2	1735	RC
Oxford	17	1730	RC
RUTLAND			
Uppingham	9	1730	RC
SHROPSHIRE			
Bridgnorth	7	1691	Sh, 177
Ludlow*	16	1728	Sh, 180
Market Drayton	1	1729	Sh, 180
Much Wenlock	—	1733	Sh, 181
Newport	1	1738	RC
Oswestry	8	1728	Sh, 181

Place	Meetings Recorded In Calendar Sample (Max. No. = 17)	Earliest Reference	Source
Shawbury	—	1768	Sh, 180
Shrewsbury	10	1717	Sh, 177
Whitchurch	12	1600	Sh, 181
SOMERSET			
Bath*	7	1723	Hobhouse, *Diary of a West Country Physician*, 100.
Bridgwater	7	1738	RC
Wells	6	1739	RC
STAFFORDSHIRE			
Burton-upon-Trent	—	Early 18th cent.	Kettle, 'Lichfield Races', 39.
Eccleshall	2	1730	RC
Etchinghill	1	1736	RC
Hednesford	1	1770	RC
Lichfield	17	1682	Kettle, 'Lichfield Races', 39.
Newcastle-under-Lyme	1	1730	RC
Offlehay	1	1735	RC
Penkridge	1	1735	RC
Stafford	1	1770	RC
Stone	5	1735	RC
Tamworth	3	1738	RC
SUFFOLK			
Beccles	15	1723	SM, 20 May 1723.
Bungay	5	1723	SM, 22 Apr. 1723.
Bury St Edmunds	7	1722	SM, 16 July 1722.
Ipswich	17	1726	SM, 30 May 1726.
New Buckenham	1	1738	RC
Newmarket*	17	*c*.1613	*VCH Cambridgeshire*, v. 279.

Place	Meetings Recorded In Calendar Sample (Max. No. = 17)	Earliest Reference	Source
SURREY			
Carshalton	7	1730	RC
Cobham	6	1735	RC
Croydon	4	1574	L, 30
Egham	6	1735	RC
Epsom*	16	1625	Hunn, *Epsom Racecourse*, 32.
Guildford	16	Early 18th cent.	Macky, *Journey*, i. 89.
Hurst Park	1	1737	RC
Kingston-upon-Thames	3	1735	RC
Limpsfield	3	1730	RC
Wimbledon	6	1730	RC
SUSSEX			
Chichester	2	1735	RC
Eastbourne	4	1730	RC
Lewes	17	1730	RC
Midhurst	5	1730	RC
Steyning	6	1735	RC
WARWICKSHIRE			
Atherstone	4	1730	RC
Birmingham	2	1739	RC
Coleshill	—	1711	L, 73
Coventry	4	1735	RC
Nuneaton	—	1751	Newdigate Diaries, 31 July 1751.
Rugby	12	1730	RC
Stratford-upon-Avon*	11	1718	*Evening Post*, 2–5 Aug. 1718.
Warwick*	17	1707	*VCH Warwickshire*, viii. 512.
WESTMORLAND			
Appleby	1	1736	RC
Kirby Lonsdale	3	1727	FB, ii

Place	Meetings Recorded In Calendar Sample (Max. No. = 17)	Earliest Reference	Source
WILTSHIRE			
Amesbury	1	1735	RC
Chippenham	4	1737	RC
Cricklade	2	1736	RC
Market Lavington	2	1738	RC
Marlborough	12	1730	RC
Salisbury*	17	1584	G, 184
Warminster	2	1735	RC
WORCESTERSHIRE			
Bromsgrove	4	1736	RC
Hampton	1	1739	RC
Lickey	1	1757	RC
Tenbury Wells	3	1736	RC
Worcester*	10	1718	G, 229
YORKSHIRE			
Askrigg	2	1738	RC
Barnsley	1	1717	FB, ii
Bedale	10	1726	FB, ii
Beverley*	17	1690	G, 33
Bishop Burton	5	1738	RC
Boroughbridge	9	1595	L, 30
Bramham	2	1702	FB, ii
Bridlington	2	1730	RC
Catterick Bridge*	—	Early 17th cent.	G, 50
Doncaster*	16	1595	FB, ii
Follifoot	1	1753	FB, ii
Fremington	3	1735	RC
Gatherley Moor	4	Early 16th cent.	FB, i
Guisborough	—	1550	FB, ii
Halifax	4	1736	RC
Hambleton	17	1612 or 1613	FB, i

Place	Meetings Recorded In Calendar Sample (Max. No. = 17)	Earliest Reference	Source
Hedon	2	1738	RC
Hull	7	c.1734	FB, ii
Hunmanby	4	1730	RC
Kiplingcotes	17	1555	FB, ii
Knaresborough	4	1730	RC
Leeds	7	1682	FB, ii
Malton	17	1692	FB, ii
Middleham	6	1726	FB, ii
Northallerton	1	1750	FB, ii
Nunnington	—	1630	FB, ii
Penistone	—	1726	FB, ii
Pontefract*	6	1735	RC
Richmond	6	1576	FB, i
Ripon*	1	1664	G, 179
Rotherham	5	1727	FB, ii
Scarborough	6	1736	RC
Selby	6	1730	RC
Sheffield	4	1711	FB, ii
Stokesley	—	1752	FB, ii
Tollerton	—	Early 17th cent.	FB, ii
Wakefield	17	1678	FB, ii
Yarm	4	1729	FB, ii
York*	17	1530	FB, ii

BIBLIOGRAPHY

A. Manuscript Sources

Bath City Archives, City Record Office
Council Minutes 1690–1760
Chamberlain's Accounts 1690–1715

Bath Reference Library
38/43, 'Diary of A Tour Undertaken by Three Students' (1725)

Beinecke Library, Yale
Osborne Shelves, f.c.80, Diary of E. Pigott (1770–83), 2 vols.

Bristol Archives Office
04479(2), printed 'Proposals for Erecting by Subscription an Assembly House
    in the City of Bath'
Bristol Common Council Proceedings 1687–1702

Hereford City Library
Hereford Common Council Minutes 1693–1736

Lancashire Record Office
DDKe, Kenyon MSS
DDX/146/2, Subscriptions to the Union Hunt in Preston 1770
PR.2847, Miscell. (5), 4, Rules and Orders for the Establishment of a Book
    Club, 1 Jan. 1756, Ulveston

Preston Corporation Manuscripts, Preston Town Hall
White Book (Council Minutes and Orders 1660–1761)
Small Order Book 1694–1703
Council Minutes 1703–64
Guild Rolls 1662–1762

Shakespeare Birthplace Trust, Stratford-upon-Avon
ER.2/188, Subscription Lists, Stratford-upon-Avon Races 1755 and 1758
PR.64, printed Bills for Stratford-upon-Avon and Warwick Races (1769)

Somerset Record Office
DD/L, Luttrell MSS

Suffolk Record Office, Bury St Edmunds
E2/20/1-3, Cullum Correspondence 1756-85, based on typescript catalogue of E. Byers
E2/25/1-3, Hanson Letters 1741-1816, based on typescript catalogue of E. Byers
E2/44/1, Revd Sir J. Cullum's Journal of a Tour of the Yorkshire Area (1771)

Warwickshire County Record Office
CR.15/96, Unsorted Collection of Solicitor's Papers
CR.136, Newdigate MSS
CR.143/A, J. Fish, 'The Survey of the Manor of Rusden with the Honour and Part of the Manor of Kenilworth'
CR.217, J. Fish and C. Bridgeman, Plan of Warwick (*c.*1711)
CR.229 (Shirley MSS), Box 2/2, Articles and Subscription List, Warwick Races 1754
CR.1368, Mordaunt MSS, 7 vols.
CR.1618 (Warwick Borough Records), W.10, Petitions to the Fire Court, 3 bundles
—— W.13/5, Corporation Accounts 1693-1728
—— WA.4 (Fire Records), 'Memorials of . . . the Late Dreadful Fire'
—— WA.4, 'An Estimate of the Loss Sustained in and by the Late Fire . . . 1694'
—— WA.6/116 (Ann Johnston's Charity), Landor House: Articles of Agreement and Proposed Elevation
L6, Lucy MSS
QS/11 (Hearth Tax Returns) /3 (Kineton Hundred 1662), 5 (Warwickshire 1663), 7 (Warwick Borough 1670), 50 (Warwick Borough 1674)
Warwick Castle MSS, Castle Accounts 1695-8

Wiltshire Record Office
947, Long MSS

York City Archives, York City Library
House Book, 40 (1692-1706), 41 (1706-19), 42 (1720-39), 43 (1739-56), 44 (1756-80)
M.23/1, Assembly Rooms: Directors' Minute Book 1730-58
M.23/3, printed 'Proposals for Building, by Subscription, Assembly Rooms, in the City of York'
M.23/4/A, Assembly Rooms Ledger and Register of Subscribers 1732-47

B. Acts of Parliament

18 & 19 Car. II, c. 7, 8, London Rebuilding Acts (1667)
27 Car. II, Northampton Rebuilding Act (1675)
6 Gul. III, c. 1, Warwick Rebuilding Act (1695)
5 Geo. II, c. 16, Blandford Forum Rebuilding Act (1732)
10 Geo. II, c. 28, Theatre Act (1737)
12 Geo. II, c. 28, Gaming Act (1739)
13 Geo. II, c. 19, Horse-Racing Act (1740)

C. Newspapers

Bath Advertiser
Evening Post
Gloucester Journal
Lancashire Journal
Leeds Mercury
Post-Boy (London)
Preston Weekly Journal; also known as *Preston Journal*
True British Courant or the Preston Journal; also known as *British Courant or
the Preston Journal*
Stratford, Shipston, and Alcester Journal; also known as *Keating's Stratford
and Warwick Mercury: Or Cirencester, Shipston, and Alcester Weekly
Journal*
Suffolk Mercury or St Edmund's Bury Post

D. Maps

A New and Correct Plan of the City of Bath and Places Adjacent (1750).
CHADWICK, J., *The Map of all the Streets, Lanes, and Alleys within the Town
of Liverpool* (1725).
COSSINS, J., *A New and Exact Plan of the Town of Leeds* (1725).
DOIDGE, W. and H., *A Plan of the Ancient City of Canterbury* (1752).
DONN, B., 'A Plan of the City and Suburbs of Exeter', sheet 42 in *A Map of
the County of Devon* (1765), reprinted, Devon and Cornwall Record Soc.
(1965).
DRAKE, F., *A Plan of the City of York* (1736), in Drake, *Eboracum*, opposite
244.
GILMORE, J., *The Map or Topographical Description of the City of Bath* (1694).
MILLERD, J., *An Exact Delineation of the Famous City of Bristol and Suburbs*
(1673).

NASH, T., *Plan of . . . Worcester*, in Nash, *Worcestershire*, ii.

NOBLE and BUTLIN, *A Plan of the Town of Northampton* (1746).

WESTLEY, W., *The Plan of Birmingham, Surveyed in the Year 1731*.

WINTER, S., *Plan of Stratford on Avon* (1759).

WOOD, J., *A Plan of the City of Bath*, surveyed 1735 (1736).

E. Printed Sources and Unpublished Theses

ABRAM, W. A., *Memorials of the Preston Guilds* (Preston, 1882).

ACTON, G., and LLOYD, D., *Ludlow Walks* (n.p. [1983]).

ADEY, K. R., 'Seventeenth-Century Stafford: A County Town in Decline', *Midland History*, ii, No. 3 (1974), 152-67.

AGNEW, J.-C., *Worlds Apart: The Market and the Theatre in Anglo-American Thought 1550-1750* (Cambridge, 1986).

AIKIN, J., *A Description of the Country from Thirty to Forty Miles round Manchester* (London, 1795).

AIRS, M., *The Buildings of Britain: Tudor and Jacobean* (London, 1982).

ALBERT, W., *The Turnpike Road System in England 1663-1840* (Cambridge, 1972).

ALLEN, T., *A New and Complete History of the County of York*, 3 vols. (London, 1828-31).

ALTHAM, H. S., and SWANTON, E. W., *A History of Cricket*, 2nd edn. (London, 1938).

AMERY, C. (ed.), *Period Houses and their Details* (London, 1978).

ANDREW, D. T., 'The Code of Honour and its Critics: The Opposition to Duelling in England 1700-1850', *Social History*, v, No. 3 (1980), 409-34.

—— 'Aldermen and Big Bourgeoisie of London Reconsidered', *Social History*, vi (1981), 359-64.

ANDREWS, J. H., 'The Port of Chichester and the Grain Trade 1650-1750', *Sussex Archaeological Collections*, xcii (1954), 93-105.

ANSTEY, C., *The New Bath Guide*, 1766, repr. (Bath, 1970).

APPLEBY, A. B., 'The Disappearance of Plague: A Continuing Puzzle', *EcHR*, 2nd ser., xxxiii, No. 2 (1980), 161-73.

ASTILL, G. G., *Historic Towns in Berkshire: An Archaeological Appraisal*, Berkshire Archaeological Committee, Publication No. 2 (Reading, 1978).

ASTON, M., and BOND, J., *The Landscape of Towns* (London, 1976).

AUSTEN, J., *Persuasion*, 1818, ed. D. W. Harding, repr. (Harmondsworth, 1971).

AVISON, C., *An Essay on Musical Expression* (London, 1752).

BAINES, E., *History, Directory, and Gazetteer of the County Palatine of Lancaster*, 1824, repr., 2 vols. (Newton Abbot, 1968).

BAKER, C. H. Collins and M. I., *The Life and Circumstances of James Brydges, First Duke of Chandos* (Oxford, 1949).

BAKER, M., *Discovering the Bath Road* (Tring, 1968).

BARBEAU, A., *Life and Letters at Bath in the Eighteenth Century* (London, 1904).

BARKER, K., *Bristol at Play: Five Centuries of Live Entertainment* (Bradford-on-Avon, 1976).

BARKER, T., 'Lancashire Coal, Cheshire Salt, and the Rise of Liverpool', *Trans. of the Historic Soc. of Lancashire and Cheshire*, cii (1951), 83–101.

BARLEY, M. W., *The English Farmhouse and Cottage* (London, 1972).

BARLEY, M. W. (ed.), *The Plans and Topography of Medieval Towns in England and Wales*, Council for British Archaeology, Research Report, xiv (1976).

BARNETT, W., *et al.*, *Whitehaven: A New Structure for a Restoration Town* (n.p., n.d.).

BARRELL, J., *The Political Theory of Painting from Reynolds to Hazlitt* (New Haven, Conn., and London, 1986).

BARRETT, J., 'Spas and Seaside Resorts 1660–1780', in J. Stevenson *et al.*, *The Rise of the New Urban Society*, Open University Urban History Course (Milton Keynes, 1977), 37–70.

BARRY, J., 'Popular Culture in Seventeenth-Century Bristol', in Reay, *Popular Culture*, 59–90.

—— 'The Cultural Life of Bristol 1640–1775', D.Phil. thesis (Oxford, 1985).

—— 'Religion in the Georgian Town', in *Life in the Georgian Town*, 34–42.

BARTON, M., *Tunbridge Wells* (London, 1937).

The Bath and Bristol Guide: Or, the Tradesman's and Traveller's Pocket-Companion, 3rd edn. [1755], repr. (Bath, 1969).

Bath: A Poem (London, Bath, and Bristol, 1748).

Bath Assembly Rooms, National Trust Guide (1979).

The Bath Miscellany for the Year 1740 (Bath, 1741).

BECKETT, J. V., 'English Landownership in the Later Seventeenth and Eighteenth Centuries: The Debate and the Problems', *EcHR*, 2nd ser., xxx, No. 4 (1977), 567–81.

—— 'The Lowthers at Holker: Marriage, Inheritance, and Debt in the Fortunes of an Eighteenth-Century Landowning Family', *Trans. of the Historic Soc. of Lancashire and Cheshire*, cxxvii (1978), 47–64.

—— *Coal and Tobacco: The Lowthers and the Economic Development of West Cumberland 1660–1760* (Cambridge, 1981).

—— 'Land Tax Administration at the Local Level', in M. Turner and D. Mills (eds.), *Land and Property: The English Land Tax 1692–1832* (Gloucester, 1986), 161–79.

BEIER, A. L., 'The Social Problems of an Elizabethan Country Town: Warwick 1580–90', in Clark, *Country Towns*, 46–85.

BEIER, A. L., and FINLAY, R. (eds.), *London 1500-1700: The Making of the Metropolis* (London, 1986).

BELL, C. and R., *City Fathers: The Early History of Town Planning in Britain* (Harmondsworth, 1972).

BELLINGHAM, T., *Diary of Thomas Bellingham*, ed. A. Hewitson (Preston, 1908).

BENEVOLO, L., *The Architecture of the Renaissance*, 2 vols. (London, 1978).

BERESFORD, M., *New Towns in the Middle Ages* (London, 1967).

—— *History on the Ground*, rev. edn. (London, 1971).

BISSE, T., *A Sermon Preached in the Cathedral Church of Hereford, at the Anniversary Meeting of the Three Choirs, Gloucester, Worcester, Hereford, September 3, 1729* (London, 1729).

BLACK, J., *The British and the Grand Tour* (London, 1985).

BLOMEFIELD, F., *An Essay towards a Topographical History of the County of Norfolk*, 1739-75, 2nd edn., 11 vols. (London, 1805-10).

BLUNDELL, N., *The Great Diurnal of Nicholas Blundell*, ed. J. J. Bagley, Record Soc. of Lancashire and Cheshire, 3 vols., cx, cxii, cxiv (1968-72).

BONSER, K. J., and NICHOLS, H., 'Printed Maps and Plans of Leeds 1711-1900', *Publications of the Thoresby Soc.*, xlvii, No. 106 (1958).

BORSAY, P., 'A County Town Renaissance: Warwick 1660-1760', typescript deposited in Warwickshire CRO.

—— 'The English Urban Renaissance: The Development of Provincial Urban Culture *c*.1680-*c*.1760', *Social History*, No. 5 (1977), 581-603.

—— 'The English Urban Renaissance: Landscape and Leisure in the Provincial Town *c*.1660-1770', Ph.D. thesis (Lancaster, 1981).

—— ' "All the Town's a Stage": Urban Ritual and Ceremony 1660-1800', in Clark, *Provincial Towns*, 228-58.

BOUCH, C. M. L., and JONES, G. P., *A Short Economic and Social History of the Lake Counties 1500-1830* (Manchester, 1961).

BOURNE, H., *Antiquitates Vulgares: Or, the Antiquities of the Common People* (Newcastle-upon-Tyne, 1725).

—— *The History of Newcastle-upon-Tyne* (Newcastle-upon-Tyne, 1736).

BOYCE, B., *The Benevolent Man: A Life of Ralph Allen of Bath* (Cambridge, Mass., 1967).

BOYLE, E. C. (ed.), *The Orrery Papers*, 2 vols. (London, 1903).

BRAILSFORD, D., *Sport and Society* (London, 1969).

BRAND, J., *Observations on Popular Antiquities* (Newcastle-upon-Tyne, 1777).

—— *History and Antiquities of the Town and County of Newcastle-upon-Tyne*, 2 vols. (London, 1789).

BRETT-JAMES, N. G., *The Growth of Stuart London* (London, 1935).

BREWER, J., 'Commercialization and Politics', in McKendrick *et al.*, *Birth of a Consumer Society*, 195-262.

BRIDBURY, A. R., 'English Provincial Towns in the Later Middle Ages', *EcHR*, 2nd ser., xxxiv, No. 1 (1981), 1-24.

BRIGGS, M. S., *Wren the Incomparable* (London, 1953).

British Sporting Painting 1650–1850, Arts Council of Great Britain (London, 1974).

BROOKES, C., *English Cricket: The Games and its Players through the Ages* (Newton Abbot, 1978).

BROWN, A. F. J., 'Colchester in the Eighteenth Century', in L. Munby (ed.), *East Anglian Studies* (Cambridge, 1968), 146–73.

—— *Essex at Work 1700–1815* (Chelmsford, 1969).

BROWN, P. S., 'The Vendors of Medicines Advertised in Eighteenth-Century Bath Newspapers', *Medical History*, xix (1975), 352–69.

BRUNSKILL, R. W., *Illustrated Handbook of Vernacular Architecture*, 2nd edn. (London, 1978).

BRUNSKILL, R. W., and CLIFTON-TAYLOR, A., *English Brickwork* (London 1977).

BRUSHFIELD, T. N., 'Andrew Brice and the Early Exeter Newspaper Press', *Trans. of the Devonshire Association*, xx (1888), 163–214.

BUCK, S. and N., *Buck's Antiquities*, 3 vols. (London, 1774).

BUCKLEY, G. B., *Fresh Light on 18th Century Cricket* (Birmingham, 1935).

—— *Fresh Light on Pre-Victorian Cricket* (Birmingham, 1937).

The Buildings of England:

N. Pevsner, *Bedfordshire and the County of Huntingdon and Peterborough* (Harmondsworth, 1968).

N. Pevsner, *Berkshire*, repr. (Harmondsworth, 1975).

N. Pevsner, *Buckinghamshire*, repr. (Harmondsworth, 1973).

N. Pevsner, *Derbyshire* (London, 1953).

N. Pevsner, *South Devon* (Harmondsworth, 1952).

J. Newman and N. Pevsner, *Dorset* (Harmondsworth, 1972).

N. Pevsner, *Essex* (Harmondsworth, 1954).

D. Verey, *Gloucestershire: The Cotswolds* (Harmondsworth, 1970).

N. Pevsner and D. Lloyd, *Hampshire and the Isle of Wight*, repr. (Harmondsworth, 1973).

N. Pevsner, *Herefordshire*, repr. (Harmondsworth, 1977).

N. Pevsner, *Hertfordshire* (London, 1953).

J. Newman, *West Kent and the Weald* (Harmondsworth, 1969).

N. Pevsner, *North Lancashire* (Harmondsworth, 1969).

N. Pevsner, *North-East Norfolk and Norwich* (Harmondsworth, 1962).

N. Pevsner, *North-West and South Norfolk* (Harmondsworth, 1962).

N. Pevsner, *Northamptonshire*, 2nd edn. rev. B. Cherry (Harmondsworth, 1973).

N. Pevsner and J. Sherwood, *Oxfordshire* (Harmondsworth, 1974).

N. Pevsner, *Shropshire*, repr. (Harmondsworth, 1974).

N. Pevsner, *North Somerset and Bristol* (Harmondsworth, 1958).

N. Pevsner, *South and West Somerset* (Harmondsworth, 1958).

N. Pevsner, *Staffordshire*, repr. (Harmondsworth, 1975).

N. Pevsner, *Suffolk*, 2nd edn. rev. E. Radcliffe (Harmondsworth, 1974).

N. Pevsner and I. Nairn, *Sussex* (Harmondsworth, 1965).

N. Pevsner and A. Wedgwood, *Warwickshire* (Harmondsworth, 1966).

N. Pevsner, *Wiltshire*, 2nd edn. rev. B. Cherry (Harmondsworth, 1975).

N. Pevsner, *Worcestershire* (Harmondsworth, 1968).

N. Pevsner, *Yorkshire: The North Riding* (Harmondsworth, 1966).

N. Pevsner, *Yorkshire: The West Riding*, 2nd edn. rev. E. Radcliffe, repr. (Harmondsworth, 1979).

N. Pevsner, *Yorkshire: York and the East Riding* (Harmondsworth, 1972).

BURKE, P., *Popular Culture in Early Modern Europe* (London, 1979).

BURLEY, K. H., 'The Economic Development of Essex in the Later Seventeenth and Early Eighteenth Centuries', Ph.D. thesis (London, 1957).

BURLEY, T. L. G., *Playhouses and Players of East Anglia* (Norwich, 1928).

BURR, T. B., *A History of Tunbridge Wells* (London, 1766).

BUTLER, D. J., *The Town Plans of Chichester 1595-1898* (Chichester, 1972).

BUTLER, R. M., 'A Late Seventeenth-Century Plan of York', *Antiquaries Jnl.*, ii, Part 2 (1972), 320-9.

CALAMY, E., *An Historical Account of My Own Life*, ed. J. T. Rutt, 2 vols. (London, 1829).

CAMIDGE, W., *The Mansion House at York* (York, 1902).

CAMPBELL, R., *The London Tradesman*, 1747, repr. (Newton Abbot, 1969).

CANNON, J. (ed.), *The Whig Ascendancy* (London, 1981).

CAPP, B., 'Popular Literature', in Reay, *Popular Culture*, 198-243.

CARR, R., *English Fox-Hunting: A History* (London, 1976).

CARTWRIGHT, J. L., 'Oundle in the Eighteenth Century through the Eyes of John Clifton', *Northamptonshire Past and Present*, v, Part 4 (1976), 339-46.

CHALKLIN, C. W., 'A Seventeenth-Century Market Town: Tonbridge', *Archaeologia Cantiana*, lxxvi (1961), 152-62.

—— *The Provincial Towns of Georgian England* (London, 1974).

—— 'The Making of Some New Towns c.1600-1720', in Chalklin and Havinden, *Urban Growth*, 229-51.

—— *Seventeenth-Century Kent*, repr. (Rochester, 1978).

—— 'Capital Expenditure on Building for Cultural Purposes in Provincial England 1730-1830', *Business History*, xxii (1980), 51-70.

—— 'The Financing of Church Building in the Provincial Towns of Eighteenth-Century England', in Clark, *Provincial Towns*, 284-310.

CHALKLIN, C. W., and HAVINDEN, M. A. (eds.), *Rural Change and Urban Growth 1500-1800* (London, 1974).

CHAMBERLAYNE, E., *Angliae Notitia*, 18th edn. (London, 1694).

CHAMBERS, J. D., 'Population Change in a Provincial Town: Nottingham 1700-1800', in D. V. Glass and D. E. C. Eversley (eds.), *Population History* (London, 1965), 334-53.

CHANDAMAN, C. D., *The English Public Revenue 1660-1688* (Oxford, 1975).

CHANDLER, G., *Liverpool* (London, 1957).

CHANDLER, M., *A Description of Bath: A Poem* (London, 1734).

CHARTIER, R., 'Culture as Appropriation: Popular Cultural Uses in Early Modern France', in S. L. Kaplan (ed.), *Understanding Popular Culture: Europe from the Middle Ages to the Nineteenth Century* (Berlin, New York, and Amsterdam, 1984), 229-53.

CHARTRES, J., 'Markets and Marketing in Metropolitan Western England in the Late Seventeenth and Eighteenth Centuries', in M. A. Havinden (ed.), *Husbandry and Marketing in the South West 1500-1800* (Exeter, 1973), 63-74.

—— *Internal Trade in England 1500-1700* (London, 1977).

—— 'Road Carrying in England in the Seventeenth Century: Myth and Reality', *EcHR*, 2nd ser., xxx, No. 1 (1977), 73-94.

—— 'The Marketing of Agricultural Produce', in J. Thirsk (ed.), *The Agrarian History of England and Wales*, Vol. 5: *1640-1750, Part 2, Agrarian Change* (Cambridge, 1985), 406-502.

CHATWIN, P. B., 'The Rebuilding of St Mary's Church, Warwick', *TBAS*, lxv (1943-4), 1-40.

—— 'The Great Fire of Warwick 1694', *TBAS*, lxvii (1947-8), 35-41.

CLARK, F. L., 'A History of Epsom Spa', *Surrey Archaeological Collections*, lvii (1960), 1-41.

CLARK, J. C. D., *Revolution and Rebellion: State and Society in England in the Seventeenth and Eighteenth Centuries* (Cambridge, 1986).

CLARK, P. (ed.), *The Early Modern Town* (London, 1976).

—— (ed.), *Country Towns in Pre-Industrial England* (Leicester, 1981).

—— *The English Alehouse: A Social History 1200-1830* (London, 1983).

—— 'Visions of the Urban Community: Antiquarians and the English City before 1800', in Fraser and Sutcliffe, *Urban History*, 105-24.

—— (ed.), *The Transformation of English Provincial Towns 1600-1800* (London, 1984).

—— 'The Civic Leaders of Gloucester 1580-1800', in Clark, *Provincial Towns*, 311-45.

CLARK, P., and SLACK, P. (eds.), *Crisis and Order in English Towns 1500-1700* (London, 1972).

CLARK, P., and SLACK, P., *English Towns in Transition 1500-1700* (London, 1976).

CLARKE, B. F. L., *The Building of the Eighteenth-Century Church* (London, 1963).

CLEGG, A. L., *A History of Dorchester, Dorset* (London, 1972).

CLEMENS, P. G. E., 'The Rise of Liverpool 1665-1750', *EcHR*, 2nd ser., xxix, No. 2 (1976), 211-25.

CLERK, J., 'A Journie to Carlyle and Penrith in 1731', ed. W. A. J. Prevost,

Trans. of the Cumberland and Westmorland Antiquarian and Archaeological Soc., new ser., lxi (1961), 202-37.

CLIFTON-TAYLOR, A., *The Pattern of English Building* (London, 1962).

—— *Six English Towns* (London, 1978).

'Coffee-Houses Vindicated. In Answer to the Late Published Character of a Coffee-House', 1675, repr. in *The Harleian Miscellany*, vi (1745), 433-6.

COHEN, R. A., 'Documents Concerning Dr William Johnston, Physician, of Warwick', *TBAS*, lxxviii (1962), 55-60.

COLEMAN, D. C., *The Economy of England 1450-1750* (London, 1977).

COLEMAN, D. C., and JOHN, A. H. (eds.), *Trade, Government, and Economy in Pre-Industrial England* (London, 1976).

COLLEY, L., *In Defiance of Oligarchy: The Tory Party 1714-60* (Cambridge, 1982).

COLLINSON, J., *The History and Antiquities of the County of Somerset*, 3 vols. (Bath, 1791).

COLVIN, H. M., 'The Bastards of Blandford: Architects and Master-Builders', *Archaeological Jnl.*, civ (1948), 178-95.

—— 'Fifty New Churches', *Architectural Review* (Mar. 1950), 189-96.

—— 'Domestic Architecture and Town Planning', in A. L. Poole (ed.), *Medieval England*, 2 vols. (Oxford, 1958), i. 37-97.

—— 'Francis Smith of Warwick 1672-1738', *Warwickshire History*, ii, No. 2 (1972/3), 3-13.

—— (ed.), *The History of the King's Works*, Vol. 5: *1660-1782* (London, 1976).

—— *A Biographical Dictionary of British Architects 1600-1840* (London, 1978).

COLVIN, H. M., and WODEHOUSE, L. M., 'Henry Bell of King's Lynn', *Architectural History*, iv (1961), 41-62.

CONNELY, W., *Beau Nash* (London, 1955).

CONZEN, M. R. G., 'The Use of Town Plans in the Study of Urban History', in H. J. Dyos (ed.), *The Study of Urban History* (London, 1976), 113-30.

COOK, T. A., *A History of the English Turf*, Vol. 1, Division 1 (London, 1901).

COOPER, A. A., Earl of Shaftesbury, *Characteristics of Men, Manners, Opinions, Times*, 4th edn., 3 vols. (London, 1727).

COOPER, J. P., 'The Social Distribution of Land and Men in England 1436-1700', *EcHR*, 2nd ser., xx, No. 3 (1967), 419-40.

CORFIELD, P. J., 'A Provincial Capital in the Late Seventeenth Century: The Case of Norwich', in Clark and Slack, *Crisis and Order*, 263-310.

—— 'Urban Development in England and Wales in the Sixteenth and Seventeenth Centuries', in Coleman and John, *Pre-Industrial England*, 214-47.

—— 'Economic Growth and Change in Seventeenth-Century English Towns', in Phythian-Adams *et al.*, *Traditional Community under Stress*, 31-71.

—— *The Impact of English Towns 1700-1800* (Oxford, 1982).

COWARD, B., *The Stuart Age: A History of England 1603-1714* (London, 1980).

COX, T., *Magna Britannia et Hibernia, Antiqua et Nova*, 6 vols. (London, 1720-31).

CRAIK, T. W. (ed.), *The Revels History of English Drama*, Vol. 3: *1576-1613* (London, 1975).

—— *The Revels History of English Drama*, Vol. 5: *1660-1750* (London, 1976).

CRANFIELD, G. A., *A Handlist of English Provincial Newspapers and Periodicals 1700-1760*, Cambridge Bibliographical Soc. Monographs, No. 2 (Cambridge, 1952).

—— 'Handlist of English Provincial Newspapers and Periodicals 1700-1760: Additions and Corrections', *Trans. of the Cambridge Bibliographical Soc.*, ii, No. 3 (1956), 269-74.

—— *The Development of the Provincial Newspaper 1700-1760* (Oxford, 1962).

CRESSY, D., 'Levels of Illiteracy in England 1530-1730', *Historical Jnl.*, xx (1977), 1-23.

—— *Literacy and the Social Order: Reading and Writing in Tudor and Stuart England* (Cambridge, 1980).

CROFTS, J., 'A Lakeland Journey 1759', ed. B. G. Hutton, *Trans. of the Cumberland and Westmorland Antiquarian and Archaeological Soc.*, new ser., lxi (1961), 288-93.

CROSSLEY, F. H., *Cheshire* (London, 1949).

CRUICKSHANK, D., *A Guide to the Georgian Buildings of Britain and Ireland* (London, 1985).

CRUICKSHANK, D., and WYLD, P., *London: The Art of Georgian Building* (London, 1975).

CRUMP, M., and HARRIS, M. (eds.), *Searching the Eighteenth Century* (London, 1983).

CUNLIFFE, B., *The City of Bath* (Gloucester, 1986).

CUNNINGTON, H. (ed.), *Some Annals of the Borough of Devizes* (Devizes, 1925).

DARLEY, G., *Villages of Vision* (London, 1978).

DAVIS, D., *A History of Shopping* (London, 1966).

DAVIS, R., *The Rise of the English Shipping Industry* (Newton Abbot, 1972).

DAVISON, D. (ed.), *The Penguin Book of Eighteenth-Century English Verse* (Harmondsworth, 1973).

DEAN, W., *The New Grove Handel* (London, 1982).

DEFOE, D., *Moll Flanders*, 1722, repr. (London, 1971).

—— *A Tour through the Whole Island of Great Britain*, 1724-6, ed. G. D. H. Cole and D. C. Browning, 2 vols. (London, 1962).

DEFOE, D., *The Complete English Tradesman*, 1725-7, 1745 edn., repr. (New York, 1970).

—— *The Compleat English Gentleman*, composed 1728-9, ed. K. D. Bülbring (London, 1890).

DENVIR, B., *The Eighteenth Century: Art, Design, and Society 1689-1789* (London, 1983).

DERRICK, S., *Letters Written from Liverpool, Chester, Cork, the Lake of Killarney, Dublin, Tunbridge Wells, Bath*, 2 vols. (London, 1767).

'A Description of the Bath', in *Tunbridge and Bath Miscellany . . . 1714*.

A Diary of a Journey through the North of England Made by William and John Blathwayt of Dyrham in 1703, ed. N. Hardwick (n.p., 1977).

The Diseases of Bath: A Satire (London, 1737).

DODD, D., *Mompesson House, Salisbury*, National Trust Guide (1984).

DODDRIDGE, P., *The Correspondence and Diary of Philip Doddridge*, ed. J. Doddridge Humphreys, 2 vols. (London, 1829).

DOOLITTLE, I. G., 'The Effects of the Plague on a Provincial Town in the Sixteenth and Seventeenth Centuries', *Medical History*, xix (1975), 333-41.

DOWNES, K., *English Baroque Architecture* (London, 1966).

—— *Hawksmoor* (London, 1969).

—— *The Georgian Cities of Britain* (Oxford, 1979).

DRAKE, F., *Eboracum: Or, the History and Antiquities of the City of York*, 1736, repr. (East Ardsley, 1978).

DUNCAN, A. G., 'Bideford under the Restored Monarchy', *Trans. of the Devon Association*, xlvii (1915), 306-33.

DUTHIE, R. E., 'English Florists' Societies and Feasts in the Seventeenth and First Half of the Eighteenth Centuries', *Garden History*, x (1982), 17-35.

DYER, A., *The City of Worcester in the Sixteenth Century* (Leicester, 1973).

—— 'Warwickshire Towns under the Tudors and Stuarts', *Warwickshire History*, iii, No. 4 (1976/7), 122-35.

—— 'Growth and Decay in English Towns 1500-1700', *Urban History Yearbook* (1979), 60-72.

—— 'The Market Towns of Southern England', *Southern History*, i (1979), 123-34.

—— 'Urban Housing: A Documentary Study of Four Midland Towns 1530-1700', *Post-Medieval Archaeology*, xv (1981), 207-18.

ELLIS, A., *The Penny Universities: A History of the Coffee-Houses* (London, 1956).

ELLIS, J., 'The Decline and Fall of the Tyneside Salt Industry 1660-1790: A Re-examination', *EcHR*, 2nd ser., xxxiii, No. 1 (1980), 45-58.

—— 'A Dynamic Society: Social Relations in Newcastle-upon-Tyne 1660-1760', in Clark, *Provincial Towns*, 190-227.

ELLWOOD, M., 'Library Provision in a Small Market Town 1700-1929', *Library History*, v (1979), 48-54.

ENFIELD, W., *An Essay towards the History of Liverpool* (Warrington, 1773).

England Illustrated or, a Compendium of the Natural History, Geography, Topography, and Antiquities Ecclesiastical and Civil, of England and Wales, 2 vols. (London, 1764).

'An Epistle to a Friend', in *Tunbridge and Bath Miscellany . . . 1714*.

ESDAILE, K. A., 'The Small House and its Amenities in the Architectural Handbooks of 1749-1827', *Trans. of the Bibliographical Soc.*, xv (1917-19), 115-32.

EVELYN, J., *The Diary of John Evelyn*, ed. E. S. De Beer (London, 1959).

EVERITT, A., 'The Food Market of the English Town 1660-1760', in *Third International Conference of Economic History* (Munich, 1965), 59-71.

—— 'Social Mobility in Early Modern England', *Past and Present*, xxxiii (1966), 56-73.

—— 'Urban Growth 1570-1770', *Local Historian*, viii, No. 4 (1968), 118-25.

—— *Change in the Provinces: The Seventeenth Century* (Leicester, 1969).

—— *Ways and Means in Local History* (London, 1971).

—— (ed.), *Perspectives in English Urban History* (London, 1973).

—— 'The English Urban Inn 1560-1760', in Everitt, *Urban History*, 91-137.

—— 'The Market Towns', in Clark, *Early Modern Town*, 168-204.

—— 'Country, County, and Town: Patterns of Regional Evolution in England', *TRHS*, 5th ser., xxix (1979), 79-108.

FAIRFAX-BLAKEBOROUGH, J., *Northern Turf History*, 6 vols. (London, n.d.).

FALKUS, M., 'Lighting in the Dark Ages of English Economic History: Town Streets before the Industrial Revolution', in Coleman and John, *Pre-Industrial England*, 248-73.

FAWCETT, T., 'Eighteenth-Century Norfolk Booksellers: A Survey and Register', *Trans. of the Cambridge Bibliographical Soc.*, vi (1972-6), 1-18.

—— *Music in Eighteenth-Century Norwich and Norfolk* (Norwich, 1979).

—— 'Measuring the Provincial Enlightenment: The Case of Norwich', *Eighteenth-Century Life*, new ser., xviii, Part 1 (1982), 13-27.

—— 'Self-Improvement Societies: The Early "Lit. and Phils." ', in *Life in the Georgian Town*, 15-25.

FEATHER, J., *The Provincial Book Trade in Eighteenth-Century England* (Cambridge, 1985).

FERDINAND, C. Y., 'Benjamin Collins: Salisbury Printer', in Crump and Harris, *Searching the Eighteenth Century*, 74-92.

FERGUS, J., 'Eighteenth-Century Readers in Provincial England: The Customers of Samuel Clay's Circulating Library and Bookshop in Warwick 1770-72', *Papers of the Bibliographical Soc. of America*, lxxviii (1984), 155-213.

FIELD, W., *An Historical and Descriptive Account of the Town and Castle of Warwick*, 1815, repr. (East Ardsley, 1969).

FIELDING, H., *Joseph Andrews*, 1742, ed. A. R. Humphreys (London, 1973).

FIELDING, H., *The History of Tom Jones*, 1749, ed. R. P. C. Mutter (Harmonds-worth, 1971).

—— 'An Enquiry into the Causes of the Late Increase in Robbers', 1751, in *The Works of Henry Fielding*, ed. J. P. Browne, 10 vols. (London, 1871), x. 343–483.

FIENNES, C., *The Journeys of Celia Fiennes*, ed. C. Morris (London, 1947).

FITZSIMMONS, L., 'The Theatre Royal, York', *York History*, iv (n.d.), 169–92.

FORD, J., *Cricket: A Social History 1700–1835* (Newton Abbot, 1975).

FOX, L., *The Borough Town of Stratford-upon-Avon* (Stratford-upon-Avon, 1953).

FRANÇOIS, M. E., 'The Social and Economic Development of Halifax 1558–1640', *Proceedings of the Leeds Philosophical and Literary Soc.*, Literary and Historical Section, xi, Part 8 (1966), 217–80.

FRASER, D., and SUTCLIFFE, A. (eds.), *The Pursuit of Urban History* (London, 1983).

FURNIVALL, F. J. (ed.), 'Harrison's Description of England in Shakespeare's Youth', *New Shakespere Soc.*, ser. 6, i (London, 1877).

GARDINER, H. C., *Mysteries' End: An Investigation of the Last Days of the Medieval Religious Stage*, repr. (n.p., 1967).

GEERTZ, C., 'Deep Play: Notes on the Balinese Cock-Fight', in C. Geertz, *The Interpretation of Cultures* (London, 1975), 412–53.

GENNEP, A. van, *The Rites of Passage* (London, 1977).

Gentleman's Magazine.

GIBSON, J. S. W., 'The Three Tuns in the Eighteenth Century', *Cake and Cockhorse*, viii (1979), 3–12.

GILBERT, E. W., 'The Growth of Inland and Seaside Health Resorts in England', *Scottish Geographical Magazine*, lv (1939), 16–35.

—— *Brighton: Old Ocean's Bauble* (London, 1954).

GILBOY, E. W., 'Wages in Eighteenth-Century England', *Jnl. of Economic and Business History*, ii, No. 4 (1930), 603–29.

GILL, C., *History of Birmingham*, Vol. 1: *Manor and Borough to 1865* (London, 1952).

GILL, J., *Racecourses of Great Britain* (London, 1975).

GILLETT, E., and MACMAHON, K. A., *A History of Hull* (Oxford, 1980).

GILYARD-BEER, R., *The County Hall, Abingdon* (London, 1956).

GIROUARD, M., *Life in the English Country House* (Harmondsworth, 1980).

—— 'The Georgian Promenade', in *Life in the Georgian Town*, 26–33.

GLANVILLE, P., *London in Maps* (London, 1972).

GOAMAN, M., *Old Bideford and District* (Bideford, 1970).

GODFREY, W. H., *The English Almshouse* (London, 1955).

GOLDSMITH, O., 'The Life of Richard Nash', in *Collected Works of Oliver Goldsmith*, ed. A. Friedman, 5 vols. (Oxford, 1966), iii. 279–398.

GOMME, A., JENNER, M., and LITTLE, B., *Bristol: An Architectural History* (London, 1979).

Goose, N. R., 'Decay and Regeneration in Seventeenth-Century Reading: A Study in a Changing Economy', *Southern History*, vi (1984), 53-74.

—— 'In Search of the Urban Variable: Towns and the English Economy 1500-1650', *EcHR*, 2nd ser., xxxix, No. 2 (1986), 165-85.

Grady, K., 'The Provision of Public Buildings in the West Riding of Yorkshire c.1600-1840', Ph.D. thesis (Leeds, 1980).

Green, V., *A Survey of the City of Worcester* (Worcester, 1764).

—— *The History and Antiquities of the City and Suburbs of Worcester*, 2 vols. (London, 1796).

Gretton, M. S., *Burford Past and Present* (London, 1945).

Griffin, N., 'Epidemics in Loughborough 1539-1640', *Trans. of the Leicestershire Archaeological and Historical Soc.*, xciii (1967-8), 24-34.

Griffiths, I., *Berrow's Worcester Journal: An Examination of the Antiquity of Britain's Oldest Newspaper* (Worcester, 1941).

The Guild Merchant of Preston, with an Extract of the Original Charter (Preston, [1762]).

Habakkuk, H. J., 'English Landownership 1680-1740', *EcHR*, x (1939-40), 2-17.

Halfpenny, W. and J., Morris, R., and Lightoler, T., *The Modern Builder's Assistant* (London, 1757).

Hall, I. and E., *Historic Beverley* (York, 1973).

—— *Georgian Hull* (York, 1978/9).

Hamill, J., *The Craft: A History of Freemasonry* (n.p., 1986).

Hamilton, A., *Count Grammont at the Court of Charles II*, ed. and trans. N. Deakin (London, 1965).

Hamlyn, H. M., 'Eighteenth-Century Circulating Libraries in England', *The Library*, 5th ser., i (1946-7), 197-222.

Hampson, N., *The Enlightenment*, repr. (Harmondsworth, 1984).

Hare, G., *The Georgian Theatre in Wessex* (London, 1958).

Harley, J., *Music in Purcell's London* (London, 1968).

Harley, J. B., *Maps for the Local Historian* (London, 1972).

Harris, J., *Hermes: Or, a Philosophical Inquiry Concerning Language and Universal Grammar*, 1751, repr. (Menston, 1968).

Harris, J., 'The Architecture of Stamford', in Rogers, *Making of Stamford*, 77-90.

—— *The Palladians* (London, 1981).

Hart, G., *A History of Cheltenham* (Leicester, 1965).

Harte, N. B., and Ponting, K. G. (eds.), *Textile History and Economic History* (Manchester, 1973).

Hartnoll, P., 'The Theatre and the Licensing Act of 1737', in A. Natan (ed.), *Silver Renaissance: Essays in Eighteenth-Century History* (London, 1961), 165-86.

Harvey, P. D. A., *The History of Topographical Maps* (London, 1980).

Heape, R. G., *Buxton under the Dukes of Devonshire* (London, 1948).

HENSTOCK, A., 'Group Projects in Local History: Buildings and Society in a
    Georgian Market Town', *Bulletin of Local History: East Midlands Region*,
    xiii (1978), 1–7.
—— 'Town Houses and Society in Georgian Country Towns. Part 1: Architec-
    ture', *Local Historian*, xiv, No. 2 (1980), 68–75.
HERVEY, J., *Letter-Books of John Hervey, First Earl of Bristol*, ed. S.H.A.H.,
    3 vols. (Wells, 1894).
HEWITSON, A. (ed.), *Preston Court Leet Records* (Preston, 1905).
—— *History of Preston*, repr. (East Ardsley, 1969).
HEY, D., *Packmen, Carriers, and Pack-Horse Roads: Trade and Communica-
    tions in North Derbyshire and South Yorkshire* (Leicester, 1980).
HILL, J. W. F., *Tudor and Stuart Lincoln* (Cambridge, 1956).
—— *Georgian Lincoln* (Cambridge, 1966).
HILL, J., and DENT, R. K., *Memorials of the Old Square* (Birmingham, 1897).
HILLABY, J., *The Book of Ledbury* (Buckingham, 1982).
An Historical List of . . . Horse Matches, compiled at various times by J. Cheny,
    R. Heber, and B. Walker, annual vols. (London, 1730–71).
HISTORICAL MANUSCRIPTS COMMISSION, *Bath MSS*, i.
—— *Dartmouth MSS*, iii.
—— *Egmont MSS*, ii.
—— *Egmont MSS*, Diary i.
—— *Egmont MSS*, Diary iii.
—— *Grimstone MSS*.
—— *Hastings MSS*, ii.
—— *Hastings MSS*, iii.
—— *Portland MSS*, vi.
—— *Verulam MSS*.
The History and Proceedings of the House of Commons, xi (London, 1743).
HOBHOUSE, E. (ed.), *The Diary of a West Country Physician* (London, 1934).
HODGKINSON, J. L., and POGSON, R., *The Early Manchester Theatre* (London,
    1960).
HOGWOOD, C., 'Thomas Tudway's History of Music', in Hogwood and Luckett,
    Music in Eighteenth-Century England, 19–47.
HOGWOOD, C., and LUCKETT, R. (eds.), *Music in Eighteenth-Century England*
    (Cambridge, 1983).
HOLDERNESS, B. A., 'The English Land Market in the Eighteenth Century: The
    Case of Lincolnshire', *EcHR*, 2nd ser., xxvii, No. 4 (1974), 557–76.
HOLMES, G. S., *British Politics in the Age of Anne* (London, 1967).
—— (ed.), *Britain after the Glorious Revolution* (London, 1969).
—— 'The Achievement of Stability: The Social Context of Politics from the
    1680s to the Age of Walpole', in Cannon, *Whig Ascendancy*, 1–22.
—— *Augustan England: Professions, State, and Society 1680–1730* (London,
    1982).

HOLMES, G. S., and SPECK, W. A. (eds.), *The Divided Society: Party Conflict in England 1694-1716* (London, 1967).

HOPKINS, M. A., *Dr Johnson's Lichfield* (London, 1956).

HOSKINS, W. G., 'The Rebuilding of Rural England 1570-1640', *Past and Present*, iv (1953), 44-59.

—— *Devon* (London, 1954).

—— 'The Great Rebuilding', *History Today*, v (1955), 104-11.

—— *Provincial England* (London, 1963).

—— *Industry, Trade, and People in Exeter 1688-1800*, 2nd edn. (Exeter, 1968).

—— *The Making of the English Landscape* (Harmondsworth, 1970).

—— *Old Devon* (London, 1971).

HOTSON, L., *The Commonwealth and Restoration Stage* (New York, 1962).

HOUSTON, R. A., 'The Development of Literacy: Northern England 1640-1750', *EcHR*, 2nd ser., xxxv, No. 2 (1982), 199-216.

—— *Scottish Literacy and the Scottish Identity: Illiteracy and Society in Scotland and Northern England 1600-1800* (Cambridge, 1985).

HOWELL, R., *Newcastle-upon-Tyne and the Puritan Revolution* (Oxford, 1967).

HOWGRAVE, F., *An Essay of the Ancient and Present State of Stamford* (Stamford, 1726).

HOWLETT, R. H., *The Royal Pastime of Cock-Fighting*, 1709, repr. (Liss, 1973).

HUGHES, A., 'Warwickshire on the Eve of the Civil War: A "County Community"?', *Midland History*, vii (1982), 42-72.

HUGHES, E., *North Country Life in the Eighteenth Century*, 2 vols. (London, 1952, 1965).

HUME, D., *Essays Moral, Political, and Literary*, ed. T. H. Green and T. H. Grose, 2 vols. (London, 1875).

HUNN, D., *Epsom Racecourse: Its Story and its People* (London, 1973).

HUNTER, M., *Science and Society in Restoration England* (Cambridge, 1981).

HUTCHINS, J., *The History and Antiquities of the County of Dorset*, 2 vols. (London, 1774).

HUTCHINSON, J., and PALLISER, D. M., *York*, Bartholomew City Guides (Edinburgh, 1980).

HUTTON, W., *An History of Birmingham to the End of the Year 1780* (Birmingham, 1781).

HYDE, F., *Liverpool and the Mersey: The Development of a Port 1700-1970* (Newton Abbot, 1971).

HYDE, R., *Gilded Scenes and Shining Prospects: Panoramic Views of British Towns 1575-1900* (New Haven, Conn., 1985).

INGRAM, M., 'Ridings, Rough Music, and the "Reform of Popular Culture" in Early Modern England', *Past and Present*, cv (1984), 79-113.

ISON, W., *The Georgian Buildings of Bristol*, repr. (Bath, 1968).

Ison, W., *The Georgian Buildings of Bath*, repr. (Bath, 1969).

Itzkowitz, D. C., *Peculiar Privilege: A Social History of English Fox-Hunting 1753-1885* (Hassocks, 1977).

Jackson, G., *Hull in the Eighteenth Century* (Oxford, 1972).

James, P. R., *The Baths of Bath in the Sixteenth and Early Seventeenth Centuries* (Bristol, 1938).

James, T. M., 'The Inns of Croydon 1640-1840', *Surrey Archaeological Collections*, lxviii (1971), 109-29.

Jenkins, P., *The Making of a Ruling Class: The Glamorgan Gentry 1640-1790* (Cambridge, 1983).

Jenkins, R., 'Fire-Extinguishing Engines in England 1625-1725', *Trans. of the Newcomen Soc.*, xi (1930-1), 15-25.

Jennings, B. (ed.), *A History of Harrogate and Knaresborough* (Huddersfield, 1970).

Johnson, S., *Johnson: Prose and Poetry*, ed. M. Wilson (London, 1970).

Jones, E. L., 'The Reduction of Fire Damage in Southern England 1650-1850', *Post-Medieval Archaeology*, ii (1968), 140-9.

Jones, E. L., and Falkus, M. E., 'Urban Improvement and the English Economy in the Seventeenth and Eighteenth Centuries', in P. J. Uselding (ed.), *Research in Economic History*, Vol. 4 (Greenwich, Conn., 1979), 193-233.

Jones, E. L., Porter, S., and Turner, M., *A Gazetteer of English Urban Fire Disasters 1500-1900*, Historical Geography Research Ser., No. 13 (Norwich, 1984).

Jones, M. G., *The Charity School Movement: A Study of Eighteenth-Century Puritanism in Action* (Cambridge, 1938).

A Journey from London to Scarborough (London, 1734).

A Journey to Bath: An Heroic-Comic-Historic-, and Geographical Poem (London, [1717]).

Kaufman, P., 'English Book Clubs and their Role in Social History', *Libri*, xiv, No. 1 (1964), 1-31.

—— 'The Community Library: A Chapter in English Social History', *Trans. of the American Philosophical Soc.*, new ser., lvii, Part 7 (1967), 1-67.

—— *Libraries and their Users* (London, 1969).

—— 'Readers and their Reading in Eighteenth-Century Lichfield', *The Library*, 5th ser., xxviii, No. 2 (1973), 108-15.

Kemp, T., *History of Warwick and its People* (Warwick, 1905).

—— 'Warwick Registers', *TBAS*, xlv (1919), 1-21.

Kenyon, G. H., 'Petworth Town and Trades 1610-1760, Part One', *Sussex Archaeological Collections*, xcvi (1958), 35-107.

Kersley, G. D., *The Three Rs: Rheumatism Rehabilitation Research as Viewed from Bath* (Bath, n.d.).

Kettle, A. J., 'Lichfield Races', *Trans. of the Lichfield and South Staffordshire Archaeological Soc.*, vi (1964-5), 39-44.

KETTON-CREMER, R. W., 'Assize Week in Norwich in 1688', *Norfolk Archaeology*, xxiv (1932), 13–17.

KEVERNE, R., *Tales of Old Inns*, 2nd edn. (London, 1947).

KNOTT, J., 'Circulating Libraries in Newcastle in the Eighteenth and Nineteenth Centuries', *Library History*, ii, No. 6 (1972), 227–49.

[KUERDEN, R.], *A Brief Description of the Borough and Town of Preston*, with occasional notes by J. Taylor (Preston, 1818).

LAITHWAITE, M., 'The Buildings of Burford: A Cotswold Town in the Fourteenth to Nineteenth Centuries', in Everitt, *Urban History*, 60–90.

—— 'Totnes Houses 1500–1800', in Clark, *Provincial Towns*, 62–98.

LAITHWAITE, P., *The History of Lichfield Conduit Land Trust* (Lichfield, 1947).

LAMPARD, E. E., 'The Nature of Urbanization', in Fraser and Sutcliffe, *Urban History*, 3–53.

LANG, R. G., 'Social Origins and Social Aspirations of Jacobean London Merchants', *EcHR*, 2nd ser., xxvii, No. 1 (1974), 28–47.

LANGLEY, B., *The Builder's Chest-Book*, 1727, repr. (Farnborough, 1971).

LANGTON, J., 'Residential Patterns in Pre-Industrial Cities: Some Case Studies from Seventeenth-Century Britain', *Trans. of the Institute of British Geographers*, lxv (1975), 1–27.

LASLETT, P., *The World We Have Lost* (London, 1965).

LATIMER, J., *The Annals of Bristol in the Seventeenth Century*, repr. (Bath, 1970).

LAW, C. M., 'Some Notes on the Urban Population of England and Wales in the Eighteenth Century', *Local Historian*, x, No. 1 (1972), 13–26.

LEADER, J. D., *The Records of the Burgery of Sheffield* (London, 1897).

LEECH, R., *Early Industrial Housing: The Trinity Area of Frome*, RCHM, Supplementary Ser., 3 (London, 1981).

LENNARD, R., 'The Watering-Places', in R. Lennard (ed.), *Englishmen at Rest and Play: Some Phases of English Leisure 1558–1714* (Oxford, 1931), 1–79.

'A Letter from Tunbridge to a Friend in London', in *Tunbridge and Bath Miscellany . . . 1714.*

Life in the Georgian Town, papers given at the Georgian Group symposium 1985 (London, 1986).

LILLYWHITE, B., *London Coffee-Houses* (London, 1963).

LINSTRUM, D., *Historic Architecture of Leeds* (Leeds, 1969).

A List of the Nobility, Quality, and Gentry at Scarborough, during the Spa Season in the Year 1733. Taken from the Subscription Books at the Spa and the Long Room, the Bookseller's Shop, and the Coffee-House (London, 1734).

LITTLE, B., *The City and County of Bristol* (London, 1954).

—— *Birmingham Buildings: The Architectural Story of a Midland City* (Newton Abbot, 1971).

—— 'The Gloucestershire Spas: An Eighteenth-Century Parallel', in

P. McGrath and J. Cannon (eds.), *Essays in Bristol and Gloucestershire History*, Bristol and Gloucester Archaeological Soc. (1976), 170-99.

'A Little King and his Little State', *Chambers Jnl.*, xxxii (1859), 250-4.

LLOYD, D., *Broad Street*, Ludlow Research Paper No. 3 (Birmingham, 1979).

LLOYD, D., and MORAN, M., *The Corner Shop*, Ludlow Research Paper No. 2 (Birmingham, n.d.).

LOBEL, M. (ed.), *Historic Towns Atlas*, i (London, 1969).

—— 'Some Reflections on the Topographical Development of the Pre-Industrial Town in England', in F. Emmison and R. Stephens (eds.), *Tribute to an Antiquary* (London, 1976), 141-63.

LOFTIS, J., *The Politics of Drama in Augustan England* (Oxford, 1963).

London Magazine.

LONGRIGG, R., *The History of Horse-Racing* (London, 1972).

LOONEY, J., 'Advertising and Society in England 1720-1820: A Statistical Analysis of Yorkshire Newspaper Advertisements', Ph.D. thesis (Princeton, 1983).

LOUW, H. J., 'The Origin of the Sash-Window', *Architectural History*, xxvi (1983), 49-72.

LOVE, H. (ed.), *The Penguin Book of Restoration Verse* (Harmondsworth, 1968).

The Lover's Miscellany: Or, Poems on Several Occasions, Amorous and Gallant (London, 1719).

LOWTHER, J., *The Correspondence of Sir John Lowther 1693-1698*, ed. D. Hainsworth, Records of Social and Economic History, new ser., vii (Oxford, 1983).

LYSONS, D. and S., *Magna Britannia: Being a Concise Topographical Account of the Several Counties of Great Britain*, 6 vols. (London, 1806-22).

MACCAFFREY, W. T., *Exeter 1540-1640*, 2nd edn. (Cambridge, Mass., and London, 1975).

MCGUINNESS, R., 'The Music Business in Early Eighteenth-Century London', *Quarterly Jnl. of Social Affairs*, i, No. 3 (1985), 249-59.

MACHIN, R., 'The Great Rebuilding: A Reassessment', *Past and Present*, lxxvii (1977), 33-56.

MCINNES, A., *The English Town 1660-1760*, Historical Association (London, 1980).

MCINTYRE, S., 'Towns as Health and Pleasure Resorts: Bath, Scarborough, and Weymouth 1700-1815', D.Phil. thesis (Oxford, 1973).

—— 'Bath: The Rise of a Resort Town 1660-1800', in Clark, *Country Towns*, 198-249.

MCKENDRICK, N., 'The Consumer Revolution of Eighteenth-Century England', in McKendrick *et al.*, *Birth of a Consumer Society*, 9-33.

—— 'The Commercialization of Fashion', in McKendrick *et al.*, *Birth of a Consumer Society*, 34-99.

McKENDRICK, N., BREWER, J., and PLUMB, J. H., *The Birth of a Consumer Society* (London, 1983).

MACKERNESS, E. D., *A Social History of English Music* (London, 1964).

MACKY, J., *A Journey through England and Scotland*, 3 vols. (London, 1722–3).

McLOUGHLIN, G., *A Short History of the First Liverpool Infirmary 1749–1824* (London and Chichester, 1978).

MACMAHON, K. A. (ed.), *Beverley Corporation Minute-Books 1707–1835*, Yorkshire Archaeological Soc., Record Ser., cxxii (1956).

MALCOLMSON, R. W., *Popular Recreations in English Society 1700–1850* (Cambridge, 1973).

MANDEVILLE, B., *The Fable of the Bees*, 1714, ed. P. Harth (Harmondsworth, 1970).

MARSHALL, J. D., 'The Rise and Transformation of the Cumbrian Market Town 1660–1900', *Northern History*, xix (1983), 128–209.

MARTIN, G. H., 'Street Lamps for Kendal: A Note on Inland Transport in the 1770s', *Jnl. of Transport History* (1965), 37–43.

MARTIN, J. M., 'A Warwickshire Market Town in Adversity: Stratford-upon-Avon in the Sixteenth and Seventeenth Centuries', *Midland History*, vii (1982), 26–41.

MAY, P., *The Changing Face of Newmarket: A History from 1600 to 1760* (Newmarket, 1984).

MEE, J. H., *The Oldest Music Room in Europe: A Record of Eighteenth-Century Enterprise at Oxford* (London and New York, 1911).

MELVILLE, L., *Bath under Beau Nash* (London, 1907).

'Memoir of Beau Nash', in *Bentley's Miscellany*, ii (1837), 414–25.

MERCER, E., *English Vernacular Houses* (London, 1975).

MEYRICK, R., *The John Gershom Parkington Memorial Collection of Time Measurement Instruments*, Catalogue Mark III (1979).

MIÈGE, G., *The New State of England*, 3rd edn. (London, 1699).

—— *Present State of Great Britain*, 11th edn. (London, 1748).

MILLWARD, R., 'The Cumbrian Town between 1600 and 1800', in Chalklin and Havinden, *Urban Growth*, 202–28.

MINCHINTON, W. E., 'Bristol: Metropolis of the West in the Eighteenth Century', *TRHS*, 5th ser., iv (1954), 69–89.

—— (ed.), *The Growth of English Overseas Trade in the Seventeenth and Eighteenth Centuries* (London, 1969).

MINGAY, G. E., *English Landed Society in the Eighteenth Century* (London, 1963).

—— *The Gentry: The Rise and Fall of a Ruling Class* (London, 1976).

MISSON, H., *M. Misson's Memoirs and Observations in his Travels over England*, trans. Mr Ozell (London, 1719).

MITCHELL, B., *An Illustrated Guide to the Pump Room, Bath* (Bath, 1981).

MITCHELL, I., 'The Development of Urban Retailing 1700-1815', in Clark, *Provincial Towns*, 259-83.

'The Monarch of Bath', *Blackwood's Magazine*, xlviii (1840), 773-92.

MONEY, J., *Experience and Identity: Birmingham and the West Midlands 1760-1800* (Manchester, 1977).

MONTAGU, E., *The Letters of Mrs Elizabeth Montagu*, ed. M. Montagu, 1809-13, repr. 4 vols. (New York, 1974).

MOORE, E., *Liverpool in King Charles the Second's time*, ed. W. F. Irvine (Liverpool, 1899).

MOORE, N., *Chester Clocks and Clockmakers* (Chester, n.d.).

MORANT, P., *The History and Antiquities of the County of Essex*, 2 vols. (London, 1768).

MORGAN, F. C. and P. E., *Hereford Cathedral Libraries and Muniments* (Hereford, 1970).

MORGAN, P., 'Early Booksellers, Printers, and Publishers in Stratford-upon-Avon', *TBAS*, lxvii (1947-8), 55-70.

—— 'St Mary's Library, Warwick', *TBAS*, lxxix (1960-1), 36-60.

MORRICE, R., *The Buildings of Britain: Stuart and Baroque* (London, 1982).

MORRIS, R., *Select Architecture: Being Regular Designs of Plans and Elevations Well Suited to Both Town and Country*, 1757, repr. (New York, 1973).

MORTIMER, R., *The Jockey Club* (London, 1958).

'Mrs C——'s Complaint for the Loss of the Ace of Hearts', in *Bath Miscellany . . . 1740*.

MUMFORD, L., *The City in History* (Harmondsworth, 1975).

MUSSON, A. E. (ed.), *Science, Technology, and Economic Growth in the Eighteenth Century* (London, 1972).

NAISH, T., *A Sermon Preached at the Cathedral Church of Sarum, Novemb. 22, 1700, before a Society of Lovers of Music* (London, 1701).

—— *A Sermon Preached at the Cathedral Church of Sarum, November the 30th, 1727* (London, 1727).

—— *The Diary of Thomas Naish*, ed. D. Slatter, Wiltshire Archaeological and Natural History Soc., Records Branch, xx (1964).

NASH, T., *Collections for the History of Worcestershire*, 2 vols. (London, 1781-2), Supplement (1799).

NEALE, R., *Bath 1680-1850: A Social History* (London, 1981).

NEVE, R., *The City and Country Purchaser and Builder's Dictionary*, 1703, 1726, repr. (Newton Abbot, 1969).

The New Grove Dictionary of Music and Musicians, ed. S. Sadie, 20 vols. (London, 1980).

The New History, Survey, and Description of the City and Suburbs of Bristol (Bristol, 1794).

NEWTON, R., *Eighteenth-Century Exeter* (Exeter, 1984).

NICHOLS, J., *The History and Antiquities of the County of Leicester*, 4 vols. (London, 1795-1815).

NOBLE, M., 'Growth and Development in a Regional Urban System: The Country Towns of Eastern Yorkshire 1700-1850', *Urban History Yearbook* (1987), 1-21.

The Norwich Survey 1971-1980, 2nd edn. (Norwich, 1980).

'On a Young Gentleman's Marrying an Old Lady for Her Riches', in *The Lover's Miscellany*.

'On Mr Nash's Going from the Bath', in *Bath Miscellany . . . 1740*.

ONSLOW, R., *The Heath and the Turf: A History of Newmarket* (London, 1971).

'On the Game of Whisk', in *Bath Miscellany . . . 1740*.

OSWALD, A., *Old Towns Revisited* (London, 1952).

OWEN, D. M. (ed.), *The Minute-Books of the Spalding Gentlemen's Society 1712-1755*, Lincoln Record Soc., lxxiii (1981).

PALLADIO, A., *The Four Books of Andrea Palladio's Architecture*, trans. I. Ware 1738, repr. (London, 1965).

Pallant House Gallery, Chichester (Chichester, 1982).

PALLISER, D., *Tudor York* (Oxford, 1979).

PARKER, R. D., 'The Changing Character of Preston Guild Merchant 1762-1862', *Northern History*, xx (1984), 108-26.

PARKER, V., *The Making of King's Lynn* (Chichester, 1971).

PATTEN, J., 'Population Distribution in Norfolk and Suffolk during the Sixteenth and Seventeenth Centuries', *Trans. of the Institute of British Geographers*, lxv (1975), 45-65.

—— *English Towns 1500-1700* (Folkestone, 1978).

PATTEN, R., *The History of the Late Rebellion*, 2nd edn. (London, 1717).

PATTERSON, A. T., *A History of Southampton 1700-1914*, Vol. 1, Southampton Record Ser., xi (1966).

PAYNE, H., 'Élite versus Popular Mentality in the Eighteenth Century', in R. Runte (ed.), *Studies in Eighteenth-Century Culture*, viii (Wisconsin, 1979), 3-32.

PENROSE, J., *Letters from Bath 1766-1767*, ed. B. Mitchell and H. Penrose (Gloucester, 1983).

PEPYS, S., *The Diary of Samuel Pepys*, ed. R. Latham and W. Matthews, 11 vols. (London, 1970-83).

PERKIN, H. J., 'The Social Causes of the Industrial Revolution', *TRHS*, 5th ser., xviii (1968), 123-43.

PHILLIPS, C. B., 'Town and Country: Economic Change in Kendal *c*.1550-1700', in Clark, *Provincial Towns*, 99-132.

PHYTHIAN-ADAMS, C., 'Ceremony and the Citizen: The Communal Year at Coventry 1450-1550', in Clark and Slack, *Crisis and Order*, 57-85.

—— *Local History and Folklore: A New Framework* (London, 1975).

PHYTHIAN-ADAMS, C., 'Urban Decay in Late Medieval England', in P. Abrams and E. A. Wrigley (eds.), *Towns in Societies* (Cambridge, 1978), 159-85.
—— *Desolation of a City: Coventry and the Urban Crisis of the Later Middle Ages* (Cambridge, 1979).
PHYTHIAN-ADAMS, C., *et al.*, *The Traditional Community under Stress*, Open University English Urban History Course (Milton Keynes, 1977).
PICTON, J. A. (ed.), *City of Liverpool: Municipal Archives and Records* (Liverpool, 1886).
PIMLOTT, J. A. R., *The Englishman's Holiday* (Hassocks, 1976).
PLATT, C., *Medieval Southampton: The Port and Trading Community* AD *1000-1600* (London, 1973).
—— *The English Medieval Town* (London, 1976).
PLAYFORD, H., *The Second Book of the Pleasant Musical Companion*, 4th edn. (London, 1701).
The Pleasures of Bath: With the First and Second Part of the Tipling Philosophers (Bristol, 1721).
PLOMER, H., *et al.*, *A Dictionary of Printers and Booksellers . . . in England, Scotland, and Ireland 1641-1775*, 3 vols., repr. (Oxford, 1968).
PLUMB, J. H., *The Growth of Political Stability in England 1675-1725* (Harmondsworth, 1969).
—— *The Commercialization of Leisure in Eighteenth-Century England* (Reading, 1973).
—— 'The Public, Literature, and the Arts in the Eighteenth Century', in M. R. Marrus (ed.), *The Emergence of Leisure* (New York, 1974), 11-37.
—— 'The New World of Children in Eighteenth-Century England', *Past and Present*, lxvii (1975), 64-95.
—— *Georgian Delights* (London, 1980).
—— 'The Acceptance of Modernity', in McKendrick *et al.*, *Birth of a Consumer Society*, 316-34.
POCOCKE, R., *The Travels through England*, Camden Soc., 2nd ser., 2 vols., xlii, xliv (1888-9).
POOLE, B. L., 'Liverpool's Trade in the Reign of Queen Anne', M.A. thesis (Liverpool, 1960).
POPE, A., *The Correspondence of Alexander Pope*, ed. G. Sherburn, 5 vols. (Oxford, 1956).
—— *The Poems of Alexander Pope*, ed. J. Butt (London, 1965).
PORTER, R., 'Science, Provincial Culture, and Public Opinion in Enlightenment England', *British Jnl. for Eighteenth-Century Studies*, iii (1980), 20-46.
—— *English Society in the Eighteenth Century* (Harmondsworth, 1982).
PORTER, S., 'Fires in Stratford-upon-Avon in the Sixteenth and Seventeenth Centuries', *Warwickshire History*, iii, No. 3 (1976), 97-105.
—— 'Fire Precautions in Early Modern Abingdon', *Berkshire Archaeological Jnl.*, lxxi (1981-2), 71-7.

—— 'The Fire-Raid in the English Civil War', *War and Society*, ii, No. 2 (1984), 27–40.

—— 'The Oxford Fire of 1644', *Oxoniensia*, xlix (1984), 289–300.

—— 'The Oxford Fire Regulations of 1671', *Bulletin of the Institute of Historical Research*, lviii, No. 138 (1985), 251–5.

—— 'The Destruction of Axminster in 1644', *Devon and Cornwall Notes and Queries*, xxv (1985), 243–5.

—— 'Property Destruction in the English Civil Wars', *History Today*, xxxvi (Aug. 1986), 36–41.

PORTMAN, D., *Exeter Houses 1400–1700* (Exeter, 1966).

POTTS, W., *A History of Banbury* (Banbury, 1958).

POUND, J. F., 'The Social and Trade Structure of Norwich 1525–1575', *Past and Present*, xxxiv (1966), 49–69.

POWELL, J., *A Parson and his Flock: Kenilworth 1690–1740* (Kenilworth, 1981).

POWYS, P. L., *Passages from the Diaries of Mrs Philip Lybbe Powys*, ed. E. J. Climenson (London, 1899).

PRIESTLEY, E. J., 'All the Cities of England', *Local Historian*, x, No. 3 (1972), 139–41.

PRIESTLEY, U., and FENNER, A., *Shops and Shopkeepers in Norwich 1660–1730* (Norwich, 1985).

PRITCHARD, J. E., 'A Hitherto Unknown Original Print of the Great Plan of Bristol by Jacobus Millerd, 1673', *Trans. of the Bristol and Gloucestershire Archaeological Soc.*, xliv (1922), 203–20.

—— 'Old Plans and Views of Bristol', *Trans. of the Bristol and Gloucestershire Archaeological Soc.*, xlviii (1926), 325–53.

RASMUSSEN, S. E., *London the Unique City* (Harmondsworth, 1960).

RATH, T., 'The Tewkesbury Hosiery Industry', *Textile History*, vii (1976), 140–53.

REAY, B. (ed.), *Popular Culture in Seventeenth-Century England* (London and Sydney, 1985).

REDDAWAY, T. F., *The Rebuilding of London after the Great Fire*, repr. (London, 1951).

REED, M., 'Economic Structure and Change in Seventeenth-Century Ipswich', in Clark, *Country Towns*, 88–141.

—— *The Georgian Triumph 1700–1830* (London, 1983).

REYNOLDS, J., *Discourses on Art*, ed. R. R. Wark (London, 1969).

REYNOLDS, S., *An Introduction to the History of English Medieval Towns* (Oxford, 1977).

—— 'Decline and Decay in Late Medieval Towns', *Urban History Yearbook* (1980), 76–8.

RICE, J., *History of the British Turf*, 2 vols. (London, 1879).

RIMMER, W. G., 'The Evolution of Leeds', in Clark, *Early Modern Town*, 273–91.

RIPLEY, P., 'Poverty in Gloucester and its Alleviation 1690-1740', *Trans. of the Bristol and Gloucestershire Archaeological Soc.*, ciii (1985), 185-99.

RODGERS, H. B., 'The Marketing Area of Preston in the Sixteenth and Seventeenth Centuries', *Geographical Studies*, iii (1956), 46-55.

ROGERS, A. (ed.), *The Making of Stamford* (Leicester, 1965).

ROGERS, K. H., 'Trowbridge Clothiers and their Houses 1660-1800', in Harte and Ponting, *Textile History and Economic History*, 138-62.

ROGERS, N., 'Money, Land, and Lineage: The Big Bourgeoisie of Hanoverian London', *Social History*, iv (1979), 437-54.

ROSEN, A., 'Winchester in Transition 1580-1700', in Clark, *Country Towns*, 144-95.

ROSENAU, H., *The Ideal City* (London, 1959).

ROSENFELD, S., *Strolling Players and Drama in the Provinces 1660-1765* (Cambridge, 1939).

ROSS, A. (ed.), *Selections from The Tatler and The Spectator of Steele and Addison* (Harmondsworth, 1982).

ROSSITER, A. P., *English Drama from Early Times to the Elizabethans*, repr. (London, 1969).

ROWLANDS, M., *Masters and Men in the West Midlands Metalware Trades before the Industrial Revolution* (Manchester, 1975).

ROWNTREE, A. (ed.), *The History of Scarborough* (London and Toronto, 1931).

ROY, I., 'The English Civil War and English Society', in B. Bond and I. Roy (eds.), *War and Society: A Yearbook of Military History* (London, 1975), 24-43.

—— 'England Turned Germany? The Aftermath of the Civil War in its European Context', *TRHS*, 5th ser., xxviii (1978), 127-44.

ROYAL COMMISSION ON HISTORICAL MONUMENTS, *Dorset*, iii, Part 1 (London, 1970).

—— *City of Oxford* (London, 1939).

—— *Stamford* (London, 1977).

—— *York*, iii (London, 1972).

RUDDER, S., *A New History of Gloucestershire* (Cirencester, 1779).

SADIE, S., 'Concert Life in Eighteenth-Century England', *Proceedings of the Royal Musical Association*, lxxxv (1958-9), 17-30.

SANDELL, R., *Devizes Town Trail* (Devizes, n.d.).

SARGEANT, H., *A History of Portsmouth Theatres*, Portsmouth Papers No. 13 (1971).

SAVIDGE, A., *Royal Tunbridge Wells* (Tunbridge Wells, 1975).

—— *The Story of the Church of King Charles the Martyr*, 2nd edn. (1978).

SAXON, E., *The Story of St Ann's Church, Manchester* (n.d.).

SCOTT, G. R., *The History of Cock-Fighting* (London, 1957).

SEABY, W. A., *Clockmakers of Warwick and Leamington to 1850* (Warwick, 1981).

—— *The Paris Family of Warwick 1670-1750* (Warwick, n.d.).

SHARP, T., *English Panorama* (London, 1950).

SHAW, W., *The Three Choirs Festival* (Worcester and London, 1954).

SILTZER, F., *Newmarket: Its Sport and Personalities* (London, 1923).

SIMMONS, J., *Leicester Past and Present*, Vol. 1: *Ancient Borough to 1860* (London, 1974).

SKELTON, R. A., 'Tudor Town Plans in John Speed's *Theatre*', *Archaeological Jnl.*, cviii (1952), 109–20.

SKELTON, R. A., and HARVEY, P. D. A. (eds.), *Local Maps and Plans from Medieval England* (Oxford, 1986).

SKIPP, V., *The History of Greater Birmingham: Down to 1830* (Birmingham, 1980).

SLACK, P., 'Poverty and Politics in Salisbury 1597–1666', in Clark and Slack, *Crisis and Order*, 164–203.

—— 'Social Problems and Social Policies', in Phythian-Adams *et al.*, *Traditional Community under Stress*, 73–101.

—— 'The Disappearance of Plague: An Alternative View', *EcHR*, 2nd ser., xxxiv, No. 3 (1981), 469–76.

—— *The Impact of Plague in Tudor and Stuart England* (London, 1985).

SLATER, M., 'The Weightiest Business: Marriage in an Upper-Gentry Family in Seventeenth-Century England', *Past and Present*, lxxii (1976), 25–54.

SMITH, B. S., *A History of Malvern* (Leicester, 1964).

SMITH, G. G. (ed.), *The Spectator*, 8 vols. (London, 1907).

SMITH, J. S., *The Story of Music in Birmingham* (Birmingham, 1945).

SOUDEN, D., 'Migrants and the Population Structure of Later Seventeenth-Century Provincial Cities and Market Towns', in Clark, *Provincial Towns*, 133–68.

SPEAIGHT, G., *The History of the English Puppet Theatre* (London, 1955).

SPECK, W. A., 'Conflict in Society', in Holmes, *Glorious Revolution*, 135–54.

—— *Tory and Whig* (London, 1970).

—— *Stability and Strife: England 1714–1760* (London, 1977).

SPERSHOTT, J., *The Memoirs of James Spershott*, ed. F. W. Steer, Chichester Papers, No. 30 (1962).

SPUFFORD, M., *Contrasting Communities: English Villagers in the Sixteenth and Seventeenth Centuries* (Cambridge, 1979).

—— *Small Books and Pleasant Histories: Popular Fiction and its Readership in Seventeenth-Century England* (London, 1981).

STATHAM, M. P., 'The Bury Fairs', *Suffolk Review*, iv (1974), 126–34.

A Step to the Bath (London, 1700).

STERENBERG, A., 'The Spread of Printing in Suffolk in the Eighteenth Century', in Crump and Harris, *Searching the Eighteenth Century*, 28–42.

STEWART, R. J., *The Myth of King Bladud* (Bath, 1980).

STEWART-BROWN, R., 'The Stationers, Booksellers, and Printers of Chester to about 1800', *Trans. of the Historic Soc. of Lancashire and Cheshire*, lxxxiii (1932), 101–52.

STONE, L., 'The Educational Revolution in England 1560–1640', *Past and Present*, xxviii (1964), 41–80.

—— 'Social Mobility in England 1500–1700', *Past and Present*, xxxiii (1966), 16–55.

—— 'Literacy and Education in England 1640–1900', *Past and Present*, xlii (1969), 69–139.

—— *The Family, Sex, and Marriage in England 1500–1800* (Harmondsworth, 1979).

—— 'The Residential Development of the West End of London in the Seventeenth Century', in B. C. Malament (ed.), *After the Reformation* (Manchester, 1980), 167–212.

—— *An Open Élite? England 1540–1880*, abr. (Oxford, 1986).

STOUT, W., *The Autobiography of William Stout of Lancaster 1665–1752*, ed. J. D. Marshall (Manchester, 1967).

STRUTT, J., *Glig-Gamena Angel-Deod, or the Sports and Pastimes of the People of England*, 2nd edn. (London, 1810).

STYLES, P., 'The Corporation of Warwick 1660–1835', *TBAS*, lix (1935), 9–122.

—— 'The Heralds' Visitation of Warwickshire 1682–3', *TBAS*, lxxi (1955), 95–134.

—— 'The Social Structure of Kineton Hundred in the Reign of Charles II', *TBAS*, lxxviii (1962), 96–117.

—— *Studies in Seventeenth-Century West Midlands History* (Kineton, 1978).

SUMMERSON, J., 'John Wood and the English Town-Planning Tradition', in J. Summerson, *Heavenly Mansions* (London, 1949), 87–110.

—— *Georgian London* (Harmondsworth, 1962).

—— *Architecture in Britain 1530 to 1830* (Harmondsworth, 1970).

SURRY, N. W., and THOMAS, J. H. (eds.), *Portsmouth Record Series: Book of Original Entries* (Portsmouth, 1976).

SYDENHAM, S., *Bath Pleasure Gardens of the 18th Century, Issuing Metal Admission Tickets*, repr. (Bath, 1969).

TALBUT, G., 'Worcester as an Industrial and Commercial Centre 1660–1750', *Trans. of the Worcestershire Archaeological Soc.*, x (1986), 91–102.

The Tatler and The Guardian (Edinburgh, 1880).

TAYLOR, G., *The Problem of Poverty 1660–1834* (London, 1969).

TAYLOR, J., 'Plague in the Towns of Hampshire: The Epidemic of 1665–6', *Southern History*, vi (1984), 104–22.

TEBBUTT, C. T., *St Neots* (Chichester, 1978).

THIRSK, J., 'Stamford in the Sixteenth and Seventeenth Centuries', in Rogers, *Making of Stamford*, 58–76.

—— 'The Fantastical Folly of Fashion: The English Stocking Knitting Industry

1500-1700', in Harte and Ponting, *Textile History and Economic History*, 50-73.

—— *Horses in Early Modern England: For Service, for Pleasure, for Power* (Reading, 1978).

THOMAS, J. H., *Town Government in the Sixteenth Century* (London, 1933).

THOMAS, K., *Religion and the Decline of Magic: Studies in Popular Beliefs in Sixteenth and Seventeenth-Century England* (Harmondsworth, 1973).

—— *Man and the Natural World* (Harmondsworth, 1984).

—— 'The Meaning of Literacy in Early Modern England', in G. Baumann (ed.), *The Written Word: Literacy in Transition* (Oxford, 1986), 97-131.

THOMPSON, E. P., 'Patrician Society, Plebeian Culture', *Jnl. of Social History*, vii, Part 4 (1974), 382-405.

—— 'Eighteenth-Century English Society: Class Struggle without Class?', *Social History*, iii, No. 2 (1978), 133-65.

THOMPSON, F. M. L., 'The Social Distribution of Landed Property in England since the Sixteenth Century', *EcHR*, 2nd ser., xix, No. 3 (1966), 505-17.

THOMSON, G. S. (ed.), *Letters of a Grandmother 1732-1735* (London, 1943).

THORESBY, R., *Ducatus Leodiensis: Or, the Topography of the Ancient and Populous Town and Parish of Leeds*, 1715, 2nd edn., ed. T. D. Whitaker (Leeds, 1816).

THORPE, H., *Lichfield: A Study of its Growth and Function*, repr. from Staffordshire Historical Collections (1950-1).

TILMOUTH, M., 'The Beginnings of Provincial Concert Life in England', in Hogwood and Luckett, *Music in Eighteenth-Century England*, 1-17.

TITTLER, R., 'The Building of Civic Halls in Dorset *c*.1560-1640', *Bulletin of the Institute of Historical Research*, lviii (1985), 37-45.

[TOLAND, J.], *The Description of Epsom with the Humours and Politics of the Place* (London, 1711).

TOLDERVY, W., *England and Wales Described in a Series of Letters* (London, 1762).

TOUT, T. F., *Medieval Town Planning* (Manchester, 1934).

The Tunbridge and Bath Miscellany for the Year 1714 (London, 1714).

TUPLING, G. H., 'Lancashire Markets in the Sixteenth and Seventeenth Centuries', *Trans. of the Lancashire and Cheshire Antiquarian Soc.*, lviii (1945), 1-34.

TURNER, A. J., *Science and Music in Eighteenth-Century Bath* (Bath, 1977).

TURNER, M., 'The Nature of Urban Renewal after Fires in Seven English Provincial Towns, *circa* 1675-1810', Ph.D. thesis (Exeter, 1985).

TURNER, T., *The Diary of Thomas Turner 1754-1765*, ed. D. Vaisey (Oxford, 1984).

TURNER, V. W., *The Ritual Process: Structure and Anti-Structure* (Chicago, 1969).

TYTE, W., *Bath in the Eighteenth Century* (Bath, 1903).

UNWIN, R. W., 'Tradition and Transition: Market Towns of the Vale of York 1660-1830', *Northern History*, xvii (1981), 72-116.

VALE, M., *The Gentleman's Recreations* (Cambridge, 1977).

VAMPLEW, W., *The Turf: A Social and Economic History of Horse-Racing* (London, 1976).

Victoria County History: Cambridgeshire, v (London, 1973).

—— *Gloucestershire*, viii (London, 1968).

—— *Lancashire*, vii (London, 1912).

—— *Northamptonshire*, iii (London, 1930).

—— *Oxfordshire*, x (London, 1972).

—— *Shropshire*, ii (London, 1973).

—— *Warwickshire*, vii (London, 1964).

—— *Warwickshire*, viii (London, 1969).

—— *Wiltshire*, vi (London, 1962).

—— *Wiltshire*, viii (London, 1965).

—— *York* (London, 1961).

—— *Yorkshire: East Riding*, i (London, 1969).

WAITE, V., 'The Bristol Hotwell', in P. McGrath (ed.), *Bristol in the Eighteenth Century* (Newton Abbot, 1972), 109-26.

WALKER, B., 'Some Eighteenth-Century Birmingham Houses, and the Men Who Lived in Them', *TBAS*, lvi (1932), 1-36.

WALTERS, J., *Splendour and Scandal: The Reign of Beau Nash* (London, 1968).

WALTON, J. K., *The English Seaside Resort: A Social History 1750-1914* (Leicester, 1983).

WALTON, M., *Sheffield: Its Story and its Achievements*, 3rd edn. (Sheffield, 1952).

WARE, I., *A Complete Body of Architecture*, 1756, 1768, repr. (Farnborough, 1971).

WARNER, R., *The History of Bath* (Bath, 1801).

WATERHOUSE, E., *Painting in Britain 1530 to 1790*, 4th edn. (Harmondsworth, 1978).

WATSON, S. F., 'Some Materials for a History of Printing and Publishing in Ipswich', *Proceedings of the Suffolk Institute of Archaeology and Natural History*, xxiv, Part 3 (1949), 182-227.

WATTS, G. T., *Theatrical Bristol* (Bristol, 1915).

WEBB, S. and B., *The Manor and the Borough: English Local Government from the Revolution to the Municipal Corporations Act*, 2 vols. (London, 1908).

WEINSTOCK, M. B., 'Blandford in Elizabethan and Stuart Times', *Somerset and Dorset Notes and Queries*, xxx (1975), 118-22.

Wells Cathedral Library, 2nd edn. (Wells, 1978).

WHIFFEN, M., *Stuart and Georgian Churches* (London, 1947-8).

WHINNEY, M., *Wren* (London, 1971).

WHITTET, T. D., 'The Apothecary in Provincial Guilds', *Medical History*, viii, No. 3 (1964), 245-73.

WHYMAN, J., 'A Hanoverian Watering-Place: Margate before the Railway', in Everitt, *Urban History*, 138-60.

WICKHAM, G., *Early English Stages 1300-1660*, 3 vols. (London, 1959-81).

WILES, R. M., 'Further Additions and Corrections to G. A. Cranfield's Handlist', *Trans. of the Cambridge Bibliographical Soc.*, ii, No. 5 (1958), 385-9.

—— *Freshest Advices: Early Provincial Newspapers in England* (Columbus, Ohio, 1965).

—— 'Crowd-Pleasing Spectacles in Eighteenth-Century England', *Jnl. of Popular Culture*, i (1967), 90-105.

WILLAN, T. S., *River Navigation in England 1600-1760* (London, 1964).

WILLIAMS, J. B., 'Henry Cross-Grove, Jacobite, Journalist, and Printer', *Library*, 3rd ser., v (1914), 206-19.

WILLIAMS, J. E., 'Whitehaven in the Eighteenth Century', *EcHR*, 2nd ser., vii (1956), 393-404.

WILLIAMS, M., *Lady Luxborough Goes to Bath* (Oxford, [1945]).

WILLIAMS, R., *The Country and the City* (London, 1973).

WILLIAMSON, F., 'George Sorocold, of Derby: A Pioneer of Water Supply', *Jnl. of the Derbyshire Archaeological and Natural History Soc.*, new ser., x, No. 57 (1936), 43-93.

WILSHERE, J. E. O., 'Plague in Leicester 1558-1665', *Trans. of the Leicestershire Archaeological and Historical Soc.*, xciv (1968-9), 45-69.

WILSON, C., *England's Apprenticeship 1603-1763* (London, 1967).

WILSON, J. (ed.), *Roger North on Music* (London, 1959).

WILSON, R. G., *Gentlemen Merchants: The Merchant Community in Leeds 1700-1830* (Manchester, 1971).

WISE, M., 'Birmingham and its Trade Relations in the Early Eighteenth Century', *University of Birmingham Historical Jnl.*, xi (1949), 53-79.

WITTKOWER, R., 'Frederico Zuccari and John Wood of Bath', *Jnl. of the Warburg and Courtauld Institutes*, v (1943), 220-2.

—— *The Earl of Burlington and William Kent*, York Georgian Soc., Occasional Paper No. 5 (1948).

—— *History of York Assembly Rooms* (York, 1951).

—— *Architectural Principles in the Age of Humanism*, 3rd edn., repr. (London, 1967).

WOOD, A. C., *The Rebuilding of the Shire Hall, Warwick, in the Mid Eighteenth Century* (Warwick, 1983).

WOOD, J., *The Origin of Building*, 1741, repr. (Farnborough, 1968).

—— *A Description of Bath*, 1742-4, 2nd edn. 1749, reissued 1765, repr. (Bath, 1969).

—— *A Description of the Exchange of Bristol*, 1745, repr. (Bath, 1969).

WOOD, J., *A Dissertation upon the Orders of Columns* (London, 1750).

WOODFORDE, J., *Georgian Houses for All* (London, 1978).

WRIGHT, R., 'The Early Plans of Bath', *Proceedings of the Somerset Archae-ological and Natural History Soc., Bath and District Branch* (1929-33), 441-6.

WRIGHTSON, K., *English Society 1580-1680* (London, 1982).

—— 'Alehouses, Order, and Reformation in Rural England 1590-1660', in E. and S. Yeo (eds.), *Popular Culture and Class Conflict 1590-1914: Explorations in the History of Labour and Leisure* (Brighton, 1982), 1-27.

WRIGHTSON, K., and LEVINE, D., *Poverty and Piety in an English Village: Terling 1525-1700* (New York, San Francisco, and London, 1979).

WRIGLEY, E. A., 'A Simple Model of London's Importance in Changing English Society and Economy 1650-1750', *Past and Present*, xxxvii (1967), 44-70.

WRIGLEY, E. A., and SCHOFIELD, R. S., *The Population History of England 1541-1871* (London, 1981).

WROTH, W., *The London Pleasure Gardens of the Eighteenth Century*, repr. (Michigan and London, 1979).

YOUNG, P. M., *A History of British Music* (London, 1967).

INDEX

Abingdon 23, 105, 108-9, 325, 356
Abingdon, Lord 187
Adams, Roger and Elizabeth 128
Addison, Joseph 263, 264, 281
advertising 130-1, 214, 217, 219, 293
Ager, Thomas 144, 228
Aikin, John 55
Aire and Calder, rivers 23, 352
Alberti, Leone Battista 50
Alcester 6, 132
Alford (Lincs.) 361
Allen, Ralph 34, 213, 232-3
almshouses 61, 67, 97, 104, 109-10
Alnwick 363
Amersham 356
Amesbury 366
Andover 25, 359
Andrews, John 208
Anne, Queen 170, 182, 187, 241, 354
antiquarianism 84, 136, 145
Appleby (Westmorland) 365
Archer, Thomas 111
architectural books 49-50, 219, 232,
    290-1, 306-7
architecture:
    baroque 61, 93, 237, 305, 306
    classical 42, 45, 46, 49-59, 60, 61,
        105, 107, 232, 236, 260, 265,
        270-1, 289-91, 294, 305
    Palladian 49, 109, 159, 235, 305-7
    vernacular 42, 45, 46, 47-9, 51, 52,
        54, 60-3, 236, 289-91
Ascot 187-8, 356
Ashdown (Berks.) 233
Askrigg 366
assemblies, assembly rooms, and
    balls 28, 29, 66, 125, 147, 150-62,
        177, 179, 192-3, 213, 220, 221,
        245, 251, 257-8, 275, 276, 279,
        325, 332, 336-49
    see also Bath; York
assizes 7, 123, 124, 143-4, 150, 155-6,
    271, 337, 343, 344, 345, 347
Astrop 34, 336, 350
Atherstone 135, 145, 174, 365

Atkinson, John 233, 251
Aughton Moss (Lancs.) 360
Augusta, Princess of Wales 156, 241-2
Austen, Jane 224
Avison, Charles 126, 269-70
Avon (Som.), river 25, 166, 350, 351
Avon (War.), river 6, 25
Axminster 15
Aylesbury 6, 356

Bakewell 357
Baltic 25
Banbury 16, 45, 47, 56, 175, 332, 336,
    363
Banister, John 122
Barham (Kent) 360
Barnard Castle 358
Barnet 359
Barnsley (Yorks.) 27, 43, 194, 214, 336,
    366
Barnstaple 20, 358
Barton, George 132, 133-4
Basingstoke 5, 359
Baskerville, John 128-9
Bastard, John 237
Bath 31-4, 56, 85, 203, 213, 222,
    238-43, 266, 292 n.
    assemblies, assembly rooms, and
        balls 139, 147, 150, 151-3, 154,
        156, 158-9, 160, 161, 172, 215,
        220, 238, 239, 242-3, 246, 249,
        250, 261-2, 266, 271, 272, 273,
        275, 276, 292, 294, 304, 332,
        336-7
    baths 258, 264, 272, 299, 300, 332
    bookshops and libraries 134-5, 243
    bowling-greens 150, 165, 172, 174,
        175, 336
    chairmen 293-4
    churches and chapels 78, 111, 125,
        139, 242, 247, 272, 273, 297
    Circus 100, 101, 234, 236, 270,
        273-4, 290
    civic ceremony 255
    civilizing influence 258, 261-2

HBL 1 A